China Since Tiananmen

The Politics of Transition

China Since Tiananmen is the first book to offer a comprehensive look at the intellectual and political trends, and to assess how China has changed, since the Tiananmen Square events in 1989. Fewsmith describes the maneuverings of the top leadership and political debates among intellectuals, offering a coherent and credible narrative of deep political conflict in China in the years after Tiananmen. He puts the rise of neoconservatism and nationalism in China today into historical context, and he contrasts it with the growing pluralization of Chinese society and governance. Fewsmith depicts the growing tensions between these two trends as China's version of America's culture wars, but with arguably higher stakes. This book is filled with new information not discussed in Western media. Fewsmith's thorough and realistic assessment of the forces that drive China today is critical reading for anyone trying to understand Sino–U.S. relations, China's most recent evolution, and its future.

Joseph Fewsmith is Professor of International Relations at Boston University and Director of the East Asian Interdisciplinary Studies Program. He is the author of *Party, State and Local Elite in Republican China: Merchant Organizations and Politics in Shanghai, 1890–1930* (1985), *The Dilemmas of Reform in China: Political Conflict and Economic Debate* (1994), and *Elite Politics in Contemporary China* (2001). He has written extensively on contemporary politics in China, with articles appearing in such journals as *Asian Survey, Current History, Journal of Contemporary China, Problems of Communism, Modern China, The China Journal,* and *Comparative Studies in Society and History.*

Cambridge Modern China Series

Edited by William Kirby, Harvard University

Other books in the series:

Warren I. Cohen and Li Zhao, eds., *Hong Kong under Chinese Rule: The Economic and Political Implications of Reversion*

Tamara Jacka, *Women's Work in Rural China: Change and Continuity in an Era of Reform*

Shiping Zheng, *Party vs. State in Post-1949 China: The Institutional Dilemma*

Michael Dutton, ed., *Streetlife China*

Edward Steinfeld, *Forging Reform in China: The Fate of State-Owned Industry*

David Shambaugh, ed., *The Modern Chinese State*

Jing Huang, *Factionalism in Chinese Communist Politics*

Xin Zhang, *Social Transformation in Modern China: The State and Local Elites in Henan, 1900–1937*

Edmund S. K. Fung, *In Search of Chinese Democracy: Civil Opposition in Nationalist China, 1929–1949*

Susan H. Whiting, *Power and Wealth in Rural China: The Political Economy of Institutional Change*

Xiaoqun Xu, *Chinese Professionals and the Republican State: The Rise of Professional Associations in Shanghai, 1912–1937*

Yung-chen Chiang, *Social Engineering and the Social Sciences in China*

China Since Tiananmen

The Politics of Transition

JOSEPH FEWSMITH

Boston University

CAMBRIDGE
UNIVERSITY PRESS

PUBLISHED BY THE PRESS SYNDICATE OF THE UNIVERSITY OF CAMBRIDGE
The Pitt Building, Trumpington Street, Cambridge, United Kingdom

CAMBRIDGE UNIVERSITY PRESS
The Edinburgh Building, Cambridge CB2 2RU, UK
40 West 20th Street, New York, NY 10011-4211, USA
10 Stamford Road, Oakleigh, VIC 3166, Australia
Ruiz de Alarcón 13, 28014 Madrid, Spain
Dock House, The Waterfront, Cape Town 8001, South Africa

http://www.cambridge.org

First published 2001

Printed in the United States of America

Typeface Times 10/13 pt.   *System* AMS-T$_E$X   [FH]

A catalog record for this book is available from the British Library.

Library of Congress Cataloging in Publication Data
Fewsmith, Joseph, 1949–
China since Tiananmen : the politics of transition / Joseph Fewsmith.
p.   cm. – (Cambridge modern China series)
Includes bibliographical references and index.
ISBN 0-521-80634-8 – ISBN 0-521-00105-6 (pb.)
1. China – Politics and government – 1976–.   2. China – Economic policy – 1976–2000.
3. China – History – Tiananmen Square Incident, 1989.   4. Political leadership – China.
I. Title: Politics of transition.   II. Title.   III. Series.

JQ1510.F48   2001
951.05'9 – dc21   2001018436

ISBN 0 521 80634 8 hardback
ISBN 0 521 00105 6 paperback

For Stephanie and Andrew

Contents

Acknowledgments

This book has its origins in an earlier attempt to come to grips with the political trends in China since the tragic crackdown on student demonstrations on June 4, 1989, an event usually referred to simply as "Tiananmen" after the central square in Beijing that had been the focus of student activities for the preceding six weeks (though most of the violence took place outside the square). Roderick MacFarquhar asked me to analyze events in the first three years since that time for a revised edition of his *The Politics of China,* which appeared in 1997. I thank him for his encouragement to write that chapter and for his later suggestion to expand that chapter into a book – though doing so took longer and involved more than I could have anticipated at the time. His intellectual support and friendship have been critical to this enterprise.

A grant from the Smith Richardson Foundation and a sabbatical leave from Boston University in 1997–98 gave me the time to pursue this research. Alas, it became apparent in that year that understanding politics in the years since Tiananmen required delving into the new intellectual moods that grew up in the 1990s and reflected a very different China from the one I had grown accustomed to in the 1980s – and that required additional time and effort. Fortunately, I knew or came to know many of the intellectuals whose works are discussed in the pages that follow. They have helped me understand not only the different ideas that gained currency but also why those ideas came into being and evolved as they have. I hope that I have repaid their time and guidance by conveying the trends of the 1990s accurately.

In trying to understand post-Tiananmen China, I have often worked closely with Stanley Rosen, whose translations of debates in this period are cited frequently in the text. I thank him for his insights and support. I have also benefited from the friendship and support of my colleague Merle Goldman, who read the manuscript in draft form and whose comments have improved the final form. Similarly, Cheng Li and Timothy Cheek read the manuscript and provided valuable comments, as did an anonymous reviewer. William C. Kirby supported the project and provided encouragement along the way.

As anyone who has worked on such a book knows, scholarship depends on those who collect, organize, and know the material they put on the shelves of libraries. I have been fortunate to work with the best. Nancy Hearst of the Fairbank Center at Harvard University has provided critical support, not only bibliographically but also by proofreading the final manuscript. James Cheng and his staff at the Harvard-Yenching Library at Harvard have been similarly helpful. Jean Hung and the staff at the Universities Service Centre at the Chinese University of Hong Kong were of great assistance in locating much material used in this study, and Annie Chang of the Center for Chinese Studies Library at the University of California at Berkeley has also been of great help in finding material. I also appreciate the help that Jennifer Sova has provided in running down sources and checking footnotes.

Parts of this volume are adapted from articles previously published by the National Bureau of Asian Research, the Asia Society, and *Current History*. Permission to do so is gratefully acknowledged.

Mary Child, the editor for Asian Studies, Sociology, and History of Science at Cambridge University Press, has provided invaluable guidance and support. Matt Darnell did a splendid job copyediting the manuscript, and Pamela Dean painstakingly compiled the index.

My wife Irene has been unfailing in her support. Our children, Stephanie and Andrew, have tolerated with uncommon grace my frequent trips to China and the time I've spent locked away in my study. Because of their patience, and just because they are such great kids, this book is dedicated to them.

Chronology

1989

June 4	Tiananmen crackdown
June 23–24	Fourth Plenary Session of the Thirteenth Central Committee
November 6–9	Fifth Plenary Session of the Thirteenth Central Committee

1990

January 10	Premier Li Peng announces the lifting of martial law in Beijing
September	Economic Work Conference
November	*Yearnings* broadcast
December	National Planning Conference

1991

March 22	First Huangfu Ping commentary
March	NPC promotes Zhu Rongji to vice-premier
July 1	Jiang Zemin calls for opposing "peaceful evolution"
August 19–21	Attempted coup d'état in Soviet Union

1992

January 18– February 21	Deng Xiaoping's "southern tour"
March 10–12	Politburo meeting supports Deng Xiaoping
September 28	Conservative theoretician Hu Qiaomu dies at age 81
October 12–18	Fourteenth Party Congress
October 19	First Plenary Session of the Fourteenth Central Committee

1993

March 5–7	Second Plenary Session of the Fourteenth Central Committee
Summer	Huntington's article "The Clash of Civilizations?" published

August 3	Chinese ship, *Yin He,* stopped by U.S. Navy
September 23	2000 Olympics awarded to Sydney, Australia, instead of Beijing
November	*Strategy and Management* starts publication
November 11–14	Third Plenary Session of the Fourteenth Central Committee

1994

March	*Looking at China through a Third Eye* published
September 25–28	Fourth Plenary Session of the Fourteenth Central Committee

1995

April 10	Chen Yun, advocate of a planned economy, dies at age 90
April 27	Chen Xitong removed as Beijing Party secretary for corruption
September 25–28	Fifth Plenary Session of the Fourteenth Central Committee

1996

March 8	China tests surface-to-surface missiles into the sea off the coast of Taiwan
May	*China Can Say No* published
October	*Heart-to Heart Talks with the General Secretary* published
October 7–10	Sixth Plenary Session of the Fourteenth Central Committee

1997

February 2	Former Minister of Defense Qin Jiwei dies at age 82
February 19	Deng Xiaoping dies at age 92
May 29	Jiang Zemin speaks at Central Party School
July 1	Hong Kong is returned to China
September 12–18	Fifteenth Party Congress convenes in Beijing
September 19	First Plenary Session of the Fifteenth Central Committee
October 28	Jiang Zemin arrives in Washington, DC

1998

February 25–26	Second Plenary Session of Fifteenth Central Committee
March	*Crossed Swords* published

March 5–19	NPC meeting announces major government restructuring
May 4	Beijing University celebrates its 100th anniversary
June 27	President Clinton arrives in Beijing
July 22	Jiang Zemin calls on Chinese military to withdraw from business
September 14	Former president Yang Shangkun dies at age 91
October 12–14	Second Plenary Session of the Fifteenth Central Committee
December 21	Democratic activists Wang Youcai and Xu Wenli sentenced to jail

1999

March 23	United States starts bombing Serbian forces in Kosovo
April 6	Premier Zhu Rongji arrives in Washington to discuss WTO
April 20	Task force established to investigate corruption in Xiamen
April 25	Adherents of Falun Gong demonstrate around Zhongnanhai
May 7	U.S. bombs hit Chinese embassy in Belgrade
July 9	Taiwan President Lee Teng-hui describes relations with PRC as "special state-to-state" relations
September 19–22	Fourth Plenary Session of the Fifteenth Central Committee
October 1	50th anniversary of the founding of the PRC celebrated
November 15	United States and China reach agreement on China's accession to WTO

2000

January 20	*Wall Street Journal* reports that Lin Youfang, wife of Politburo member Jia Qinglin, detained for questioning
February	Jiang Zemin raises "three representatives" slogan
March 29	*Enlightenment Daily* carries letter implicitly criticizing Liu Junning
October 9–11	Fifth Plenary Session of the Fifteenth Central Committee

2001

April 1	Chinese F-8 fighter collides with American E-P3 surveillance plane off coast of Hainan

Schematic Overview of Chinese Political Spectrum

STATE

The Political Center

Left		Right
	Jiang Zemin	
Li Peng	Zeng Qinghong	Zhu Rongji
	Wang Huning	
Ding Guan'gen		Wang Daohan
Tang Wensheng		Liu Ji
Wang Renzhi		

SOCIETY

The Old Left
Deng Liqun
Yu Quanyu
Leftist Journals
Contemporary Trends
Quest for Truth
Mainstream

Liberals
Wan Li

Li Shenzhi
Shen Jiru
Ling Zhijun
Ma Licheng

The New Left

New Nationalists	Post-Modernists	Neo-Statists
China Can Say No	Wang Hui	Hu Angang
Wang Xiaodong	Cui Zhiyuan	Wang Shaoguang
Yang Ping	Gan Yang	
Fang Ning	Zhang Kuan	

Liberals
Liu Junning
Qin Hui
Xu Youyu
Zhu Xueqin
Lei Yi

Note: This schematic is arranged horizontally from the center outward, showing those who are far to the left and right of the political center (the Old Left and Liberals, respectively) as well as those with left and right tendencies within the political center. Vertically, those farther from the top exercise less political influence. Thus, the Old Left and Liberals influence the political center but are not as powerful; similarly, intellectuals such as Li Shenzhi are not in the same category as former Vice-Premier Wan Li. Other intellectuals, whether New Left or Liberal, are even more distant from the political center and are depicted as societal actors.

Abbreviations and Tables

Abbreviations

ASEAN   Association of Southeast Asian Nations
CAC   Central Advisory Commission
CAS   Chinese Academy of Sciences
CASS   Chinese Academy of Social Sciences
CCP   Chinese Communist Party
CDIC   Central Discipline Inspection Commission
CMC   Central Military Commission
CPSU   Communist Party of the Soviet Union
CYL   Communist Youth League
GATT   General Agreement on Trade and Tariffs
IMF   International Monetary Fund
MOFTEC   Ministry of Foreign Trade and Economic Cooperation
NATO   North Atlantic Treaty Organization
NPC   National People's Congress
NMD   National Missile Defense
PRC   People's Republic of China
SETC   State Economic and Trade Commission
SEZ   Special Economic Zone
SOE   State-Owned Enterprise
SPC   State Planning Commission
TVE   Township and Village Enterprise
TMD   Theater Missile Defense
USTR   United States Trade Representative
WTO   World Trade Organization

Tables

INTRODUCTION

State and Intellectuals at the Turn of the Century

TWO recent incidents, one receiving extensive international coverage and the other more passing notice, suggest the distance China has traveled over the past decade. The first was the reaction of students and others in the aftermath of the 1999 U.S. bombing of the Chinese Embassy in Belgrade. What was surprising was the readiness with which students and many intellectuals believed that the bombing was deliberate. Although the best evidence to date upholds the U.S. government's explanation that it was accidental,[1] most Chinese then and now believe that it was only one more (albeit a particularly bold) measure to "contain," and humiliate, China. Visiting China shortly after the bombing, I asked many people whether – if it had been, for instance, the Japanese Embassy that was struck – the reaction of the Japanese people would have been the same. Everyone I talked to said "no" but saw this apparent contradiction as perfectly logical. The United States was not trying to hold Japan down, but it *was* trying to contain China. The assumption that the bombing was deliberate rested on a perceived pattern of behavior, and the anger flowed from that perception. The outpouring of anger – and the bricks, ink bottles, and Molotov cocktails thrown at the U.S. Embassy in Beijing and its Consulates elsewhere – stood in such striking contrast to the raising of the "goddess of democracy" in Tiananmen Square by Chinese students just ten years earlier that it was difficult to comprehend how this could be the same country. Understandable anger at a shocking bombing of the Chinese Embassy is not enough to explain the sea change in Chinese public sentiment.

The second incident was the report in June 2000 that a Chinese publisher had declined to publish a translation of Ha Jin's acclaimed novel *Waiting*, winner of the National Book Award. The publishing house decided to back off after a scathing review appeared in a Chinese journal, *Chinese Reading News*. Censorship and attacks on writers are nothing new in China, so this item probably attracted little attention. What was different, however, was that the person who denounced Ha Jin's novel was no hidebound Marxist ideologue – the sort who routinely criticized liberal writers a decade ago – but rather a Western-educated professor of literature at Beijing University, the font of liberal thinking in modern China. The professor, Liu Yiqing, who had a Ph.D. from the University of Chicago, criticized Ha Jin not for poor writing (though she did feign shock at the "coarseness" of some of his words) but instead for engaging in a polemic that portrayed the Chinese as ignorant and repressed. Liu charged that Ha Jin tried to please the American literary establishment by "curs[ing] his own compatriots and [becoming] a tool used by the American media to vilify China."[2] How does one explain such a harsh critique by an internationally educated professor of a book whose quality is widely recognized?

More than a decade has passed since the violent crackdown that ended the student-led demonstrations of the spring of 1989, but American views are still heavily influenced by memories of the Tiananmen tragedy. Perhaps no image of China lingers more strongly than the photograph of a lone citizen standing in front of a column of tanks. That photo came to symbolize the American understanding that all that stood between China and democracy was a brutal government. The student demonstrators in Tiananmen Square and elsewhere, many believed, represented the wave of the future; few doubted that Chinese society, in contrast to the government, favored liberalism and democracy. China, it was assumed, would soon resume its trajectory toward democratic transition, and those who formulated policy toward China in the early Clinton administration wanted to be on the right side of history.

The enormous gap between the images of Tiananmen and the two recent incidents just cited needs to be explained. In trying to understand the evolution of Chinese society over the past decade, one may also hope to contribute to an improved U.S. understanding of China. Unfortunately, considerable differences have emerged in public perceptions of what type of polity China embodies and the challenges that China might pose to the United States. For example, Richard Bernstein and Ross Munro depict a China whose dictatorial elite, growing nationalism, and increasing economic strength will take China along a course intended to dominate Asia and bring it inevitably into conflict, perhaps militarily, with the United States.[3] In contrast, Ezra Vogel depicts a China that can be engaged and integrated into the world, a proposition that has been explored carefully in two recent books.[4] Others array themselves along this very long continuum, with most observers placing themselves some place in between.[5]

The debate over China's future is not a sterile or merely academic one. For years, the U.S. Congress hotly debated whether to continue to extend "most favored nation" (MFN, now known as "normal trade relations") status to China.

Meanwhile, the White House (under two administrations) has gone from trying to separate MFN from human rights, to trying to link the two, to trying once again to separate them and rebuild a constructive relationship. The rhetoric has often been heated. It has extended from the time of Tiananmen to the present, and both left and right have come uncomfortably together in their assaults on China and China policy. For instance, the liberal *New Republic* asserted in an editorial that "in Deng's China, the politics of communism was joined to the economics of fascism" and concluded that "the United States, in the name of its values and its interests, must engage China adversarily. This, too, is a form of engagement."[6] On the other hand, the conservative *Weekly Standard* has similarly campaigned against engagement; for example, Robert Kagan argued that "[a]s long as China maintains its present form of government, it cannot be peacefully integrated into the international order."[7] On the eve of President Clinton's June 1998 visit to China, the *Weekly Standard* editors declared that the Clinton administration's engagement policy – which essentially continued the China policy pursued by the previous five administrations[8] – was "looking more and more like outright appeasement."[9] Such negative images of China were reinforced when allegations of illegal donations to the Democratic party surfaced in the winter of 1997–98 and especially when the hearings presided over by Congressman Christopher Cox resulted in a 1999 report alleging far-reaching Chinese efforts to obtain U.S. nuclear weapons secrets.

The issues of Tiananmen and U.S. relations with China have recently been thrust back into the limelight by the publication of *The Tiananmen Papers* (which appear to be authentic accounts of leadership deliberations during the spring 1989 crisis), by the activism of a number of conservative Congressional aides and policy advisors (dubbed the "Blue Team") who advocate a more confrontational approach toward China, by the publication of new and provocative works (such as *The China Threat* by *Washington Times* columnist Bill Gertz), and by the apparent commitment of the new Bush administration to build Theater Missile Defense (TMD) and National Missile Defense (NMD).[10]

China has always defied simple understanding. The images that prevailed at the time of Tiananmen greatly distorted the reality of China even at the time, as a close reading of *The Tiananmen Papers* demonstrates. A decade later, these simple images are even less adequate. One reason such impressions linger is that Americans have paid too little attention to the domestic development of China. This is understandable, of course, since China is a highly complex society undergoing rapid change. Even those who dedicate their professional lives to studying China find themselves overwhelmed both by the amount of information available and by the opaqueness of the Chinese political process, which

3

makes it extremely difficult to sort through and make sense of the available information. Misunderstanding and simplification arise also because China at the beginning of the twenty-first century is a country riddled with contradictions. There are signs of interest in political reform, as demonstrated by the development of village elections, but there is no indication that the central government desires the democratization of China. The economy continues to develop, sometimes impressively, although the economic system evinces deep and systemic problems. There are reports of widespread urban and rural discontent even as overall social stability has been maintained. In short, the picture of contemporary China has not resolved itself with sufficient clarity that one might say with confidence just where China is headed.

Nevertheless, it is necessary to make an effort to come to grips with contemporary China, not only as a matter of intellectual inquiry but also because American understandings of China are important. They matter because the debate about China policy in the United States is not something that occurs in a vacuum but instead is actually an intrinsic part of that transition. The 1993 resolution of the U.S. Congress that opposed Beijing's bid to host the 2000 Olympic Games – a resolution that contributed to the defeat of that bid by only two votes – provoked widespread outrage in China, as did the U.S. decision to stop a Chinese ship, the *Yin He* (*Milky Way*), before it could enter the Persian Gulf and proceed to Iran. Suspicions that the ship was carrying material to be used in the production of chemical weapons were later proved to be false; Americans quickly forgot the incident, but the Chinese did not. Ezra Vogel and others (including this author) believe that U.S. attitudes and actions will be factors that contribute to whether China, as a rising power, can be peacefully integrated into the world order or whether it will try to challenge that order – perhaps with serious consequences to itself and the world.[11]

One purpose of this book is to move beyond some of the generalizations and rhetoric of recent years by presenting a careful discussion of the evolution of elite politics over the past decade and by looking at the emergence of an intellectual universe that is very different from that of the previous decade. China's rulers have often been described as hardliners, geriatric leaders (at least until Deng's death at age 93 in 1997), or bland technocrats, as if there were no substantial and meaningful differences among them. Such unidimensional generalizations ignore the problems that China's leaders face – with their changing society, with the world, and with each other – and assume away the very complexities that are likely to determine the direction in which China evolves. Focusing in addition on intellectual discussions not only gives a sense of China's problems as those in China perceive them; it also highlights the very different atmosphere that has prevailed in the 1990s (compared with the 1980s) and underscores the changed relationship that has emerged between intellectuals and the state. In looking at both elite politics and intellectual discourse, the book will suggest some of the reasons why China has evolved along lines that are quite different from those predicted a decade ago.

ELITE POLITICS IN TRANSITION?

Mao Zedong famously remarked that a "revolution is not a dinner party"; the same might be said of the conduct of elite politics in twentieth-century China. Major changes in political direction have always been brought about by one actor or coalition of actors decisively defeating another actor or coalition of actors.[12] This winner-take-all tradition of political contestation appears to be rooted both in cultural norms that conceive of political power as "monistic, unitary, and indivisible" and in the broad history of twentieth-century politics, which has dealt repeated setbacks to more pluralistic visions.[13] The specific history of the Chinese Communist Party (CCP), in which revolutionary struggle and ideology strongly reinforced a centralization of power and the articulation of a "Party line," has only strengthened that tradition.

It is not difficult to understand that the emergence of a more stable political order – much less a democratic system – requires limits to political contestation and the acceptance of a more pluralistic sense of political power. As Giovanni Sartori pointed out over twenty years ago, one of the critical breakthroughs in the emergence of British democracy was the acceptance of parts existing within a larger whole.[14] Political constraints that can nurture such notions of pluralism may be found in the emergence of institutions and a tolerant rhetorical environment.

Institutions matter. As Linz and Stepan note, "[m]any people tend to assume that what is challenged [in the course of political transition] is the nondemocratic regime and that with democracy a new legitimate system is established."[15] Democratic transition is not that easy. Among other things, there needs to be basic agreement on the territorial limits of the state and on who constitutes the nation. Given the beliefs of people living in Tibet and in the largely Muslim northwestern province of Xinjiang, and given the continued separation of Taiwan from the mainland, this basic agreement is quite problematic. In the case of China, the probability of a democratic transition setting off new and intense disputes over territory and nation seems high. Unfortunately for those who hope for an early democratic transition in China, "agreements about stateness are logically *prior to the creation of* democratic institutions."[16]

5

Part of state building is the creation of a "usable bureaucracy."[17] It is possible to have too much state as well as too little state – and indeed even to have too much and too little at the same time.[18] Much of the development literature in the 1980s prescribed reductions in the size of states as a correction for such problems as distorted markets and overcentralization of decision making. In recent years there has been a greater emphasis on building capable states – states that have sufficient capacity to maintain social order as well as the competence to know what action to take and what actions *not* to take in order to allow markets to grow.[19] The *World Development Report, 1997* focused high-level attention on the problem of building effective states.[20] As Stephen Holmes has argued, the transition in Russia has been so difficult not because Russia suffers from too much of a state but because it suffers from too little.[21] Democracy is simply not possible without a state bureaucracy functioning at a certain minimal level and in ways that enhance economic performance.

Without a basic consensus on the territorial limits of the state or on who is a citizen and without an adequately functioning bureaucracy, it seems impossible to develop the other characteristics that Linz and Stepan identified as necessary for successful democratic transition: rule of law (a *Rechtsstaat*), a "free and lively" civil society, an institutionalized economic society, and a "relatively autonomous" political society.[22]

The history of political contestation in twentieth-century China in general and the heritage of Leninism in particular make it difficult for both institution building and pluralist understandings of political power. The historical record to date suggests that Leninist systems do have difficulty reforming politically. Those in the Soviet Union and Eastern Europe imploded, while those in Cuba and North Korea have resisted reform; China and Vietnam have reformed economically but political reform has been limited. Can China chart a path that might lead to liberalization and perhaps to democratization? Can political reform follow the same, incremental path of "crossing the river while feeling the stones" as the economic reforms?[23]

Academic discussion on China in recent years has been dominated by explorations of social and economic trends and their implications for state–society relations. The focus here on elite politics is not intended to ignore social and economic changes but rather to see how, if at all, such changes are reflected in elite politics. The way in which socioeconomic and other changes are reflected in (or resisted by) the political elite is central to the process of political transition. Economics and other factors are clearly important, but the actions and decisions of political elites in rapidly changing times when the "rules of the game" are themselves unclear and changing are absolutely central to the process of transition.[24] The decisions such actors make are clearly constrained by a variety of pressures – from other elites, from Party and government bureaucracies, and from society – but political actors also make decisions to bind themselves and hopefully their successors. The decisions they make bequeath the institutions and the rules of the game with which their successors must deal. Sometimes such rules and institutions will prove binding and successful; at other times, they are subject to challenge and remaking. This is another way of saying that some transitions are more successful than others. Some transitions create states that are capable of dealing with the social, economic, and political problems that their countries face, while others fail to do so – sometimes miserably.

If the rules of political struggle in the twentieth century have been dominated by the perception that actors were in a "game to win all," it is nevertheless true that the inauguration of reform has posed a significant challenge to this perception. Indeed, one of the major thrusts of reform was to curtail the abuses of authority that had been associated with Mao's later years.[25] It was widely believed among the veteran cadres who returned to power in the late 1970s that "normal" Party life had been badly disrupted and was in urgent need of restoration. The mantra of the day was "collective leadership," meaning both that decisions should be made after inner Party discussions in which views could be freely expressed and that those who disagreed with the resulting decision should be allowed to retain their views as long as they agreed to implement the decision. The norm of democratic centralism also contained a sense that there were procedures to be followed in convening Party meetings so that one person could not arbitrarily impose his or her will on the Party or its management – including, for example, such issues as recruitment, evaluation, and promotion. Although such norms had never been fully adhered to, they continued to exert a moral force. It was toward that end that the Party passed in 1980 the Guiding Rules on Inner Party Life and adopted a new Party constitution two years later. In this way, the reaction of the CCP as an organization paralleled that of the Communist Party of the Soviet Union following Stalin's death in 1953.

Though Deng did not always adhere to the norms of collective leadership – his position as the "core" of the Party connoting something more than simply first among equals – he nevertheless advocated it in principle. Deng voiced the need to create sound political institutions in his famous 1980 speech on reforming the Party and state systems: "If these [leadership] systems are sound, they can place restraints on the actions of bad people; if they are unsound, they may hamper the efforts of good people or indeed, in certain cases, may push them in the wrong direction."[26] It was on these grounds that Deng declined to accept the positions of Party chairman (which was abolished in 1980) and general secretary (which was taken up by Hu Yaobang). It was also in deference to the norm of collective leadership that Deng played down the role of personality cult, though it should be noted that he was not above pushing his ideas in a cultlike fashion at critical junctures.[27]

This restoration of Party norms was gradually supplemented by the adoption of new, or nearly new, norms. Melanie Manion has traced the growth and gradual acceptance of a retirement norm, which is of increasing importance in the transition to the post-Deng era.[28] Similarly, Hong Yong Lee has carefully studied the professionalization of the cadre force. By the time of the Thirteenth Party Congress in 1987, college-educated, professional cadres had largely replaced the poorly educated, largely peasant cadre force that had come to power in 1949.[29] Moreover, Yasheng Huang has argued persuasively that the control and management of the cadre force has become more centralized, more professional, and more effective over the course of reform.[30]

While these inner Party norms were being developed, Chinese society, economy, and culture became far more complex and more integrated with the world economy. Not only has the Chinese economy more than quadrupled in size since 1978, state control has also retreated significantly from direct management of the economy. Whereas most prices in 1978 were controlled and development of new products to meet market demand was rare, by the mid-1990s the state controlled only a few prices and some two thirds of the economy was market-oriented.[31] In 1978, China had only $38 billion of foreign trade; by 1997 this trade had grown to $300 billion. Perhaps more important than the size of the trade was the fact that international commerce was bringing about major changes in the organization of China's economy. The virtual monopoly once enjoyed by the Ministry of Foreign Trade (later the Ministry of Foreign Trade and Economic Cooperation, MOFTEC) has yielded to the emergence of some 4,000 trading organizations, with the prospect that most companies will be allowed to conduct foreign trade directly on their own after China joins the World Trade Organization (WTO).[32] At the same time, some 300,000 joint ventures and wholly owned foreign firms were operating in China, employing millions of workers and accounting for perhaps half of China's foreign trade.

These economic changes, which have been paralleled by social changes less easy to capture with statistics, have forced the Chinese government to increasingly adopt indirect ways of managing the economy, thus changing in important ways the state–society relationship. They have also fostered the growth of law.

Since the revival of the National People's Congress (NPC) in the late 1970s, the process of lawmaking has become more institutionalized and rationalized – though there is still a long way to go.[33] As will be noted in the pages that follow, in recent years China has placed increasing weight on the role of law.

In addition, the 1978 reform decision to turn from class struggle to economic modernization has gone further than anyone could have predicted at that time. With the emphasis on economic growth has come a change in the basis of the regime's legitimacy. Although the Party still claims legitimacy on the basis of Marxism–Leninism and this claim has important consequences for the political system, everyone is aware that performance legitimacy has become far more important than ideology in justifying the government's continued rule. This was true during the 1980s but has become even more important in the years since 1989, in large part because the Tiananmen Square tragedy destroyed what little belief in Marxism–Leninism was left.

The change in the role of Party ideology, the reassertion of Party norms and the emergence and growth of new norms, the increasing complexity of the society and economy, the growing integration of the Chinese economy into the world economy, the growing body of laws and of lawyers, and the increasing role played by quasi-representative organs such as the NPC have all been justly heralded as charting a path of gradual political transition. At the same time, however, it should be recognized that these emerging norms and institutions stand in tension with rule by a Leninist party and the traditional game of winner-take-all politics. Whereas the former trends point to a growing pluralization of Chinese society and governance, the latter suggest a continuing institutional and cultural rejection of pluralism. In "normal" times, when the economy is growing steadily and political and ideological conflicts are confined within certain (if not easily defined) bounds, the inherent tension between these two impulses is merely implicit. However, when the political system faces crisis, these two trends come into conflict; to date, monistic political impulses have continued to trump pluralizing trends.

In short, one should not assume that changes observed in Chinese life will necessarily be reflected in the Chinese political system. Certainly there will not be a one-to-one correspondence. Political systems confronted by socioeconomic change can respond in a variety of ways, not all of which are "rational" from the perspective of enhancing the overall performance of the system. Political systems can simply ignore socioeconomic change, leading to stagnation (both economic and political) and collapse. Individual actors in the political system may also seek personal financial benefit from such changes and so drive what economists term "rent seeking" to new heights, hobbling the emergence

9

of more effective administration. However, political systems can also respond positively, generating more efficient public bureaucracies and more democratic political systems.

How political systems respond depends on a variety of factors, including the perceived threat that socioeconomic changes pose to the political system as well as to individual leaders within that system. Individual leaders will command varying resources and thus will respond differently to the challenges confronting the system. Some leaders will resist change while others will seek to respond positively, hoping that they can ride such changes to continued or greater success within the political system. In the course of responding to such change, individual political leaders are operating within the political culture of the regime – in China's case, within the contours of the CCP and within the context of winner-take-all rules of the game – even if they are trying to change the system.

THE ROLE OF INTELLECTUALS

Social pressures of various sorts are an important part of any political transition. Przeworski and others who have looked at democratic transitions have generally concluded that some form of "pacted" transition provides the best chance of successful transition (where "successful" means "leading to a consolidated democracy"). The notion of a pacted transition derives from a simple 2×2 matrix in which both the leadership and the social opposition are divided between hardliners and moderates. Successful transition seems most likely to occur when the moderates within the leadership and within society can reach accommodation, marginalizing hardliners and preventing large-scale violence.[34] This is no easy process. Przeworski emphasizes that the window of opportunity is often small and fleeting; the experience of Tiananmen reinforces that view, providing a tragic example of what can happen when the political dynamic reinforces hardliners on both sides and leads to the collapse of the moderate middle.[35]

Although broad social pressures – including those that emanate from workers, farmers, and entrepreneurs – provide the impetus for political change, inevitably intellectuals play a critical role in articulating interests and pushing for change. This is particularly the case in China, where intellectuals have traditionally played the role of social conscience. Although that role has significantly eroded in the 1990s, the concerns of intellectuals play a sociopolitical role by reinforcing, pressuring, or even ignoring the government. Thus, at the broadest level, the rationale for looking at the intellectual community is to

10

"take the temperature" of Chinese society in the 1990s. Intellectuals provide a large corpus of written work that reflects the concerns, outlooks, and hopes of a group of people who are closely attuned to their society regarding socioeconomic and political trends within China as well as to the broader international environment, including intellectual trends, economic changes, and political relations. Political leaders face the same environment, but they are neither at liberty nor professionally equipped to write about such concerns in the way intellectuals can. Thus, paying attention to what intellectuals are saying tells one much about the environment in which the political system exists.

Looking at intellectuals in China, one might expect that they would continue to push for liberalization of the political system and for eventual democratic change. That is basically the role that they have played over the past century, though they have often submerged their quest for a more liberal order into what they believed was a broader and more urgent quest for national sovereignty.[36] Nonetheless, whenever international and domestic tensions have relaxed, intellectuals have resumed their efforts to bring greater rationality to the political process, normalize the state–society relationship, and integrate China more fully into the international order. This was certainly the case following the Cultural Revolution. When Mao's death in 1976 brought that cataclysm to an end, intellectuals once again resumed their "proper" role in Chinese society.

Nothing expressed more vividly the hopes for a new era than Deng Xiaoping's humble statement in 1978 that he wished to serve as the "director of support services" for China's scientists and technicians so that they could devote themselves wholeheartedly to their work and to China's modernization.[37] But simple expressions of good wishes could hardly change fundamentally the relationship that had grown up between the Party and intellectuals since the Yan'an era. Mao had made it clear in his 1942 speech to the Yan'an Forum on Literature and Art that intellectuals must overcome their natural petty bourgeois nature by self-consciously "integrating" themselves with the "masses" – with the Party as judge of how successfully they had done so.[38] With the perspective of thirty years of persecution, intellectuals naturally were critics of the Party/state even when they served it. Indeed, some of the most prominent and outspoken of the liberal intelligentsia worked for the state, often in high places, and their self-assigned mission was to change the state from within. Drawing on the liberal tradition in Marxism, they sought to build a state that placed unprecedented emphasis on human beings – and that meant creating a more liberal, democratic order.

Even as high-ranking cadres, then, such liberal intellectuals were critics of the state and constituted what X. L. Ding termed a "counterelite."[39] As critics,

Introduction

they inevitably turned to the May Fourth tradition for moral inspiration – particularly its emphasis on science, democracy, cosmopolitanism, and the leading role for intellectuals as societal conscience. The May Fourth Movement (1919) was part of a broader New Culture Movement (1915–1920), which drew inspiration from the European enlightenment and hence was dubbed the "Chinese Enlightenment." Accordingly, liberal intellectuals in the 1980s were often referred to (and saw themselves) as "enlightenment intellectuals"; indeed, one of the liberal journals founded in the late 1980s was known as *The New Enlightenment* (*Xin qimeng*).

As the 1980s wore on, China's intellectual establishment diversified. Anticipating trends that would continue, albeit with significantly different content, in the 1990s, intellectuals with only minimal attachment to the state started to become active. The most important of these groups were gathered around book series and journals: the *Toward the Future* (*Zouxiang weilai congshu*) book series, created by Jin Guantao, Bao Zunxin, and others; the Academy of Chinese Culture, organized by Tang Yijie, Li Zhonghua, Wang Shucang, and others; and the *Culture: China and the World* (*Wenhua: Zhongguo yu shijie congshu*) book series, started by Gan Yang, Liu Xiaofeng, and others. These groups fueled the "cultural fever" (*wenhua re*) of the late 1980s, epitomized by the film *River Elegy* (*He Shang*).[40] The self-assigned mission of these groups was to carve out a "public space" that was independent of the state; it was a mission that assumed a common discourse based on enlightenment ideals.

The ideals and hopes of these and other intellectuals were shattered by Tiananmen. Some lost their positions (indeed, many had lost them in the course of political battles during the 1980s), some were jailed for various periods of time, and others went abroad. Yet neither political suppression nor exile (voluntary or otherwise) can fully account for the change in intellectual atmosphere in the 1990s or for the changed relationship between the state and intellectuals that began to emerge in the years after Tiananmen. Indeed, the single most important change in China's intellectual scene since then is that the common discourse that had given vitality to discussions in the 1990s has disintegrated as enlightenment ideals have – for the first time since the May Fourth Movement – been questioned or rejected by a substantial portion of intellectuals. At the start of the new century, liberalism still exists and has even shown new vigor of late, but it is no longer the common faith of intellectuals. Indeed, it has been subjected to withering criticism by intellectuals, politicians, and popular forces who reject liberalism and the neoclassical economics they associate with it. Ironically, as China has moved to enter the WTO, a significant intellectual opposition to capitalism and globalization has emerged.

As will be discussed in the chapters that follow, some intellectuals changed their minds while others emerged with new ideas. The political atmosphere and concerns changed. Enlightenment intellectuals came increasingly under fire. Just as important, the professionalization of the bureaucracy turned some intellectuals into technocrats; others turned to academic specializations, giving up to some extent the traditional role of social critic. At the same time, the commercialization of culture challenged traditional understandings of the role of intellectuals from below.[41]

The new mood of the 1990s generated a mixture of traditionalism, conservatism, utopianism, and nationalism.[42] The new mix has not extinguished liberalism; indeed, a new generation of liberal intellectuals is emerging to replenish the voices of the 1980s that were silenced by politics or exile. However, for much of the 1990s (except in the economic realm, where liberal ideas continue to receive a good hearing), liberal thinking was largely marginalized in public discourse. Liberal writings continue to be published, though when and to what extent depends very much on the political atmosphere, and some liberals remain optimistic about the future – though others feel very much besieged. The government has encouraged nationalistic feelings through its campaign of patriotic education and has generally discouraged writing about the "black spots" in its history. This campaign has no doubt generally encouraged the conservative mood, and to a certain extent the rise of nationalism has redounded to the benefit of the government, restoring some of the legitimacy lost in June 1989. But nationalism and utopian strains of thought (which have emerged simultaneously) are clearly double-edged swords, of which the government is very much aware. So even if the decline of enlightenment thinking has ameliorated some of the alienation between state and society that evolved in the 1990s, the new trends are hardly reassuring in the long run.

Probing new intellectual currents and the reasons they have emerged can tell us much about contemporary China, the social problems the state faces, the way social critics see the state, and the issues that arouse political passion and provoke engagement. That alone can clear away some of the gross generalizations that have been made and so give us a more nuanced understanding of present-day China. But intellectual currents and the relationship between intellectuals and the state are also part of the broader problem of institution building. Whether the state can explain its efforts to deal with the problems society faces and secure the acceptance of intellectuals for emerging institutional arrangements are important factors in building legitimacy. To the extent that intellectual currents support state efforts and "public opinion" is mollified, the odds of repeating a Tiananmen-type situation are reduced. Conversely, extreme alienation exacerbates political tensions, while cynicism undermines the effectiveness of nascent institutions. It is open to question whether the past decade's turn away from the enlightenment ideals of the May Fourth Movement can continue to pressure the political system in ways that promote greater openness, accountability, and restraint. It is also of some concern whether the more illiberal declarations emerging in recent years could form a basis for xenophobic mobilization. In any event, understanding the changes that have already occurred is the first step in thinking more clearly about China's present and future.

THE STATE AND INTELLECTUALS

To look at the evolution of both intellectuals and the political elite is to raise questions about the relationship between these two communities and the ways in which that relationship has changed over time. When Merle Goldman looked at the "democratic elite" in the 1980s, she inevitably turned to "Hu Yaobang's intellectual network" because most of those who were exploring democratization of the political system were tied into this network in some fashion, trying to influence the policies of the CCP.[43] Similarly, when I explored arguments over economic policy in the 1980s, the intellectuals involved were invariably tied into either the conservative network that surrounded Chen Yun, the senior Party leader and economic specialist, or Zhao Ziyang, the premier and later general secretary who led efforts to reform the economy and thus increasingly came into conflict with the policy preferences of Chen Yun.[44] Intellectuals were, to an overwhelming degree, "establishment intellectuals."[45]

This situation began to change in the mid-1980s as intellectuals, frustrated by the lack of political reform, began to carve out an autonomous realm from which they could push for cultural reform. Although the "cultural fever" that developed allowed for continued links between the state and intellectuals, the growing autonomy of intellectuals soon led them on a collision course with the state.[46]

In some ways, the relationship between the state and the intellectuals in the 1990s continued this trend toward separation, but both the character of the state and that of the intellectuals – not to mention the content of intellectual discussions – have changed greatly, so the relationship between the two arenas is substantially different from what prevailed in the 1980s. On the one hand, political leaders are themselves much better educated than any previous Chinese leadership of the twentieth century. Chinese Communist Party General Secretary and PRC President Jiang Zemin is a graduate of Shanghai's famous technical institute, Jiaotong University; Premier Zhu Rongji is a graduate of the equally prestigious Qinghua University. Many of those who advise the leadership are highly qualified intellectuals. However, they are intellectuals who have entered government and gained the expertise that comes with dealing with specific issue areas over a long period of time; they are, in short, not the generalists of before but rather technocrats (though one hastens to add that many continue to keep in touch with broad intellectual trends).[47]

In sum, as government leaders and their advisors have become better educated and more specialized, the distance between them and the broader intellectual community has both narrowed *and* broadened. It has narrowed in the sense that government leaders are themselves often intellectuals and thus share the same general background as other intellectuals. This trend should, ceteris paribus, narrow the gap between the two communities and facilitate communication. However, the increasing specialization of many government leaders and advisors means that they are often better informed on specific issues than are their intellectual counterparts. They no longer need to be given broad advice about whether to reform but instead need highly specific advice – which intellectuals are seldom in a position to provide – about *how* to reform.[48] When intellectuals raise broad concerns about the state of contemporary Chinese society, government bureaucrats tend to view them as irrelevant, and in this sense the gap between state and intellectuals is widened.

If the nature of government leadership has changed, often more so than is recognized abroad, then the nature of the intellectual community has changed even more. In particular, there has been a distinct trend away from the traditional role of intellectuals as the conscience of society, a role that has deep roots in China's Confucian past. Assaulted by commercialization on the one hand and professionalization on the other, the tradition of the intellectual as generalist giving wise moral advice to the political leadership – the role assigned to the intellectual in the story of Qu Yuan, the second-century B.C.E. advisor who drowned himself when disaster befell the king who had ignored Qu's advice – has largely disappeared (though, as we shall see, there are exceptions). This does not mean that there is not still a large and important group of public intellectuals who articulate what they believe to be the important concerns of the moment; indeed, this book focuses largely on this group of intellectuals. For them, as for their predecessors of the past century and more, the questions of identity continue to loom large: China's relationship to the outside world (inevitably summed up as "the West"), the state's relationship to society, and the present's relationship with the past. Nevertheless, this group is distanced from the halls of government and thus has less direct impact on policy than did their counterparts in the 1980s. They are nonetheless important both because they articulate broadly held concerns and perspectives that are held (at least to some degree) by the political leadership and because they express an emergent public opinion.

The role of public opinion remains modest in China, but its significance has clearly grown.[49] One aspect of this growing realm of public opinion has been the commercialization of culture, a trend that has forced intellectuals to compete in or against a real marketplace of ideas. As we will see, this too has affected the role of intellectuals in Chinese society. However, the commercialization of culture has not been restricted to the world of entertainment but has also created an audience for a wide variety of ideas – from popular histories to global issues and nationalism. To a certain extent, the government must compete in this marketplace of ideas as well. Thus one finds, for instance, an explosion in the number of books dealing with foreign policy – a subject that was virtually taboo in the 1980s. Some of these works defend the government's position while others are openly critical. In either case, the realm of public opinion can no longer be ignored.

Apart from public opinion in the traditional sense, there is also an obvious effort to use publication to bring ideas to the attention of policy makers or for policy makers to defend their ideas in public against others in government. The lines linking the state and intellectuals have multiplied, and different interests within the state have tried to manipulate intellectuals to support their preferred positions – just as intellectuals have tried to rally opinion to push their ideas on the state. The interaction between the state and public opinion is complex, subtle, and often obscure to the outside observer; nonetheless, it is an important part of the political process. Still, glimpses can be gained by looking at specific issues and events. Even if our knowledge of this process is not as good as we would like, ignoring it would miss an important dimension of the contemporary scene.

To say that public opinion has been of growing importance is not to say that the political leadership always pays attention to what intellectuals say. Indeed, there are times when political concerns dominate intellectual discussion to the point where the latter are nearly irrelevant. This was largely true of the period immediately following Tiananmen. Intellectuals were largely shocked into silence by the enormity of what had happened; alienated from the political leadership, they had little desire to participate in discussions – and the political leadership, caught up in its own conflicts, had little patience with intellectual expression.

This relative absence of state–intellectual communication in the immediate aftermath of Tiananmen points to the temporal aspect of this relationship. The

16

debate in the wake of Tiananmen was a very political debate that pitted defenders of Marxist orthodoxy (known as the "Old Left" in China) against the reformers allied with Deng Xiaoping. This was the culmination of long-festering differences of opinion that had been building for a decade within the Party, and there was little that intellectuals could do or say to sway the outcome.[50] This period lasted until Deng Xiaoping's famous journey to the south of China in early 1992 and the subsequent affirmation of his views at the Fourteenth Party Congress later that year.

With the basic distribution of power and the affirmation of reform settled by the Congress, at least temporarily, attention could turn to what type of state the political leadership wanted to (or could) build in the post-Tiananmen period. Indeed, these problems were made worse by the lack of attention given to many issues in the 1989–92 period. Given the state's weakened legitimacy and the important role always accorded to ideology in Communist China, there was a role for China's intellectuals to play. What was surprising to outside observers was that, as intellectuals began to partake again in public discourse, much of the antagonism they had directed toward the state only a few years before had largely dissipated. Indeed, one of the real ironies of recent Chinese society is that in the 1980s, a time in which the leadership pushed hard to make reforms against an opposition that was both dubious and entrenched, intellectuals were increasingly alienated by the government and disbelieving of its propaganda.[51] Contrarily, in the 1990s, a time when most outsiders would agree that the government had little interest in political (unlike economic) reform, students and the intellectual community were more believing of government propaganda (despite access to more sources of news) and more supportive of their government generally. The students at Beijing University who questioned American policy and intentions when President Clinton spoke there in June 1998 may have been put to the task by officials, but their cynicism was certainly widespread on college campuses by the middle and late 1990s.[52] Understanding why this new mood has developed is important for those who seek to comprehend contemporary China.

Part of the answer to this question is globalization. As we shall see, a significant portion of Chinese intellectuals (like Western critics of globalization) are very skeptical of the process of globalization – including what it means for China's economic, cultural, and political independence. This orientation dramatically reverses the prevailing mood of the 1980s, and on this point it can be argued that much of the intellectual community is to the "left" of the governmental mainstream. Worry over globalization partly explains the rise of nationalism in the 1990s.

By the mid-1990s, intellectuals and the state were each exploring in their own ways the issues of state legitimacy, state–society relations, and China's relationship to the outside world. Sometimes there was obvious influence and collaboration; for example, Wang Huning, a well-known political scientist at Shanghai's Fudan University, was invited by Jiang Zemin to join the government in an important think-tank role. Sometimes there seemed to be a commonality of interest, as intellectuals and the government each explored what was considered the baleful influence of the West; and sometimes there were clashes as government and intellectual views diverged.

By the middle to late 1990s, there was a more obvious contestation over public discourse. Different segments of the intellectual community vied with each other over ideas, while the government (indeed, different parts of the government) reached out to different groups of intellectuals in an effort to influence public discourse. By the end of the decade, there was renewed conflict between at least some intellectuals and the government. Unlike ten years earlier, however, by the end of the 1990s it was the government that was generally more cosmopolitan in its outlook,[53] whereas students and intellectuals took to the streets to angrily denounce the U.S. bombing of the Chinese Embassy and to contest the government's acceptance of American terms for entering the WTO.

Part I

LINE STRUGGLE REVISITED: THE ATTACK ON DENG'S REFORM PROGRAM

1

Tiananmen and the Conservative Critique of Reform

THE violence of June 4 stunned China's intellectual community. Although reflections and introspections began almost immediately, it would be over two years before intellectuals began to regain their voice, and when they did it was not only a different voice that emerged but also a very changed and divided community. Chinese intellectuals would re-emerge in a very different society, and their reactions to the surrounding socioeconomic and political events polarized them in a way not apparent in the 1980s or even, perhaps, before.

The silence and general irrelevance of the intellectual community in the wake of Tiananmen contrasted vividly with the turmoil among the political elite. The Party leadership was neither cowed into silence nor irrelevant, but it was shaken badly. Questions about the goals of reform had simmered just below the surface for years. Was reform, as Party documents repeatedly proclaimed, about the "self perfection" of socialism or was reform leading China away from socialism? Zhao Ziyang was a lightning rod for such issues. Conservative Party leaders believed that Zhao had been leading reform farther and farther from socialism and that Tiananmen was the inevitable and foreseeable denouement of the reform program that Zhao led and symbolized. It is apparent from the tone of many of the denunciations of Zhao appearing in the weeks and months following Tiananmen that such conservatives resented Zhao personally; they believed that he had ignored and insulted them, treating their concerns contemptuously. But beyond their personal dislike of Zhao was a broader concern about the content of reform as a whole, and that concern centered on the figure of Zhao's patron, senior leader Deng Xiaoping. The question thrown open by Tiananmen, then, was the nature of Deng's leadership and thus whether or not the Party should continue reform as it had been defined by Deng. Many believed that it should not.

The question of the content of reform – or, in Chinese jargon, the political line[1] – was related to a number of state–society questions: the relations between the central government and the localities, the rapidly changing social structure of Chinese society (including the emergence of a *nouveau riche* class, the growing independence of the intellectual elite, and the rising expectations of society), and the very real fears of many people that reform might hurt rather than help their interests. In other words, reform had generated a profound range of social changes, and the question that had racked the Party for years was how it should respond to these changes. How should it channel, suppress, or incorporate the demands that increasingly emanated from this changing society?

Another broad area of questions generated by Tiananmen revolved around China's relations with the outside world. Deng Xiaoping himself raised this issue in his June 9, 1989, address to martial law troops. Deng declared the Tiananmen incident to be "the inevitable result of the domestic microclimate and the international macroclimate."[2] This sense that Tiananmen was influenced (if not instigated) by outside forces raised the issue of readjusting China's relations with the outside world, particularly the United States. The issue of China's relations with the outside world has continued to intrude into Chinese domestic politics throughout the post-Tiananmen period as first Eastern Europe and then the Soviet Union rejected communism, as relations with the United States have remained generally strained, and as closer ties with East Asia have suggested alternative development models.

In June 1989, a shaken and divided Party leadership tried to begin the process of reconstituting itself while sorting out how its domestic and foreign policies should or should not be changed. This was a highly contentious process. There is little question that Deng's prestige plummeted with Tiananmen. Deng, however, was not without resources; he was still the "core" of the Party. The term "core" was added to China's political vocabulary by Deng himself, but it clearly reflects a phenomenon that has characterized CCP politics at least since Mao and one that certainly has roots deep in China's history. Although vague, the term "core" suggests a leader who occupies the center of a wide-ranging web of formal and informal relations that confer an authority not easily displaced.[3] Mao developed his core position in the Party by leading the Party through the most traumatic phase of its history, bringing the Party back from the debacle in Jiangxi to become a vigorous and growing movement in the heady days of Yan'an and the Sino–Japanese War. In 1943, the Party recognized Mao's unique status by declaring that he would have the decisive vote even if his colleagues on the Secretariat (the equivalent of the later Politburo) disagreed.[4] Mao's immediate successor, Hua Guofeng, never attained core status because he lacked the range of experience and connections essential to that position. Deng did have that status within the Party, and thus replaced Hua and emerged as the core of the "second generation" of CCP leadership (as Deng put it, ignoring the fact that he was really part of the first generation of leadership).

In 1989, Deng could use his core status to stress continuity and to dominate decisions on leadership. When Deng met with leaders of martial law troops on June 9, he declared that the line of "one center and two basic points" (economic development was the center; the two basic points were reform and opening up on the one hand and opposition to "bourgeois liberalization" on the other), which had been officially adopted at the Thirteenth Party Congress in 1987, was correct and that reform and opening up needed to be pursued even more vigorously.[5] Deng also tried to forestall an all-out attack on Zhao's policies (and himself) by declaring that "the political report of the Thirteenth Party Congress was passed by the representatives of the Party to the congress; even one character must not be changed."[6]

JIANG ZEMIN EMERGES AS GENERAL SECRETARY

Perhaps the most important advantage that Deng's core status conferred was the authority to have the final word on high-level leadership decisions. No doubt, given the defense of the Party against the so-called counterrevolutionary rebellion and the discrediting of Zhao Ziyang, conservatives hoped that one of their own – perhaps Premier Li Peng, economic planner Yao Yilin, or even former Propaganda Department head Deng Liqun – might replace Zhao as general secretary. Dashing their hopes, Deng on May 31 informed Li Peng and Politburo Standing Committee member Yao Yilin that the Party leadership (Deng said that he had conferred with Party elders Chen Yun and Li Xiannian, giving a fairly accurate sense of who constituted the Party leadership) had decided that Jiang Zemin, then CCP secretary of Shanghai, would be plucked from relative obscurity to become the "core" of the third generation of CCP leadership.[7] In explaining the decision, Deng almost contemptuously told Li and Yao, "[t]he people see reality. If we put up a front so that people feel that it is an ossified leadership, a conservative leadership, or if the people believe that it is a mediocre leadership that cannot reflect the future of China, then there will be constant trouble and there will never be a peaceful day."[8]

Thus began Deng's efforts to install a new leadership – his third attempt following the dismissals of Hu Yaobang and Zhao Ziyang – and so guarantee the continuation of his policies after his death. The choice of Jiang Zemin surprised insiders and outsiders alike, but in fact there were not many viable candidates from whom to choose. In 1989 there were five members of the Politburo Standing Committee. Two of these, Zhao Ziyang and Hu Qili, were disqualified because they had been too tolerant toward the Tiananmen demonstrations. Li Peng and Yao Yilin, as Deng scornfully noted, were too conservative to satisfy him. Deng might have added that the choice of either one would have decisively shifted the balance of the Party; maintaining balance – albeit with a bias toward reform – was the only way to maintain both a semblance of stability within the Party and the continuation of Deng's line of reform and opening up. That left Qiao Shi. Some reports maintain that Deng asked Qiao to be general secretary, but that seems unlikely. Qiao seems not to have been the power player that his background in intelligence led many to believe he was, and in any case he was too close to Zhao Ziyang to satisfy conservatives.

Thus, Deng cast his eye toward other members of the Politburo. Chen Xitong might have been a logical choice; he had long served in the Beijing Municipal Party apparatus and had cultivated ties with Deng and other Party elders. However, his well-known hardline response to the student demonstrations undoubtedly disqualified him – as was the case with Li Peng and Yao Yilin. Li Ruihuan was another possibility; according to *The Tiananmen Papers,* Deng nominated Li as general secretary, describing him as "energetic, effective, and thoughtful."[9] The other elders, however, demurred.

Just as Chen and Li were Party secretaries of Beijing and Tianjin, respectively, Jiang Zemin was secretary of China's largest city, Shanghai. If Jiang lacked the illustrious credentials of his revolutionary predecessors, as all members of his generation necessarily did, his background and career were solid. Born in the Jiangsu city of Yangzhou in 1926, Jiang received a mixed classical Chinese and Western education. In 1937 he tested into the prestigious Yangzhou Middle School, where he pursued his interests in literature and music. In 1939, at the age of 13, Jiang was adopted into the family of his uncle, Jiang Shangqing, who had been martyred as a result of his revolutionary activities. In 1943, Jiang began to study electrical engineering at Nanjing's Central University, which was subsequently merged with Shanghai's Jiaotong University. It was at this time that Jiang became actively involved in the Shanghai underground, and in June 1946 he joined the CCP.[10]

In 1947 Jiang Zemin began a career characterized by a gradual climb upward, though mostly in technical fields. In 1953 he was recruited into Shanghai's No. 2 Design Bureau by his political mentor, Wang Daohan (later mayor of Shanghai). In 1955 he was selected to study automotive engineering at the Stalin Autoworks in Moscow. When he returned to China the following year, he was sent to the Changchun No. 1 Automobile Factory, where he spent the next six years. When the Cultural Revolution broke out, Jiang inevitably came under attack as a "person in authority taking the capitalist road," but he quickly resumed his career when he was selected in 1971 to lead a technical delegation to Romania.[11]

In 1980, Wang Daohan was appointed mayor of Shanghai and recommended that Jiang take his place on the State Import–Export Management Commission and the State Foreign Investment Management Commission, organs that were responsible for the newly established Special Economic Zones in Guangdong and Fujian provinces. In 1982, Jiang was appointed first vice-minister of the newly established Ministry of the Electronics Industry and was selected as a member of the CCP Central Committee. He was appointed Minister of the Electronics Industry in June 1983. In 1985, again with Wang Daohan's support, Jiang was named mayor of Shanghai. Two years later, at the CCP's Thirteenth Congress, Jiang Zemin was named as Shanghai CCP secretary and concurrently a member of the Politburo.[12]

In short, Jiang's career was one of steady promotions. His ability to resume his career in 1971 reflects both his junior status and his technical credentials. That he was able to survive in the Ministry of Machine Building in the 1970s no doubt reflects his cautious nature, something that might have cost him further promotion in the reform era if he had not been technically trained and not had the support of patrons such as Wang Daohan. Later, as mayor and then Party secretary of Shanghai, Jiang had many opportunities to host the top leadership when they visited Shanghai. Deng Xiaoping often spent part of the winter there, as did Chen Yun, who was born just outside the city and had spent his early revolutionary career in the city. Jiang's relationship with Li Xiannian seems to have been particularly close. He was thus acceptable to the leading figures in the Party, and that in itself was an important qualification for leadership.

No doubt the single most important reason for Jiang's promotion at that critical time was his decision in May to close down the reform-minded newsweekly *World Economic Herald* (*Shijie jingji daobao*). On April 19, the *World Economic Herald* had convened a joint meeting in Beijing with the *New Observer* (*Xin guancha*) to memorialize Hu Yaobang. Run by the veteran revolutionary Ge Yang, the *New Observer* had been one of the principal outlets for liberal thinking in the 1980s and was at least as controversial as the *World Economic Herald*. In speeches, Su Shaozhi, Yan Jiaqi, Chen Ziming, and others called for "reversing the verdict" on Hu Yaobang as well as for criticism of the 1983 campaign against "spiritual pollution" and the 1987 campaign against "bourgeois liberalization." These speeches were printed in an issue of the *World Economic Herald* that was to go to press on April 24. By this time, there were deepening debates within the Party leadership about how to respond to the student demonstrations, which had started eight days earlier on April 16; on April 25, Deng would endorse a hardline approach by saying that the demonstrations were aimed at "fundamentally negating the leadership of the Chinese Communist

Party and at negating the socialist system." It was that judgment, written into a *People's Daily* editorial the next day, that inflamed student opinion and brought the student movement to a new crisis point.[13]

Aware of the controversies raging within the Party, Jiang Zemin's close confidante Chen Zili, head of the Shanghai Propaganda Department (and appointed in 1998 to head the Ministry of Education), was upset when she saw galley proofs of the forthcoming issue of the *World Economic Herald,* fearing that it would give new stimulus to the demonstrations. On hearing of the situation, Jiang Zemin called the editor of the *World Economic Herald,* Qin Benli, and told him to delete sensitive paragraphs from the offending issue. When, despite Jiang's order, part of the issue was printed and distributed, Jiang immediately ordered the presses stopped and Qin Benli removed from his post. Liu Ji, another close associate of Jiang Zemin who would play an important role in the 1990s, headed a work team that took over the paper. At the time, Liu was deputy head of the Shanghai Propaganda Department. Oddly enough, he was also on very good terms with Qin Benli; not only was Liu himself a contributor to the paper, but Qin's wife had taught Liu in middle school.[14]

The *World Economic Herald* had been one of the icons of liberal reformers in the 1980s and a beacon of expanding press freedom, so the removal of the respected Qin Benli and the paper's closure prompted an immediate outcry among press circles. For the first time since the demonstrations had started, journalists took to the streets. Carrying banners that identified their papers – *People's Daily* (*Renmin ribao*), *Workers Daily* (*Gongren ribao*), *Enlightenment Daily* (*Guangming ribao*), and so on – journalists hoisted signs declaring that they would not be forced to lie again.

At the same time, Zhao Ziyang, who had journeyed to North Korea April 23–30 in one of the worst-timed diplomatic trips imaginable, returned and convened a meeting of the Politburo on May 10. Referring to the *World Economic Herald* incident, Zhao declared that the Shanghai Party Committee "was hasty and careless" and had "turned a simple issue into a mess."[15] Before the meeting concluded, an anxious Jiang followed Li Ruihuan to the men's room to seek his advice. Li, who did not have a good opinion of Jiang, merely laughed.[16] Returning to Shanghai, Jiang tried to repair the damage. Despite interventions by Liu Ji and Su Shaozhi, Qin Benli refused to reconsider his actions, and Jiang seemed to be left hanging.[17] Perhaps, if Jiang's efforts to reverse his "decisive" handling of the *World Economic Herald* case had succeeded, he would not have been chosen as general secretary. However, Jiang emerged looking both decisive in opposing "bourgeois liberalization" and capable in handling the local situation; unlike Beijing, Shanghai was under control.

THE QUESTION OF ZHAO

Following the ouster of Zhao Ziyang and the subsequent crackdown in Beijing and elsewhere, the question of how to deal with Zhao became central. This issue was inevitably linked with the question of Deng Xiaoping's leadership, not just because Zhao's selection first as premier and then as general secretary now seemed to reflect poorly on Deng Xiaoping's judgment (for a second time – the ouster of Hu Yaobang in 1987 marking the first) but also because Zhao had been implementing a political *cum* economic line long supported by Deng.[18] Deng was famous as the exponent of the pragmatic advice, "black cat, white cat, whichever cat catches the mice is a good cat." Zhao had come to Beijing in 1980 as a pragmatist known for his concentration on economic development.

What lay behind this argument were distinctly different understandings of what "reform" meant. For Zhao – and for Deng – economic development was primary, and the only way to develop the economy was to marketize and join the international economy. In practice, this meant undermining and going around much of the old planned economy, allowing a market economy to grow outside the scope of the planned economy, and thus continuously reducing the relative importance of the planned economy. It also meant, to a greater or lesser extent, playing down much of socialist ideology. For Deng, the "four cardinal principles" (upholding the socialist road, the dictatorship of the proletariat [later, the people's democratic dictatorship], the leadership of the Communist Party, and Marxism–Leninism–Mao Zedong Thought), which he had enunciated in the spring of 1979 to curtail liberal criticisms of Mao and the socialist system, did not constitute a vision of socialist ideology but rather a boundary line defining the limits of acceptable public expression. When expression diverged too far from what he deemed acceptable, Deng cracked down. Such crackdowns allowed more ideologically oriented conservatives to criticize "bourgeois liberalization" for a while, but inevitably Deng would dampen the expression of such themes and re-emphasize economic development. Deng was interested in defining a middle path, using "reform and opening up" to oppose "leftism" and using the "four cardinal principles" to oppose "bourgeois liberalization."[19] It was a way to prevent ideological disputes from tearing the Party apart as they had in the past, and it was a political strategy that allowed Deng to build a coalition that upheld the center of the political spectrum. The adoption of the formula "one center and two basic points" in the spring of 1987 (in the course of the campaign against bourgeois liberalization that followed Hu Yaobang's ouster) merely formalized long-standing practice.

27

Leftists, on the other hand, emphasized ideology. They did so for several reasons. Many were products of the propaganda "system" (*xitong*) and thus had a vested interest in maintaining the political relevance of their competencies. Central ministries also had a vested interest in conservative ideological interpretations, because emphasizing such themes as "the planned economy as primary" or "state-owned enterprises as pillars of the economy" bolstered their importance in the political system. Leftist ideology also appealed to the vast numbers of Party cadres who worked in state-owned enterprises, whose relevance was thrown into question by the economic reforms. By 1979 Deng had already raised the issue of removing Party committees from enterprises, an issue that continues to fester two decades later. Thus, leftists saw Deng's reforms as undermining ideology and weakening the "fighting strength" of the Party. Market-oriented reforms, decentralization, and opening to the outside world all threatened these beliefs and interests.

These very different orientations underlay the mounting tensions in the Party in the late 1980s, and the anger and frustration of the left wing of the Party came pouring out in the aftermath of Tiananmen. Even though much of this hostility was directed at Zhao Ziyang, it was clear that the criticism of Zhao was also intended to curb Deng's authority. Deng's sharp defense of the Thirteenth Party Congress resolution – "not one character should be changed" – was no doubt intended to staunch this antireform tide.

The decision to declare martial law had effectively been made in a meeting of the Politburo Standing Committee at Deng's house on the morning of May 17. Prior to the meeting, Zhao solicited the views of his Politburo Standing Committee colleagues and Central Military Commission deputy head Yang Shangkun, who as a close political ally of Deng had the right to attend such meetings (as did Party elder Bo Yibo). Premier Li Peng and State Planning Commission (SPC) head Yao Yilin supported declaring martial law; the others – Hu Qili, Qiao Shi, Yang Shangkun, and Zhao – all opposed it. (Bo's views prior to the meeting are unknown.) Thus, prior to the critical meeting, the majority opposed imposing martial law. But Deng's mind was made up. When the meeting opened, Deng announced his own support for martial law and then asked each person to express his views. It soon became apparent that the majority opposing martial law had evaporated and that martial law would be declared. Such was Deng's "core" power. A meeting of the Politburo Standing Committee later that evening formally endorsed Deng's view – though Zhao Ziyang and Hu Qili voted against martial law and Qiao Shi abstained.[20] It was on the morning of the 19th when a tearful Zhao Ziyang appeared in Tiananmen Square, telling students that he had "come too late." Indeed he had; he no longer functioned as general secretary.[21]

According to Party custom, Zhao was expected to support the "majority" opinion, but Zhao embarrassed and angered the Party leadership by failing to attend the public meeting called to announce the implementation of martial law in Beijing on the evening of May 19. He also refused to make the self-criticism that was expected of him. If he had, he probably would have been retained as a member of the Central Committee. Instead, Zhao chose to defend his actions.

Sorting out leadership issues was the task of the Fourth Plenary session of the Thirteenth Central Committee, which convened in Beijing on June 23–24 following a three-day enlarged meeting of the Politburo. The plenum approved the removal of three Zhao associates: Hu Qili from the Politburo Standing Committee and Rui Xingwen and Yan Mingfu from the Secretariat. Veteran economic planner Song Ping and Tianjin mayor Li Ruihuan were added to the Politburo Standing Committee along with Jiang Zemin, while Li Ruihuan and Ding Guan'gen (Deng's bridge partner) were added to the Secretariat. The new Politburo Standing Committee was more conservative than before, but it was more balanced than might have been expected. Li Peng, Yao Yilin, and Song Ping made up a conservative block, while Li Ruihuan and Qiao Shi represented more moderate views. Jiang Zemin, no ideologue by nature, would have to feel his way in these turbulent waters.

On the question of Zhao, the Fourth Plenum charged that, "[a]t the critical juncture involving the life and death of the Party and state, he made the mistake of supporting turmoil and splitting the Party, and he bears unshirkable responsibility for the formation and development of the turmoil. The nature and consequences of his mistakes are very serious."[22] The public case for this judgment was made by Beijing mayor Chen Xitong, who presented a long and detailed report to the Standing Committee of the National People's Congress (NPC) on June 30. Despite declaring that Tiananmen had been brewing and had been "premeditated" for a long time, Chen's report focused narrowly on the alleged actions of Zhao and some of his supporters only in the months immediately preceding the crisis and during the demonstration itself. Chen sharply criticized Zhao for his opposition to the closing of the *World Economic Herald,* his speech to the Asian Development Bank, and his revelation to Gorbachev of the Thirteenth Party Congress resolution referring important Party matters to Deng – which Chen described as "deliberately directing the fire of criticism at Deng Xiaoping ...."[23] In his criticism of some of the intellectuals linked to Zhao, however, Chen hinted at the depth of the struggle within the Party. For instance, referring to a widely publicized conversation between senior intellectuals Yan Jiaqi and Wen Yuankai intimating that Zhao might be removed as Liu Shaoqi had been, Chen declared that this dialogue was intended to "whip up public opinion for covering up Zhao Ziyang's mistakes, keeping his position and power, and pushing bourgeois liberalization even more unbridledly."[24]

Li Peng's report to the Fourth Plenum, which unlike Chen's report to the NPC was not publicized in PRC media, makes it even clearer that the dispute between the two wings of the Party had existed for a long time. Li declared that bourgeois liberalization "spread rampantly" after Zhao became general secretary; Zhao, the premier charged, "accommodated, encouraged, and supported bourgeois liberalization." Specifically, he alleged that, at a Secretariat meeting in January 1987, Zhao had declared that of the four cardinal principles they should emphasize only Party leadership and not mention the other three – the socialist road, Marxism–Leninism–Mao Zedong Thought, and the people's democratic dictatorship. Moreover, Zhao allegedly declared that no one can explain what the socialist road is and, on other occasions, stated that corruption is inevitable at the initial stage of socialism. Li declared that in the future the Party should "carry out the struggle against bourgeois liberalization for a long time to come rather than do it perfunctorily or give it up halfway as in the past."[25]

Zhao Ziyang was allowed to attend the Fourth Plenum and respond to Li Peng's report. Oddly, the *People's Daily* even ran a picture of Party leaders attending the Fourth Plenum that included the back of Zhao's head. Zhao argued that everything he had done had been intended to "ease the confrontation" and to "gradually calm down the student unrest." He also refuted many of the charges raised by Premier Li. For instance, he said that he could not remember ever saying "corruption is inevitable at the initial stage of socialism." He rejected the accusation of neglecting political and ideological education by saying that he was worried that the "old methods" of ideology would not work and "might even arouse people's repugnance." Even while admitting responsibility for grasping economic work firmly but being lax with regard to bourgeois liberalization, he defended himself by citing Deng's words from April 1987, a time when Deng was trying to dampen an earlier campaign against bourgeois liberalization: "The struggle against bourgeois liberalization is a long-term struggle and is also a prolonged process of education. We cannot launch political movements, but should successfully carry out reform and develop the economy, thus demonstrating the superiority of the socialist system. Practice will convince people who doubt the socialist system."[26]

Zhao's speech also reveals that differences of opinion within the Party were long-standing. Describing discussions over the text of Li Peng's "Government Work Report" made to the NPC in the spring of 1989, Zhao said that Li's draft had "repeatedly" used the words "for many years" when discussing problems in economic work. The impasse was resolved by focusing the work report on just the preceding year, but Zhao reported that "[s]ome comrades" had criticized him for not allowing Li to discuss the mistakes of the "past few years" in the report.[27]

Although the Fourth Plenum accused Zhao of supporting the turmoil and splitting the Party – charges Zhao asked the Party to reconsider in his rebuttal – it could not reach a resolution on his case, declaring only that the Party would "continue to investigate his problem."[28] The plenum's failure to conclude Zhao's case reflected the depth of division within the Party. Some wanted to pursue the issue of Zhao's guilt, apparently to the point of criminal prosecution. For instance, Yuan Mu, hard-line spokesman for the State Council and protégé of Premier Li Peng, stated that Zhao's case would be handled "in accordance with the criterion based on law," suggesting the possibility of legal prosecution.[29] Some Party elders were even blunter. Li Xiannian, President of the People's Republic of China (PRC), allegedly called Zhao the "root cause of the riots and rebellion," while Party elder Peng Zhen accused Zhao of "attempting to topple the Communist Party and wreaking havoc with the socialist system in coordination with hostile powers at home and abroad."[30]

Putting Zhao on trial, as Deng had the Gang of Four, would have had profound implications for Deng Xiaoping and the continuation of reform. Shortly after such speculation appeared, the PRC-owned Hong Kong paper *Ta kung pao* reported that Deng Xiaoping had set a two-year period for "reflection" and declared that it is "highly unlikely" that Zhao would be put on public trial.[31]

Although Deng's "prediction" that Zhao would not face trial ultimately proved correct, his call for a period of reflection was largely ignored. During the campaign against "bourgeois liberalization" that was unleashed following Tiananmen, it was impossible to separate criticism of Zhao Ziyang from issues of ideology and Party line, and there is every indication that hardliners within the Party wished to press such issues with an eye to curtailing Deng's authority and returning the Party to the more limited notion of reform that had prevailed in the late 1970s and early 1980s. In his 1989 National Day (October 1) address, Jiang Zemin asserted that there were two types of reform: one that upholds the four cardinal principles and one that is based on "bourgeois liberalization." The question, Jiang said, was whether the socialist orientation would be upheld.[32] Deng had opened the way for this line of analysis in his May 31 talk with Li Peng and Yao Yilin. In that talk, Deng said that the "center of their [Zhao Ziyang and others'] so-called 'reform' is to become capitalists. The reform I talk about is different...."[33] In picking up Deng's thought and posing the question the way he did, Jiang raised the issue that would dominate Chinese politics for much of the next two years: What was socialist and what was capitalist?

By the same reasoning, if Zhao had advocated a reform that was based on "bourgeois liberalization" and hence was capitalist in nature, then Zhao's mistake would not have been a simple error of implementation (one hand firm and the other lax, as Deng put it) but an error of line. Although the Party, in the interest of putting ideological battles behind it at the beginning of the reform era, had ceased to describe intra-Party conflicts as "line struggles," the notion of political line and hence of line struggle remained very much a part of Party life at the elite level.

This assumption about inner-Party struggles comes through clearly in a talk Song Ping gave to a national meeting of organization department heads, where he implicitly criticized Zhao for making line errors. For Song, Tiananmen was the inevitable outcome of a trend of bourgeois liberalization that extended back to the democratic movement of 1978, had never been effectively opposed, and had resulted in such "absurd theories" (*miaolun*) as the "criterion of productive forces." The theory of productive forces, a phrase used (primarily by critics) to describe the view that anything that improves the economy is ipso facto socialist, was voiced prominently in an article by Zhao Ziyang that appeared in the *People's Daily* in February 1988,[34] but Song's reference was clearly to Deng Xiaoping as well. This trend of bourgeois liberalization, Song asserted, went against the Marxist political line set by the Third Plenum in 1978, and Tiananmen was the "bitter fruit of violating this [Marxist] *line.*"[35] Similarly, Chen Yun referred to "line struggle" in the "six points" that he conveyed to the Central Advisory Commission in November 1991. The third point reads, "Marxists must admit that there are line struggles within the Party, which is part of normal Party life, and it is necessary to actively launch inner-Party criticism and self-criticism."[36]

Both personal animosity toward Zhao and broader criticism of the "line" that Zhao was supposedly heading came through in press commentary in the summer and fall of 1989. A meeting of conservative writers and artists in July, for instance, declared that Zhao was the "biggest umbrella for bourgeois liberalization in literature and art circles" and accused him of "rudely critic[izing] comrades who adhered to the four cardinal principles" and who, as a result, were "vilified, suppressed, and attacked by others."[37]

Other articles criticized Zhao for putting forth the idea of "transforming the ideological and political work" and thus weakening the Party's ideological work.[38] For instance, one author complained that "[i]n recent years the viewpoint that class struggle in society will certainly find expression within the Party has been criticized as being a 'leftist' viewpoint."[39] The weakening of ideological and political work was held, among other things, to undermine the sense of class struggle, which Deng was certainly every bit as guilty of as Zhao.

DENG'S STRATEGY

In certain ways, the situation following Tiananmen resembled that in 1987 when, in the wake of student demonstrations, Deng and the Party elders had unceremoniously dumped General Secretary Hu Yaobang. After a four-month, often vitriolic, campaign against bourgeois liberalization that targeted three well-known intellectuals – astrophysicist Fang Lizhi, investigative journalist Liu Binyan, and writer Wang Ruowang – Deng and Zhao engineered a dramatic turnaround in the political atmosphere. In April, Deng told visiting Spanish Socialist Workers Party leader Alfonso Guerra that leftism was the "main danger" facing the Party.[40] Shortly thereafter, on May 13, Zhao Ziyang gave a major inner-Party speech, asking rhetorically but sharply: "Who would be responsible if the current [economic] policies were interpreted as liberalization?"[41] On the July 1 anniversary of the Party's founding, the *People's Daily* reprinted Deng's controversial 1980 speech "On Reform of the Party and State Leadership Structure," setting the tone for the upcoming Thirteenth Party Congress, which for the first time addressed the issue of political reform.[42]

In 1989, however, Tiananmen opened divisions within the Party that far exceeded those existing two years before. Among Party conservatives there was a deep sense of "we told you so." Their warnings, they believed, had not been listened to, and Tiananmen was the fulfillment of their predictions. Whereas previously they had held strong reservations about the direction of economic and cultural change in China, in 1989 they were convinced that reform was on the wrong track. Deng Xiaoping's prestige within the Party was correspondingly diminished by Tiananmen and the disgrace of Zhao. Chen Yun summed up the feelings of many conservatives when he accused Deng of being rightist in his economic policies and leftist in his use of the military.[43] Unlike before, Deng could no longer dominate China's policy agenda. Turning around the political atmosphere as he had in 1987 would prove far more difficult; indeed, it would take him three years (until 1992).

Deng's task was made even more difficult by the tense international atmosphere that prevailed in the months after Tiananmen. Deng had always coupled "reform" with "opening up" not only because he believed that China's economic modernization needed capital, technology, and export markets that only the West could provide, but because he recognized that jettisoning the Maoist emphasis on international class struggle was necessary for dampening domestic calls for a continuing emphasis on class struggle, something that would (and did) make the implementation of economic reform more difficult, perhaps impossible. The unraveling of communism in Eastern Europe would make Deng's position even more difficult as the dangers of "peaceful evolution" were brought home vividly to China's leaders, Deng included.

In short, in 1989 Deng was fighting a rear-guard action. Although damaged politically, he was hardly without resources. Despite considerable doubt about the wisdom of many of his policies and even a determination to cut back those policies, no one made an effort to remove Deng from his "core" position within the Party. Chen Yun was the only one in the Party with the stature to challenge Deng, but just as he had never challenged Mao, with whom he disagreed, he never challenged Deng's political position. Indeed, Chen seemed to enjoy prestige in the Party at least in part because he was not personally ambitious. Chen was more interested in policy than power, and he seemed both content and determined to force Deng to accept a diminished role in policy making.

In terms of political strategy, Deng clearly tried to relax the political atmosphere by responding to the popular resentments that had underlain the Tiananmen demonstrations, by trying to play down ideological tensions, and by ameliorating international tensions to the greatest extent possible. On the eve of the Fourth Plenum, Deng urged the leaders not to dissipate the energies of the Party in futile ideological disputes: "If at this time we open up some sort of discussion on ideology, such as a discussion regarding markets and planning, then not only would bringing up this sort of issue be disadvantageous to stability but it would cause us to miss an opportunity."[44] Yet it was, of course, precisely this sort of discussion – whether the given policies were "socialist" or "capitalist" – that was already beginning to fill the media and would dominate policy discussions until Deng's trip to the south in 1992.

Li Ruihuan, the former carpenter whom Deng had put in charge of ideology, made an effort to relax the ideological atmosphere in the summer by calling for a campaign against pornography. The campaign started on July 11, 1989, when the Press and Publications Bureau issued a circular on rectifying the cultural market. Over the summer, Li spoke on the issue of pornography many times.[45] It was a clever ploy that left conservatives nonplussed. After all, pornography was associated with Western influences, but it hardly raised the central ideological issues that conservatives desired to pursue. In September, Li asked in a sharply worded interview with the PRC-owned Hong Kong paper *Ta kung pao*: "Why do we always have to go to excess?" Berating conservative ideologues, Li said that "[w]e must not use dogmatic and rigid methods to criticize bourgeois liberalization."[46]

34

In Deng's talk on the eve of the Fourth Plenum, he also called for "doing some things to satisfy the people."[47] In response, the State Council in July passed a resolution on resolving problems the people were concerned about, especially restricting the activities of leading cadres' families, and on reorganizing suspect companies.[48]

Similarly, Deng harped on the issue of stability – eventually coining the phrase "stability overrides everything" (*wending yadao yiqie*)[49] – and emphasized the continuity of reform and opening up. In September, on the eve of the Party's Fifth Plenum, Deng told American physicist T. D. Lee that "reform and opening up will certainly be continued."[50] The message of reform and opening up was pressed by a *People's Daily* editorial six days later which strongly reiterated that reform would be continued and declared, "[w]e certainly must not stop eating for fear of choking."[51]

CONSERVATIVES PRESS THEIR ADVANTAGE

As Deng and Li Ruihuan tried to cool the ideological atmosphere and refocus the Party's attention on reform and opening up, conservatives were determined to press their advantage. Throughout the reform period a major debate had raged within the Party over the economic line to be pursued. Conservatives, led by Chen Yun, had argued that the "planned economy is primary, the market economy supplementary." That line, which had been enshrined at the Party's 1980 Central Work Conference and Twelfth Party Congress in 1982, was rejected (albeit implicitly) by the 1984 Third Plenum, which had adopted the "Decision on the Reform of the Economic Structure." The plenum decision endorsed the view that the economy was a "commodity economy" rather than, as conservatives had maintained, a "planned economy."[52] This was a significant ideological breakthrough that served to justify further liberalization of the economy and marked a major parting of the ways.[53] The rift between Deng and Chen widened in the ensuing years.

With the suppression of the protest movement in Beijing and elsewhere and with the ouster of Zhao Ziyang, conservatives seized the opportunity to criticize Zhao's leadership over the economy and impose their own interpretation of economic reform. This effort began with the editing of Deng Xiaoping's remarks. In Deng's June 9 talk, he referred to the "integration of planned economy and market regulation."[54] This expression restored the preferred usage of conservatives, which they had been able to impose during the 1981–82 retreat from more market-oriented reforms.[55] As later revealed, Deng had originally called for the integration of the "planned economy and the market economy," a formulation that put the two economic types on the same plane. However, before his remarks could be published in the *People's Daily,* conservatives edited them to fit their agenda.[56] The term "market economy" would not reappear until Deng's trip to the Shenzhen Special Economic Zone (SEZ) in January 1992.

In November 1989, Chen Yun's economic thought was restored as orthodoxy by the Fifth Plenary Session of the Thirteenth Central Committee. The "CCP Central Committee Decision on Furthering Improvement and Rectification and Deepening Reform" (frequently referred to as "The 39 Points") that was adopted by the plenum laid out a systematic, though implicit, critique of Zhao's management of the economy. That decision, like much commentary in the months since Tiananmen, hinted at the implicit line struggle that had existed within the Party by suggesting that the economy had begun to go awry in 1984 – when the Decision on the Reform of the Economic Structure was adopted. Since that time, the Fifth Plenum decision declared, economic policy had ignored China's "national strength," allowed aggregate demand to "far, far" exceed aggregate supply, permitted the balance between industry and agriculture to be thrown off, ignored basic industries, and overly dispersed financial resources, thus eroding the state's ability to exercise macroeconomic control. These problems, the decision declared, constituted a "mortal wound" (*zhimingshang*) to the economy.[57] All these charges were part of the conservative critique of reform that had been ongoing at least since 1984.

In Jiang Zemin's speech to the plenum, he declared that the "greatest lesson" to be derived from the PRC's economic past was that the country must not "depart from its national conditions, exceed its national strength, be anxious for success, or have great ups and downs."[58] These, like the charges listed in the preceding paragraph, were all well-known theses of Chen Yun, so Jiang's endorsement of Chen Yun's thought over Deng's line of reform and opening up was apparent.

Just as Party conservatives rejected Deng's economic line, they spurned efforts to reduce ideological tensions. Their rejection of Deng's efforts to reduce tensions was based not only on the depth of division within the Party but also on the collapse of socialism in Eastern Europe.[59] On December 15, Wang Renzhi, the conservative head of the Propaganda Department, launched a blistering attack on bourgeois liberalization in a talk to a Party building class. In direct opposition to Deng's theses that economic development would promote social stability and that ideological debates should be put off – or better, not taken up – Wang argued that stability could only be built on the basis of Marxist ideology. Only in this way, Wang argued, could economic work be carried out without deviating from the socialist orientation. As Wang put it, "[o]nly by criticizing and struggling against the ideological trend of bourgeois liberalization will we be able to consolidate and develop the political situation of stability and unity and to promote the smooth development of socialist construction." In effect, Wang reinterpreted Deng's slogan "stability overrides everything" – a phrase coined to relax ideological tension – as a clarion call for ideological struggle as the basis of some presumed future stability. Lest anyone think that the time had come to relax the campaign against bourgeois liberalization, Wang declared that "[w]e have only just started" to clarify ideological errors and that "[t]he logic of struggle is cruel and merciless."[60]

Wang's speech was followed by a full-page article in the *People's Daily* praising the notorious "Zhuozhuo meeting" of 1987. At that meeting, conservative Party leaders, concerned that Zhao and others would blunt the campaign against bourgeois liberalization that had unfolded in the wake of Hu Yaobang's ouster, tried to breathe new fire into the movement. It was after that meeting, and apparently because of it, that Deng authorized Zhao's famous May 13, 1987, speech that closed off the campaign against bourgeois liberalization and prepared the political atmosphere for the Thirteenth Party Congress in the fall. Now, in the wake of Zhao's ouster, conservative writer Chen Daixi (writing under the pseudonym "Yi Ren") accused Zhao of using "all kinds of dirty tricks with the most malicious motives" to suppress the Zhuozhuo meeting.[61] Obviously, Chen, as well as other conservative writers at the time, was aware that Deng had fully supported the stoppage of the 1987 campaign and they hoped to prevent him from doing so again.

REINFORCING STATE PLANNING

The strength of the conservative wing of the Party in the winter of 1989–90 was indicated not only by the directness of the challenge to Deng's ideological authority but also by a major effort to restore at least a significant measure of state planning to the economy. For years, conservatives had complained that reform had directed investment into small-scale, less efficient industries (mostly township and village enterprises, TVEs) that competed with large- and medium-sized state-owned industries for scarce energy, transportation, and raw materials. As a result, basic energy and material sectors were drained of investment capital while transportation and energy supplies were always strained by demand. Moreover, reform strategy had led to a regional bias as TVEs along the east coast grew and developed while industry and living standards in the interior lagged behind.

A major effort to strengthen the "pillars" of the economy, as the large- and medium-sized state-owned industries were called, came in late 1989 when Li Peng announced that a State Council Production Commission (*Guowuyuan shengchan weiyuanhui*) was being established to "promptly resolve major problems regarding production."[62]

The new commission was headed by Ye Qing, a specialist in the coal industry who had become a vice-minister of the State Economic Commission (SEC) before being named vice-minister of the State Planning Commission (SPC) when the former office was abolished in 1988. The State Council Production Commission incorporated offices that had once belonged to the SEC, including the production control and technological transformation departments, which had been placed under the SPC, and the Enterprise Administration Office, which had been assigned to the State Economic Restructuring Commission.[63]

Rather than resurrecting the SEC, which had often acted as a spokesperson for industry interests and had often clashed with the more conservative SPC, the new State Council Production Commission was clearly intended to be subordinate to the SPC. The idea behind the establishment of the State Council Production Commission was apparently to better coordinate the functions of planning and plan implementation through a newly established "double guarantee" system to be administered by the Production Commission, which in turn would be overseen by the SPC. The double guarantee system was intended, on the one hand, to guarantee the supply of the necessary raw materials and funds to important state-owned enterprises and, on the other hand, for the enterprises to guarantee delivery of profits, taxes, and output to the state.[64] The double guarantee system was initially imposed on 50 major enterprises in northeast China and then extended to cover 234 of China's largest enterprises.

Establishing the Production Commission and implementing the double guarantee system were clear victories for the conservative wing of the Party and especially for Li Peng, who would have a chance to try out his policies for strengthening socialist management. The victory for Li Peng was underscored by the appointment of Zou Jiahua, Li's close colleague of many years, as head of the SPC in December 1989 (replacing the conservative planner, Yao Yilin).

RENEWED DEBATE OVER THE DIRECTION OF THE ECONOMY

In the weeks and months after Tiananmen, there was virtually no debate over the course of the economy – at least not in the major newspapers. In fact, most economic commentaries carried by the *People's Daily* and *Enlightenment Daily* in those early months were by unknown reporters or economists. It was only after the Party's Fifth Plenum in November 1989 that the *People's Daily* began running serious economic views again. A number of well-known economists – including Ma Hong, Zhang Zhuoyuan, Li Chengrui, and Wang Jiye – argued the case for the Fifth Plenum's call for continuing retrenchment in measured, academic terms in the pages of the *People's Daily*.[65] These economists defended continued retrenchment as more liberal economists began to suggest that the policy of reform and readjustment had already achieved the major goal of controlling inflation and was beginning to hurt the development of the economy by excessively reducing demand. The emergence of this debate over retrenchment policies marked the first time in nearly half a year that a tone of rational discussion had entered the press.

This trend continued the following spring with Li Peng's address to the NPC in March 1990. Although Li was uncompromising on the need to continue "improvement and rectification," the name given to the retrenchment policies adopted in the fall of 1988, he called for finding a way to successfully "integrate" planning and market regulation.[66] This talk inaugurated a public discussion on this topic, the third such discussion in the history of the PRC. The previous two rounds of discussion, however, had been inaugurated in the wake of economic difficulties in 1959 and 1979 and were meant to justify an expansion of market forces. In contrast, this new discussion was intended to justify integration on the basis of planning. But at least an opening for rational discourse on the economy had been created.

Even as Li Peng was seeking to define and defend a policy that would recentralize the economy and reimpose a significant degree of planning, economic trends were revealing just how wrong such conservative views of the economy were. As Naughton has argued, China's economy in 1989 was far healthier than the conservatives' declaration of profound economic crisis would suggest.[67] The harsh restrictions on credit and investment were so successful in reducing demand that, by September 1989, consumer prices were actually falling – though China's planners, calculating inflation on a year-to-year rather than a month-to-month basis, were unaware of this dramatic turnaround.[68] Even calculating on a year-to-year basis, inflation in the first half of 1990 was only 3.2 percent, making it apparent to everyone that the urgency behind the retrenchment policies had passed. Meanwhile, the profitability of large state firms – the very sector that conservative policies had been designed to shore up – was collapsing. In 1990, profits of in-budget state firms fell 57 percent.[69] At the same time, inventory stocks shot up, enterprise losses jumped 89 percent over the same period the previous year, and the retail sales of commodities fell 1.9 percent.[70] Difficulties in the state-owned sector would force the government to pump an additional 270 billion yuan of loans into that sector in 1990 on top of the 126 billion yuan of loans issued in the fourth quarter of 1989.[71]

The combination of subsiding inflationary fears and stagnating industrial production brought renewed calls to revive reform, although it is surprising how slowly such calls were heeded given the debacle produced by conservative control of the economy. In May and June of 1990, some leaders solicited input from economists by raising the question of whether or not China's economy had come out of the economic trough.[72] This call stirred a new round of economic debate, and that summer the Economic Situation Group of the Chinese Academy of Social Sciences, headed by Liu Guoguang, proposed that the "weight" of reform be increased.[73] This proposal by no means rejected the austerity program adopted in 1988 (indeed, Liu had been one of the authors of that program), but it did emphasize that improvement and rectification were intended to bring about an atmosphere for a market-oriented reform rather than a reinstitution of the planned economy.

CENTER–PROVINCIAL CONFLICT OVER
THE EIGHTH FIVE-YEAR PLAN

One of the conservatives' biggest complaints about Zhao's management of the economy was that the strategy of decentralization pursued in the 1980s was leading to Beijing's loss of economic, and perhaps political, control over the provinces. In July 1988, as conservatives were mounting increasing attacks on the economic policies of Zhao Ziyang, Minister of Finance Wang Bingqian complained that the "financial situation is grim," largely because decentralization had led to a steady decline of central government revenues as a percentage of national income and as a percentage of all government revenues. The former figure, said Wang, had fallen over the course of reform from 31.9 percent in 1979 to only 22 percent in 1987.[74] Conservative economists complained loudly that the decentralization policies pursued in the course of reform had brought about a system of "feudal-lord economies" (*zhuhou jingji*), where each province was essentially a self-contained economic unit over which Beijing had little control.[75] Conservatives demanded a recentralization of economic and political power.

Conservative complaints were not without some validity. Central government revenues as a percentage of gross domestic product had fallen to under 20 percent by 1990 (from 31 percent in 1978), which put China in a range with such countries as Italy. Some experts predicted that if this trend continued it could lead to the virtual inability of the central government to control the macroeconomy.[76] However, the central question was: Which powers were to be recentralized and by what means?

Conservative instincts were to recentralize by exercising more direct control over the economy. This was the route mapped out by the draft of the Eighth Five-Year Plan as it neared completion in the summer of 1990. Zou Jiahua, vice-premier and head of the State Planning Commission (the organization with primary responsibility for drafting the plan), put it as follows: "The integration of central planning and market regulation is a basic principle" of economic policy making, but "the two do not have equal status. Central planning is of primary importance. Market regulation is supplementary."[77] This, of course, was standard conservative rhetoric.

The difference between this concept of planning and the provincial interest in continuing the existing patterns of reform came to a head at the September 1990 Economic Work Conference. Two issues were central to the conflict. One was an evaluation of reform: whereas Li Peng insisted that reform had led to various "dislocations" in the economy, the provinces insisted that reform be affirmed and written into the Eighth Five-Year Plan. The other issue concerned the financial interests of the provinces. The central government wanted to replace the local financial contract system, under which the provinces were responsible only for delivering a specified sum to Beijing, with a "dual tax system" that would designate clearly which taxes would go to the central government and which to the localities. Led by Ye Xuanping (governor of Guangdong), Zhu Rongji (CCP secretary and mayor of Shanghai), and Zhao Zhihao (governor of Shandong), the provinces virtually rebelled against the authority of the central government.[78]

The September work conference is often taken as a symbol of the growing independence of the provinces, and to a certain extent it was. Over the years, reform had allowed the provinces to accumulate considerable resources, primarily in the form of extrabudgetary revenues, which freed them from dependence on the central government. Provincial authorities went to elaborate lengths to nurture (and conceal) such funds, and they would not willingly yield their economic interests.

There was, however, another important aspect of this provincial "rebellion" – namely, that the central government was itself divided, with some political leaders and organizations sympathizing with the provinces. The most important of these was none other than Deng Xiaoping, who feared that the conservative agenda being pushed by Li Peng would negate the contributions of reform (and therefore of Deng Xiaoping) and would also lead to lower growth rates. Throughout the 1980s, Deng had emerged as the champion of higher growth

41

rates, not only because the economic achievements of China would reflect favorably on his own leadership and place in history but also because he believed that, as the economy developed, political and social conflicts would be more easily resolved, thus reducing the possibility that major conflicts could lead to another Cultural Revolution.[79] Thus, on the eve of the Economic Work Conference, Deng sent Yang Shangkun to talk to such provincial leaders as Zhu Rongji and Ye Xuanping, letting them know that they had Deng's support in their opposition to Li Peng.[80]

SINO–U.S. RELATIONS

A significant part of reformers' efforts to regain the initiative in 1990 lay in their hopes to improve Sino–U.S. relations. In the immediate aftermath of Tiananmen, however, Deng Xiaoping appears to have shared some of the suspicions of his more conservative colleagues. In fact, he inadvertently laid the foundation for the campaign against "peaceful evolution" by declaring that the June 4th "storm" had been an inevitable product of the "international macroclimate." A week later, Deng was more explicit, saying that "[t]he entire imperialist Western world plans to make all socialist countries discard the socialist road and then bring them under the control of international monopoly capital and onto the capitalist road"; he stated further that if China did not uphold socialism then it would be turned into an appendage of the capitalist countries.[81] Moreover, in his October 1989 talk with former President Richard Nixon, Deng charged that the "United States was too deeply involved" in the student movement.[82]

Conservative leaders, often quite hostile to the United States, were – on the basis of Deng's comments – able to whip up a campaign against "peaceful evolution." Such conservatives charged that the United States, having failed to contain and overthrow socialism in the 1950s and 1960s, had pinned its hopes on the later generations of Chinese, who might be susceptible to Western influences and thus bring about change from within. Such officials argued in the summer of 1989 that China should reorient its foreign policy away from the West to build better ties with the remaining socialist states and the Third World.[83]

Although such advocates did not carry the day, their views certainly influenced China's top leadership. In Jiang Zemin's October 1, 1989, speech marking the 40th anniversary of the founding of the PRC, the Party general secretary charged that "international reactionary forces have never given up their fundamental stance of enmity toward and [desire to] overthrow the socialist system."[84] Although conservatives were never able to bring about a fundamental reorientation of Chinese foreign policy, they certainly were able to constrain the ability of the Chinese government to take initiatives that might have improved relations. Thus, as Deng told Nixon, "[t]he United States can take a few initiatives; China cannot take the initiative."[85]

The United States responded to Deng's advice by sending Deputy Secretary of State Lawrence Eagleburger and National Security Advisor Brent Scowcroft to Beijing in December 1989. The timing of the trip, it turned out, was not good. The collapse of socialism in Eastern Europe, as noted previously, was provoking new debate in Beijing and bringing about a new upswing in conservative influence. Thus, China was able to make only minor concessions in return for the visit: it lifted its own restrictions on cultural and academic exchanges and promised not to sell medium-range missiles to the Middle East.[86] Beijing finally lifted martial law on January 10, 1990. It was not until June 1990 that Fang Lizhi, the Chinese astrophysicist who had taken refuge in the U.S. Embassy in Beijing after the June 4 crackdown, was finally permitted to leave the country.

Fang's release, like the other concessions, was too little and too late to win notice in the U.S. Congress, which was increasingly vocal and hostile, but it did begin to ease the tensions in Sino–U.S. relations. In late 1990, ties improved again with Chinese Foreign Minister Qian Qichen's visit to the United States, which culminated in a meeting with President Bush. After meeting with the President, Qian declared that the visit would "help open vast vistas for bilateral relations."[87] Qian's optimistic appraisal, however, did not materialize. Deep suspicions on both sides kept relations tense, and in China conservatives used opposition to "capitalism" to slow the pace of reform. Even after Deng's reform program was restored in 1992, this hostility left a legacy of suspicion that fed into the very different intellectual atmosphere that would emerge in the 1990s.

2

Deng Moves to Revive Reform

BY late 1990, Deng seemed visibly distraught by China's situation and his own inability to reassert his leadership. There were moments of small progress. For instance, in November he met with Jiang Zemin and Yang Shangkun before their trip to Shenzhen to commemorate the tenth anniversary of the SEZs' (Special Enterprise Zones') founding.[1] This meeting no doubt accounts for Jiang's high evaluation of the zones at the meeting late that month.[2] Then, on the eve of the Seventh Plenum in late December, Deng gave a short speech to several leaders emphasizing that planning and markets are not the distinguishing characteristics of socialism and capitalism, respectively. "Don't think that engaging in a little market economy is [taking] the capitalist road; it is not like that," Deng told his colleagues. He also urged his colleagues to be bolder and to take some risks.[3] These remarks evidently caused Jiang Zemin to revise his speech to the Seventh Plenum to declare that it was necessary to persist unswervingly in reform and opening up.[4] One report indicates that Jiang made the opening remarks to the plenum – but, if so, they have not been publicized; his closing remarks do contain a section called "firmly persist in reform and enlarge the scope of opening up."[5]

Such verbal reaffirmations of Dengist policy, however, did not amount to a resurrection of Deng's reform line. For instance, whereas the communiqué adopted by the Party's Seventh Plenum in December 1990 "highly evaluated" China's "tremendous achievements" in reform and opening up, it nevertheless went on to stress the "integration of the planned economy with market *regulation*" and to repeat such staples of Chen Yun's economic thought as calling for "sustained, stable, and coordinated" economic development and "acting according to one's capability" (*liangli erxing*).[6]

Such limited endorsement of Deng's views apparently left the patriarch frustrated. "Nobody is listening to me now," Deng allegedly complained. "If such a state of affairs continues, I have no choice but to go to Shanghai to issue my articles there."[7] So saying, Deng traveled to the east-coast metropolis and proceeded to give a number of talks intended to rekindle reform. In his talks, Deng declared that market and planning were both economic "methods" (rather than distinguishing characteristics of capitalism and socialism, respectively) and argued that whatever promoted the socialist economy was socialist. The Hong Kong press quickly dubbed Deng's comments as his "new cat thesis" (because of the idea that anything that promotes production is socialist) after his famous aphorism from the 1960s that the color of the cat does not matter.

The gist of Deng's talks in Shanghai was summarized in four commentaries carried in the Shanghai Party paper, *Liberation Daily,* under the pen name "Huangfu Ping" (which can be translated as "Shanghai Commentator"). Their writing and publication was overseen by Deng's daughter Deng Nan and Shanghai Party secretary Zhu Rongji.[8] The first commentary was published under photographs of Deng Xiaoping, Yang Shangkun, and Li Xiannian conveying lunar New Year's greetings to Shanghai leaders, thus visually emphasizing the authoritative nature of the commentary. Using language not seen since the heyday of reform in the late 1980s, the commentaries excoriated "ossified thinking" and repeatedly called for a new wave of "emancipating the mind." For instance, one article declared that China would "miss a good opportunity" if it got bogged down in worrying about whether something was capitalist or socialist,[9] while another quoted Deng as saying that capitalist society is "very bold in discovering and using talented people" and urging the promotion of a large number of "sensible persons."[10] A third article directly refuted conservative ideologue He Xin's argument (see Chapter 3) that foreign investment had led to the poverty of the Third World by calling on Shanghai leaders to "courageously take a risk, boldly use foreign capital, and turn Shanghai into a commercial, financial, and information center."[11]

RESPONSE FROM THE PROVINCES

It did not take long for several of China's provincial leaders to respond to Deng's initiative. On March 11, 1991, Guangdong's Party secretary Lin Ruo, who had close ties to Zhao Ziyang, published an article in the Guangdong Party paper *Southern Daily* (*Nanfang ribao*) and a shorter, somewhat watered down, version in the *People's Daily.* Lin pointedly attributed the rapid growth that Guangdong had enjoyed over the previous decade to the implementation of market-oriented policies. In the *Southern Daily* version of his article, Lin argued that planning had to be based on "commodity exchange and the law of value" and declared that "this is an objective law whether people recognize it or not."[12]

Another provincial leader who responded to Deng's initiative was Tan Shaowen, the Party secretary of Tianjin. Tan, an ally of Politburo Standing

Committee member Li Ruihuan, was subsequently promoted to the Politburo at the Fourteenth Party Congress in 1992 (and subsequently died in February 1993). In a major speech, Tan urged cadres to "emancipate the mind" and declared that "it was because of the reform and opening up that we conducted that we withstood the severe tests of the changes in the international situation, the political storms in the country, and numerous difficulties." In good Dengist fashion, Tan argued that "[e]conomic stability is the foundation of political and social stability."[13]

At the same time that Tianjin publicized Tan Shaowen's address, Hebei Governor Cheng Weigao echoed Deng's Shanghai comments, saying that "the development of the market and display of the market's regulatory functions must not be regarded as a practice of capitalism." Reflecting provincial (and Dengist) impatience with conservative leaders, Cheng sharply criticized planners in Beijing who had recentralized authority over the economy, and he demanded that central policies regarding enterprise autonomy be enforced and the Enterprise Law (passed in 1988 but never put into effect) be implemented. Cheng also berated conservatives as people who "have doubts and misgivings" about reform and have "lost courage to make positive explorations."[14]

Some of the strongest provincial comments came from Jiangxi governor Wu Guanzheng, who called on his colleagues to "emancipate the mind" and "increase the weight of reform." Sharply criticizing those who feared that the economic inequalities brought about by reform would lead to polarization, Wu declared that, "if the work initiative of the workers is not effectively aroused and if production does not grow, there will be only common poverty for all people."[15]

Most surprising of all was the call from Beijing mayor Chen Xitong to "emancipate the mind." One of the most conservative of China's high officials and a hardliner who had actively encouraged the use of force in suppressing the 1989 protest movement, Chen was nevertheless a close follower of Deng and responded to his call. In an interview with *Fortnightly Chats* (*Banyue tan*), Chen repeatedly invoked Dengist rhetoric, criticizing "ossified thinking" and giving explicit support to Deng's "new cat thesis."[16] In contrast, Beijing Party secretary Li Ximing, who would be ousted for his conspicuous resistance to Deng's policies following the patriarch's 1992 trip to Shenzhen, avoided the use of similar reformist rhetoric.

CAMPAIGN TO PROMOTE SCIENCE AND TECHNOLOGY

Even as Deng traveled to Shanghai to launch his "northern expedition" (as the Hong Kong press quickly dubbed his campaign), the dramatic outcome of the

Gulf War was forcing the Chinese leadership to reassess the impact of science and technology – and, by implication, that of ideology – in the contemporary world. This reassessment apparently began as early as March 1991 when Li Peng, in an internal address, elevated science and technology to first place in the four modernizations (up from their normal third-place listing).[17] Then, in April, reportage on Jiang Zemin's trip to Sichuan province quoted the Party head as saying that "comrades of the whole party, leading cadres at all levels in particular, should deeply understand the Marxist viewpoint advanced by Deng Xiaoping, that science and technology are the primary force of production."[18] Shortly thereafter, Deng Xiaoping's office wrote and forwarded an article to the *People's Daily*. The article revived many of the themes associated with discussions of the new technological revolution held in the 1983–84 period, when that theme had been used by Zhao Ziyang and others to turn back the campaign against "spiritual pollution."[19] Jiang Zemin himself made clear that the performance of high-tech weapons in the Gulf War had prompted him to stress the importance of science and technology.[20]

ZHU RONGJI ENTERS THE LEADERSHIP

One major success for Deng in the spring of 1991 was the elevation of Zhu Rongji to the position of vice-premier during the annual session of the NPC – though his elevation was balanced by the simultaneous selection of the conservative Zou Jiahua as another vice-premier. After the NPC meeting, there were five vice-premiers: Yao Yilin, Tian Jiyun, Wu Xueqian, Zou Jiahua, and Zhu Rongji. Yao was a member of the Politburo Standing Committee, and Tian and Wu were members of the Politburo. Zou was a full member of the Central Committee, but Zhu was only an alternate member. It was highly unusual for an alternate member of the Central Committee to be promoted to vice-premier. Zhu has drawn intense interest from domestic and foreign observers alike because he is unique in Chinese politics. Named a rightist in 1957, Zhu has nevertheless risen to the inner circles of power; moreover, Zhu has firm ideas on economic reform and the personality to push them against strong opposition. That Deng would reach out to such a person suggests his need and determination to counterbalance the conservative bureaucrats who had come to dominate the top of the system in the wake of Tiananmen – much as Mao decided to dilute Lin Biao's power by "mixing in sand" to the military command structure in the early 1970s.

Deng appears to have been familiar with Zhu's work and talents since at least the early 1980s, when Zhu was promoted to vice-chairman of the State Economic Commission.[21] When the State Economic Commission was abolished in 1988, a new assignment had to be found for Zhu. Although one school of thought argues that Zhu was personally selected by Zhao Ziyang to go to Shanghai to break up Chen Yun's powerful network there, it seems more likely that Zhu's background in the State Planning Commission and State Economic Commission reassured Chen that Zhu would not unduly disrupt the planned economy in Shanghai. Indeed, it seems likely that Zhu was able to maintain good relations with both Zhao and Chen and not become too closely identified with either; otherwise, it would have been difficult for Zhu to rise.

Like Li Ruihuan in Tianjin, Zhu seems to have drawn Deng's interest by his skillful handling of the 1989 demonstrations in Shanghai. Despite pressure, Zhu rejected calls to declare martial law in the city, opting instead for organizing worker pickets to restore order. After the violent suppression of protesters in Beijing, Zhu became famous for his ambiguous but suggestive remark that "the facts will eventually be made clear."[22] But Zhu was no liberal. When a train accident led an inflamed crowd to beat the driver and set fire to the train, Zhu oversaw the arrest, conviction, and execution of three people within eight days.[23]

When Zhu first came to Beijing as vice-premier, Li Peng apparently declined to assign him a portfolio. Three months later, under pressure from Deng, Li finally allowed Zhu to take over the State Council Production Commission, the group established under the State Planning Commission to oversee implementation of the "double guarantee" system. The Production Commission had failed in that task, allowing interenterprise debts to balloon.[24] Zhu promptly renamed the group the State Council Production Office (*Guowuyuan shengchan bangongshi*).[25] To put Zhu in charge of the State Council Production Office and of clearing up interenterprise debts marked an obvious policy failure for Li Peng, Zou Jiahua, and Ye Qing, but it did pass the hottest of hot potatoes to their rival Zhu Rongji. Zou maintained his position as a vice-premier and head of the SPC (until 1993), but his influence in policy circles was beginning to fade despite his subsequent elevation to the Politburo (but not its Standing Committee) in 1992.

Nevertheless, Zhu had been given a chance to develop a bureaucratic apparatus. Zhu quickly recruited his former associates from the old State Economic Commission, including former vice-chairmen Zhang Yanning and Zhao Weichen, who were made deputy directors of the new Production Office. The roles of Zhu and the Production Office were further enhanced in May 1993 when the office was expanded and reorganized as the State Economic and Trade Commission. The new office had a bureaucratic standing equivalent to the SPC and effectively hollowed out the latter organization by taking over day-to-day management of the economy, leaving the SPC to deal with the macroeconomy.[26] Moreover, Zhu was successful, at least temporarily, in reducing the problem of interenterprise debt. In June 1991, such debts had amounted to some 300 billion yuan; about two thirds of that was cleared by the end of 1992.[27] His successes would eventually allow him to enter the Politburo Standing Committee at the Fourteenth Party Congress in fall 1992.

CONSERVATIVE RESPONSE

Deng's offensive from the fall of 1990 through the spring of 1991 would prove to be a trial run for his efforts of the following year, but in 1991 he came up short. He had indeed used provincial officials to undermine the draft of the Eighth Five-Year Plan and then to publicize and promote his own thought, and he had laid the foundation of a later breakthrough by promoting Zhu Rongji and giving him an institutional basis from which to compete with Li Peng. But conservative opposition remained fierce. Despite Li Ruihuan's formal position as head of the Ideological Leading Small Group, conservatives had dominated the top reaches of the Propaganda and Organization Departments, as well as economic policy making, since 1989.[28] They would not give up without a fight.

This opposition was led by the father–son combination of Chen Yun and Chen Yuan, the deputy governor of the People's Bank of China. Even as Deng carried his message to Shanghai, the *People's Daily* carried a long article by Zhejiang Party Secretary Li Zemin disclosing comments made by the normally reclusive Chen Yun the previous year. Chen had long felt that Deng had, like Mao, created his own "one voice chamber" (*yiyantang*) and had thereby not abided by the tenets of collective leadership. Thus, Chen was quoted as saying, "[a]s leading cadres, we must pay attention to exchanging views with others, especially those who hold views opposite from our own."[29]

At the same time that the father's thought was being publicized, the son made a splash in intellectual circles. In December 1990, Chen Yuan organized a forum of many prominent economists at which he presented a paper entitled "China's Deep-Seated Economic Problems and Choices (Outline)." The paper was subsequently published in *China Youth News* in January, in the prestigious economic journal *Economic Research* in April, and in the Party theoretical journal *Seeking Truth* in June. Chen's article picked up where the conservative critique of reform in 1989 and 1990 had left off. Lambasting the decline in central authority that had resulted from a decade and more of devolving economic power, Chen called for a "new centralization" to deal with the emergence of "feudal lords" and "this disintegration of macrocontrol."[30]

In May 1991, the elder Chen was back in the public eye with a rare televised report of Chen meeting with Shanghai leaders. Subtly reiterating his own opposition to Deng's unwillingness to yield to collective leadership, Chen presented Shanghai leaders with a rhymed couplet that enjoined them to "not simply follow what superiors or books say" but to "act only according to reality."[31]

If Chen's reminders to Deng were gentle – almost obscure – others were willing to be much more direct. Indeed, as soon as the Huangfu Ping commentaries appeared, conservatives launched an investigation into their background, an effort that apparently concluded only when Deng's office let it be known that Deng himself lay behind the commentaries.[32] The knowledge that the commentaries expressed Deng's views apparently did not impress conservative leaders any more than had Deng's previous efforts to promote his views in the capital, and conservatives launched a variety of direct and indirect assaults on Deng's policies and the Huangfu Ping commentaries.

The sharpest attack on them, and hence on Deng, was a commentator article in the conservative journal *Contemporary Trends* (*Dangdai sichao*) that was excerpted shortly thereafter in the *People's Daily*. *Contemporary Trends* was one of several conservative journals that began publication in the wake of June 4 (others include *The Quest for Truth* [*Zhenli de zhuiqiu*] and *Mainstream* [*Zhongliu*]) and was edited by conservative ideologue Duan Ruofei, who had previously worked at the Party journal *Hongqi* (*Red Flag*). Since its founding, *Contemporary Trends* had published several articles by leading hardline officials, including Deng Liqun and Wang Zhen, and had carried numerous articles criticizing bourgeois liberalization in extremely harsh terms.

The April commentator article warned that those in favor of "bourgeois liberalization" remained "resolute" and that "we must be soberly aware that the liberalized trend of thought and political influence, which was once a major trend, will not disappear because we have won a victory in quelling the rebellion, but will again stubbornly manifest itself in a new form, spar with us, and attack us." Harkening back to themes raised by Song Ping and Wang Renzhi the previous year, the commentary argued that opposing bourgeois liberalization – not developing productive forces – was the key to ensuring political stability. Moreover, the article argued that the issue of bourgeois liberalization could never be confined to the ideological sphere because it was inherently a political issue involving the question of whether to take the socialist or capitalist road.[33]

REFORM HITS A TROUGH

With the publication of the *People's Daily*'s excerpt of the article from *Contemporary Trends* and other attacks on the themes raised by the Huangfu Ping commentaries, reformers fell quiet. For the summer, central and provincial leaders stopped voicing concerns about "emancipating the mind" or not worrying about whether a given reform was socialist or capitalist. This hiatus in the slow but steady progress that advocates of reform had been making at least since the September 1990 economic conference is difficult to explain. Four explanations seem possible.

The first is that, in the spring of 1991, Deng simply lacked the political strength to reinstate his vision of reform. Such an explanation assumes not only that Deng failed to win over (or intimidate) his opponents, but also that he failed to win the support of the "silent majority" of Party elders who seem to move to one side or the other in periods of political conflict, thereby affecting the political center of gravity. Second and more plausibly, one can assume that Deng, faced with opposition and uncertainty, yielded once again, as he had apparently done several times over the preceding two years – biding his time until a more opportune moment arose to renew his assault. This explanation assumes that Deng possessed the power necessary to prevail (which he would demonstrate a year later), but that he believed the cost in terms of Party unity outweighed the importance of prevailing at that time. Third, events in the Soviet Union – namely, Gorbachev's turn to the right, which culminated in cracking down on the Baltic republics in January 1991 – may have bolstered conservatives in Beijing, who are likely to have seen such a shift as a sign that the Soviet Union, too, was finally backing away from radical reform.[34] Fourth, the swift American victory in the Gulf War, which caught China off guard, may very well have renewed fears in Beijing that the world was becoming unipolar and that the United States would apply new pressures on China. Such a concern is likely to have reinforced the tendency among Party leaders to hunker down, assess the situation, and avoid divisive conflicts.

Such explanations are not mutually exclusive, and it is probable that a combination of internal and external factors convinced Deng to back off. In any event, with the publication of Jiang Zemin's speech on the 70th anniversary of the CCP on July 1, 1991, it became clear that reform was once again on hold.

Jiang's speech reflected the sharply conflicting opinions within the Party, affirming reformist themes but stressing conservative concerns. For instance, Jiang paid homage to Deng's emphasis on economic construction, saying that "from beginning to end, we must take economic construction as the center," and he even managed to incorporate (minimally) Deng's remarks in Shanghai by saying, "[p]lan and market are methods of market regulation" and that they "are not signs by which to differentiate socialism and capitalism." Nevertheless, conservative themes predominated. For instance, Jiang returned to the issue he had raised in his 1989 National Day address: the need to differentiate two types of reform. He also linked domestic class struggle to international class struggle and emphasized that "the ideological arena is an important arena for the struggle between peaceful evolution and anti-peaceful evolution." Moreover, with regard to economic policy, Jiang emphasized that "large- and medium-sized state-owned enterprises are the backbone strength of the socialist economy" and that "shaking public ownership of the means of production would shake the economic foundation of socialism and harm the fundamental interests of the whole people, to say nothing of socialism."[35] In short, it was a speech that, despite its bows in a reformist direction, clearly reflected conservative dominance over the overall ideological and policy agenda. More important, whatever reformist sentiments were in Jiang's speech were soon played down as the Party responded to renewed liberalization in the Soviet Union by circling the wagons even more tightly.

In late July 1991, the Soviet Communist Party (CPSU) surrendered its monopoly on political power and moved its ideological stance toward democratic socialism. This move caused obvious anxieties in China and prompted conservatives to take an even harder line. In particular, an August 16 commentator article in the *People's Daily* put an even more conservative spin on Jiang's CCP anniversary speech, calling for building a "great wall of steel against peaceful evolution" in order to protect the country from "hostile forces" at home and abroad. If such hostile forces win, the commentator article warned, it would be a "retrogression of history and a catastrophe for the people."[36] The tone of other, less authoritative articles likewise suggests a major conservative push in reaction to events in the Soviet Union. For instance, one article made a thinly veiled allusion to the Huangfu Ping commentaries of the previous spring and asked whether the orientation of the author of those commentaries was "socialist or capitalist."[37] Moreover, deputy director of the Propaganda Department Xu Weicheng, writing under his pen name Yu Xinyan, attacked the "Western monopoly capitalist class" for gloating over its success in promoting peaceful evolution, declaring that it had "rejoiced too soon."[38]

THE SOVIET COUP

Given the reaction of Chinese hardliners to what they regarded as the downward spiral of events in the Soviet Union, it is no wonder that they could barely contain their glee when they heard the news of the conservative coup d'état launched on August 19. China's ambassador congratulated the perpetrators of the coup, and conservative elder Wang Zhen, then in Xinjiang, called on China's Party leaders "never to deviate" from Marxism–Leninism–Mao Zedong Thought and to "fight to the death" for communism.[39] While in Xinjiang, Wang gave a number of "fiery speeches."[40] There were apparently a variety of meetings of leftists called to consider their response.

The ebullient mood did not last long. When the coup collapsed after only three days, Chinese leaders were despondent. Even Deng worried that if Yeltsin banished the CPSU, China would be the only major state practicing socialism. "Then what shall we do?", he reportedly asked.[41] The abortive coup in the Soviet Union posed, in the starkest possible terms, the fundamental question of the period: Should the CCP try to preserve its own rule by emphasizing ideology and socialist values, or should it try to win popular support and strengthen the nation through continued economic reform? Leftists in the Party clearly wanted to take the former route. Chen Yun, in a scarcely veiled attack on newly promoted Vice-Premier Zhu Rongji, reputedly warned against allowing a "Yeltsin-like figure" to emerge in China.[42]

If Deng was initially despondent over events in the Soviet Union, he did not stay that way long. Reacting quickly to conservatives' efforts to assert themselves following the Soviet coup, Deng intervened to insist on accelerating reform and opening up. As a PRC-affiliated Hong Kong magazine later put it, "Deng played a crucial role in preventing China from incorrectly summing up the experiences of the Soviet coup and in rendering the 'leftist' forces in the Party unable to use the opportunity to expand their influence."[43] Internationally, Deng reiterated his call for caution, saying that China should "tackle calmly, observe coolly, and pay good attention to our own national affairs."[44] Domestically, he inaugurated a determined campaign to reassert his own leadership and to put his understanding of reform back in the center. That campaign would last from the time of the abortive Soviet coup until the convening of the Fourteenth Party Congress in October 1992.

The first public sign that political winds were shifting came on September 1, when the Xinhua News Service transmitted the text of an editorial to be run the following day by the *People's Daily*. The editorial contained some of the most reformist language to be used since the previous spring, and did so in a more authoritative context. However, the first sentence contradicted and effectively negated the rest of the editorial. It read: "While carrying out reform and opening up to the outside world, we must ask ourselves whether we are practicing socialism or capitalism, and we must uphold the socialist orientation." Seven hours after this version of the editorial was transmitted, Xinhua released a new version in which the first sentence was changed dramatically to read, "While carrying out reform and opening up to the outside world, we must firmly adhere to the socialist course and uphold the dominant role of public ownership."[45] The critical question of whether a reform was "socialist" or "capitalist" had been cut.

It turned out that the second version was actually the editorial as originally approved, but prior to transmission the director of the *People's Daily*,[46] Gao Di, rewrote the first sentence to insert the conservative's pet thesis. This change was spotted, and at Deng's behest Li Ruihuan ordered that the offending sentence be removed. Thus, the editorial that appeared in the *People's Daily* on September 2 differed from what listeners had heard on the radio the evening before. Deng angrily declared that the *"People's Daily* wants to comprehensively criticize Deng Xiaoping."[47]

This incident underscores the deadly serious nature of "documentary politics" in the PRC, but it also makes clear that reformers were responding quickly to evolving events in the Soviet Union and restoring the push that had stalled the previous spring.[48] Just how difficult that task would be was indicated by an article by former Organization Department head Chen Yeping that appeared in the *People's Daily* on September 1. Taking the unusual step of criticizing former general secretary Zhao Ziyang by name (attacks by name had largely died out more than a year earlier), Chen accused him of advocating "productivity as the criterion for selecting cadres" – essentially what the Huangfu Ping commentaries had called for the previous spring – and claimed that his "erroneous viewpoint still has some effect in the cadre work of some regions and departments."[49] Reformers responded almost immediately. In late September, Deng instructed Jiang Zemin and Yang Shangkun to persevere in reform and opening up,[50] and Yang subsequently gave a ringing endorsement of reform on the 80th anniversary of the 1911 Revolution. Reform was, he said, a part of the historical effort to revive and develop China that had begun with Sun Yat-sen.[51]

In its stress on patriotism and its assessment that economic development is the common goal of all Chinese, Communist or not, Yang's speech echoed the 1986 Third Plenum resolution on building socialist civilization. That resolution played down the importance of Communist ideology in favor of a "common ideal" to which all patriotic Chinese could subscribe.[52] More important in terms of the immediate political debate, Yang declared unequivocally that *"all* other work must be subordinate to and serve" economic construction and that the Party must not allow its "attention to be diverted or turned away" from economic construction.[53]

Despite such clear signals from Deng and his supporters, conservatives continued to resist. During his November visit to Shanghai, Li Peng could not resist telling Zhu Rongji, who had overseen the compilation of the Huangfu Ping articles, that "[t]he influence of the 'Huangfu Ping' articles was terrible.

It caused the unified thinking that the center had expended a great deal of effort to bring about to become chaotic again."[54]

On October 23, the *People's Daily* published a hard-hitting article by leftist ideologue Deng Liqun, entitled "Have a Correct Understanding of Contradictions in Socialist Society, Take the Initiative in Grasping and Handling Contradictions." In stark contrast to Yang Shangkun's speech two weeks earlier, Deng declared that class struggle was more acute than at any time since the founding of the PRC. An editor's note stated that "the harsh reality of struggle has made clear to us that pragmatism can make a breach for peaceful evolution."[55] The term "pragmatism" seemed a clear allusion to the policies of Deng Xiaoping.

At the meeting of the Central Advisory Commission (CAC) convened on November 29, Party elder Bo Yibo conveyed six points raised by Chen Yun that stressed strengthening Party organization, the threat of peaceful evolution posed by the United States, and the danger posed by overzealous efforts to speed up economic development.[56] In late November, Deng Xiaoping urged the leadership to improve relations with the United States by not raising the issue of peaceful evolution so much and by compromising with the United States on human rights issues. On hearing Deng's suggestion, Party elder Wang Zhen apparently flew into a rage, declaring that Deng's policies were leading the country down the road to capitalism.[57] At the time, as Wang Zhen's outburst showed, the Party remained deeply divided over the danger posed by "peaceful evolution." In September, Propaganda Department head Wang Renzhi and others had organized an "anti–peaceful evolution" study group at the Central Party School which warned that peaceful evolution could be boosted by "pragmatists" in the leadership. Conservatives participating in the group denounced Li Ruihuan as "a person who wants to be Gorbachev" and called Qiao Shi a "fence sitter."[58]

DENG'S "SOUTHERN TOUR"

On January 19, almost eight years to the day since Deng's first visit to Shenzhen inaugurated a new push in opening China to the outside world, Deng once again set foot in the SEZ. Accompanied by Yang Shangkun and other officials, Deng spent the next several days touring Shenzhen and then the Zhuhai SEZ, talking about the importance of reform and blasting his opponents as he went.

Perhaps the most critical point in his talks was his contention that, without the ten years of reform and opening up, the CCP would not have survived an upheaval such as the Party had faced in spring 1989. This judgment was Deng's response to his opponents' contention that reform had led to the Tiananmen incident and would lead to the downfall of the CCP, just as it had to that of the CPSU and the various communist parties of Eastern Europe.

In order to defend his vision of reform against his critics' arguments, Deng reiterated the theoretically unsophisticated but ultimately effective argument that he had put forth in Shanghai the previous year: planning and markets, far from being distinguishing characteristics of socialism and capitalism, were simply economic "methods" possessed by both types of systems. The two systems, Deng declared, were distinguished by their respective ownership systems – public ownership in the former and private ownership in the latter – rather than by the existence or extent of the market. Moreover, Deng hit back directly at the numerous derogatory criticisms of the so-called "criterion of productive forces" made over the previous two years. In the baldest statement of that thesis since Zhao Ziyang had championed it on the front page of the *People's Daily* four years before, Deng declared that socialism could be defined in terms of three "advantages": whether or not something was "advantageous to the development of socialist productive forces, advantageous to increasing the comprehensive strength of a socialist nation, and advantageous to raising the people's standard of living."[59]

In addition to dismissing conservatives' concerns over whether a particular reform was "socialist" or "capitalist," Deng blasted his cautious colleagues with one of Mao's most famous metaphors. Deng urged them not to act like "women with bound feet"; reform needed to be bolder and the pace of development faster. "To develop a large, developing country like ours," Deng said, "economic development must be a bit faster; it cannot always be calm and steady." Underscoring his implicit but pointed criticism of Chen Yun's thought, which had just been endorsed again by the Seventh Plenum in December 1990, Deng went on: "We must pay attention to the steady and coordinated development of the economy, but being steady and coordinated is relative, not absolute." He then called on Guangdong to catch up to the "four small dragons" (South Korea, Taiwan, Singapore, and Hong Kong) in twenty years.[60]

The most eye-catching passages in Deng's talks, however, were his blunt criticisms of the "left." In sharp contrast to the constant criticism of bourgeois liberalization and peaceful evolution over the preceding two years, Deng pointed out that the main danger to the Party lay on the "left." "The right can bury socialism, the 'left' can also bury socialism," declared the patriarch. Moreover, in a direct criticism of Deng Liqun, Deng Xiaoping declared that "saying that reform and opening up is introducing and developing capitalism and believing that the main danger of peaceful evolution comes from the economic arena are 'leftist'." Deng also declared that anyone who opposed reform should "step down" – a threat that would be carried out against several conservative leaders the following fall and was clearly intended to shake up the cautious Jiang Zemin as well. Throwing down the gauntlet, Deng declared: "Whoever changes the line, orientation, and policies of the [1978] Third Plenum will be stopped by the common people (*lao baixing*) and will be struck down."[61]

THE STRUGGLE FOR DOMINANCE

Initially, the PRC media did not report Deng's trip and the CCP did not relay his comments internally. It was only after the Hong Kong media began reporting on Deng's trip that the PRC-owned Hong Kong papers *Wen wei po* and *Ta kung pao* began covering it. *Wen wei po* claimed that failure of the PRC media to cover Deng's trip was at Deng's insistence.[62] If that was the case (and it seems highly unlikely), Deng soon changed his mind.

The obvious resistance to publicizing Deng's trip – and the subsequent process of yielding partially while continuing to resist – reflects the very ambiguous nature of authority relations at the highest level of the CCP in the early 1990s. Deng began to shed his formal authority by stepping down from the Politburo Standing Committee at the Thirteenth Party Congress in September 1987 and then yielding leadership over the Party's Central Military Commission (CMC) to Jiang Zemin in November 1989. However, it seems that Deng was unwilling to shed all vestiges of formal authority and rule solely through informal politics. Thus, the Thirteenth Party Congress passed a secret resolution to refer all major decisions to Deng Xiaoping as the "helmsman" of the Party.[63] The authority conferred by this resolution is ambiguous, though, since "helmsman" was not a formal position and it was not clear whether Deng's wishes still needed to be obeyed in the same way as before his retirement. With the Tiananmen incident, Deng's prestige within the Party plummeted, weakening his ability to exercise informal authority. Conservative strategy in the three years following that incident was apparently to hamstring Deng's ability to exercise authority but not to challenge directly his "core" position. The effort was to turn Deng into the titular leader of the Party, much as Liu Shaoqi and Deng himself may have hoped to do to Mao in the early 1960s.

As the struggle for dominance in the spring of 1992 would show, Deng had (or had regained) enough authority to force nominal compliance with his wishes but not enough to immediately subdue opposition. Unlike in the spring of 1991, when Deng had backed off a decisive confrontation with his opponents, in 1992 – with the Fourteenth Party Congress looming on the horizon – Deng was determined to raise the stakes to the level of a contest for Party leadership. In such a contest, the advantages of being "core," ambiguous as they were, would eventually secure the victory for Deng, but his opponents would not yield without staunch resistance.

A turning point in this struggle for dominance – the first of several – came when a Politburo meeting on February 12, 1992, under obvious pressure from Deng, decided to relay the content of Deng's talks orally only to cadres at or above the ministerial, provincial, and army ranks.[64] This limited dissemination of Deng's views reflected a pattern that would hold throughout most of the spring: namely, yielding to pressure from Deng (thereby sidestepping direct confrontation) but doing so only as little as possible (in the hopes that Deng would yield to resistance).

In the face of this passive resistance, Dengist forces used local media to step up the pressure on Beijing's still silent official media. On February 15, Shanghai's *Liberation Daily* (*Jiefang ribao*) published a full page of pictures of Deng taken by Yang Shaoming, Yang Shangkun's son. Five days later, on February 20, Shenzhen's paper launched a series of eight articles that gave new details about Deng's visit and summarized the content of his remarks – the first such coverage in PRC media.[65]

Finally, the *People's Daily* began to yield to the pressure. On February 22, it published an authoritative editorial, apparently reflecting the Politburo meeting ten days earlier, that called for strengthening reform. In contrast to the emphasis on slow and steady economic growth that had dominated press coverage in recent months, the *People's Daily* now declared that "the fundamental point for upholding socialism is developing the economy as fast as possible."[66] The editorial made clear its criticism of "leftists" within the Party by pointing out the "catastrophes" caused in the past by "taking class struggle as the key link." Two days later, a second editorial urged people to "be more daring in carrying out reform" and cited Deng's dictum, "Practice is the sole criterion of truth."[67]

What attracted even greater attention, though it carried less weight, was a vigorous defense (the likes of which had not been seen in over two years) of learning from capitalism by Fang Sheng, an economist at Chinese People's University. Decrying "leftist" influences in the past that had led China to take a "tortuous" path, Fang urged "absorbing certain views, models, and methods from contemporary bourgeois economic theories" – even if it meant that "exploitation" would exist in China for a while.[68] However, despite publication of the two editorials and of Fang Sheng's article, Beijing's media remained silent about Deng's trip to the south, indicating the deep opposition within the Party to Deng and his views. Indeed, Deng's opponents took active measures to resist Deng's new offensive. Deng Liqun made his own trip, visiting the cities of

Wuhan and Xining, where he declared, "[t]here is the core of economic work but also another core of fighting peaceful evolution and waging class struggle. And sometimes, the campaign against peaceful evolution is more important."[69] Chen Yun himself presided over a meeting of the CAC held in Beijing on February 17 at which he declared that the only way for the CCP to avoid a CPSU-style collapse was to emphasize Communist ideology and strengthen Party building. Thirty-five senior leaders at the meeting drafted a strong letter to Deng demanding that Communist ideology continue to be propagated and that the Party strongly oppose peaceful evolution.[70] It was not until March 1 that Deng's remarks were officially spread within the Party in the form of Central Document No. 2. This official compilation followed the dissemination of Deng's remarks in five versions in different bureaucratic hierarchies and was intended not only to put out an official version but also to delete some of Deng's harshest comments. Nonetheless, the propaganda system limited circulation of the document.[71] Yet the dissemination of Document No. 2 did not squelch opposition. Conservative Party elder Song Renqiong declared in early March that he could not detect leftist influences in current political, ideological, and economic work.[72] Similarly, the conservative director of the *People's Daily,* Gao Di, declared on March 9 that "[w]e have already published two or three comments, and that is enough for the moment. No more articles will be published."[73]

In the midst of this acrimonious dispute, an enlarged meeting of the Politburo was convened for March 10–12. Yang Shangkun, Deng's close associate and permanent vice-chairman of the CMC, led the charge by demanding that the body endorse Deng's view of economic work at the center. Jiang Zemin offered a self-criticism for his laxity in promoting reform and opening and echoed Yang's views.[74] Politburo member and NPC Chairman Wan Li also strongly endorsed Deng's views, and Politburo Standing Committee member Qiao Shi argued pointedly that the leadership of the Party remained hindered by leftist ideology that interfered with the effective implementation of the Party's principles and policies. In opposition, Politburo Standing Committee member Yao Yilin argued that Deng's comments on guarding against leftism referred to the economic field; there were no indications of leftism in other fields. Yao's comments were echoed by Song Ping, also a member of the Standing Committee.[75] The outcome favored Deng. The communiqué issued by the Politburo meeting endorsed the "necessity" of upholding the "one center" of economic development and called on the Party to "accelerate the pace of reform and opening to the outside world." Moreover, it affirmed Deng's thesis that the main danger the Party faced was leftism.[76] Accordingly, China's central media finally publicized Deng's trip. On March 31, the *People's Daily* reprinted a long, flowery but detailed account of

Deng's activities in Shenzhen entitled, "East Wind Brings Spring All Around: On-the-Spot Report on Comrade Deng Xiaoping in Shenzhen."[77]

Despite this important endorsement, the meeting decided to delete a reference to guarding against leftism from the draft of Li Peng's Government Work Report to the upcoming session of the NPC on the grounds that it would be inappropriate to include any reference to differences of opinion in a government (as opposed to Party) work report.[78] A fusilade of criticism from the floor, clearly abetted by NPC Chairman Wan Li, forced the premier to add a warning to his report that the main danger lay on the left – as well as to make 149 other large and small changes.

The enormous stakes involved and Deng's willingness to use any and all methods to carry the day were clearly revealed at the NPC meeting when Yang Baibing, vice-chairman of the CMC, declared that the People's Liberation Army (PLA) would "protect and escort" (*baojia huhang*) reform.[79] This military intervention in domestic politics was a clear indication of the degree of tension in the Party. Moreover, the military kept up the pressure. Over the ensuing months, four delegations of senior PLA officers visited the Shenzhen SEZ to demonstrate their support for reform and opening up; also, the army newspaper, the *Liberation Army Daily*, repeatedly ran articles in support of reform.[80] The effort to professionalize and depoliticize the military, which had suffered badly with its crushing of the 1989 movement, was again set back. It became clear that military backing was the ultimate support for Deng's rule, and trying to secure that support would soon become central to Jiang Zemin in his quest to become "core" of the Party in reality as well as name.

THE DEBATE CONTINUES

The March 1992 Politburo meeting and the subsequent NPC session marked important, if not unambiguous, victories for Deng. The battle over reform continued. On April 8, members of the CAC held a meeting to draft a letter to the Central Committee, which was subsequently forwarded on April 14. The letter warned against the tendency to "completely negate" the theories of Marxism–Leninism–Mao Zedong Thought and declared, in direct opposition to Deng's comments in Shenzhen, that "the biggest danger is the 'rightist' tendency and bourgeois liberalization in the last 10 years."[81]

Shortly thereafter, on April 14, the *People's Daily* ran a long article by Li Peng confidante Yuan Mu, head of the State Council Research Office. Entitled "Firmly, Accurately, and Comprehensively Implement the Party's Basic Line," Yuan's article did to Deng what Deng had previously done to Mao: reinterpreted the leader's thought by insisting that it be viewed "comprehensively." For instance, while endorsing Deng's view about the importance of guarding against the left, Yuan went on to stress the need to maintain "vigilance against bourgeois liberalization" in order to prevent the sort of "evolution" experienced by Eastern Europe and the Soviet Union.[82] Similarly, a joint Propaganda Department and State Council Information Office writing team published an article under the pen name Leng Rong that used Deng's words to blunt Deng's own offensive. The article cautioned against bourgeois liberalization by quoting Deng as saying, "[h]enceforth, if necessary, when elements of turmoil just emerge, we must go to any lengths to eliminate them as soon as possible." This was not the message that Deng was trying to promote in the spring of 1992.[83]

In response, Deng's supporters rallied. On April 6, Qiao Shi – in an apparent criticism of Jiang Zemin – derided "some leading comrades" who only feign compliance with the line of reform and opening up. Such people, Qiao urged, should step down from power.[84] Similarly, during his April 16–22 tour of Shanxi province, Qiao touted Dengist themes, calling for an "ideological leap" in people's awareness of the need for reform.[85] On April 13, Gong Yuzhi (former deputy head of the Propaganda Department and a long-time supporter of Deng) gave a talk called "Emancipate Thought, Liberate Productive Forces" at the Central Party School. Gong sharply criticized those who questioned further reform on the grounds that it was capitalist, saying that such views had prevented the emergence of reforms for many years prior to the 1978 Third Plenum. China needed to renew the spirit of "emancipating the mind" that had prevailed then. This talk marked an important signal to intellectuals and opened the way to harsher attacks on leftism.[86]

In late April, Vice-Premier Tian Jiyun went to the Central Party School and lambasted leftists for having "basically repudiated all the most fundamental and substantial elements that we have upheld since reform and opening up." In a barb apparently directed at General Secretary Jiang Zemin, Tian declared that "[t]o do away with 'leftist' influence, one must particularly guard against those who bend with the wind, the political acrobats who readily vacillate in attitude." With a parody rare in Chinese politics, Tian told his listeners that leftists should go to a "special leftist zone" in which there would be total state planning, supplies would be rationed, and people could line up for food and other consumer items.[87] Soon, pirated copies of Tian's talk were being sold on the streets of Beijing.

Deng's demonstration that he would not back off this time, underscored by the mobilization of the army on his behalf, stirred Chen Yun to make some concessions. Appearing in Shanghai on the eve of Labor Day, the Party elder encouraged leaders there to "emancipate their minds" and "take bold steps." According to one report, Chen's declaration came on the heels of a high-level meeting with Deng, Peng Zhen, Li Xiannian, Bo Yibo, and Yang Shangkun.[88] Chen, who in 1978–79 had opposed the establishment of the SEZs and especially opposed the establishment of one in Shanghai, was now quoted as saying, "I very much favor the development and opening of Pudong!"[89]

Despite Chen's partial concession in Shanghai, Deng Xiaoping obviously remained frustrated at the lack of meaningful response from the leadership. On May 22, Deng showed up at Capital Iron and Steel (usually referred to by its Chinese abbreviation, Shougang) and listened to Zhou Guanwu, the long-time leader of the model enterprise, report on the enterprise's reform experience. Deng complained that many leaders were "merely going through the motions" of supporting reform and that they were in danger of losing their jobs.[90] Just as important, Deng signaled his strong support for Zhu Rongji, whom he had sponsored to become vice-premier in March 1991. Zhu, Deng said, is "quite capable" in economics.[91]

Deng's criticism of China's leadership finally stirred Jiang Zemin to action. On June 9, the general secretary followed in the wake of Qiao Shi and Tian Jiyun by giving a major speech at the Central Party School. Jiang at last openly endorsed the view that the "primary focus must be guarding against the 'left'." Quoting liberally from Deng's talks in Shenzhen, Jiang now argued that reform is like "steering a boat against the current. We will be driven back if we do not forge ahead." The Party chief nevertheless refrained from calling for a "socialist market economy," which would become the keynote of the Fourteenth Party Congress, continuing to refer instead to "market regulation" (though he dropped the formulation "integration of planned economy and market regulation").[92] Jiang's speech was the occasion of the *People's Daily*'s first authoritative comment on reform since February.[93]

Reform was given new momentum in late May with the circulation of Document No. 4, "The CCP Central Committee's Opinions on Expediting Reform, Opening Wider to the Outside World, and Working to Raise the Economy to a New Level in a Better and Quicker Way." The document, apparently drafted under the auspices of Zhu Rongji, marked a major new stage in China's policy of opening to the outside by declaring that five major inland cities along the Yangtze and nine border trade cities would be opened and that the thirty capitals of China's provinces and municipalities would enjoy the same preferential treatments and policies as the SEZs. Moreover, the document stated formally what Deng had said in January – namely, that Guangdong was to catch up with the four small dragons in twenty years.[94]

The more open political atmosphere of the spring encouraged long-silenced liberal intellectuals finally to raise their voices again in protest against leftism. A collection of essays by such famous intellectuals as Wang Meng (former Minister of Culture), Hu Jiwei (former editor-in-chief of the *People's Daily*), and Sun Changjiang (former deputy editor of *Science and Technology Daily* [*Keji ribao*]) created a storm when it was published under the title *Historical Trends*.[95] The book's sharp criticism of leftism quickly brought the wrath of the Propaganda Department, which banned the book.[96] Shortly after the book's publication, Yuan Hongbing – the law lecturer from Beijing University who had edited the book – presided over a gathering of more than 100 well-known intellectuals in Beijing. Such people as Wang Ruoshui, the former deputy editor of the *People's Daily*, and Wu Zuguang, the famous playwright who had been expelled from the Party in 1987, addressed the forum.[97] In the months that followed, other books denouncing leftism came off the press.[98]

The renewed activities of such liberal intellectuals was certainly grist for the leftists' mill. Shortly after the forum in Beijing, Deng Liqun launched a new attack. In an internal speech at the Contemporary China History Institute, Deng called for "extra vigilance over the recent rise in rightist tendencies."[99]

Many intellectuals had taken heart from Deng Xiaoping's trip to the south and his harsh denunciations of the left. They hoped that the patriarch would at last deal a fatal blow to such leftist leaders as Deng Liqun, Wang Renzhi, and Gao Di. Deng's calculus, however, remained different from that of the intellectuals. Deng's goals were twofold. First, he wanted to reassert his dominance in the Party. His southern tour, his harsh rhetoric, and his willingness to use the military in an intra-Party struggle demonstrated his determination; the Fourteenth Party Congress' enshrinement of Deng's thought would signal his success. Second, however, Deng sought a path that might ensure stability after his passing, and the terrible intra-Party struggles that Tiananmen and the ensuing changes in the international environment had set off demonstrated just how precarious that goal was. In 1989 Deng had endorsed the concept of neo-authoritarianism, the idea that the authority of the state could be used to build a strong economy and stable society à la the authoritarian regimes on China's periphery. During his trip to the south, Deng praised the example of Singapore. During his visit to Shougang, he signaled that he had found his tool to build such a society: Zhu Rongji.

Thus, the Fourteenth Party Congress that convened in October 1992 sought to attain two seemingly contradictory goals: establish the dominance of Deng (and his line of reform and opening up) over the left and deny the fruits of victory to the "bourgeois liberals" within the Party.

THE FOURTEENTH PARTY CONGRESS

Deng's efforts over the preceding year and more, starting with his early 1991 trip to Shanghai and building momentum following the abortive coup in the Soviet Union and with his trip to Shenzhen, finally culminated in October 1992 with the adoption by the Fourteenth Party Congress of the most liberal economic document in CCP history. Whereas a year earlier Deng Liqun had been calling reform and opening up the source of peaceful evolution,[100] the Fourteenth Party Congress report declared that "the most clear-cut characteristic of the new historical period is reform and opening up" and that the "new revolution" inaugurated by Deng Xiaoping was "aimed at *fundamentally* changing the economic structure rather than patching it up." Underlining the profound changes called for by Deng's revolution, the political report endorsed the creation of a "socialist *market* economic system" as the goal of reform, thereby advancing well beyond the 1984 thesis of building a "socialist planned commodity economy" – which had itself been a controversial step forward.[101]

Moreover, the political report endorsed the important theses of Deng Xiaoping's southern tour, including his statement that planning and market are merely economic "means" for regulating the economy, his proposition that the 1978 Third Plenum line should be pursued for 100 years, and – most important – that it was necessary "mainly to guard against 'leftist' tendencies within the Party, particularly among the leading cadres."[102]

The Fourteenth Party Congress was certainly a personal victory for Deng. Although his policies had been under nearly constant attack since 1989 and Chen Yun's economic thought had been repeatedly written into speeches and policy documents, the Fourteenth Party Congress lauded Deng for his "tremendous political courage in opening up new paths in socialist construction and a tremendous theoretical courage in opening up a new realm in Marxism." No other plenum or congress report in the reform era had been so personal or so laudatory. Rhetorically at least, Deng's status became comparable to, if not higher than, that of Mao.

Personnel changes at the Fourteenth Party Congress (see Table 1) supported to some extent the policies favored by Deng. Conservative leaders Yao Yilin and Song Ping were removed from the Politburo Standing Committee and Zhu Rongji, Liu Huaqing (a senior military modernizer who was also promoted to be vice-chairman of the CMC), and Hu Jintao (a 50-year-old former Communist Youth League cadre and former Party secretary of Tibet) were added. The conservative Li Ximing, targeted by Deng during his southern tour, was removed from the Politburo and subsequently replaced as Beijing Party secretary

Table 1. *Leadership of the*
Chinese Communist Party

Prior to the 14th Party Congress	Following the 14th Party Congress
Politburo	
Standing Committee	Standing Committee
Jiang Zemin (age 66)	Jiang Zemin (age 66)
Li Peng (64)	Li Peng (64)
Qiao Shi (68)	Qiao Shi (68)
Yao Yilin (76)	Li Ruihuan (59)
Song Ping (76)	Zhu Rongji (64)
Li Ruihuan (59)	Liu Huaqing (76)
	Hu Jintao (50)
Other Full Members	Other Full Members
Li Tieying (57)	Chen Xitong (62)
Li Ximing (67)	Ding Guan'gen (59)
Qin Jiwei (79)	Jiang Chunyun (62)
Tian Jiyun (64)	Li Lanqing (60)
Wan Li (77)	Li Tieying (57)
Wu Xueqian (72)	Qian Qichen (64)
Yang Rudai (67)	Tan Shaowen (63)*
Yang Shangkun (86)	Tian Jiyun (64)
	Wei Jianxing (61)
	Wu Bangguo (51)
	Xie Fei (60)
	Yang Baibing (72)
	Zou Jiahua (66)
Alternate Member	Alternate Members
Ding Guan'gen (59)	Wang Hanbin (67)
	Wen Jiabao (50)
Secretariat	
Ding Guan'gen (59)	Hu Jintao (50)
Li Ruihuan (59)	Ding Guan'gen (59)
Qiao Shi (68)	Wei Jianxing (61)
Yang Baibing (73)	Wen Jiabao (51)
	Ren Jianxin (67)
Alternate Member	
Wen Jiabao (50)	

* Died February 1993.

65

by Chen Xitong, who had responded loyally to Deng's "emancipate the mind" campaign in 1991, despite his hardline stance during the 1989 protest movement. Overall, the number of full Politburo members was increased to 20 from 14 as a number of provincial and younger leaders joined the august body while several elders retired (Yang Shangkun, Wan Li, Qin Jiwei, Wu Xueqian, and Yang Rudai).[103] Moreover, the Central Advisory Commission, of which Chen Yun was the head and which had long served as a bastion of conservative opposition to Deng, was abolished.

Although these changes reflected a major shift in China's top-level policy-making body, Deng stopped short of a fundamental overhaul. In particular, Deng was determined to prevent supporters of former General Secretary Zhao Ziyang from moving into the highest positions. Thus, Vice-Premier Tian Jiyun, a protégé of Zhao who had pushed Deng's themes with such devastating effectiveness the previous spring, was denied a Politburo Standing Committee seat. Moreover, such Zhao associates as Hu Qili and Yan Mingfu, partially rehabilitated in June 1991, did not rejoin the Politburo and Secretariat (respectively) as some had hoped.[104] Indeed, the promotion of Hu Jintao to the Politburo reflected this effort to make sure that Zhao would never stage a comeback. As a Communist Youth League (CYL) leader, Hu had good ties with Hu Yaobang and other reformers, but he had emerged following the Cultural Revolution as head of the CYL in Gansu province, where the conservative Song Ping was Party secretary. Hu, who is open-minded but circumspect, got along well with Song, and Song became his primary supporter. In the period prior to Tiananmen, Zhao Ziyang arranged for Hu to go to Guizhou as Party secretary, much to Hu's dismay. Hu was a victim of the internecine battles then raging between Hu Yaobang and Zhao Ziyang. Hu Jintao's turn came following Tiananmen, when Jiang and others needed cadres who were hostile to Zhao. By using Hu, Jiang was able to appease those in Hu Yaobang's camp, appeal to conservatives like Song Ping, and freeze out supporters of Zhao.[105]

Most important, the changes stopped short of affecting the "Jiang–Li structure" at the top of the system. Many had expected Zhu Rongji or Tian Jiyun to be elevated to the second slot, in line to succeed Li Peng as premier, at the NPC meeting the following spring. Such predictions *cum* hopes were unrealistic. Zhu had already made a "helicopter"-like ascent by jumping three levels from alternate member of the Central Committee to the Politburo Standing Committee; to go one level further would have roused intense opposition. And Tian had offended many conservatives by his caustic ridicule – not to mention by his close relationship with Zhao.

Deng's most important consideration, however, may have been to maintain balance between reformers and conservatives. As the well-known writer Bai Hua put it: "It was as though he [Deng] were afraid that once the leftists had been wiped out, the [factional] balance would be upset and another wave of 'bourgeois liberalization' would set in."[106] Bai's estimate was, no doubt, correct.

Deng did at least two things that bolstered Jiang. After thinking seriously of removing Jiang from office, Deng was persuaded not only to retain him but also to strengthen his position by removing Yang Baibing as vice-chairman of the powerful CMC, a move that also undercut the authority of Yang Shangkun, Deng's long-time confidant and supporter. Yang Baibing had made no bones about his disdain for Jiang Zemin, conferring major promotions himself rather than deferring to Jiang as head of the CMC, and that meant the leadership situation was unstable. In addition, there was growing resentment in the military establishment at the concentration of authority in the hands of the Yang brothers (who were derided for creating a "Yang family army"). This antagonism was particularly concentrated among veterans of the New Fourth Army who had fought in east China during the war against Japan. These veterans, who included Zhang Aiping, Li Xiannian, Ye Fei, Hong Xuezhi, and Zhang Zhen, resented being passed over by th e Yang brothers, who had risen through the ranks as political commissars rather than as commanders.[107] They also rallied to Jiang Zemin as one of their own. Zhang Aiping, one of the founders of the PLA Navy and a leader of China's nuclear program, had been close to Jiang Zemin's uncle, Jiang Shangqing. Zhang had served as commander of the Fourth Division of the New Fourth Army. Li Xiannian was commander of the Fifth Division, Ye Fei was commander of the First Division, and Hong Xuezhi was chief of staff of the Third Division. Zhang Zhen, who would be promoted at the Fourteenth Party Congress, had been Zhang Aiping's chief of staff.

Moreover, senior conservative Party leaders also supported Jiang Zemin. The key person was Bo Yibo, the veteran economic planner who somehow maintained close relations with both Chen Yun and Deng Xiaoping. When Jiang first came to Beijing as general secretary, he cultivated a close relationship with Bo, often visiting his house and seeking his guidance. Now Bo supported Jiang. In a reference to Deng's removal of first Hu Yaobang and then Zhao Ziyang, Bo told Deng that he could not repeatedly (*yi er zai, zai er san*) change general secretaries. No doubt Bo's advice reflected the counsel of other conservative leaders.

To turn against his long-time associate Yang Shangkun and support Jiang Zemin, whose desultory support of reform had prompted Deng's trip to the south, must have been difficult. In retrospect, it appears to have been Deng's most statesmanlike act. Perhaps he reflected on the unstable situation Mao had left behind and worried that if he, Deng, left a situation of political tension then his legacy might well end up like that of Mao – overturned.

To replace the Yangs, Deng turned to the elderly (76 in 1992) Liu Huaqing, who was given a Politburo Standing Committee seat and named vice-chairman of the CMC, and Zhang Zhen (78 in 1992), who was named second vice-chairman of the CMC. The surprise elevation of Liu and Zhang certainly underscored a renewed professionalism in the PLA (Liu is one of the leading modernizers in the PLA – particularly of the navy, which he led for many years – and Zhang was commandant of the National Defense University before his promotion), but their promotion also highlighted the inability to turn the leadership of the military over to a younger generation, even as the age of the civilian leaders of the country continued to fall.

Second, in order to stabilize the political situation, Deng limited his purge of leftists. As noted previously, Song Ping and Yao Yilin were removed from the Politburo Standing Committee, and the CAC, a bastion of conservative influence, was abolished. In addition, Li Ximing was removed from the Politburo and from his position as secretary of the Beijing Municipal CCP Committee, and Gao Di was removed as director of the *People's Daily*. These moves already cut deeply into conservative influence, so Deng allowed others to remain in influential positions. For instance, Xu Weicheng, who had once written on behalf of the Gang of Four and more recently had been editor of the conservative *Beijing Daily,* remained as deputy head of the Propaganda Department. Wang Renzhi, who had excoriated Deng's policies as head of the Propaganda Department, was removed from that position (he was replaced by Deng loyalist Ding Guan'gen) but took over as Party secretary of the Chinese Academy of Social Sciences (CASS). Moreover, Deng Liqun organized many of his leftist colleagues – including former State Education Commission head He Dongchang, former CASS vice-president You Lin, former vice-chairman of the State Planning Commission Fang Weizhong, and director of the Party Literature Research Center Pang Xianzhi – into a newly established PRC Historical Society. It was apparent that this group of leftists intended to maintain a voice in Party councils and to maintain vigilance against bourgeois liberalization.[108]

BACK TO THE MIDDLE

The effort to strike a new balance was apparent in the aftermath of the Fourteenth Party Congress. Whereas Deng's new reform push had dominated Chinese politics since his trip to Shenzhen at the beginning of the year, China's leaders began to warn liberal intellectuals not to go too far shortly after the congress closed. Thus, in late November, Jiang Zemin warned cadres to exercise caution in criticizing Marxism–Leninism–Mao Zedong Thought, saying that their viewpoints represented "the most updated reflection of class struggle inside society and inside the Party in a certain realm." Similarly, Chen Xitong, who had come out in vigorous support of Deng's "emancipate the mind" campaign in the spring of 1991, told a December 1992 meeting of the Beijing Party committee that "[t]he bourgeois liberalization elements in some superstructure departments and activists in the 1989 counterrevolutionary riot have resumed their activities again, and have dished up all sorts of viewpoints on thoroughly dumping Marxism, while propagating a Western capitalist multiparty system."[109]

As the political atmosphere began to shift in a more conservative direction, Yao Yilin, who had stepped down from the Politburo Standing Committee at the Fourteenth Party Congress, sharply criticized economic czar Zhu Rongji at a State Council meeting and then at a conference for Politburo members and state councilors. Yao argued that capital investment had exceeded the plan by too much (38 percent), that bank credits had likewise greatly exceeded the plan (120 percent), and that debt chains and stockpiles were again building up. His criticisms were echoed by Wang Bingqian, the conservative former minister of finance, who warned against a repetition of the sort of fevered atmosphere that had prevailed during the Great Leap Forward in the late 1950s. Zhu reportedly defended himself by arguing that, although there were problems with the economy, it was not "overheated."[110] Nevertheless, both Jiang Zemin and Li Peng warned at the year-end National Planning Conference and National Economic Conference against the "overheated economy."[111]

This renewed attack on rapid economic growth, which can be directly attributed to Deng's efforts to build momentum for reform in 1992, prompted the patriarch to intervene again. For the third year in a row, Deng appeared in Shanghai to encourage high growth and reform. This time, Deng was quoted as saying, "I hope you will not lose the current opportunities. Opportunities for great development are rare in China." Deng also used the occasion to heap praise on Shanghai, which had grown a remarkable 14.8 percent since his last visit: "In 1992 people in Shanghai accomplished what other people could not do."[112]

Deng's intervention was apparently intended not only to keep up reform momentum in general but also specifically to influence the NPC meeting scheduled for March. In early March, the Second Plenary Session of the Fourteenth Central Committee met to consider policy prior to the NPC and endorsed Deng's view that "at present and throughout the 1990s, the favorable domestic and international opportunities should be grasped to speed up the pace of reform, opening up, and the modernization drive." On the basis of this optimistic assessment, the plenum endorsed an upward revision of the annual growth target set by the Eighth Five-Year Plan (1991–95) from 6 percent to 8–9 percent.[113]

Following this plenum resolution, Li Peng and his drafting team had to rewrite the text of the Government Work Report, much as he had been forced to rewrite the text of the previous year's work report. According to the PRC-owned Hong Kong paper *Wen wei po,* the work report was revised to "more positively, more comprehensively, and more accurately" reflect the guiding principles of the Fourteenth Party Congress – an admission of just how far the initial draft had deviated from Deng's policies. The revised version highlighted the essence of Deng's talk in Shanghai: it was necessary to "grasp the opportunity, because there will not be many big opportunities for China."[114]

The issues that roiled the political elite in the years from 1989 to 1992 were basically those that had shaped Chinese politics from the late 1970s until Tiananmen. On the one hand, those who looked to the 1950s as a "golden age" emphasized ideology, political loyalty, and the planned economy, whereas those who believed in more radical change stressed "reform and opening up." The tensions between these two lines had coursed through Chinese politics for more than a decade before exploding in the cataclysm of Tiananmen and the vitriolic struggles of the years immediately thereafter.

Deng won the battle. His ideas were enshrined in the Fourteenth Party Congress report. Targets for growth were raised, new measures to attract foreign investment were adopted, and, most important, the nonstate sector would be permitted to develop – indeed, explode. But in another sense, the Fourteenth Party Congress really marked the end of the Dengist era (though Deng would not die until 1997). Although the issues with which that congress dealt would remain relevant throughout the 1990s, they would be joined by new issues as the problems bequeathed by the Dengist reforms became increasingly apparent. Income inequality, corruption, and decline of state revenues could not be addressed adequately simply by more reform and opening up, at least as that program had been understood in the 1980s, and greater efforts at state building did not necessarily mean a retreat from reform and opening. Moreover, the changed international environment of the post–Cold War era began to have a profound impact on the thinking of Chinese elites, and a new nationalism inevitably emerged. In short, a rethinking of the issues of domestic reform and China's place in the world would mark the 1990s as a very different decade from the one before it. The post-Deng era was arriving in China even as Deng had his greatest personal success in forging the Fourteenth Party Congress report. To understand the issues that shaped the post-Deng era, we need to shift our attention from the rarified atmosphere of elite politics to the broader arena of intellectual contention. The next three chapters explore the reshaping of the intellectual landscape that occurred in the 1990s.

Part II

REDEFINING REFORM:
THE SEARCH FOR A NEW WAY

3

The Emergence of Neoconservatism

IN the years following Tiananmen, new currents of thought began to emerge and play a significant role in social, intellectual, and political circles. Most of these currents had roots in the 1980s, but either they were more peripheral ideas that moved toward the center of intellectual concern or they underwent a significant evolution in the context of post-Tiananmen China, or both. In all cases, they reflect an effort to come to grips intellectually with the political failure of reform in the 1980s, the economic and social problems that emerged (or became more acute) in the 1990s, and the type of political system that might be effective in coping with the problems facing China, both domestically and internationally. As we will see in this and the next two chapters, deep divisions opened up within the intellectual community, even as the place of that community in Chinese society changed significantly. In broad terms, even as the government maintained its own ideological line, a new arena of public discourse developed. Over time, the government took increasing account of this public opinion, sometimes absorbing ideas from it, sometimes engaging it, and sometimes suppressing it. The purpose of Part II is to focus on intellectual developments in the 1990s; in Part III, we will look more closely at the government–intellectual interaction.

One trend that emerged in the 1980s was that of "new authoritarianism," which re-emerged in the 1990s as "neoconservatism." Although few in government, or even in intellectual circles, would lay claim to the title "neoconservative," the impact of the ideas associated with it on the thinking of the political leadership was clear, particularly in the early to mid-1990s.

The first public glimpse of this trend came on January 16, 1989, when Shanghai's reform-oriented newspaper, the *World Economic Herald,* published an article by Wu Jiaxiang, then a young researcher with the General Office of the Central Committee. In apparently self-conscious imitation of *The Communist Manifesto,* Wu began, "there is a strange spirit that has sprouted wings and flown through the forest of the intellectual world, and that is the intellectual tide of the new authoritarianism" (*xin quanwei zhuyi*). Society needed to develop through three stages, Wu maintained: first a stage of traditional authoritarianism, then an intermediate stage in which individual freedom could develop under the protection of new authoritarianism, and finally a stage of freedom and democracy. The intermediate stage of new authoritarianism was necessary, Wu argued, because otherwise the crumbling authority of traditional authoritarian rule would be captured by a variety of social structures and forces, preventing both individual freedom and necessary central authority. Freedom would not develop and authority would be dispersed. The "new" in new authoritarianism referred to self-conscious use of authority to guide society through this treacherous intermediate stage, blocking those forces that would otherwise prevent the development of individual freedom from forming and thus guiding society safely through to a free, democratic, and modern society.[1]

Chinese intellectuals began exploring the idea of new authoritarianism in 1986. Wu himself refers to a 1986 report written by Wang Huning – then a professor of international politics at Fudan University and, since 1995, head of the Political Section of the Central Committee's Policy Research Office under Jiang Zemin – discussing the need for "necessary concentration" of central authority in the course of reform.[2] Wang's report set off a major internal policy battle when it was read by Hu Qili. Hu was favorably impressed by the report and forwarded it to Hu Yaobang. The general secretary, however, was not impressed and referred to it, in a marginal note, as "rubbish." Later he took Hu Qili to task for accepting the ideas in the report.[3]

At roughly the same time that Wang was forwarding his report to the top leadership, another intellectual, Zhang Bingjiu (then a Ph.D. candidate at Beijing University) wrote an article saying that China needed a "semi-authoritarian" (*banjiquan*) political system in order to develop a commodity (i.e., market-oriented) economy.[4] What Zhang meant by the creation of a semi-authoritarian political system was the separation of politics from economics. In traditional authoritarian systems, Zhang maintained, economics and politics were conflated so that economic units could not have real autonomy. Democracy could only develop on the basis of such economic autonomy, so the current need was to use the political system to consciously separate politics from economics. Zhang believed – similarly to Wu – that if China tried to move too quickly to democracy then the conflation of economics and politics would continue and there would be no basis for real, stable democracy. Just as Yuan Shikai in 1915 could abort Song Jiaoren's efforts to bring about a democratic system by ordering his assassination, so democracy would not have an adequate foundation today unless the political elite consciously used the political system to force through the separation.[5]

Following Hu Yaobang's ouster as general secretary, his replacement Zhao Ziyang felt the need to concentrate greater authority in his office, both to be able to push reform forward against the resistance of local officials and to ward off political threats at the central level. Thus, a debate on the merits of new authoritarianism opened up among Zhao's advisors, with some favoring the concept and others opposed. Zhao indicated his sympathy for the concept by reporting on the discussion in April 1989 to Deng Xiaoping. Deng indicated general agreement, saying "[t]his is also my idea" while registering reservations about the terminology (saying that the "specific word for this notion can be reconsidered").[6]

Over the early months of 1989, the pages of China's newspapers and journals filled with discussions of the new authoritarianism and related issues. The emphases of different authors varied. Some favored "elite democracy"[7] while others emphasized "strongman politics."[8] However, the basic thrust of these various discussions was that, at this particular stage in China's reform, it was necessary to have a powerful authoritarian central government to push through economic reforms and bring about full marketization. Advocates of the new authoritarianism argued that unless a powerful central government could oversee the implementation of market-oriented reforms, the reform process itself might stall and a democracy might never appear. Those in favor of the new authoritarianism were not opposed to democracy but, on the contrary, believed that only a step-by-step, gradualist approach could ultimately achieve it.[9]

The contentions of the new authoritarians were quickly challenged by liberal intellectuals. For instance, Yu Haocheng, a legal scholar and chief editor of the Masses Publishing House (*Qunzhong chubanshe*), argued that the new authoritarians fundamentally misunderstood their facts; the conditions in the "four small dragons" (South Korea, Taiwan, Singapore, Hong Kong), on which much of the new authoritarian thinking was modeled, were fundamentally different from conditions in China.[10] In the four dragons, the economy was free and so intertwined with the international economy that their governments really could only have a "minuscule" impact on determining their economies. The example of a "honeymoon" period between the common citizens and monarchs of Europe (another argument made by the new authoritarians) was irrelevant to China, which had not had a manorial economy in the two millennia since the first emperor of the Qin. What China had seen was an autocratic government and a lack of democracy. Indeed, it was this lack of democracy, Yu argued, that had led to the alternation of autocracy and anarchy in Chinese history. Only by developing democracy could this cycle be broken. Contrary to the reasoning of the new authoritarians, Yu argued that only a democratic system could bring the stability and solidarity desired by the new authoritarians, and democracy could not be achieved by building a new autocracy.[11]

Proponents of the new authoritarianism and of democracy each focused on real, but different, features of the Chinese polity in the late 1980s. New authoritarians worried about two problems. On the one hand, they worried that the decentralizing reforms that reformers themselves had helped bring about were now creating new centers of power at lower levels that were preventing the continuation of marketizing reforms. Whereas lower levels had welcomed reforms earlier in the decade, now they had developed interests in the semireformed institutions of local society and opposed efforts that would erode their newfound power. New authoritarians hoped to use the power of the state to break through these obstacles and push marketization forward. On the other hand, both the reform program and individual reformers, particularly Premier (and then General Secretary) Zhao Ziyang, were facing a rising barrage of criticism. Some advocates of the new authoritarianism no doubt hoped to use the theory to concentrate greater power in Zhao's hands and thus turn back challenges to his authority. For them, Zhao's personal role and the fate of marketizing reforms were two sides of the same coin.

Liberal intellectuals, such as Yu Haocheng, saw the same problems but arrived at very different conclusions. In their opinion, political reform had to precede economic reform. Unless the political system could be democratized, they believed, there could never be guarantees for the sanctity of law or property, without which a market economy could never function well. Moreover, they believed that a recentralization of authority, however good the intentions of the new authoritarians might be, would inevitably lead China back into the sort of autocracy from which the country had only recently begun to escape.

It might be said that the new authoritarians underestimated the likelihood that a recentralized authority would be used to shore up personal authority (not necessarily that of Zhao Ziyang!) instead of being used to push through the marketizing reforms that they hoped for, just as liberal intellectuals underestimated the very real problems in maintaining social stability and in continuing economic reform – some of which required the creation of a stronger, or at least more effective, state. Both new authoritarians and liberal intellectuals were strongly influenced by the example of the "East Asian development model" that had seemed so effective in that part of the world, but whereas new authoritarians hoped to emulate their neighbors, liberal intellectuals stressed the differences between China and its neighbors. Liberal intellectuals contrasted the independence of state administration, law, market institutions, and "civil society" in other East Asian societies with the pervasive role the CCP played in China and concluded that China could not follow the developmental path of its neighbors; without political reform, the Chinese Communist Party could not be extricated from the other institutions of society and hence China could never develop either a market economy or a professional state administration.

Although the public nature of this debate ended with the crackdown of June 1989, the themes that it raised informed thinking among intellectuals and policy makers alike and laid the bases for new debates in the 1990s, debates that reprised the themes of those debates on new authoritarianism but also developed in new directions. By the 1990s, there were new concerns with the problems of stability, the complexities of reform, and the difficult international environment. Whereas reformers in the 1980s had largely seen themselves as moving away from the planned economy and ideological orthodoxies of the past, by the 1990s the problems of partial reform had become evident; the need to build a new system, rather than merely tear down the old one, came to the fore. This trend had been evident in the discussions of the new authoritarianism, but it was the trauma of Tiananmen that imparted new urgency to the task.

In the immediate aftermath of Tiananmen, as described in Part I, there was a knee-jerk effort to reimpose ideological orthodoxies and strengthen planning. By late 1990, the failure of that effort was evident, though it took until 1992 for the Dengist reform program to be publicly reaffirmed. But even the reaffirmation of reform did not mean a return to the problematique of the 1980s. Below the highest levels, policy makers and intellectuals – sometimes in conjunction but more often following their own paths – began to chart policies and rationales that could no longer be understood simply in terms of "reform" measures and "conservative" opposition.

There were many issues driving this new agenda. First and foremost was the issue of stability. In the 1980s, the only choices appeared to be between "reform" and "conservatism"; Tiananmen and the subsequent collapse of the Soviet Union confronted Chinese policy makers and intellectuals alike with the specter of an unpleasant third alternative: social and political collapse. Foreign observers, focusing on hopes for political democratization, tend not to consider the downside risk of political change, in part because worries about "chaos" can and have been used by the political authorities in Beijing to justify repressive measures. Chinese policy makers (not just "hardliners") and intellectuals, however, are keenly aware of the turmoil of twentieth-century politics and worry openly about the costs of political implosion. Even such a liberal observer of contemporary China as Ding Xueliang has warned: "If an anarchic situation appears in China, the violence that Chinese will inflict on each other will far exceed the barbarism inflicted by the Japanese army when it invaded in the 1930s."[12]

The shock of Tiananmen, which was soon followed by the collapse of socialism in Eastern Europe and the subsequent disintegration of the Soviet Union, led many in China to rethink the course of reform. This rejection of enlightenment thinking (which stressed science and democracy) and at least partial reaffirmation of more statist approaches to reform has often been referred to as neoconservatism; this term has been rejected by many of those who are said to advocate it, but it was used by some of the participants in the debates in the early 1990s. Although one can see some of its concerns continuing into the mid-1990s, by 1993 many people had developed beyond the concerns of neoconservatism as it was expressed in the 1989–92 period. If we confine our use of the term to the period prior to 1993, it does not seem inappropriate to use the term neoconservative.

Nevertheless, neoconservatism must be understood as a loose term, indicating a set of concerns and a broad intellectual orientation rather than a well-developed and consistent body of thought. In general, neoconservatism indicated a desire to find a middle path between the traditional conservatism of the Old Left (as exemplified ideologically by more orthodox Marxist–Leninists such as Hu Qiaomu and Deng Liqun and economically by such traditional planners as Chen Yun) and "radical reformers" (as epitomized culturally by the film *River Elegy* and economically by advocates of privatization). In general, neoconservatism accepted market economics, albeit with some caveats, but desired a greater role for the state. Here, it is useful to view the development of neoconservatism by looking at the following themes: incrementalism, central–local relations, its roots in the new authoritarianism, state-centered nationalism, and the turn away from cultural cosmopolitanism.

INCREMENTALISM

The disintegration of the Soviet Union stood in stark contrast to China following Tiananmen. Whereas the Soviet Union broke up into its fifteen constituent republics, lost its superpower status, and experienced rapid economic and social decline, China held together and after a short while resumed an impressive rate of growth. Although some argued that such a contrast justified the Tiananmen crackdown, most people drew the more modest but nevertheless potent lesson that "incremental" reform was better than "shock therapy" (the idea of instituting price and property reforms in a short period of time). This was a lesson that perhaps came easily to Chinese, for it seemed embedded in their reform experience: "Crossing the river by feeling the stones" (*mozhe shitou guohe*) was the mantra of the 1980s. Moreover, it did not take long before foreign economists affirmed the wisdom of their Chinese counterparts.[13]

The transformation of incremental reform from a necessity of circumstance into a distinct "Chinese model"[14] was rooted in the economic discussions of the 1980s. In the first decade of reform, young and middle-aged economists increasingly introduced Western neoclassical economics in opposition to the political economy of Marxism. Although some focused more on macroeconomics while others emphasized microeconomics, there was a common understanding among these reformers that economics as developed in the West was applicable to China. By 1986–87, however, "institutional economics" as developed by Ronald Coase, James Buchanan, Mancur Olson, Douglass North, and others came increasingly to the attention of young economists, many of whom had studied overseas. Institutionalist economics appealed to Chinese economists because it provided a framework for studying China's transition to a market economy. As Sheng Hong (a leading institutional economist and former student of Ronald Coase) wrote, neoclassical economics "supposes that institutions are constant factors, that transaction costs are zero, and that a human being's rationality is perfect; it also ignores research into the distribution of interests."[15] These were all dubious assumptions in the very imperfect market conditions in China, and they did not explicate the problems China faced in the course of transition. Perhaps more importantly, then, institutional economics provided an intellectual rationale for rejecting "shock therapy." Neoclassical economics, in Sheng's opinion, lacked a concept of time; shock therapy was thus a logical corollary to neoclassical economics – and neither was suitable to China.[16]

What was striking about the Chinese "model" of incremental reform for Sheng and many others was that China had gone a long way toward the reform of prices, property rights, stock markets, and so forth at a relatively low cost. This was particularly important in light of Tiananmen, which, as Sheng wrote, "raised from a negative perspective the question of the cost of reform" and caused "some young economists to give up their romantic attitude toward reform issues."[17] The experience of Tiananmen persuaded some economists not only to doubt neoclassical economics but also to pay increasing attention to avoiding conflicts of interest and reducing the cost of reform.[18] One might say that incremental reform was elevated from an unarticulated strategy to a theory, one that some economists held was applicable not just to China but elsewhere as well.[19]

For Sheng Hong, there was also an important cultural dimension to China's transition. For Sheng, who would soon draw widespread attention as a cultural nationalist, China's culture emphasizes the harmony between individuals, reconciling their interests and promoting cooperation. This cultural disposition, in Sheng's opinion, forms a broad background to government efforts to work out reforms in a way that maximizes benefits and minimizes costs.[20] Whether or not China's culture has influenced its reform strategy, Sheng's attitude toward China's culture has certainly influenced his advocacy of transitional economics as a model. There is an evident self-satisfaction in the rejection of "romantic" notions of reform derived from Western neoclassical economics and in the identification of a uniquely "Chinese" path to reform.

If a belief in incrementalism derived primarily from China's reform experience, it also had roots, perhaps ironically, in a historical and cultural critique of the Chinese revolution. Cultural debates in the 1980s, as noted in the Introduction, were dominated by a cosmopolitanism, a desire to "enter the world" (*zouxiang shijie*), and a corresponding fervor to critique the "feudal" values of China's past. By the late 1980s, however, some were questioning this cosmopolitan orientation. One critique came from a group of scholars, many of whom were based abroad, who argued that China needed to revive its traditional Confucian values. This interest in Confucianism, as we will see in the next chapter, was inspired by the same search for values that underlay much of the cultural fever in the 1980s. Such scholars argued that China needed to recover those timeless Chinese values that could be of value in the present. They believed that the loss of values felt by so many intellectuals was because the Chinese revolution had moved too far from China's tradition – indeed, that the revolution in 1949 had marked a radical rupture in China's cultural history.

This argument was presented most forcefully by Princeton University Professor Yu Yingshi in a speech presented at The Chinese University of Hong Kong in 1988 (though not published until almost two years later). Yu argued that Chinese intellectual thought in the twentieth century has been characterized by the dominance of radicalism and that it became increasingly radical from the late nineteenth century through the Cultural Revolution. Yu firmly placed the origins of this trend in the reform movement of 1898, led by Kang Youwei and Liang Qichao. At this time, the demand was for "rapid change." Kang had argued that incremental change was useless; change must be immediate and comprehensive. Of all the leaders of the reform movement, the one who most thoroughly exemplified the radical spirit of the times was Tan Sitong, whose 1897 *Study of Humaneness* (*Renxue*), in Yu's opinion, "completely denied 2,000 years of Chinese tradition" (*yi kou foukenle Zhongguo liangqian nian de chuantong*).[21] From political radicalism, China moved to cultural radicalism in the May Fourth Movement, and then to social radicalism with the victory of the Communist revolution. The Cultural Revolution, in Yu's opinion, was the logical culmination of this century of unchecked radicalism. In a follow-up article, Yu took issue with trends in contemporary American studies of China that see contemporary China as a continuation of tradition. Yu held a completely opposite view: "Since 1949, a group of marginal people in China, relying on an especially radical theory and using a new type of totalitarian organization, completely destroyed the traditional social structure of China."[22]

Yu's ideas certainly had an impact on mainland scholars. "Incrementalism" began to have much more positive connotations. The French Revolution, glorified in the Chinese Marxist tradition, began to lose its luster, while the English Revolution, previously denigrated as insufficiently radical, came to be seen in a much more positive light. Some years later, the impact of Yu's ideas were clearly visible in Li Zehou and Liu Zaifu's controversial 1996 book *Farewell to Revolution* (just as Li Zehou's ideas had an impact on Yu's thinking). Li and Liu argued that most of China's political difficulties over the past century have been caused by a powerful tendency to see problems in revolutionary terms. That is to say, when confronted by obstacles or opposition, there has been a tendency to see the solution not in discussion and compromise but in terms of "struggle" and revolution. Political conflicts become total: "You die and I live." Tracing the modern history of this revolutionary impulse, Li and Liu, like Yu, found its *locus classicus* in Tan Sitong. Reviewing the history of the period, they arrived at the controversial conclusion that the Revolution of 1911 was "not necessarily necessary,"[23] a judgment that undermined the legitimacy of the Communist revolution as well.

CENTRAL–LOCAL RELATIONS

As stability and incrementalism became one important impulse informing Chinese discourse in the 1990s, concern over the changing relationship between the central government and the local governments was another. Between 1978 and 1992, central government revenues as a percentage of GDP had fallen from 31.2 percent to 14.7 percent, suggesting that the central government had been weakened to the extent that it could no longer maintain control over macroeconomic policy – and inflation was then a major concern. The publicity given to several major instances of regional protectionism (the "cocoon war," the "cotton war," etc.) all reinforced the notion that the central government was losing control over the provinces. In 1988, CASS economists Shen Liren and Dai Yuanchen, in a highly influential article, introduced the term "feudal lord economy" (*zhuhou jingji*) to describe this phenomenon.[24]

In the wake of Tiananmen, conservatives had (as discussed in Chapter 1) tried to turn the clock back, but even they soon realized that the goal of restoring anything resembling the old planned economy was no longer practical. This realization prompted new efforts to explore ways of combining political control and economic marketization and to justify a tightening of central control. One of the most important exponents of neoconservative thinking in this area was Chen Yuan, son of Party elder and economic policy specialist Chen Yun.

Born in 1945, Chen Yuan entered the department of automatic control (*zidong kongzhi*) at Qinghua University in 1965. Chen received his degree in 1970, even though classes were suspended because of the Cultural Revolution, and was sent to work in a factory in Hunan. In 1973 he returned to Beijing to work as a technician in the Aeronautics Ministry. When entrance exams were restored in 1978, Chen tested into the economic management department of the graduate school at CASS, where he studied under the guidance of senior economists Ma Hong and Yu Guangyuan (interestingly, Zhu Rongji was in the same institute at that time). After a short stint in the State Planning Commission, Chen was appointed deputy and then first Party secretary of the West City District Party Committee in Beijing. In 1984 he became head of Beijing Municipal Commerce and Trade Department (*bu*) and concurrently deputy director of the city Economic Reform Commission (under then-mayor Chen Xitong). At this time, Chen organized a group of people as the Beijing Young Economists Association (*Beijing qingnian jingji gongzuozhe xiehui*) to study economic theory and formulate Beijing development strategy. This organization was intended to serve as Chen Yuan's own think tank, and many of the connections between Chen and young economists in the late 1980s continued into the 1990s.

In 1987, in one of the first uses of multicandidate elections (*cha'e xuanju*, which have more candidates than positions though not as many as two candidates for each position), Chen Yuan failed to be elected to the Beijing Party Committee. Chen's failure was primarily a reflection of widespread resentment of the rapidly growing power of the children of high-level cadres (*taizi*, "princes"), a trend that continues to this day. In the same election, Chen Haosu (son of Marshal Chen Yi) and Bo Xicheng (son of Party elder Bo Yibo) both withdrew their names from consideration rather than face defeat; Chen Yuan proved overly confident. With Chen's defeat, Zhao Ziyang quickly arranged a position for him as vice-governor of the People's Bank of China; Zhao's concern was motivated by his desire to placate Chen Yun, with whom he was then having increasing difficulties.

In the summer of 1987, Chen Yuan organized a large-scale seminar to discuss a "Report on the Stages of the Socialist Economic Operating Mechanism."

At this seminar, Chen presented a report stressing that the chief characteristic of China's economy in the primary stage of socialism is the "tightness" of the economy. That is to say, the "primary contradiction" facing China's economy is "shortage" created by growing aggregate social demand and the limited resources available to produce the requisite supply. This was, in Chen's view, a structural problem that could not be allowed to continue without serious social consequences, including inflation and the distortion of the structure of production. The solution to this problem, Chen argued, was to strengthen planning and thereby gradually build the capacity to meet demand. Only planning would allow China to use its scarce resources in a way that would maximize supply in a socially beneficial manner.[25]

In December 1990, Chen Yuan presented a paper entitled "China's Deep-Seated Economic Problems and Choices – Several Issues Regarding China's Economic Development Situation and the Operating Mechanism (Outline)," which decried many of the decentralizing consequences of reform. As pointed out in the previous chapter, this paper was very much a part of the critique of the Dengist reform program that unfolded in the period after Tiananmen. Although it was no doubt connected with his father's (Chen Yun) critique of Deng, it was not simply a repetition of his father's formulations. Rather, Chen Yuan was exploring an approach that was conservative in terms of its critical evaluation of Deng's decentralizing policies but also more accepting of Western economics. In this way, Chen Yuan's paper tried to lay out a neoconservative approach to economic policy.

Chen objected to decentralization both on the grounds that it led to local protectionism and the fragmentation of the national market and, more seriously, on the grounds that the erosion of central resources was resulting in a "weak and powerless central government" surrounded by numerous "feudal lords." These trends would, he warned, result in "the great socialist mansion that we have built laboriously over many years collapsing" if nothing were done.[26] Faced with this dire situation, Chen recommended a "new centralization," but one, he declared, that would be different from the old planned economy.[27] Although Chen wanted to recentralize authority and use the power of the state to readjust China's industrial structure, he was also very clear that he wanted to develop the role of the market (by breaking down local protectionism and ministerial interference in enterprises) even as he would give a greater role to the state.

Chen obviously had the East Asian developmental state in mind. He argued that the successful experiences of the late industrializing nations proved that the central government has certain unique functions; not everything can be left to the whims of the market.[28] Chen's understanding of the role of the central government was also influenced by his view of China's role in the world economy: whereas China should participate in the international division of labor and economic exchange, at the same time, "China must develop as an economic great power that is not dependent on any other country or group of countries." China's developmental path cannot be like that of small countries; China must have a complete and fairly advanced industrial system.[29] Market forces alone will never bring about such an economic system; the government should have a clear industrial policy and should direct scarce resources to strategic industries.

A year later, Chen Yuan reflected on the usefulness of Western economics for China in another article. He firmly rejected the ideas of deficit financing and expansionary monetary policy that were then closely associated with the name of Keynes, but he praised Keynes for "pointing out in clear-cut terms that the function of macroeconomic quantitative regulation and control can only be performed by the government, not the market mechanism." He praised Milton Friedman for his emphasis on monetary control but rejected his laissez-faire economic philosophy. By selecting what was useful and rejecting the rest, Chen argued that "Western economics can be turned to serve our socialist revolution." It is difficult to imagine Chen Yuan's father citing the works of Keynes or Friedman, but not difficult to imagine the elder Chen agreeing that the state is an "indispensable actor" and not simply a "passive referee."[30]

NEW AUTHORITARIANISM AND NEOCONSERVATISM

While Chen Yuan began to articulate a neoconservative vision of economics in the post-Tiananmen period, others began to explore the political dimensions. As just discussed, intellectuals such as Wu Jiaxiang and Zhang Bingjiu argued that authority needed to be recentralized in the hands of the central government – not, as conservatives would have it, to restore the old Marxist–Leninist order, but to use the strength of the central government to push the marketization of the economy against local forces that supported decentralization but not marketization. Although such people argued for strengthening the center's authority, there was a liberal goal within their vision. The marketization of the economy would lead to the growth of a middle class, which in turn would foster the growth of democratic governance. This was the lesson that many intellectuals at the time had drawn from the development of several East Asian economies and the wave of democratization then starting to spread across the region. For these intellectuals, the government would take the place of the middle class until a middle class could develop.

86

Although the public discussion on new authoritarianism is generally identified with a number of intellectuals close to then–General Secretary Zhao Ziyang, the earliest discussions were held in Shanghai. Two important people in these discussions were Wang Huning and Xiao Gongqin.

Wang Huning, who in 1995 was to be brought to Beijing by Jiang Zemin in order to head the Political Section of the CCP's Policy Research Office, was born in 1955. He entered Shanghai's East Normal University during the Cultural Revolution as a "worker-peasant-soldier student" in 1974. After three years of studying French, Wang studied for a master's degree at Fudan University's Department of International Politics. Completing the program, he stayed on at Fudan University, eventually heading the Department of International Politics.[31]

In the late 1980s, Wang wrote a series of essays that drew attention to himself as one of the bright young lights on the intellectual scene. Political science was a new and precarious discipline in China, and it was impossible to write rigorous political science. Nevertheless, Wang managed to infuse his writings with some of the concerns of Western political science, giving his essays a freshness lacking in many of the writings then being published. Many of these essays appear in *The Collected Writings of Wang Huning,* which was published in 1989. Written mostly in 1987 and 1988, a time when discussion of political structural reform filled the air, these essays give the sense of a liberal, open-minded writer. Pointing to phenomena as diverse as the call for further democratization by the 27th Party Congress of the CPSU, the implementation of multicandidate elections in Hungary, the election of the French Socialist Party, and the democratic movement in South Korea, Wang declared that political reform is a universal phenomenon in the world. China's culture itself is changing from being "conservative, closed, subjective, and arbitrary" to one that is "renewed, open, objective, and democratic." "Without a highly democratic political system," Wang warned, "it is difficult to establish oneself as a modernized, strong country among the advanced people of the world."[32]

Unlike much of the democratic discussions then taking place in China, however, Wang constantly registered a note of caution. First, Wang's notion of democracy, though never explicitly defined, appears to be one of substantive rather than procedural democracy. Wang seemed more interested in building a stable and efficient government that could make good decisions based on widespread consultation – what might be called "elite democracy" – than democracy per se. For instance, Wang called for better policy research and brain trusts, powerful and effective administrative organs, effective propaganda to win the trust of the people, and better feedback.[33] Second, and perhaps more important,

Wang insisted that political reform is part of a complex process of change and that "[a] given political structure must fit the given historical, social, and cultural conditions."[34] This implied a lengthy period of transition. As Wang wrote: "In China, the construction of democratic politics implies overcoming the feudal political tradition and political consciousness that extended for more than 2,000 years since the Zhou–Qin period; it implies changing the undemocratic political traditions formed under semi-colonialism and semi-feudalism; it implies solving the contradiction between establishing an advanced political system on the basis of backward forces of production; and it implies enriching our thinking through practice." Such a process must take, as Wang put it, a "rather long time" (*jiaochang de shijian*).[35] Moreover, unless one develops democracy "scientifically," the results will be the opposite.[36]

In general, Wang's essays combine an almost Parsonian understanding of the way in which everything is linked to everything else with a Huntingtonian understanding of the need to build institutions and maintain stability through a strong government over a long period of transition. Hence, Wang is interested in political culture: how the turbulent history of twentieth-century China has led to an uneasy overlapping of traditional, modern, and post-1949 cultural concerns; and how the political system might play a role in shaping a modern political culture that will support reform. At the same time, Wang sees China as evolving slowly from what he calls a "culture-centered political culture" to an "institution-centered political culture." The key is to strengthen the cadre force and other elements that can support institutionalization while China's political culture completes its long and painful transition.

Whereas the focus in Wang's *Collected Writings* is on political reform and democratization, his concerns are quite different in a number of articles published in the late 1980s and early 1990s that were not included in this volume. In these other essays, Wang took up the issue of public, particularly central, authority under the conditions of reform and limited resources. In Wang's view, devolving greater authority to China's industrial enterprises during the 1980s took place at a time when the level of economic development was low and markets were far from perfect. The role of local government therefore expanded to fill the gap; local government took over economic regulation and helped enterprises secure supplies of materials and markets for their products – functions that would normally be fulfilled by the market. As he put it, as the central government began to "wean" enterprises, local governments took up "breast feeding."[37]

The decrease in the functions of the central government and corresponding increase in the functions of local government resulted in a system in which the power to redistribute resources and satisfy interests was divided; in other words, local governments began to have the political power and economic resources to pursue their own interests at the expense of the central government. Wang argued that local governments had previously passed all resources on to the central government, which then redistributed them to the localities. Reform was greatly changing the relationship between central and local governments by diminishing the role of the central government in redistribution and by encouraging localities to satisfy their own interests.

At the same time, economic reform was stimulating a rapid increase in the number of interests and demands in society. Such demands were focused on local government, forcing the localities to concentrate ever more attention on their own needs. Accordingly, local governments increasingly concentrated on expanding their fiscal resources, and the fiscal contract responsibility system – under which governments promised to remit specific revenue targets to the central government while retaining any excess – provided the resources to pursue those interests. In Wang's view, the restructuring of incentives seriously undermined the ability of the central government to define and implement a policy that took the long-term best interests of the nation into account. As he put it: "Because the central government depends on the local government to guarantee its fiscal revenue and also depends on the local policies to satisfy localized interests (*difanghua de liyi*), it must make concessions to regional protectionism."[38]

The political implications of such trends were potentially ominous. Wang pointed to the rise of regional inequality in China and to the weakness of the Yugoslav Federal Government (then still in existence) as consequences of localism. He also cited the 1988 elections, in which a number of candidates favored by the Party failed to be elected, to show that local interests were reducing the central government's prerogatives with regard to the appointment of local personnel.[39]

Wang's interest in the rise of a multiplicity of demands and interests was the focus of yet another article, one that appears to have been heavily influenced by Samuel Huntington's (1968) *Political Order in Changing Societies*. Like Huntington, Wang is concerned with the relationship between social demands and institutions, though he views them in somewhat different terms from Huntington. For Wang, the emphasis is on "social aggregate resources" (*shehui ziyuan zongliang*), which he views broadly to encompass not only material resources but cultural, value, educational, and religious resources as well. Like Huntington,[40] Wang sees a public authority that cannot extract sufficient resources from the society as being sharply constrained by social demands and hence ineffective. A paucity of social resources makes the creation of effective

89

public authority more difficult even as it gives rise to greater social tension, so it is important in such societies to maintain and strengthen public authority. Wang sees China's socialist system as contributing to the strengthening of public authority and to the concentration of resources needed to maintain social equilibrium; without such authority, there would be an "anarchic struggle for resources among individuals, groups, and regions" leading to general social instability.[41] It should be noted that Wang's prescription for strong public authority was not necessarily a plea for authoritarian rule. In his writings, Wang sees the changes in Chinese society and the growth of the economy as demanding corresponding adjustments on the part of government, including greater efficiency and more democracy, though he also sees the development of democracy as a process that would take an extended period of time.[42]

Wang was also interested in the role of public values in forging political unity. As he put it: "The political life of a society must seek a fair degree of unity and homogeneity; otherwise, contradictions will appear everywhere and political development will be unstable."[43] In order to promote such unity, Wang advocated cultivating what he called "political aesthetics" (*zhengzhi shenmei*), a vague term that appears to mean the ability to apprehend and appreciate the political values and ideals appropriate for the time. In a passage reminiscent of Sun Yat-sen's discussion of "thinker-inventors" (*xianzhizhe,* those who were able to comprehend the trends of their time), their disciples (*houzhizhe*), and the unconscious performers (*buzhizhe*), Wang noted the elitism inherent in his concept: "Advanced elements in a society first apprehend (*tiren*) the aesthetic ideals that represent the direction in which history is developing, and then they energetically propagate these aesthetic ideals so that they spread to every member of society, creating an atmosphere conducive to the realization of these aesthetic ideals."[44] In short, the creation and maintenance of political values and ideals, like the extraction of resources and the development of strong and efficient public authority, was a necessary part of maintaining social order in the course of modernization.

Xiao Gongqin is a more historically minded thinker than Wang Huning. Born in Hunan in 1946, Xiao spent the Cultural Revolution as a worker in Shanghai's suburbs. In 1978, he tested into the history department at Nanjing University as a graduate student, receiving his master's degree in 1981. The following year, he was assigned to Shanghai Normal University and was promoted to associate professor in 1987 – highly unusual for someone without a Ph.D.[45] Although originally interested in the Yuan Dynasty, in the mid-1980s Xiao turned his attention to the late Qing–early Republican period and has concentrated on the problems of modernization and political transformation ever since. In his early work, Xiao focused on Yan Fu (1853–1921), the famed translator of Adam Smith's *The Wealth of Nations* and other major works of Western intellectual history. Yan's translations and commentaries marked a new stage in China's understanding of the West. Whereas China's efforts to introduce knowledge from abroad had previously been limited mostly to technology, particularly weapons and later light manufacturing, Yan's translations served to make the point that Western technology was part of a complex culture; it would be impossible, as Yan's contemporary Zhang Zhidong was advising, to "take Chinese culture as the essence and Western learning for practical use" (*Zhongti xiyong*) – culture and technology were not separable. Yan is usually understood as introducing Western learning as a means to make China "wealthy and powerful" (*fuqiang*).[46] Following the Revolution of 1911 and particularly in his support of Yuan Shikai's monarchical efforts, Yan is usually depicted as a tired and conservative old man who had fallen behind the spirit of his times.

Xiao argued that Yan's thinking should not be dichotomized into early reformism and later conservatism but instead should be seen as a whole. What unified Yan's thinking, in Xiao's opinion, was his understanding that societies were complex and organic wholes that could not be cut apart or transplanted lock, stock, and barrel; they had to evolve. Thus, Yan argued that modernization must be based on preserving the "national spirit" (*guoqing*), that is, on Confucianism. Western culture or technology could not simply be grafted onto China but had to find resonance within China's tradition; the task of modernization had to be based on the growth, development, and maturation of factors present in China's original culture.[47] Yan was consistent as a "neoconservative." Prior to the 1911 Revolution, Yan was critical of "radicals" (*jijin zhuyizhe*), such as Kang Youwei and Liang Qichao in the 1898 Reform Movement, who wanted to accomplish everything at once; following the 1911 Revolution, Yan continued to look to Confucianism as the essence of China's "national spirit." It was in this way that he allowed himself to be swept into Yuan Shikai's ill-fated monarchical movement and thus fall into personal tragedy.

What defined Yan as a neoconservative, in Xiao's opinion, was that he was not opposed to modernization – indeed, he harshly criticized the old autocratic system – but at the same time he was not a radical modernizer. Yan believed that radicals viewed the problems of modernization too simply and naively and ended up making matters worse; this explained Yan's disappointment with China's situation following the 1911 Revolution. What Yan advocated was combining the old and the new, neither clinging stubbornly to an ossified understanding of the national essence (*guocui*), and therefore not modernizing, nor discarding the national essence and turning the culture into an empty shell incapable of digesting the Western elements it was importing.[48] As Yan put it, "[w]ithout renewal there will be no progress; without the old there would be nothing to hold on to."[49] The trick was to modernize the national spirit while maintaining the culture as an organic whole.

Consistent with this view, in separate studies Xiao blamed the failure of the 1898 Reform Movement not on the obstinacy of the Empress Dowager or the treachery of Yan Shikai – the usual suspects – but rather on the impatience and "radicalism" (*jijin zhuyi*) of Kang Youwei and other reformers. In Xiao's opinion, the Empress Dowager Ci Xi was not completely opposed to reform, but the reformers (led by Kang) believed that reform had to rapidly make a sharp break with tradition. There was a pan-moralistic (*fan daode zhuyi*) view holding that the new and the old, like fire and water, could not coexist. The reformers had simplistic and optimistic expectations, with the result that they misjudged the situation and the reform failed completely. As Xiao concluded: "When China most needed its political elites to use their wisdom and abilities to carry out reform, those extreme (*jizhixing*) elements in traditional culture stimulated the factors in those early Chinese reform elites that were most disadvantageous to reform and most advantageous to revolution."[50]

Xiao's interest was perhaps not so much in understanding the past as in prescribing for the present. Indeed, Xiao first presented his ideas on neoconservatism to a conference on "China's Traditional Culture and Socialist Modernization" in December 1990. He Xin attended that conference, as did a number of "princes" (those whose parents were high-ranking cadres).[51] This conference was part of an increasingly heated debate between advocates of "incremental" change and those who favored "radical" change; indeed, Xiao's work was very much a part of this debate. However, Tiananmen greatly changed the terms of debate. Those who had doubts about the course of reform, or who quickly developed them following that tragedy, came to see Tiananmen not so much as a case of repression as another instance of romantic radicalism bringing about its own defeat. This conclusion was part analysis, part opportunism, and part reconciliation with a regime that had shown no tolerance for being challenged. In fact, most reformers had seen themselves as incrementalists trying to patch together a reform ("feeling the stones while crossing the river") in uncharted territory, though it is also true that, as reform developed in the late 1980s, the tensions between "reformers" and "conservatives" mounted as the gap between their visions increased and as the problems generated by reform became more apparent. Deng's ill-fated effort to introduce comprehensive price reform in 1988 by "storming the pass" (what became known in the context of the Soviet

Union as "shock therapy") was one expression of such tension, as were the debates between democrats and new authoritarians – both of whom wanted to break the tension, albeit by different means.

It should be noted that although Xiao became one of the best-known articulators of neoconservatism in the early 1990s, he remained true to the new authoritarian faith of the 1980s: namely, that the point of incrementalism was to build a political and economic system that could support liberal democracy. In this way Xiao, like Sheng Hong, was quite different from neoconservatives who simply sought to strengthen the central state as well as from the postmodernist thinkers (examined in the next chapter) who rejected economic and political liberalism in a search for a new path.

HE XIN AND STATE-CENTERED NATIONALISM

Nationalism was another force propelling changes in the way Chinese intellectuals and policy makers viewed the world in the period following Tiananmen. Nationalism is hardly a new force in China; indeed it is the leitmotif underlying twentieth-century Chinese politics. In the 1980s, China had adopted a cosmopolitan orientation, linking domestic reform with opening to the outside world. This did not mean that China was not nationalistic in this period, but rather that its nationalism was directed toward economic development and a critique of traditional socialism (which impeded that development).[52] Following Tiananmen, however, the West (and the U.S. in particular) seemed threatening and subversive. Disregarding those extreme voices associated with the Old Left, a new nationalism began to emerge. Through the 1990s it has taken on many guises, ranging from realpolitik to discussions of post-colonialism. One of the first (and certainly one of the loudest) voices of the new nationalism was that of He Xin, an erstwhile literary critic who turned his attention to economics, politics, and international relations in the late 1980s. As perhaps the only intellectual to support the government in the days following Tiananmen, He quickly became a very public, and often reviled, figure.

Although more extreme – particularly with regard to his nationalism – than other neoconservatives, He shared many of the basic orientations of this approach. Although he publicly identified himself with the regime, his writings and interviews reveal little knowledge of or interest in Marxism; what concerned He was the power of the central government vis-à-vis the localities, the stability of society, and China's position in the world. In this way, He became identified as a exemplar of what might be called a "muscular" or assertive neoconservatism.

Nationalism, particularly anti-Americanism, was central to He Xin's views. Like many writers in this period, He contradictorily depicted the United States both as a power in decline and as one bent on world domination. In late 1988, he wrote that the United States had entered a period of inevitable decline and that, by the early part of the twenty-first century, it would be reduced to a large regional power without the strength to bother the East.[53] Perhaps more concerned about Japan's global ambitions,[54] He recommended changing China's coastal development strategy, opting instead for an economic alliance with the Soviet Union. Such an alliance would not only have the advantage of strengthening China, but just as importantly it would pre-empt Japan from allying with the Soviet Union and establishing a neocolonial dominance over China.[55] Similarly, the strengthening of the Chinese economy was necessary to prevent Japan from dominating the world in the next century.[56]

A year or so later, He seemed less certain of the inevitable decline of the United States and more worried about the failure of reform in the Soviet Union.[57] The breakup of the Soviet Union would cause China to lose its last strategic shield against the United States, so China should make use of any conflict between other countries and the United States. Evidently viewing America as the more serious strategic threat (despite insisting repeatedly that it was in decline), He dropped his previous fears of Japan and urged allying with Japan (indeed, to become like "lips and teeth").[58] He also urged supporting Germany in any disputes with the United States (suggesting that China should urge Germany to withdraw from NATO) and supporting Southeast Asia, lest America return to that region of the world and threaten China.[59]

He argued that the world was headed toward unity,[60] but that it could be united either under U.S. domination or be integrated on the basis of "fairness, equal sovereignty, common interest, and cooperation."[61] If America succeeds in its global ambitions, He warned, "the world will enter into a dark and chaotic age."[62] The biggest obstacle to the realization of U.S. ambitions is China.[63] In his opinion, it does not matter what type of policy China adopts internally (i.e., whether it supports human rights or becomes a democracy), since U.S. policy will not change; the United States simply does not want to see a "strong, unified, prosperous, and industrialized modern China."[64] In He's view, American demands for human rights and democracy were merely a part of its strategy to weaken and hopefully divide China.[65] It was to weaken China that the United States aggravated the political crisis of Tiananmen, using the Voice of America and other means to try to split China apart.[66] China should "comprehensively" adjust its foreign policy approach over the next decade so that it no longer facilitates U.S. designs for global hegemony.[67]

Reflecting on the decade of reform prior to Tiananmen, He regarded the 1984–88 period as one of "romanticism." In his opinion, reform in this period not only shifted from the countryside to the cities but also branched out from economics into other spheres of activity, creating an atmosphere that disregarded the difficulty and length of time that reform would take.[68] Most people have viewed this period as one of great creativity and cultural flourishing, but He expressed dismay at the decline of ideology, national spirit, values, state consciousness, and social order.[69] The film *River Elegy* epitomized the tendency in the 1980s for cultural criticism to lead to an all-round criticism of politics and social reality and then to "complete Westernization." This led to a "new dogmatism" of worshipping Western values.[70] "For a while," He said, "American culture became the main current and major tone of literature. This was a very bad development for China ...."[71] Tiananmen, He argued, was the result of such trends. As stability was re-established following Tiananmen, He argued that people came to realize that Western thought really could not solve China's problems.[72] It was on that basis that He argued for a return to Chinese values and an emphasis on nationalism and restoration of political authority.

As this argument suggests, He Xin expressed repeated concern about cultural imperialism, which he regarded as the essence of "peaceful evolution" and which, as we will see, would become a major concern of many intellectuals in the 1990s.[73] One form of "cultural imperialism" that He repeatedly railed against was neoclassical economics. Exporting neoclassical economics was one of the tools by which the United States sought to dominate the world, as was so vividly demonstrated by the results of radical price reform in the Soviet Union; shock therapy, He said, was simply "economic suicide." Chinese intellectuals were susceptible to the influence of neoclassical economics, particularly after 1984, because of their anxiousness for quick success – another manifestation of the "romantic" mood that swept China in the late 1980s.[74] Accepting neoclassical economics would lead to China's further integration in the world economy; He argued that this would benefit U.S. interests, not Chinese interests, because the United States was able to dominate international trade through its monopoly position. Obviously, joining the General Agreement on Trade and Tariffs (GATT, later the WTO) could be dangerous.[75]

THE TURN AWAY FROM CULTURAL LIBERALISM

He's criticism of late 1980s cultural liberalism was part of a broader turn against the "cultural fever" that had dominated the latter part of that decade. In the 1980s, impatient intellectuals, wondering why reforms had not developed more quickly than they had, turned increasingly to dissecting their own culture. In many ways, these intellectuals picked up where the May Fourth generation of intellectuals had left off. Indeed, one of the primary intellectual influences at the time was the work of Li Zehou, a philosopher at CASS, who argued that China's "enlightenment" project, inaugurated by the May Fourth Movement, had been constantly interrupted and deferred by "national salvation" movements that had grown up in response to foreign threat and war. It was time to get back to the enlightenment project.[76]

Enlightenment, in the view of many intellectuals, entailed a remaking of Chinese culture, exorcising the "feudal" elements of tradition, and opening up to influences from the West. This mood was well captured by Gan Yang, editor of the influential *Culture: China and the World (Wenhua: Zhongguo yu shijie congshu)* book series, who pleaded for cosmopolitanism and cultural renovation: "China must enter the world, so naturally its culture must also enter the world; China must modernize, so naturally we must realize the 'modernization of Chinese culture' – this is the common faith of every person of foresight in the 1980s, this is the logical necessity of the great historical take-off of contemporary China."[77]

This "cultural fever" culminated in the 1988 television series *River Elegy.* In this film, the dry, arid, exhausted soil – and culture – of the northwest (the cradle of Chinese civilization) is contrasted with the fertility, dynamism, and openness of the blue sea. If China hoped to revitalize its ancient civilization, the program suggested, it must look to the outside world, and particularly to the West. The film captured the confidence and optimism of many at the time that reform could be accomplished relatively quickly and easily if only the country would rally behind an enlightened leader, turn its back firmly on its "feudal" past, and embrace the outside world wholeheartedly.[78]

Although cosmopolitan in its orientation, it is important to recognize that *River Elegy* was quite nationalistic. The film asks pointedly such questions as, "Why did China fail to maintain the *great lead it used to have* ...? Why did China fail to maintain its *cultural and political domination* over the world?"[79] As Jing Wang remarked, "[t]he modern elite are, after all, dreaming the same dream as their forebears of the dynastic past: wealth, power, and hegemony."[80] *River Elegy,* like other efforts to renovate China's culture, was clearly rooted in a nationalistic response to China's problems, but this nationalism sought to modernize China by remaking it in the image of the outside world.[81]

Although it was enthusiastically supported by reform-minded intellectuals and by then–General Secretary Zhao Ziyang (who ironically presented a copy of the series to visiting Singapore senior minister Lee Kuan Yew, an outspoken champion of traditional Chinese values), *River Elegy* aroused a storm of criticism from different points along the ideological spectrum. Conservative critics of the film blasted it as a prime example of "national nihilism" and bourgeois liberalization. Most vociferous in this regard was Party elder Wang Zhen, who accused it of "completely negating" the Chinese tradition and adopting a "Eurocentric" view of history.[82] Wang's criticism represented the ideological views of the Old Left, but people quite unsympathetic to the sort of leftism Wang Zhen represented also had serious reservations about the film.

In contrast to Wang Zhen's emphasis on "national nihilism," He Xin's criticism focused on what he regarded as the misplaced romanticism of the intellectual elite's cultural project.[83] A similar sort of criticism came from Wang Xiaodong, a young intellectual affiliated with the Communist Youth League, who would emerge in the 1990s as one of the main voices of popular nationalism. Born in 1955, Wang studied mathematics at Beijing University and then went to Japan for further study. Tiring of mathematical study, Wang went on to Canada before returning to China. He returned to find the "cultural fever" of the 1980s in full bloom, and found himself deeply opposed to the cultural cosmopolitanism it expressed.

Wang was neither part of the Old Left nor a cultural conservative, yet he was as harshly critical as others in his condemnation of *River Elegy*. What bothered Wang was what he perceived as the elitism of the authors of *River Elegy* and the cultural elite of which they were a part. These people, Wang believed, identified themselves with the West and denigrated the Chinese people on the basis of Western standards – what he would later dub a "reverse racism."[84] As he put it, the authors "ridiculed the Chinese peasants' dull-witted love of the yellow soil and praised highly the courage and insight of Westerners in throwing themselves into myriad difficulties."[85] In a later article, Wang argued that, in the 1980s (and even in the 1990s), "Chinese intellectuals were swept up by the thinking that the Chinese culture was an inferior culture and the Chinese people an inferior race" – a trend of thinking that, in his opinion, the government had actually encouraged.[86] Wang argued that China needed nationalism and believed that the nationalism emerging in the 1990s, of which he was a tireless promoter, was a "normal nationalism" that corrected the abnormal situation that had prevailed in the 1980s and was not threatening to the outside world.

Wang's critique was not rooted in a Marxist–Leninist world view. Like many younger intellectuals, Wang evinced no faith in socialist values and yet rejected the Western capitalist and cultural tropes that had dominated discourse in the 1980s. Wang reflected a visceral nationalism that reacted against the cosmopolitanism of *River Elegy*; at the same time, he reflected a populist sentiment that rejected the elitism of those who had dominated discussions of Chinese culture in the 1980s. What differentiated Wang's critique from that of the Old Left (as reflected in Wang Zhen's article) and foreshadowed trends in the 1990s was the combination of populism, nationalism, and disregard of Communist values.

"REALISTIC RESPONSES"

As noted in the previous chapter, the abortive August 1991 coup in the Soviet Union marked a watershed in Chinese elite politics. At first overjoyed by news of the coup, conservative critics of Deng Xiaoping began celebrating and holding meetings. With the collapse of the coup, Deng moved quickly to reassert his vision of reform, leading to his trip to the south and the Fourteenth Party Congress. The coup proved to be a watershed in another way as well. Within days of the failure of the coup, a number of young intellectuals associated with the theoretical department of *China Youth Daily* circulated a paper entitled "Realistic Responses and Strategic Options for China after the Soviet Upheaval." This paper drew heavily on the ideas that have been discussed in the preceding pages, and indeed it marked the first systematic attempt to draw together the diverse strains into a reasonably coherent program of neoconservatism (a term used in the document). Although circulated internally, the document was soon leaked to the outside world, quickly becoming the subject of much commentary and sharp criticism.[87]

The document was written by Yang Ping, then the leading manager of the ideological and theoretical section at *China Youth Daily* and a close friend of Wang Xiaodong.[88] Yang and Wang called together perhaps a dozen young people, and "Realistic Responses" was a summary of their discussions. The article is sometimes referred to as a "manifesto of the princes' party" (*taizidang*), but no "princes" were at the meeting that evening. That does not mean, however, that Yang and Wang were unfamiliar with the thinking of some people at higher levels. One of those at the discussion meeting was Jiang Hong, who later became deputy head of the State Asset Management Bureau. Jiang reflected the sometimes erratic paths, in careers and thinking, taken by young people between the late 1970s and the 1990s. A key player in the democracy wall movement of 1978–79, Jiang shifted his thinking after Tiananmen and became deeply involved in the still shadowy maneuvers of neoconservatives in the government. Jiang was a close friend of Chen Yuan, Chen Yun's son, and Pan Yue, the son-in-law of Liu Huaqing, the PLA general promoted to the Politburo Standing Committee and vice-chairmanship of the CMC at the Fourteenth Party Congress. Pan clearly had political ambitions and fostered

98

neoconservative discussions among young intellectuals. To a certain extent, "Realistic Responses" was a result of such efforts.[89]

"Realistic Responses" tried to place itself between two ideological extremes. On the one hand, it criticized "utopian socialism" – the Old Left – for continually relying on mass movements, which (the authors believed) would end up destroying the very socialism that it purportedly wanted to save. The "ossified" thinking of such socialism only caused "resentment" among the people. On the other hand, it criticized "utopian capitalism" – liberal reformers – for advocating a type of "radical reformism" that was ultimately "unwilling to stop short of destroying the entire present order."[90] Instead of these two extremes, the authors called for a program of "social stability and gradual reform" that drew on both Western rationalism (Bertrand Russell, Karl Popper, and Frederick von Hayek are cited as examples of rational thinkers) and Chinese tradition. The new ideological orientation of the regime, the authors hoped, would fight against "ideological superstition" while maintaining control; sufficient space would be allowed for theoretical exploration.[91] Neoconservatism, the article said, converged with Western rationalism in its opposition to radicalism and emphasis on gradualism.

The central concern of the article was how the CCP had to change from a revolutionary party to a ruling party. Although the authors did not elaborate in detail, obviously they were exploring, however tentatively, efforts to establish viable political institutions. They were not abandoning the ruling role of the CCP but rather were trying to figure out institutional arrangements through which it might be able to preserve political stability. The authors reflected great awareness of the CCP's fragile legitimacy. As they noted, there were historically two bases for the CCP's legitimacy, the October Revolution in Russia and the "Marxism of the mountains and valleys" of Mao Zedong. With the first pillar severely shaken (and indeed about to disappear), it was all the more necessary to emphasize the "Chineseness" of the Chinese revolution. As the authors put it, it was necessary to emphasize "uniting Marxism with Chinese reality ..., with emphasis on China's national condition."[92] In the Yan'an days of the revolution, Mao had de-emphasized the specifically Marxist aspects of his evolving ideological system by demanding that Marxism be combined with Chinese reality. Deng had carried this process further by emphasizing "seek truth from facts" and by calling for building "socialism with Chinese characteristics." Now the authors of "Realistic Responses" were calling for taking this process another step forward. Just how big of a step they had in mind was suggested by their call to emphasize the "rational elements" of China's traditional culture. Considering that China's revolution had been made to destroy

China's "feudal" culture, reincorporating Chinese tradition into the ideology of the CCP would not be an easy or uncontested process. But the authors argued that, unless they could do so, "we will establish the Chinese value system on a dry stream-bed, on a trunkless tree."[93]

The desire to reincorporate elements of China's Confucian past into its current ideology was one aspect of a plainly expressed nationalism. In opposing "peaceful evolution," the state should emphasize nationalism and patriotism as well as the national interest and China's unique "national characteristics" (*guoqing*). In this regard, the article called for jettisoning the remaining ideological elements from China's foreign policy and focusing exclusively on China's national interest. Almost heretically – given the strong Chinese approval of the coup in the Soviet Union and the equally strong sense of despair after it failed – the authors argued that it would not necessarily have been to China's advantage had the coup succeeded. The result might well have been a stronger, more nationalistic Soviet Union on China's northern border.[94]

Finally, "Realistic Responses" emphasized the importance of stability, which in terms of economic policy meant that the emphasis should be on "digesting" previous reforms rather than on making new breakthroughs. The authors argued for "steady reform" and continued "experiments," particularly in smaller enterprises, but called for "attack[ing] and contain[ing] radical reformism" such as the continued "devolution of authority and granting of benefits" (*fangquan rangli*) and the rapid implementation of price reform and the shareholding system.[95] Thus, it combined the incrementalism called for by people like Sheng Hong with the criticism of the feudal-lord economy called for by Chen Yuan.

4

The Enlightenment Tradition under Challenge

PRIOR to 1993, neoconservatism consisted primarily of the ruminations of a handful of intellectuals. It was a diverse and not very coherent movement, drawing on people with distinctly different attitudes and statuses within the Chinese system. Although well connected with some conservative leaders, there was an unmistakable opportunism in He Xin's xenophobic defenses of the government, which contrasted with Chen Yuan's politically more important efforts to articulate an alternative economic agenda. Wang Huning, who had set off internal arguments about new authoritarianism, wrote nothing about the subject as public debate unfolded in 1989, but he would emerge as a politically important advisor to Jiang Zemin in the mid- and late 1990s. People like Sheng Hong and Xiao Gongqin wrote frequently but were intellectuals with limited policy impact, not to mention a different intellectual agenda from others. Yang Ping and Wang Xiaodong can perhaps be regarded as intellectual entrepreneurs who worked to inject previously marginal ideas into the mainstream, though their connections with parts of the political system should not be underestimated.

The appearance of "Realistic Responses" in 1991 marked a certain coming of age of these ideas, not so much a political manifesto of the "princeling faction" (*taizidang*) – though that element was present – as an argument that China's future lay in pioneering a "third way," rejecting both Marxism–Leninism (as traditionally understood) and Western capitalism.[1] Such a third way would include an assertion of nationalism, but it was not clear what such a nationalism would espouse since it somewhat paradoxically incorporated both an assertion of Chinese identity and an adoption of "Western rationalism." There were also hints of populism that coexisted uneasily with implicit assumptions of elite control. Although "Realistic Responses" called for readjusting central–local relations in favor of the center and rejected blind faith in market forces as "utopian capitalism," it did not reconcile that agenda with either its acceptance of market forces (shy of blind faith) or with the continuing poor performance of state-owned enterprises and the rapid growth of the nonstate sector that had accompanied the growth of market forces. In short, although "Realistic Responses" marked a certain maturation of neoconservative thought, it was really more of a starting point for further exploration than a full-blown political agenda.

By the 1992–93 period, China was emerging from the shock caused by Tiananmen and the heavy-handed propaganda campaign waged by the government against bourgeois liberalization. The economy had picked up and indeed had nearly careened out of control, as loose monetary policies were adopted to support Deng Xiaoping's call for a renewed period of reform. An orgy of real estate and stock speculation stimulated new income inequalities, between classes as well as between regions.

Because of these trends, Deng's call for renewed reform and economic development in 1992 did not cause many intellectuals simply to pick up where they had left off before and continue on the trajectory of liberal economic thought and Western-oriented reform that had dominated pre-1989 discussions. On the contrary, much of the discourse that emerged in the mid-1990s was affected by new concerns and new intellectual trends. First and foremost, the end of socialism in Eastern Europe and the subsequent disintegration of the Soviet Union not only set off ruminations about why those events had taken place and how China could avoid a similar fate (the concern among most intellectuals was not saving socialism but rather avoiding the economic decline and political disintegration that had accompanied the democratization of those countries, particularly Russia) but also about globalization. Despite divergent perspectives, intellectuals across the ideological spectrum believed that the demise of socialism in Eastern Europe and the former Soviet Union heralded a new global order, one dominated by international capital. What they disagreed about were the consequences of this new global order for China.

Second, with the upsurge of the economy and a loosening of the old rules governing economic activity, China was swept by a wave of commercialism that continues to the present day. Previously marginalized groups – individual entrepreneurs, joint venture employees, and entertainers – began to create a new urban consumer culture.[2] With the passing of Tiananmen, Marxist ideology lost whatever residual hold it had maintained on people, and the state implicitly but strongly reaffirmed the social contract that had emerged in the 1980s: economic prosperity in exchange for political quiescence. On the one hand, the wave of consumerism contributed to social stability by refocusing urban residents' attention from politics to material comforts,[3] but on the other hand it created resentments and marginalized those left behind. Unlike the 1980s, in which the vast majority of people benefited from reform, by the 1990s there was an increasing sense of "winners" and "losers," both economically and psychologically.[4]

Such changes set off a very different social dynamic, one that had implications for intellectuals not only in the way they thought about society but also in the way they related to it in material terms. Previously, intellectuals had thrown themselves into reform efforts without thought of material reward; now they began to find that their values were no longer society's values. In the Maoist period, intellectuals had been treated well materially, and even the campaigns that targeted them were a backhanded acknowledgment of their importance. As the 1980s gave way to the 1990s, however, intellectuals found their income shrinking relative to other groups and that their ideas and ethos were no longer esteemed.[5] One might argue, as Yu Yingshi has, that intellectuals have been increasingly marginalized throughout the twentieth century, yet intellectuals have been slow to give up the traditional notion that they are the bearers of the highest cultural values of the society. Nonetheless, the 1990s presented very strong evidence that intellectuals as a group were not valued by the society.

This change in status came about quickly. In 1988, as noted in Chapter 3, the television miniseries *River Elegy* epitomized the intellectual project of a cultural elite (indeed, that is what Wang Xiaodong found so repelling about it), one that conceived of itself as carrying on an intellectual and cultural mission that stems from the May Fourth Movement. Only two years later, another television series, China's first domestically produced soap opera, would reflect an extraordinarily different ethos. *Yearnings* (*Kewang*), which began broadcasting in November 1990, was put together hastily by a group of writers, including Wang Shuo and the respected author Zheng Wanlong, in a self-conscious effort to create a commercial success, something that does not come naturally to Chinese intellectuals. Starting with stock characters – the kindly, filial daughter, the "sappy intellectual," the "shrew," and so forth – the scriptwriters added flesh and blood and created a television drama that drew huge audiences.[6] In her brilliant portrait of the contemporary intellectual scene, Jianying Zha quotes Li Xiaoming, the chief scriptwriter, as saying: "If you're a television writer, and you know that the majority of your Chinese audience had to save up for years to buy a TV set, then you'd better come to terms with them."[7] Commercialism had come to the Chinese intellectual scene, and it was a painful transition for many. Commercialism destroyed the "feeling that a writer is the beloved and needed spokesman of the people and the conscience of society."[8]

One reflection of this commercialization of culture was the rates that top performers could charge. In the late 1980s, a headline performer might earn as much as 2,000 yuan for a performance; by 1992, such fees had risen to between 5,000 and 7,000 yuan, and by the mid-1990s top performers could earn tens of thousands of yuan for a single performance.[9] This commercialization of culture was also reflected in such popular writings as Jia Pingwa's *Abandoned Capital,* which depicts seamy sex and crass cynicism in a society that has lost ideals.[10] As literary critic Xiao Xialin put it: "Ours is the world of the abandoned capital. Everywhere you look, the basic values of civilization – justice, truth, ideals, and the sublime – are in a state of alienation. Morality itself has nothing more than a utilitarian value. All we dream of now and hope for in the future are sex and money."[11]

Reviewing the intellectual scene, the Shanghai-based critic Xu Jilin commented that intellectuals in the latter part of the 1980s really were "intellectual heroes," treated as celebrities on college campuses and urban streets. However, by the 1990s this was no longer the case, as intellectuals became marginalized by the changes in social values that accompanied the growth of the economy.[12] Similarly, Wang Hui, editor of the country's most influential intellectual journal *Dushu (Reading),* wrote that "[i]ntellectuals in the 1980s thought of themselves as cultural heroes and persons of foresight (*xianzhi*), but intellectuals in the 1990s are struggling to find a new way of adapting. Facing a commercial culture that has penetrated everywhere, they have painfully recognized that they are no longer cultural heroes and the molders of values."[13]

It was not just that commercialization presented intellectuals with a profound crisis of identity but also that intellectuals began to disintegrate as an identifiable social group. Despite deep divisions among intellectuals throughout China's modern history, there was never any doubt about intellectuals as a distinct social category with a sense of self-identity and group ethos. As Xu Jilin put it:[14]

> The difference in intellectual mode between the 1990s and the 1980s is that in the 1980s, even though there were all sorts of debates and ideological differences, the intellectual background, assumptions of thought (*sixiang yushe*), and value tendencies that lay behind these various divisions were fundamentally the same. Behind [the divisions] there still existed a common ideological platform (*sixiang pingtai*), namely enlightenment discourse. However, with the 1990s, that commonality no longer exists. A unified ideological platform has completely disintegrated ....

Even as commercialization undermined the role of intellectuals as the conscience of society, professionalization also drove some intellectuals into their ivory towers to undertake the sort of specialized research typical of their counterparts elsewhere in the world. Others joined the government as members of "think tanks." This was certainly a trend that had started in the 1980s, but by the 1990s intellectuals in government had become increasingly professionalized;

they had become "policy wonks," not generalists. Increasingly they talked mainly to those university-based intellectuals who shared their specialties rather than to intellectuals in general.

Finally, by the 1990s, the Chinese intellectual community was far more international than it had been a decade earlier. Not only had professional contacts with overseas Chinese and Western academics grown substantially, but significant numbers of Chinese intellectuals had studied for prolonged periods in the West. These intellectuals either stayed in the West, taking up university or other positions, or returned to China. In either case, they spoke more with Chinese outside of China and were more aware of intellectual and academic trends in the West. The phenomenal growth of the Internet greatly facilitated this internationalization of Chinese discourse. In many ways, these trends simply reflect the growth and internationalization of Chinese society and economy, but they also mark the profound difference between China in the 1980s and China as it enters the twenty-first century.

If globalization and commercialization were two major economic and social phenomena sweeping across the landscape in the early 1990s, a new willingness (some might say eagerness) to reflect on the failings of reform was another. In the 1980s, criticism of reform came mostly from "conservatives," primarily those ideologues with ties to the propaganda system, the planned economy, and parts of the military who tried to uphold "socialism" in the face of reform. Reformers had consistently pushed for more reform, worrying that conservative forces would stop reform but not that reform itself might create new problems. Yet by the 1990s a considerable number of intellectuals began to worry about the consequences of declining central revenues (in relative terms), increasing income gaps between both classes and regions, corruption, and other problems. In part these new reflections marked a certain maturation of economic and social thought as problems began to be conceived less in terms of "reform" versus "conservatism" and more in terms of solutions to specific problems. There was more of a sense that China should concentrate less on "isms" and more on "problems." Nevertheless, these reflections on the problems China faced raised new questions about where reform was going. Whereas reformers in the 1980s could look to the old system as the negative image they wanted to escape and to the West as holding out solutions they wanted to move toward, by the 1990s there was less certainty about the goal of reform. Even as marketization increased apace, the problems associated with it made people ask new questions about the role of the state and social fairness. And the rise of such questions meant that "isms," or (more accurately) broad intellectual orientation, could not be dissolved completely into analysis of "problems"; indeed, by

105

the end of the 1990s, a new concern with "isms" seemed to be overwhelming the discussion of "problems."

These questions were further related to wide-ranging reflections on what had gone wrong in the 1980s. The question of reform had seemed so easy then; no one thought about reform as a decades-long process. A sense of optimism had prevailed. Tiananmen burst that optimism. Whereas reform and maintaining the old system had seemed the only alternatives in the 1980s, after Tiananmen the alternative of social and political collapse had to be considered as well. Tiananmen thus had a sobering effect; even the most reform-minded intellectuals had to stop and ask questions about system building, not just (as in the 1980s) about destroying the institutions of the old order.

This reaction, it should be noted, differed greatly both from views widely held in the West and by democracy activists in both China and the West. Democracy activists and their supporters in the West continued to see issues largely as they had in the 1980s, hoping that a democratic movement would bring down the old order and bring forth a new democratic order. The possibility of such a scenario ending in social chaos was rarely discussed, and this is why democratic activists found themselves isolated not only from the Chinese government but also from many of the same intellectuals who had supported them in the heady days of spring 1989. The intellectual atmosphere in China had changed dramatically.

Finally, one must consider the very changed relationship with the United States. As the collapse of socialism in Eastern Europe and the Soviet Union defined one pole in intellectual thinking about the international environment, the United States formed the other. Intellectuals held overwhelmingly favorable views of the United States in the 1980s; many initially supported the sanctions imposed by the Bush administration on the Chinese government in the wake of Tiananmen. But by the early 1990s, that positive image began to be replaced by suspicion and sometimes hostility. The triumphalism apparent in America following the demise of socialism did not help. It was widely believed after the Soviet Union had done everything that the United States had asked, including getting rid of socialism, that the United States had done little to help the peoples of the former Soviet Union. Rather, it was believed, America was perfectly happy to watch Russia and the other republics of the former Soviet Union fall into a position from which they would never be able to challenge the United States again. The subsequent decision to expand the North Atlantic Treaty Organization (NATO) only served to confirm these suspicions. More directly, by the early 1990s, many Chinese – intellectuals and ordinary people alike – came to believe that America was not against government repression or even socialism but against China itself. The belief that the United States wanted to "hold

China down," as many put it, grew quickly and took hold. The opposition of the United States to China's bid to host the 2000 Olympics was a major turning point for many people in this regard. The bid to host the Olympics was a point of pride for many people; opposition to it could only be seen as hostility toward the Chinese people.[15]

The failure of socialism in Eastern Europe and the Soviet Union, the new awareness of globalization that that collapse brought about, the commercialization of Chinese society and culture, the changing status of intellectuals, the changed perceptions of the United States, the raising of new questions about the effects and goals of reform, heightened concerns about social and political stability, and nuts and bolts questions about how one might successfully carry out reform all pointed to an intellectual atmosphere that was vastly different from that in the 1980s.

Merely to list this range of changes is to suggest the variety of responses that began to emerge in the early 1990s. For instance, Wang Shuo, the popular novelist and champion of the underside of Chinese life, embraced the new commercialization and flaunted the opportunity to throw off the constraints imposed by the cultural elite.[16] To the surprise of many, Wang Meng, a liberal writer and Minister of Culture in the late 1980s, came out in defense of Wang Shuo. For both Wangs, the commercialization of culture was liberating, a way of burying "leftism" forever.[17]

In contrast, other intellectuals began to express concern over the decline in their traditional ethos. This was apparent in the 1993 debate, touched off by Wang Xiaoming and several colleagues, about the decline of China's "humanistic spirit" (*renwen jingshen*). Wang's essay started with a dramatic statement: "Today, the crisis of literature is very obvious. Literary magazines are changing direction in great numbers, there is a universal decline in the quality of new literature, the number of readers with an ability to appreciate [what they are reading] is declining steadily, and the number of writers and critics discovering that they have chosen the wrong career and leaping 'into the sea' [of business] is growing larger and larger."[18] Trying to uphold the ethos of a cultural elite in the face of commercial pressures was an increasingly thankless task, and even those determined to pursue such an ideal found it necessary to redefine their role in society. But the psychological pressures behind such a debate can be imagined.

It was not only the pressures of commercialization but also the loss of values in general that drove many intellectuals to search for meaning.[19] Some, such as Liu Xiaofeng, turned to Christianity. Working in Hong Kong since completing his dissertation in theology in Switzerland in 1993, Liu has indefatigably probed Christianity for an absolute truth that transcends sociohistorical and cultural–ethnic boundaries.[20]

A contrary response to the same search for values has been the revival of interest in "national studies" (*guoxue*). The rise of national studies in the 1990s marked an assertion of cultural nationalism, but it was not without a certain amount of official sponsorship. Cultural nationalism arose in response both to the perceived decline in values in China and to the belief that Western values could not solve the problems of the modern world.[21] As noted in the previous chapter, interest in China's tradition had been stimulated by the efforts of several well-known overseas Chinese scholars in the mid-1980s, and this had resulted in the establishment of one of the major popular (*minjian*) cultural groups of that era: the Academy of Chinese Culture, formed by a number of Beijing University professors.[22] Despite the interest the lectures and writings of the academy attracted, revival of traditional Chinese culture and studies on Confucianism were not viewed as being on the intellectual cutting edge in the 1980s. By the early to mid-1990s, however, "national studies" had not only achieved intellectual respectability but had become an intellectual fad (*guoxuere*), standing in counterpoint to the cosmopolitan cultural fever that had swept China only a decade before.

By the early 1990s, many believed that there had been a woeful loss of moral values in contemporary China – as reflected in corruption, commercialism, crime, and hedonistic lifestyles – and that there was much in China's tradition that was still of great value in the contemporary world. The deepening cultural and moral crises suggested that the problem lay not in China's traditional culture, as adherents of the May Fourth tradition believed, but rather in the decline of traditional values.[23] This understanding was bolstered by the rapid development of Japan and the "four small dragons" with attendant discussions of "Confucian capitalism," as Western social scientists and Asian commentators alike rediscovered the positive aspects of Confucianism for economic development: the frugality, work ethic, probity, respect for family and education, and acceptance of authority were all seen as reinforcing economic development and even as defining a uniquely Asian path to development.[24]

In 1991, Ji Xianlin, a well-known scholar of Chinese literature at Beijing University, published an article that looked at the cyclical rise and fall of civilizations and concluded that Chinese civilization would rise again. As he put it epigramically, "[t]he river flows east for thirty years and [then] flows west for thirty years."[25] He followed this with other articles arguing that Western civilization was based on an antagonistic relationship with nature and thus could not solve the ecological and environmental problems of the modern age. Chinese civilization, with its belief in harmony between humanity and nature, could provide a way out.[26]

Ji Xianlin was one of many older scholars who came together in 1993 to found the Institute of Chinese Culture (*Zhongguo chuantong wenhua yanjiu zhongxin*) at Beijing University. The establishment of this institute marked a watershed in the reconsideration of Chinese culture and raised eyebrows because it was set up at Beijing University, which for three quarters of a century stood as the symbol of the May Fourth Movement, intellectual enlightenment, and liberal thought in modern China. It also caught attention because of the way in which its creation was touted in *People's Daily*. This was one of the clearest indicators of Jiang Zemin's efforts to incorporate the glory of China's tradition into contemporary understandings of Marxism; others would come later.[27] In any event, the effort to co-opt reviving interest in China's tradition in the interest of political stability reflected the way private agendas coexisted, sometimes uneasily, with government desires in this period.

Another expression of cultural nationalism attracted a great deal of attention because it came from an unlikely source. In 1993, Sheng Hong, the economist whose views on incrementalism were discussed in the previous chapter, published an essay that drew parallels between China's pre-Qin philosophy – including such varied thinkers as Laozi, Zhuangzi, Confucius, Mencius, and Xunzi – and the insights of Western institutional economics, including the importance of property rights and the role that institutions play. In some ways this essay, which bore a curious resemblance to the efforts of some nineteenth-century scholars to find antecedents of Western thought in China's ancient tradition, seemed an effort to legitimize liberal economics in terms of China's cultural tradition. Nevertheless, Sheng's explorations of China's philosophical heritage had an edge. As he put it: "The goal of this essay ... is to reaffirm, in this time when Western centrism dominates and feelings of Chinese inferiority are pervasive, that within the great family of humankind China is an outstanding, non-Western culture, and at the same time to find commonalities between different cultures."[28]

This nationalistic edge was even more evident in his widely discussed 1995 essay, "What is Civilization?" In this article, Sheng argued that "Western culture in fact tends toward solving problems through war, whereas Chinese culture tends to solve conflicts through peace."[29] Sheng concluded that only a rebirth of China's tradition can save the world, a conclusion that he reiterated in greater detail in a follow-up piece, "From Nationalism to Universalism."[30] Although neither of these articles referred explicitly to Huntington, both use the term "clash of civilizations" (*wenming chongtu*), suggesting that Huntington's well-known article (discussed in Chapter 5) further stimulated Sheng's nationalist feelings.

Sheng's expressions of cultural nationalism are interesting because they reflect the overlapping and conflicting notions that are present in the minds of many contemporary intellectuals. Sheng spent several months studying with Nobel laureate Ronald Coase at the University of Chicago and is well known in China as an advocate of institutional economics and the clarification of property rights through mergers and acquisitions. Conservative critics frequently charge devotees of Coase with desiring "privatization," and Sheng Hong's remarks on limiting the role of government and his citations of Frederick Hayek's work did little to alleviate such concerns. It is particularly interesting, then, that such an economist – who sees himself as standing in the liberal tradition of Adam Smith and Ronald Coase – expresses the strong nationalistic feelings that he does.

A different aspect of this revival of interest in the continuing value of tradition was reflected in Yue Daiyun's 1989 article, "China's Contemporary Conservatism in the World Cultural Discourse." Yue Daiyun is well known to Western readers for her moving autobiography, *To the Storm,* which traces her tribulations as she went from being a revolutionary student activist to a "rightist" in 1957 to a scholar trying to cope with life after the Cultural Revolution.[31] As one of the leading literary critics in China, Yue has played a key role in introducing postmodernist concepts into China. Thus, it came as something of a shock when she wrote favorably about contemporary Chinese conservatism.

Conservatism has generally been denigrated in the modern Chinese value system. This is true not only within the revolutionary tradition of the CCP, but also of the GMD (*Guomindang*) and the May Fourth iconoclasts. Such evaluations have been reflected in Western narrations, and it is remarkable how little attention has been paid to Chinese conservatism in Western scholarship.[32]

In "China's Contemporary Conservatism" Yue Daiyun focused her attention on the group of scholars who founded, edited, and often wrote in the pages of *Xueheng* magazine, which published continuously from 1922 to 1926 and sporadically thereafter until closing in 1933. Many of the scholars associated with the journal – particularly Wu Mi, Mei Guangdi, Hu Xiansu, and Tang Yongdan – studied at Harvard University around 1920 with the neohumanist scholar Irving Babbitt. These scholars, then, were every bit as familiar with the Western tradition as their better-known contemporaries: liberal thinkers like Hu Shi and Carson Chang (Zhang Junmai), and radical activists such as Chen Duxiu and Li Dazhao. Those in the *Xueheng* group were not the "faked antiques" that Lu Xun had accused them of being.[33]

What attracted Yue Daiyun to the scholars of the *Xueheng* group is that, unlike the better-known "national essence" (*guocui*) group, they did not reject the West out of an obstinate clinging to tradition. On the contrary, they embraced those Western values that could be considered "universal" and compatible with Chinese tradition. In other words, as Axel Schneider has put it, their writings did not conceive "of Confucianism as a *Chinese* remedy to the *Western* illness of modernity" but rather as "one part of a classicist answer to the problems of modernity."[34] In terms of understanding history, the cultural conservatives of the *Xueheng* group formed the counterparts of the liberals and the radicals, criticizing the May Fourth Movement's rejection *in toto* of Chinese tradition. There is a hint in Yue's article that a healthy conservativism can serve as a valuable check on liberalism and radicalism – that cultural checks and balances are as important as political ones.

It should be noted that the article revived the reputation of a group of scholars long rejected by Communist orthodoxy, and in that sense the new attention focused on the *Xueheng* group also led to an emphasis on intellectual independence. This is particularly apparent in the many books and articles that have appeared discussing the life of Chen Yinke, a historian loosely associated with the *Xueheng* group who insisted on intellectual independence and suffered for it in post-1949 China. Lu Jiandong's vivid portrayal of the last twenty years of Chen's life became a widely read book after its publication in 1995, and Chen has emerged as something of an icon – an intellectual firmly rooted in tradition who upheld personal morality and intellectual integrity and concentrated on preserving the essence of Chinese tradition for later generations.[35] There is, then, in the popularity of Chen Yinke an ambiguity: a revival of traditional values and thus a turn away from the May Fourth tradition, but also a demand for intellectual freedom and hence away from Communist orthodoxy.[36]

The rise of cultural nationalism and the interest in a group of scholars who stood apart from the May Fourth mainstream criticism of traditional culture was part of a broader re-evaluation of the May Fourth tradition that took place in the early 1990s. This marks a real watershed in contemporary Chinese thought, for the May Fourth tradition has long been held sacred among China's intellectuals, encapsulating the ideals – science, democracy, cosmopolitanism – to which they have dedicated themselves.

In the late 1970s and early 1980s, as China emerged from the Cultural Revolution, intellectuals were obsessed by a desire to understand where the revolution had gone wrong and with a profound wish to prevent anything resembling the Cultural Revolution from ever happening again.[37] Intellectuals placed the blame squarely on "leftism." The enormous excesses of the Chinese revolution – from the "socialist transformation" of the mid-1950s to the antirightist movement of 1957, the Great Leap Forward of 1958–60, and finally the Cultural Revolution of 1966–76 – were attributed to a "leftism" that accepted uncritically a (contradictory) mix of Stalinist economic planning and Maoist mobilization, that rejected the importance of rationality and hence of intellectuals, that emphasized the "class nature" of human beings to the detriment of their humanity, and that turned the nation inward, rejecting the importance of learning from the West. These trends were also encompassed by the term "feudalism," a term of opprobrium that had nothing to do with its meaning for the economic and political history of the West or even its traditional meaning of local self-rule in China; instead, it connoted everything negative that had been attributed to Chinese traditional society through the long course of China's revolution: patriarchalism, authoritarianism, bureaucratism, anti-intellectualism, and fanaticism, to name a few. As China's revolution had increasingly criticized "capitalism," trying desperately in the course of the Cultural Revolution to "cut off the tail of capitalism" and to criticize "bourgeois rights," feudalism had flourished. "Leftism" was thus rooted in "feudalism," and the task of intellectuals and reform-minded Party people was to expunge these evils and thus set China on a course toward "modernity."

Given this basic (if somewhat oversimplified) diagnosis of what was wrong with China, it was natural that intellectuals turned to the May Fourth tradition for inspiration and moral sustenance. The May Fourth tradition had always contained contradictory elements: a radical critique of traditional Chinese culture and a demand to learn from the West combined with a nationalism that rejected cosmopolitanism in favor of nativism. Li Zehou, a member of the CASS Philosophy Institute, articulated for his generation of 1980s scholars the need to disentangle the "liberal" elements of the May Fourth tradition – those that emphasized "enlightenment" – from those that were caught up in nationalistic efforts to "save the nation." Li argued that every time the cultural critique seemed to offer hope of introducing new, enlightenment values into Chinese culture, it was overwhelmed by nationalism ("national salvation") as China faced one crisis after another.[38] Now, in the 1980s, it was finally time to take up the task of enlightenment and carry it through to fruition.

This enlightenment project dominated intellectual discourse in the 1980s. Whether it was discussions of "alienation" in socialism,[39] efforts to bring an end to "life-long tenure" and create a rational civil service,[40] policy proposals to marketize the Chinese economy,[41] translations of Western thinkers,[42] nascent writings about human rights and democracy,[43] or "reconceptualizations" of capitalism and socialism to emphasize their similarities, the task was to expunge "leftism" from Chinese social, economic, and political life. This focus on the dangers of leftism and feudalism assigned a lofty position to the West – particularly the United States, which took on an aura of modernity that provided a mirror opposite to the leftism that intellectuals sought to root out. Western culture provided fuel for ongoing critiques on Chinese culture, thus continuing the May Fourth rejection of traditional values, while the Western economic and political systems served as foils to criticize the planned economy and authoritarian political system of China. If discussions of the United States and other Western countries in the 1980s were superficial, it was because the point was not to understand how those systems actually worked but instead to provide a fulcrum from which faults in the Chinese system could be criticized. However superficial these discussions may have been, they clearly saw themselves as lying within the May Fourth enlightenment tradition, and they provided a cosmopolitanism that helped support the political relationship being forged with the West as well as reformers within the Party.

CRITIQUE OF THE MAY FOURTH ENLIGHTENMENT PROJECT

Although the May Fourth enlightenment project dominated intellectual endeavors in the 1980s, it was badly shaken by the end of the 1990s. Wang Hui, the editor of *Reading* mentioned previously, has argued that enlightenment thought lost its vitality because it was predicated on a fundamental acceptance of Western categories of thought – including liberal democracy,[44] neoclassical economics, individualism, and law – and because it relied on such dichotomies as China versus the West and tradition versus modernity to analyze China's problems. Such values and categories proved powerful when reflecting on the failings of socialism in the 1980s, but they lost their vigor, Wang argued, as globalization and marketization changed the relationships between state and society in China and between China and the outside world.

The basic problem was that globalization and marketization did not lead to the "good society." China's reform had indeed marketized the economy and linked it to the world, as enlightenment intellectuals had urged, but the result was not fairness and social justice – much less political democracy – but rather polarization, corruption, and a mutual penetration between political and economic power; indeed "the process of marketization itself had manifested new contradictions that were, in a certain sense, even more difficult to overcome" than those of the 1980s.[45] Enlightenment intellectuals had not changed their focus on state autocracy to the analysis of the "complicated relations between state and society that were developing in the course of the formation of the capitalist market," which in Wang's view was the central issue of the 1990s.[46]

In response to the changed circumstances of the 1990s, a number of young scholars, including Wang Hui, adopted a variety of postmodernist and critical methodologies by which they hope to move beyond the enlightenment critique of the previous decade. In China, this group is usually referred to as the "New Left" – "new" to distinguish them from old Marxist–Leninist ideologues like Hu Qiaomu and Deng Liqun (now known as the "Old Left") and "left" to suggest that their thought remains on the left side of the political spectrum, which in China is identified with "socialism" broadly (and ambiguously) defined. The opposite trend of thought (the "right") is liberalism. The term New Left is one that identifies aspects of the intellectual stance of this group, but like most labels it is also of polemical value. Because the term "left" has negative connotations for intellectuals, calling this group the New Left is intended to discredit them. Those who are generally identified with this group would prefer to think of themselves as "critical" intellectuals – in the sense of that term as used in literary criticism in the West.

Although this book will occasionally use the term New Left because it is so widespread and understood in China, it will usually refer to this group as "postmodernists," assuming that that term can be understood loosely to encompass a fairly wide range of critical methodologies including deconstructionism, postcolonialism, critical legal studies, analytic Marxism, and so forth.[47] While this group draws on a wide variety of intellectual trends (and it should be quickly added that there are many differences among these people), they do share the postmodernist concern with power relations in their various manifestations.

These postmodernists are composed primarily of scholars who have been educated extensively in the United States, some of whom have taken up jobs in American universities and others of whom have returned to China to take up prestigious university and research positions. Becoming familiar with the variety of the critiques of capitalism and capitalist society that abound in academia and reflecting on the situation in China, these scholars began to doubt whether China could, or should, follow the "Western route."[48] This made the goal of reform more obscure than it had seemed only a few years earlier. In part, as Suisheng Zhao commented, the "demythification" of the West that is central to this postmodernist critique was the product of wider and more frequent exchanges with the United States. As intellectuals have come to know the United States better, they have acquired the knowledge and the boldness to become more critical.[49] As works by such influential scholars as Edward Said, Michel Foucault, and Fredrick Jameson were introduced into China, there was a growing interest in and acceptance of postmodernism and deconstructionism.[50] The introduction of such critical methodologies marked a new turn in the old debate about the relative merits of "Eastern" (meaning Chinese) culture and "Western" (mostly U.S.) culture. In the wake of Tiananmen, postmodernism, deconstructionism, studies of neocolonialism, and other critical methodologies – like the revival of interest in traditional culture – began to mark a major departure from the May Fourth tradition.

While such methodologies can provide valuable insights by uncovering forgotten voices and offering new explanations, there has been a marked tendency in recent years to deconstruct Western narratives of Chinese history. These narratives, it is said, have not only been projected by those serving Western interests but have also been accepted by Chinese intellectuals. This line of thinking became prominent with a 1993 article by Zhang Kuan, then a literature student at Stanford University, that discussed Edward Said's books *Orientalism* and *Culture and Imperialism*. Besides giving an overview of Said's argument that Westerners have distorted and uglified the reality of the Orient for their own purposes, Zhang argued that Western images of China changed from quite favorable (indeed, idealized) views held by early Jesuit missionaries and enlightenment intellectuals to decidedly negative images as the West began to oppress and exploit China. He stated further that many contemporary American scholars of China were trained by the military in order to "understand the enemy," ignoring the many China scholars who courageously opposed U.S. policy toward China in the years after World War II.[51]

The brunt of Zhang's argument, however, is not his critique of Western distortions of China but rather the acceptance by Chinese intellectuals of these Western portrayals. In this regard, Zhang is critical both of contemporary manifestations of Orientalism in China and of the broader enlightenment tradition in modern Chinese thinking. An example of the former is Chinese artists whose works have become popular in the West, such as the film director Zhang Yimou, Zheng Nian (Cheng Nien, the author of *Life and Death in Shanghai*), and Zhang Rong (Chang Jung, author of *Wild Swans*). Zhang argues that their success is built on pandering to Western images of China; they have, he says, "used some fantastic and unreasonable things to make Westerners feel stimulated, intoxicated, or nauseated, to make Western audiences or readers feel what aesthetics call 'sublime' (*chonggaogan*) and compassionate and to have a sense of racial and cultural superiority (*zhongzu wenhua shangde youyuegan*). Thus, their works are popular and sell well."[52] The continuity and pervasiveness of this sort of postcolonial critique in contemporary China is precisely what underlay the criticism of Ha Jin's *Waiting* discussed in the Introduction.

In examining the broader question of Chinese images of the West, Zhang adopts the term "Occidentalism" as the opposite of Orientalism to indicate distorted presentations of Western reality. Although the concept of Occidentalism includes denigration of Western culture, Zhang is more concerned with the idealizations of the West that he believes have been prevalent in China since the May Fourth Movement. It was, of course, the May Fourth Movement that introduced and popularized many concepts of the European enlightenment to China; Zhang is so wary of enlightenment values that he takes Said to task for basing his criticisms of the West on those values. Zhang argues that humanism contains within it the antihumanist values that became the basis of colonialism and culminated in the Holocaust: "The evil perpetuated on the Jews under German fascism was the inevitable [result] of the logical development of enlightenment discourse; it returned the antihumanist practice hidden in the humanist faith from the colonies back to Europe."[53]

Zhang's rejection of enlightenment values is clearly intertwined with an affirmation of Chinese values – though he is vague about precisely what those values are. Zhang does not share the New Confucian agenda of resurrecting a revivified Confucian tradition, but he does share the New Confucian belief that the May Fourth Movement went too far in its criticism of Chinese traditional values, with the result that, "[f]or a fairly long period of time, we have diluted (*danhua*) our own cultural identity, excessively taking Western [views] of right and wrong to be right and wrong."[54] Elsewhere Zhang declares that it is the duty of Chinese intellectuals to build up a "discourse of resistance" so that the country can better counter Western demands regarding such issues as human rights and intellectual property rights.[55]

Zhang Kuan was one of the earliest and most influential participants in discussions on Orientalism and colonial culture, but he was by no means alone. For instance, Qian Jun recalls Edward Said writing about being invited to an Arab country to teach English literature – only to find the English department so dominated by colonial culture that they would only permit him to teach in the traditional English manner and not say anything critical. "I think," adds Qian, "that if Said were to come to China the situation would probably be about the same." For Qian, like Wang Xiaodong (whose views on culture were discussed in the previous chapter), the cultural fever of the 1980s demonstrated the enduring influence of imperialism in China, with *River Elegy* exemplifying this tendency.[56]

Liu Kang, coauthor of *Behind the Demonization of China* and a professor of comparative literature at Pennsylvania State University, argues that the issue at hand is one of defining a multiplicity of modernities, thereby escaping the dualities – "official/unofficial, autocracy/democracy, anti-Communist/

pro-Communist" – that have dominated thinking about contemporary China. For him, postmodernist approaches respond to the difficult position that post-Tiananmen intellectuals find themselves in: no longer the "social conscience" guiding and critiquing government, and pressed by the commercialization of culture.[57]

Another major assault on the presumed hegemony of modernist discourse came in an article entitled "From 'Modernity' to 'Chineseness'." Written by Zhang Fa of Chinese People's University, Zhang Yiwu of Beijing University, and Wang Yichuan of Beijing Normal University, this article called for a "new form of knowledge" that would break out of the categories of thought that had been accepted since the May Fourth Movement and enable China to view the world (i.e., the West) from its own perspective rather than viewing itself from the world's perspective. Essential to this new form of knowledge was the belief that there were unlimited possibilities for development and that every nationality could create its own path of development.[58] As Zhang Yiwu put it elsewhere, the concept of modernity is inevitably bound up with ideology and power relations, and China needs to explore its own developmental path.[59] Implicit in this was not so much the suggested pluralist vision but rather the "discourse of resistance" desired by Zhang Kuan and others.

The need to explore a uniquely Chinese path of development was also central to Gan Yang's well-known article "Reunderstanding 'Rural Economy'." Gan Yang, who helped pioneer the cultural fever of the 1980s, reversed course in recent years to champion efforts aimed at developing a distinct Chinese discourse. In his article on the Jiangcun economy, Gan takes Fei Xiaotong's well-known book, *Peasant Life in China,* and reinterprets it as being in the forefront of contemporary sociology.[60] Noting that Western sociologists have been critical of the way in which the Western experience has shaped the development of their discipline, Gan Yang suggests that the mixture of industry and agriculture – characteristic of both traditional and contemporary Chinese rural society – evinces a development pattern that differs dramatically from the narrative proposed by Western sociology (though not so much from the reality as revealed by recent social histories) and breaks down the assumption of a sharp disjuncture between tradition and modernity. As Gan puts it:[61]

What we call social sciences today is Western social sciences which were developed in the process of *Western* "social changes." [Social sciences] not only represented Westerners' self-understanding of social changes, but were also results of the interaction among various complex social and political factors in the process of social changes [in the West].

117

In calling for a "nativization" of sociology, Gan suggests that a form of decentralized and traditional rural society may yet prove to be in the forefront of "modernization."[62]

Although sympathetic to such approaches, Wang Hui, one of the leading intellectuals in contemporary China, has argued that they continue to accept Western understandings of modernity; the narrative or the developmental model may differ from that of the West, but the goal remains the same.[63] Wang believes that Chinese socialism, and modern Chinese thought in general, has sought a way to modernize that avoids the pitfalls of Western capitalist development. Marxism in China is a modernizing ideology, and Mao Zedong's socialist thought was a type of "modernist theory that was opposed to capitalist modernity."[64] Elsewhere, Wang goes further, pointing out the contradictions within the modernist project and arguing that "a modernity opposed to modernity is not only a special manifestation of Chinese thinkers but a reflection of the structural contradictions within modernity itself."[65] Arguing that the categories of "socialism" and "capitalism" are no longer meaningful in a marketized and globalized China, Wang has tried to develop an approach that transcends not only those categories but also such dichotomies as Western versus Chinese and modern versus traditional. In doing so, Wang argues that the problem of socialism in China is part of a worldwide "crisis of modernity," so any answer to China's problems cannot be based solely on Western concepts of modernity but must respond also to the problems in Western capitalism. As Wang's comments about capitalism and "complex relations" between state and society suggest, he is deeply suspicious of market forces, constantly seeing the hand of power influencing and distorting social and economic outcomes. As he puts it, it is simply "utopic" to think that "fairness, justice, and democracy can be achieved in the domestic and international arenas naturally out of the market."[66]

Given the debates that have emerged in recent years over China's integration into the world economy, it is important to note that Wang also sees globalization not as the extension of free markets but as the growth of multinational corporations that collude with domestic political forces to undermine both market forces and political democracy.[67] Hence Wang is not content with calling for political democracy (in which capitalist relations predominate) but argues further that political democracy must be coupled with economic democracy and cultural democracy.[68] Only in such a way can social fairness and justice prevail.

In surveying contemporary intellectual efforts to come to grips with the problem of modernity, Wang reserves his highest praise for Cui Zhiyuan. Cui, who received his Ph.D. from the University of Chicago and then taught at the

Massachusetts Institute of Technology, has probably worked harder than any-one else to develop a Chinese social science that is both informed by Western social science and at the same time critical of mainstream Western thinking. Cui is one of a large number of scholars who were quite young when the Cultural Revolution ended. Having no direct personal experience of Maoism, they tend to be more sympathetic toward (some would say they romanticize) the Maoist era, if not in its details then in some of the goals and social experiments.[69] Liberal thinkers in China react strongly and negatively to Cui's suggestions that Maoist practices can be shorn of their radicalism and thence provide a basis for economic democracy in contemporary China; for instance, no lib-eral would accept Cui's assertion that "[t]here are really quite a few positive factors in Mao's thought waiting to be excavated."[70] Similarly, liberals bridle at the notion that the Anshan Iron and Steel Factory Constitution, held up by Mao during the Cultural Revolution as a model of worker participation, really foreshadowed "quality circles" and can be resurrected as a model of economic democracy in the present era. Nonetheless, Cui has drawn on neoevolution-ary biology to argue that just as animals in the course of evolution might lose a characteristic while retaining the gene – and thus the ability to regain the lost characteristic at some later point in evolutionary history – contemporary Chi-nese society can draw on some of the practices of the Mao era, including that of Anshan, to create a more just and humane society in the future.[71] Cui argues strongly that only by acknowledging workers as "stakeholders" in enterprises can China create a society that is both economically efficient and socially fair.

It is important to keep in mind that Cui is writing in the post–Cold War period; he witnessed both the collapse of the Russian economy and the subse-quent corruption and social disintegration – as well as the West's triumphant reaction. Thus, he expresses the same concern that many other writers from different perspectives have, namely, that values have been lost in the sea of materialism that has swept China in the post-Tiananmen period: "How can we open up the spiritual resources that can bind (*niju*) the Chinese people together while being swept by a wave of 'looking for money in everything'?"[72] Perhaps no book irks Chinese intellectuals more than Fukayama's *The End of History,* with its argument that the combination of liberal democracy and neoclassical capitalism is the only route to modernity.[73] This argument not only renders the Chinese revolution – with its sacrifice of millions of lives – meaningless, it also stands in stark contrast to Chinese intellectuals' understanding of the Russian experience. Cui rejects Fukayama's argument, saying first that there is really no clear-cut neoliberal model for China to follow (since Japan, Germany, and the U.S. are so different) and second that many intellectual trends in the West

119

suggest that the neoliberal model, to the extent that it exists, is undergoing fundamental change (a point that Cui seems to exaggerate).[74]

Cui draws heavily on analytic Marxism (especially the work of John Roemer), neoevolutionary biology, and critical legal studies (particularly Roberto Unger) to derive what are basically social democratic solutions to China's problems.[75] For instance, in rejecting intellectual trends in China that accept the neoclassical paradigm of Western economics, including calls for the "clarification of property rights" and for privatization,[76] Cui argues that many people in the United States and other advanced capitalist nations are changing significantly their understandings of private property.[77] Indeed, Cui notes that critical legal studies have shown that there is no such thing as "absolute private property."[78] "Property rights" are not unified and exclusive but rather a "bundle of rights" that can be dissolved and recombined in a variety of ways. He cites changes in U.S. laws that recognize the rights not just of shareholders but also of stakeholders as one important instance of this. Thus, Cui argues against the permanence (*yongdongji,* "inertia") of institutions, saying that they can be altered and renewed in a variety of ways over time to make them more democratic. He believes that reformers who want to move quickly to clarify property rights are engaged in a type of "institutional fetishism" that will prematurely close off important institutional innovations and curtail economic democracy. Cui places great weight on the role of institutions both in changing individual behavior and in supporting ideals: "Human nature is not immutable."[79]

Much of Cui's writing, as this discussion suggests, is carried on at a high level of abstraction. Most contemporary social scientists would agree that property rights are best understood as a "bundle of rights," but to suggest that those arguing in favor of a clarification of property rights and other similar reforms are engaged in "institutional fetishism" leaves unclear what sort of system Cui would favor. Some insight into Cui's thinking on such issues is gained from a book that Cui coauthored on Nanjie Village in Henan province.

In the mid-1990s, Nanjie Village became very controversial because it had become wealthy but nevertheless eliminated private property and extolled Mao Zedong Thought. The Old Left claimed it as their own because it displayed the virtues of collectivism.[80] Cui teamed with Deng Yingtao, the son of Deng Liqun, and another rural researcher by the name of Miao Zhuang to explore Nanjie Village to see what lessons it could offer for China's development.[81]

Like many places in China, Nanjie Village faced problems in the mid-1980s as the rising costs of inputs and low grain prices made farming less profitable, even as new commercial opportunities were opening up in nearby areas. In order to maintain agricultural production and increase village incomes, the

120

local leadership persuaded farmers to turn over their contracted land to the collective so that all the land could be cultivated together. At the same time that land ownership and management were centralized in the collective, the village authorities built a series of large-scale village enterprises. Indeed, despite the appellation "village," Nanjie is home to one of the largest ramen (*fangbian miantiao*) factories in China, possessing a daily production capacity of 240 tons, a rice cake (*guoba*) factory with a daily production capacity of 126 tons, and a joint venture beer factory with an annual production capacity of 50,000 tons.[82] In fact, industry is so dominant in Nanjie that agricultural production accounts for less than 1 percent of total output.[83] All the industry is collective in terms of ownership, and enterprises are organized into one large corporation: the Henan Provincial Zhongyuan Industrial and Trading Corporation, headed by Wang Hongbin, Nanjie's Party secretary and concurrent deputy Party secretary of Linying County (in which Nanjie is located). The corporation draws up industrial plans and arranges production. Since the scale of production requires far more workers than live in Nanjie, some 10,000 workers have been recruited from other areas, compared with the approximately 3,000 inhabitants of Nanjie Village.[84]

Besides being held together by the concentration of ownership in the collective, there is a strong ideological component. Residents in Nanjie are required to study Mao Zedong's "five old essays" ("Serve the People," "In Memory of Norman Bethune," "The Foolish Old Man Who Moved the Mountain," "Oppose Liberalism," and "Where Do Correct Thoughts Come From?"). Study of these essays, for which residents are required to attend classes on a regular basis, is said to "destroy selfishness and establish publicness" (*posi ligong*). All individuals and families are rewarded with up to ten "stars" for living up to the demands of socialist spiritual civilization, and these stars are linked to the material benefits of individuals by withholding goods – otherwise freely distributed – from individuals and families who lose stars.

Cui Zhiyuan argues that Nanjie Village shows that it is possible to beat the "free rider" effect associated with collective action and still remain competitive economically; indeed, Cui argues that Nanjie's form of collective action actually enhances economic efficiency. It is thus possible to harness socialism, the positive legacy of the Mao era, to a market economy, achieving social fairness and market efficiency at the same time.[85]

Put in more general terms, Cui's work argues that China should not pursue single-mindedly the neoliberal economic model of the West – not only because significant questions about the validity of that model have been raised in the West[86] but also because China can build on its own legacies (and here he means the legacies of socialism) to avoid some of the problems of the West.[87] In so arguing, Cui seems to be combining a moral revulsion at the concentration of wealth and abuse of power that have occurred in the reform years with an idealism that socialist and economic democracy can be implemented in China despite the lack of stable social, economic, and legal institutions to build upon. Although Cui would deny any nationalist intent, his critiques of Western neo-liberalism and his evocation of China's Maoist heritage are very much a part of the 1990s' turn away from the new enlightenment problematique of the 1980s and an effort to build a China-centered social science in contradistinction to Western traditions.

LIBERAL THOUGHT IN CONTEMPORARY CHINA

This overview of postmodernist approaches to the problems of contemporary China suggests the outlines of a major cleavage between these intellectuals and those who identify themselves as "liberals." Although there are many streams of thought in contemporary China, the difference between postmodernists and liberals is perhaps the deepest and most politically salient (we will discuss na-tionalists separately, though, as their thinking overlaps significantly with that of postmodernists). Like the term "New Left," the term "liberal" should probably not be accepted uncritically, even though there has been less controversy over its use within China – either by liberals or their critics – than there has been of the term "New Left." Moreover, contemporary Chinese liberalism shares the broad outlines of classical Western liberalism, though the Western tradition's complexity and diversity make direct comparisons difficult. Nevertheless, it is important to keep in mind that Chinese liberalism is also informed by Chinese tradition, particularly the *minben* (people as the foundation) tradition associ-ated with Mencius, as well as by the liberals' understanding of modern Chinese history and the nature of the problems facing contemporary China.

As we have outlined, contemporary Chinese liberals identify themselves with the May Fourth enlightenment tradition. In the 1980s, they championed reform, which meant not only marketization and political liberalization (and eventual democratization) but also opposing the people, ideas, and forces that they saw as upholding the old order. These included orthodox understandings of Marxism–Leninism, the bureaucracies that lay at the core of the "planned economy," and those ideologues who wielded the "big stick" against people like themselves and who maneuvered to uphold and take advantage of the old system. For lib-erals, Tiananmen did not change their understanding of the forces that needed to be opposed; indeed, it only reinforced that understanding.

This understanding of the problems facing China points to a fundamental difference between liberals and the New Left, namely, their very deep disagreement over the nature of the problems facing China. For postmodernists like Wang Hui and Cui Zhiyuan, the Old Left of orthodox Marxist–Leninists has lost its power and influence as marketization and globalization have destroyed the old planned economy and opened (entangled) China to (with) the outside world; the problem for them is what type of China will be built upon the ruins of the old system, whether a "fair" society can emerge or whether economic and social disparities will be locked into place. As will become apparent, liberals share many of these concerns (though their approach to solving them is quite different), but they also see the Old Left as continuing to wield considerable power in China. Thus, liberals often speak in terms of "left" and "right" or "conservatives" and "reformers," while postmodernists dismiss such formulations as passé and reflective of a "Cold War mentality."

The community of liberal intellectuals was badly damaged by Tiananmen and its aftermath; many lost their voice and influence as they either took up residence overseas or were forced to remain silent in China. Nevertheless, there are several important liberal thinkers, both older and younger scholars, who have remained active or have become active again. The best-known of these include Li Rui, Mao's former secretary, who has written a series of works excoriating the leftist past;[88] Hu Jiwei, former editor-in-chief and director of *People's Daily,* who has published his memoirs and some articles in Hong Kong;[89] and Wang Ruoshui, former deputy editor-in-chief of *People's Daily,* who has similarly published a memoir in Hong Kong and has written a number of articles, mostly on Mao Zedong.[90] Such voices, quite influential in the 1980s, no longer carry the weight they once did, in part because the government is no longer sympathetic to their views and generally denies them access to mainland media, and in part because younger academics see them as not well trained (in contemporary academic terms) and hence "out of date." Nevertheless, their writings carry weight in some circles and stand in constant counterpoint to revisionist views of history. Whereas some younger scholars, such as Cui Zhiyuan, suggest that there are positive aspects of the Maoist era, these and other scholars of the older generation remind those who will listen that the Maoist era really was bad.

In general, these scholars of the older generation restrict themselves to writing about the past rather than engaging in polemics with their postmodernist colleagues. One exception is Li Shenzhi, the former head of the Institute of American Studies at CASS, who emerged in the 1990s as the dean of liberal thought. Born in 1923, Li graduated from the Sichuan campus of Yanjing College during the war against Japan and was one of several young, talented people recruited by Zhou Enlai to serve as secretaries and speech writers. Li accompanied Zhou Enlai to the Geneva and Bandung conferences but was then attacked during the antirightist movement of 1957. Although he was allowed to return to the Xinhua News Service in the 1960s, it was only in the late 1970s – when he was selected to head the newly established Institute of American Studies – that he became an influential voice in foreign policy.[91] In the aftermath of Tiananmen, Li was retired because of his liberal views. Although he maintained a low profile in the early 1990s, by the middle part of the decade he began writing prolifically. Well known for his understanding both of China's tradition and the West, Li is one of the most respected intellectuals in China. Moreover, his age and retirement from official responsibilities, as well as his concerns about political trends in China and intellectual trends among younger Chinese, make him willing to speak out in a way that few people have dared.

Li is an unapologetic and unreconstructed May Fourth enlightenment intellectual. He calls himself a true son of the Chinese enlightenment,[92] believing that China lacked the scientific tradition that informed Western philosophy and the democratic tradition that regulated state–society relations in the West.[93] In direct contrast to postmodernist thinkers, Li argues that the goals of the May Fourth Movement, laid down 80 years ago, have not been reached, so the spirit of the May Fourth Movement remains as important as ever.[94] Moreover, he argues that the essence of the May Fourth enlightenment tradition was liberalism and individualism. He quotes Hu Shi, one of the founders of the May Fourth Movement, as follows: "Now, there are some people who tell you, 'Sacrifice your individual freedom and strive for the freedom of the country!' I say to them, 'Fighting for your individual freedom is fighting for freedom for the country! Struggling for your individual dignity (*renge*) is struggling for the dignity of the country! A country of freedom and equality cannot be created by a group of slaves'."[95] Li quotes to similar effect other heroes of the May Fourth Movement – including Chen Duxiu, Cai Yuanpei, and Lu Xun – thus making clear that the values of individualism, human rights, and tolerance were embedded in the very fabric of the May Fourth Movement. This restatement of May Fourth values not only stands as a rejoinder to postmodernists (who tend to look more to collective solutions than to individualism, as Cui's study of Nanjie Village suggests), but also to the Communist Party, which perennially tries to subsume the May Fourth spirit under the rubric of "patriotism."

Li Shenzhi argues that the thinking of the founders of the May Fourth Movement was really "the liberalism and individualism of mainstream, orthodox world thought over the past three centuries."[96] It was, in other words, a conjoining of Chinese thought and Western liberalism, a manifestation of China's joining the world. This suggests a very different attitude toward globalization than that held by postmodernist thinkers. In contrast to the postmodernist views already described, Li takes a positive view of recent trends. Not unlike Wang Hui, Li takes 1989–92 as marking a watershed in the acceleration of globalization (a process he traces back to Columbus's landing in the Americas), one that has brought about global capitalism – as symbolized not only by the collapse of socialism in Eastern Europe and the breakup of the Soviet Union but also by the CCP's acknowledgment, at the Fourteenth Party Congress in 1992, of the need to continue reform in the direction of further marketization. Rather than exhibit the shock shown by conservative politicians or the sense of threat exhibited by postmodernists, Li states simply and boldly that "[t]he events that happened between 1989 and 1991 can in fact be understood as the force of information destroying the fortress of isolation."[97]

What was different in the globalization of recent years when compared with that of the past five centuries, and which gave symbolic import to the date 1992, was that the pace of globalization had increased exponentially and its nature had changed. By emphasizing "globalization," as opposed to the clash of national interests, Li and others were able to depict a process that transcended the nation–state system and hence threatened Western culture as much as it did Eastern culture. The proper response to globalization was not nationalism but modernization.

Thus, in reviewing works like Zbigniew Brzezinski's 1993 book *Out of Control*[98] and Samuel Huntington's *The Clash of Civilizations,* Li noted that the forces of globalization were affecting the United States as well as other countries – as reflected in American concerns over the decline of traditional standards of virtue and the pluralization of culture (multiculturalism) – and that these concerns were very much at the root of their broader strategic concerns over the future international role of the United States. Unlike young nationalists who pointed to social problems in the United States as indicators of the inevitable decline of American power, Li viewed such problems as common to all societies in a global era and not as a cause for national gloating.[99]

Like all Chinese intellectuals, Li is certainly nationalistic; it is impossible to read his essays without sensing the pride he has in Chinese culture and in the accomplishments of China.[100] But Li is critical, even contemptuous, of the rising voices of the new nationalists. For instance, in one article he noted that as China's economy has developed and a small number of people finally have some money in their pockets, a mood of pompous arrogance (*xuqiao*) has emerged, but "[t]his sort of crude nationalism is completely contrary to the spirit and trend of globalization."[101] In another article, Li wrote: "What is strange is that there are at the moment not a few students who have studied overseas who are quite different from their elders. They cannot see the good points in others and frequently develop a mood of what I call, 'an attitude of pompous arrogance' (*xuqiao zhi qi*). Perhaps this precisely reflects China's progress, but it lacks the attitude of 'knowing shame approaches courage' (*zhichi jinhu yong*) possessed by the generation of Sun Yat-sen, Kang Youwei, Wang Guowei, Chen Yinke, and Hu Shi."[102] What worries Li about the attitude of these young nationalists (who will be discussed in the following chapter) is that they overestimate the progress that China has made in the past few years and that their nationalism will prevent China from continuing to learn from the rest of the world. As he puts it at one point, those who declare that we should "rely on Chinese culture to save the world" are "arrogant and conceited" (*kuangwang*); not only will this approach not push forward China's modernization, it runs directly counter to China's cultural tradition.[103]

Li's response to globalization differs from that of young critics in part because of his own deep understanding of China's tradition, but being rooted in China's tradition does not mean that Li believes tradition to be without fault. On the contrary, Li blames much of modern China's tragedy on China's "little tradition," particularly what might be called the millenarian strain in peasant rebellions. In a heartfelt introduction to Wang Xuetai's *Vagrant Culture and Chinese Society* (*Youmin wenhua yu Zhongguo shehui*), Li suggests that Wang's book has really opened up a largely ignored source of influence on China's society and culture. For Li, Wang's study, which centers around such classic novels as *The Romance of the Three Kingdoms* and *Water Margin,* offers a key to understanding radicalism ("leftism") in Chinese history. He notes that a historical account recently unearthed reports that two of the heroes of *The Romance of the Three Kingdoms,* Guan Yu (better known as Guan Gong, later enshrined as the God of War) and Zhang Fei, went to each other's homes to kill the other's entire family so that neither would have any domestic pulls that might deter him from the enterprise at hand.[104] Li goes on to say that, when he discussed this story with several old friends, he learned that there were many instances of similar actions at the beginning of the Communist revolution.[105] This leads Li to comment that writings like Yu Yingshi's "Radicalism and Conservatism in the History of Modern Chinese Thought" and Li Zehou and Liu Zaifu's *Farewell to Revolution* simply place too much emphasis on the impact of intellectuals and not enough on the social roots of radicalism.[106] Radicalism, he argues, goes back at least to Chen Sheng and Wu Chang, whose uprising in 209 B.C.E. brought down the Qin Dynasty and remains embedded in China's social structure. This aspect of China's tradition presents a formidable obstacle to modernization: "Our

126

present goal is to modernize, but if we are not clear how many things in our-selves are not modern, then how can we know how to take the road forward?"[107]

Li's understanding of the strengths and weaknesses of China's cultural and social traditions informs his response to globalization; Li is not naive about its impact but welcomes it nonetheless. He hopes that globalization will foster eco-nomic development and that economic development will eventually bring about a middle class – a genuinely revolutionary change in China's social structure. Moreover, only such a social revolution can root out the sources of radicalism in Chinese culture and prepare the ground for law and democracy.[108] In this sense, globalization will supplement Chinese culture through social change.

In meeting the challenge of globalization, Li evinces greater confidence than many of his younger colleagues. Acknowledging that China's core problem was the loss of identity,[109] Li argues that there were many values in China's traditional culture that remained important for re-establishing a moral order, values that were not only compatible with globalization but could also contrib-ute to global civilization. Nationalism, he argues, was stimulated in China by the pressure of the foreign powers; once China has gained a position of equal-ity with other countries in the world, Chinese culture will, Li predicts, return to its roots in culturalism and cosmopolitanism (*tianxia zhuyi*) – which in the present world would be globalism.[110] Summing up, he states: "The moderniza-tion of China's culture must take tradition as its foundation and globalization as its goal."[111] There is, no doubt, a genuine idealism in Li's vision of the future,[112] one that clashes not only with the cynical view of global capitalism and cul-tural imperialism held by young critics but also with the hard realism of many in the foreign policy establishment.

Finally, Li makes clear that political reform is part of cultural modernization and China's joining the world. In early 1998, as China entered one of its periods of political relaxation, Li published a short essay arguing that the time had come for political reform to catch up to economic reform. Li's essay was pegged to the just-completed Fifteenth Party Congress, the most liberal in Party history, which had endorsed the "continued promotion of political reform." Jiang's re-port to the Party Congress had called for a "country with rule of law" (*fazhi guojia*), as Jiang was trying to promote his campaign to strengthen the legal institutions of the country. However, Li's essay interpreted Jiang's report as going further than Jiang apparently intended. Li argued that whereas Party documents normally called for "rule by law" (*fazhi*), the Fifteenth Party Con-gress had introduced the term "rule of law."[113] Li, no doubt with the hope of pushing the Party further in this direction, praised this breakthrough. But re-turning to the theme of China's culture, he noted that "[t]he greatest defect in

China's cultural tradition is that it lacks human rights."[114] Implementing "rule of law" would bring about fundamental political change, improve human rights in China, and let China join the world and earn the respect of other countries.[115] Thus, the only way to meet the challenge of globalization was to establish institutions that were compatible with it – democracy and rule of law – and not try to rely on market forces alone.[116]

Li Shenzhi may be an aging defender of the May Fourth tradition, but in recent years he and other older liberals have been joined by a new generation of younger thinkers. In the political area, perhaps the best known of the younger generation is the political philosopher Liu Junning, a researcher in the Institute of Politics at CASS until he was forced to leave during a tightening of the political atmosphere in early 2000. Liu Junning, like most liberals, is far more optimistic that the clarification of property rights and growth of capitalism, both domestic and international, will corrode the sorts of political relationships that lead to the outcomes postmodernists rightly decry. Liu sees private property as the anchor for individual freedom and political democracy.[117] In general, liberals are highly suspicious of direct democracy as called for in the works of Cui Zhiyuan and others. As noted in our discussion of Li Shenzhi, liberals view globalization as pushing forward the forces of capitalism, which they believe will lead to representative democracy.[118] Perhaps most of all, they are suspicious of nationalism – fearful that it might prevent the adoption of economic and political arrangements that could lead to liberal democracy.[119]

Whereas most of the older generation developed liberal interpretations of Marxism, which comported well with China's *minben* (people as the foundation) tradition and their own youthful hopes for democracy, the younger generation of liberal thinkers have drawn more directly on Western sources of inspiration. Thus, whereas liberals in the 1980s drew on Marx's *Economic and Philosophic Manuscripts,* the writings of East European reformers, and democratic socialist ideals, liberals in the 1990s have turned to Western writers – frequently to such conservative thinkers as Frederick von Hayek, Ayn Rand, and Milton Friedman, though also drawing on more liberal thinkers such as Isaiah Berlin, Alexis de Tocqueville, and James Madison. In short, while postmodernists have turned to the Marxist critique of liberalism, liberals have turned to the liberal critique of Marxism. Both groups have moved well beyond the dominant discourse of the 1980s, but they have done so by moving in very different directions.

The differences between postmodernists and liberals have revolved primarily around their very different understandings of the relationship between capitalism (both domestic and international) and power. As we have suggested, postmodernist thinking is highly suspicious of the power relationships embedded in capitalism and distrustful that liberal democracy is capable of restraining such relations sufficiently to bring about a fair society. This perspective is natural given the domestic and international situation in which China finds itself. Internationally, there has been a dramatic increase in foreign investment, stimulating the discussions of postcolonialism noted previously, but there has also been the dramatic failure of Russia to implement successful economic or political reforms after listening – too eagerly, in the eyes of many Chinese – to the advice of Westerners. It is little wonder, then, that postmodernists draw heavily on Immanuel Wallerstein's world system theory, which emphasizes the hierarchical nature of international capitalism.[120] The state of Sino–U.S. relations throughout much of the 1990s has played into this dynamic, exacerbating these tendencies.

Although the intellectual trends just described are understandable given China's circumstances, it is not difficult to detect a utopic element, influenced by nationalism, in the writings of postmodernist writers. As in Cui Zhiyuan's writings, postmodernists are suspicious of efforts to prematurely define property rights and to implement political democracy in the absence of economic democracy (and of cultural democracy, in the view of Wang Hui). When postmodernists write of democracy, they tend to cite Rousseau and his support of direct democracy.[121] In making such arguments, China's postmodernists are clearly drawing on a tradition of populism in modern China. Perhaps they turn toward China's populist tradition because they suspect – with good reason – that privatization, clarification of property rights, and even political democracy would institutionalize the privileges of the *nouveau riche* who have emerged in recent years. These people often have substantial political backing and have managed to take advantage of their positions to benefit from economic reform; they are, in the words of one report, the "never left-out class" (*bu luokong jieji*).[122] Indeed, perhaps the most potent charge that postmodernists make against liberals is that they ignore social justice in their quest for private property.[123]

In contrast, liberals believe that postmodernists are turning their backs on precisely those enlightenment values needed for economic and political reform; for this reason, liberals often accuse them of collaborating (directly or indirectly) with the government. Thus, Zhao Yiheng believes that postmodernist thinking is merely a continuation of the neoconservative thinking examined in Chapter 3,[124] Xu Ben has argued that postmodernists are "cultural explicators of official nationalism and authoritative domestic policies,"[125] and Zhang Longxi goes so far as to accuse postmodernists of being "spokespersons for the Ministry of Foreign Affairs."[126] Lei Yi, a well-known historian at the Institute of Modern History, pointed out the irony of a Third-World scholar using the

postmodernist discourse developed in the West to criticize the cultural hegemony of the West. Even in trying to escape the dominant discourse of the West,
one was almost inevitably captured by Western discourse; true escape is difficult, if not impossible. More importantly, Lei Yi argued that if Chinese scholars
were going to import postmodernist discourse, they should "sinify" it by carrying out an archaeology of dominant discourses in China.[127]

Zhang Kuan quickly picked up the implication of this suggestion and de-
fensively argued that Chinese scholars should handle postmodernism carefully.
Said's thinking, Zhang argued, could be used as a resource to mobilize Chinese by giving them a sense of identity with their own political culture. Indeed,
Zhang recognized clearly that the appeal of postmodernist discourse in the
1990s was linked directly to the emergence of nationalist feelings in the wake
of the *Yin He* incident and China's failed bid to host the Olympics. But if postmodernism were used to deconstruct the dominant discourse in China, then it
could be quickly used by minority populations to create trouble – and this was
clearly contrary to the nationalist mission of resisting external (American) cultural pressures that Zhang and others had in mind.[128]

Just as postmodernists and liberals differ in their understandings of capitalism and power, they have sharply different understandings of Chinese history.
Indeed, although they cannot fully lay out their different interpretations of modern history because of its political sensitivity, this is the area in which some of
their most profound differences lie. As noted before, they disagree most about
the relevance of the May Fourth tradition. Postmodernists see it as largely irrelevant to the problems of contemporary China; if it was once a vital tradition, it is
not so anymore. This attitude toward the May Fourth tradition is clearly related
to their understanding of the value of the Communist revolution. Although postmodernists can be quite critical of the government, they nevertheless see much
that is worthwhile in the Communist revolution, in terms both of accomplishments and moral values. For Western observers who have long since dismissed
the Communist revolution as a mistake – or at least as something whose time
has come and gone – this is the area of greatest disconnect, the place where the
change in intellectual outlook was so unexpected that it has gone largely unno-
ticed or been dismissed as an atavistic trend of "neoconservatism." But when
Wang Hui looks at Mao Zedong as exploring a path to modernity that is critical of Western modernity, and when Cui Zhiyuan resurrects the "good" aspects
of Maoism (as in the Anshan Constitution), there is something more profound
going on.

In contrast – as our discussion of Li Shenzhi makes clear – liberals have profound reservations about the value of the Chinese revolution. Although few are

willing to say (or perhaps believe) that it was unnecessary, they are intent on bringing a liberal economic and political order out of the society that the revolution has wrought. Their disagreement about the value of the May Fourth tradition has much to do with their assessments of the worth of the Chinese revolution. This is why liberals are a greater threat to the CCP's legitimacy and why they bear the brunt of political criticism.

5

The Emergence of Neostatism
and Popular Nationalism

ALTHOUGH the previous chapter laid out the major differences between postmodernists and liberals, attention was focused primarily on differences in their world views. To that extent, the discussion was fairly abstract, as are many of the writings in this genre. This chapter focuses on more specifically political issues that have arisen parallel to the discussions described in Chapter 4. In particular, we focus on two issues that at first glance appear to be contradictory: the emergence of a body of neostatist thought that has revolved around the issue of "state capacity" on the one hand, and the emergence of populist nationalism on the other. Chapter 3 discussed the nationalism of people like He Xin and the recentralizing impulses of people like Chen Yuan. However, even though He Xin's tone was populist, he was so obviously directing his views upward (toward the leadership) that he never tested the popular basis for his views. Similarly, although Chen Yuan sought ways to combine market economics with a stronger central government, he never developed a systematic conceptual approach. These limitations condemned the neoconservatism of the 1989–92 period to the margins of Chinese intellectual life, even as it expressed a prevalent mood within a segment of the political leadership.

By 1992–93, however, as noted in the previous chapter, the economic and social bases had developed for a broader intellectual acceptance of postmodernist ideas that would have been considered "conservative" only a few years earlier. Yet as social thinkers like Wang Hui, Cui Zhiyuan, and others began to explore new understandings of "modernity" and different development paths, other scholars – particularly Hu Angang and Wang Shaoguang, whose ideas are discussed shortly – turned their attention to the issue of "state capacity." State capacity is an old issue in American political science that received an infusion of new intellectual vitality in the 1980s as Joel Migdal, John Zysman, and others began to look at how strong states could bring about social change and economic development.[1]

Although the neostatist desire to increase state capacity appears at first glance to move in the opposite direction from popular nationalism and its criticisms of the existing government – and both of these seem distant from the post-modernist concerns discussed in Chapter 4 – in fact, all three of these trends share a basic intellectual orientation, and personal relations across them tend to be quite close. At least three concerns cross-cut these otherwise different approaches and bind them together. First, there is a common nationalism directed primarily against the United States, both in terms of its presumed desire to control China internationally and in terms of the American model of liberal democracy and neoclassical economics. Second, the approaches share a concern with social justice, though they differ somewhat in their preferred solutions. Finally, all three approaches share a populist orientation, although the neostatist is characterized by a concern for state building that popular nationalists like Wang Xiaodong do not display.

The greatest tension across these different groups of thinkers is centered on the figure of Zhu Rongji. At least prior to China's final push to join the World Trade Organization (WTO), neostatists like Hu Angang and Wang Shaoguang were interested in influencing state policy and in appealing to Zhu. They saw Zhu as someone who could both centralize state power and marketize the economy. In contrast, postmodernists worried about "premature" institutionalization, the clarification of property rights, the power relations hidden behind capitalist relations, and the integration of China's economy into the international economy. Hence, they have opposed much of what Zhu has been trying to do. Nationalists share the neostatists' desire to strengthen the state but are skeptical of the present political leadership's ability to govern successfully, to articulate China's national interests forcefully, or to use state power to bring about social justice. Keeping in mind these commonalities and differences, we turn first to the issue of state capacity and the work of Hu Angang and Wang Shaoguang.

Wang Shaoguang was among a cohort of bright young Chinese students who came to study in the United States in the 1980s; he went on to teach at Yale University before moving to the Chinese University of Hong Kong. Although his graduate work focused on the Cultural Revolution, he quickly developed an interest in the issue of state capacity and how that might relate to China's economic and political development.

While Wang came to the United States for advanced study, Hu stayed in China. Graduating from the Tangshan Institute of Technology, Hu got a job at the Chinese Academy of Sciences (CAS). The first book on which he was a major collaborator was *Survival and Development*. This book was published internally in 1989 but not openly until 1996. It stressed China's "national conditions" and how they prevented China from following the West's developmental path. In particular, China's large population and consequent low per-capita resource base meant that China would need a strong government that could "coordinate" (*xietiao*) the various demands on resources. China could not simply follow the Western model of allowing some people to become very affluent.[2] Fortunately for Hu, the book was passed to Deng Nan, Deng Xiaoping's daughter, who then passed it (or a summary) on to her father. Deng Xiaoping praised the work, and – not surprisingly – state resources were then lavished on the "national conditions research group" at CAS that Hu worked with.[3]

In 1991, Hu came to Yale as a visiting scholar and met Wang Shaoguang. Together they worked on a research report entitled "Strengthen the Guiding Role of the Central Government during the Transition to a Market Economy: On China's State Capacity." In trying to "operationalize" the concept of state capacity, Hu and Wang focused on the state's extractive capacity, not only because it is easy to measure – making it easy to compare trends across both time and space – but also because, in their opinion, it was the pressing issue of the day. In focusing on extractive capacity, Hu and Wang chose to ignore other, more difficult (but nonetheless important) components of state capacity, such as legitimation capacity, corruption, and bureaucratic efficiency.

Hu and Wang argued that the extractive capacity of China's central government was quite weak. They cited statistics to show that central government revenues as a percentage of GNP had fallen from 31.2 percent in 1978 to 14.7 percent in 1992, and they projected that such revenues would fall to only 11.3 percent in the year 2000.[4] At least as serious, they argued, was the ratio between central government revenues and total government revenues. In the period of the Seventh Five-Year Plan (1986–90), central government revenues accounted for only 40 percent of all government revenues, and Wang and Hu estimated that this figure would fall to only 34 percent by the year 2000.[5] In contrast, the comparable figure in France was 88 percent, in Brazil 84 percent, in India 69 percent, and in the United States – the lowest of all industrialized countries – it was still 59 percent.[6]

Central government revenues had decreased in percentage terms, they argued, largely because of the fiscal arrangements implemented in the 1980s to give local governments an interest in fostering local industry. These arrangements worked better than anyone had anticipated. Indeed, as Jean Oi has argued, rural China took off because China "got the taxes wrong."[7] However, the development of "local state corporatism" gave local governments an incentive to hide revenues from the central government.[8] This they could do through a variety of means: granting tax remissions, encouraging enterprises to retain revenue (so that it would not have to be declared), and expanding the scope of "extrabudgetary revenues." Extrabudgetary revenues, which allowed local governments to raise and retain certain funds for local purposes, had been introduced during the Great Leap Forward to give localities flexibility in meeting the demands of the center. In the course of the 1980s, however, extrabudgetary revenues grew rapidly. Although the exact size and distribution of such funds are controversial, Hu and Wang estimated that their size had grown from 31 percent of budgeted revenue in 1978 to 95 percent by 1989.[9] In other words, extrabudgetary revenues were roughly the same size as in-budget revenues. And about 80 percent of those revenues, according to Hu and Wang, were under the control of local governments.

The growing wealth of the localities and the declining capacity of the central state had clear and negative political ramifications, in the opinion of Hu and Wang. The result was a "weak center and strong localities";[10] the relationship between center and localities had become one of "negotiation and bargaining between equals."[11] The consequences of such a situation were said to be quite severe. Not only would macroeconomic stability and economic growth be undermined, but even China's political unity would be threatened. China's weakened state capacity put China at risk of disintegrating, just as Yugoslavia had. As they put it: "If we were permitted to take another step here and speculate on the worst case scenario, it seems possible that once the 'political strong man' at the center (for example, Deng Xiaoping) passes away, a situation like that in Yugoslavia after the death of Tito could take place in China.... *we could go from economic disintegration to political fragmentation, and, in the end, fall into national disintegration.*[12]

Wang and Hu argued that the relative decline in central state revenues was fundamentally due to the fiscal reforms introduced in the 1980s, reforms that gave localities incentives to build up their local economies but not necessarily to pass on increased revenue to the central government. Local revenues were not remitted to the central government not only because many were designated as extrabudgetary and thus earmarked for local purposes but also because the central government did not have tax offices in the localities. Provincial governments were supposed to pass up part of the revenues they collected, but the localities had an interest in retaining as much revenue as possible, so there was much "slippage" between what was collected and what was remitted.

Moreover, as Hu and Wang correctly noted, China's revenue system was disproportionately based on state-owned enterprises (SOEs), particularly large ones. As SOE efficiency had declined, their ability to generate revenue for the central government had declined as well. Meanwhile, as the nonstate economy – TVEs, private enterprises, joint ventures, and so forth – had grown, the state had not been able to tap this revenue source.

Thus, the crux of Hu and Wang's argument is that China was in urgent need of a comprehensive tax reform, one that would standardize rates across different categories of industry, that would be genuinely subordinate to the central government, and that would be able to tap various forms of nonstate industry. Hu and Wang wanted to raise the central government's proportion of revenue to about 60 percent.

Decrying the decline of central government revenues – the "two ratios" (the ratio of all government revenues as a percentage of GNP and the ratio of central government revenues as a percentage of all government revenues), as they were known – had been a staple of conservative political rhetoric throughout the 1980s. During that period, however, those who worried about Beijing's declining share of the wealth were primarily such bureaucracies as the Ministry of Finance and the State Planning Commission, organs that had a vested interest in strengthening the role of the planned economy and maintaining their own bureaucratic power.

In contrast to such old conservatives who argued for centralization and against marketization, Hu and Wang argued in favor of centralization *and* marketization. As they put it, "reform does not necessarily mean weakening state capacity, and a market economy does not necessarily connote the elimination of state intervention; modernization certainly does not need a weak central government."[13] In making this case, Hu and Wang drew on the tradition in American political science that argues that "strong states" are important in establishing stable societies and bringing about rapid economic development.[14]

Hu and Wang's use of this political science literature stood the mainstream Chinese intellectual perspective of the 1980s on its head. In that decade, those who viewed themselves as reformers generally argued that it was necessary to break down the "overconcentration" of power in the central government on the grounds that the government stifled the development of market forces. For many, anything that undermined the power of the Stalinist state was ipso facto reform-oriented and marketizing. There were market-oriented reformers who dissented from this view – the best known of whom was economist Wu Jinglian – but both the realities of political contestation and the understanding of reform-minded economists led the Dengist state to adopt the decentralizing strategy known as "devolving authority and granting benefits" (*fangquan rangli*).[15]

Shortly after the publication of their report on state capacity, Hu Angang and Wang Shaoguang shifted their focus to the problem of regional inequalities, which had begun to draw increasing attention. From the beginning of the reform period, the central government had encouraged the provinces along the eastern seaboard to carry out reforms that were more far-ranging than those in the inland areas. This policy was reflected in the establishment of the first four Special Economic Zones (Shenzhen, Zhuhai, Shantou, and Xiamen) and the generous fiscal contracts given to Guangdong and Fujian provinces. The Seventh Five-Year Plan (1986–90) formalized the strategy, and the policy of integrating the east coast into the international economy by putting "both ends on the outside" (*liangtou zaiwai* – i.e., importing raw materials and exporting finished products) further extended the policy. These policies clearly helped China's economic development, but they also brought about increasing inequalities as the eastern seaboard began to develop more quickly.

Following Tiananmen, the grievances of interior provinces were given greater voice, and the central government announced that it would adopt a "biased" or "slanting" (*qingxiang*) policy that would favor the interior. At the same time, the number of rural workers seeking employment in coastal cities grew significantly, drawing increased attention as rail lines were clogged (particularly around the lunar new year), shanty towns grew up, and crime rates increased.[16] Nevertheless, when Deng Xiaoping visited Shenzhen in 1992, he argued that the problem of regional differences need not be addressed too quickly: "Of course, it will not do to adopt this method [of the developed regions supporting the interior] too early. Now, we cannot weaken the vitality of the developed regions, and we cannot encourage 'eating from the common pot'."[17]

Hu Angang disagreed with this assessment and regarded growing regional inequalities as one of China's most important problems. Though regional differences raised questions of fairness, it is apparent that the more urgent problem in Hu's mind was that of social order.[18] Thus, he reported that a questionnaire given to provincial officials attending the Central Party School in 1994 showed that 84 percent identified social instability as the greatest problem generated by regional gaps; 16 percent feared such gaps could lead to national division.[19] As in their report on state capacity, Hu and Wang argued that regional inequalities cannot be left to the market, since the market alone might well increase rather than reduce income disparities. The government had an indispensible role to play.[20] A state could take effective action only if it had both a strong desire to address regional inequalities and a strong capacity to do so.[21] Thus, their research on regional inequalities reinforced their conclusions in the report on state capacity – namely, that the fiscal strength of the state needed to be increased and the strength of the state used to address the moral, social, and political problems presented by regional inequality.

Hu Angang and Wang Shaoguang opposed the negotiated relationship between the central government and the provinces (devolving authority and establishing fiscal contracts) because it had led, in their opinion, to the creation of privileged enclaves and vested interests with special privileges. The need to strengthen the state, implement a universal and centralized tax system, and establish the principle of "fair competition" among the various regions of China led them to argue that the most privileged of all enclaves – the Special Economic Zones – should be abolished. Hu Angang raised this issue in an internal report in early 1994. This argument was then picked up by the press, with *Economic Daily* writing a series of articles from July 2 to July 6 under the title, "How Will the Special Zones Continue to Be Special?" In August, Hu expanded on the views he had previously expressed internally by writing in the Hong Kong paper *Ming pao*. According to Hu, no local authorities should have the right to reduce or waive central tax levies or to enjoy any extralegal, extrasystemic economic privileges. He also expounded his views in a lecture to provincial governors at the Central Party School in June.[22]

Hu's arguments touched off a major debate. The *Shenzhen Special Zone Journal* responded with a series of highly vitriolic and personal attacks on Hu, and *Enlightenment Daily* ran an article arguing that the zones should be made even more special.[23] The crux of the responses was (1) that the SEZs were still necessary to introduce and experiment with various forms of management and government–enterprise relations and (2) that Hu's arguments did not take the realities of China into account, that to eliminate the SEZ's special role would amount to "contemporary egalitarianism": "The special zones' development does not hinder other regions. Their development and the development of other regions can only promote one another; they do not negate one another."[24] In June 1994 Jiang Zemin visited Shenzhen and tried to dampen the debate by declaring that the Party's and state's policies toward the SEZs had not changed. Nevertheless, Hu felt partial vindication when Zhu Rongji told Lee Hsien Loong (son of Singapore senior minister Lee Kuan Yew) in October of that year that, although the basic policies would remain unchanged, "some readjustment and improvement" was needed in specific measures.[25] The change in official policy on regional differences was more palpable: the 1994 NPC meeting drew considerable attention to regional inequalities, Jiang Zemin explicitly called for reducing regional gaps in his speech to the Fifth Plenum in September 1995, and in 2000 the development of western China was made a major theme of the NPC meeting.[26]

Hu and Wang's criticisms of "devolving authority and granting benefits" and of regional inequalities were clearly intended as critiques of the Deng Xiaoping reform program, and in this sense their views were clearly a part of the broader intellectual reflection on the "failings" of the 1980s and particularly of the 1990s. Like other New Left intellectuals, Hu and Wang focused on the problem of social fairness, which was both a moral and a political issue. Social fairness was a moral issue in the general sense that reforms creating winners and losers also created a moral obligation to help those who lost from reform – as well as in the specific sense that growing income inequalities undermined the egalitarian commitments that underlay much of the Communist Party's claim to legitimacy. Social fairness was a political issue because, as Hu Angang argued, the sense of injustice was fueling social tensions and outbreaks of violence.[27]

In 1994, Hu Angang added another criticism by raising the issue of economic fluctuations. In Hu's views, economic fluctuations in China were not primarily the result of the "business cycle" as they were in the West but rather the product of "political shocks." Hu started his work in this area in June 1989 when he and two collaborators published a report on maintaining "sustained, stable, and coordinated" development.[28] Of course, the phrase "sustained, stable, and coordinated" was a staple of Chen Yun's economic philosophy, and Hu – like Jiang Zemin in his October 1, 1989, National Day speech – called such development "the most important historical summation of the past forty years of China's economic development."[29] Hu focused attention on the subject of economic fluctuations in the wake of Deng Xiaoping's journey to the south, arguing that there was a clear historical trend of the political leadership artificially pumping up the economy in advance of party congresses and then trying to restore economic stability afterward.[30] Yet just as periods of rapid growth obscured political differences, periods of economic retrenchment inevitably exacerbated intra-Party differences, leading to major political struggles.[31] As Hu commented, the Chinese government still has a limited ability to control overheating but rich experience in implementing economic readjustment.[32] This uneven ability to effect macroeconomic control was clearly a legacy of China's planned economy, and it pointed to the need for both greater marketization and greater government rationality. Thus, although Hu employed the language of Chen Yun and was critical of economic policies associated with Deng Xiaoping, he did not call for a reinstitution of the planned economy but rather for strengthening of the government, regularization of government policy making, and further marketization of the economy.

One of the more controversial aspects of Hu's and Wang's writings is the relationship between their obvious desire to strengthen the central state and their parallel calls for political reform. Hu and Wang have argued that increasing the extractive capacity of the state requires granting a greater "voice" to society. Specifically, with respect to tax reform, they called for establishing a committee in the NPC to discuss and approve the state budget. Each province would elect representatives to the committee (they do not specify how the representatives would be elected, though it would probably not be by popular vote), and each province would have a single vote. Presumably, those who are able to participate in decision making are more willing to tax themselves. In a more recent work, Wang Shaoguang returns to this theme, arguing that allowing greater voice to society will serve both to strengthen the central government and to facilitate a more equal distribution of the gains and losses from reform.[33]

Such calls for greater societal voice parallel the populist calls that have arisen in the 1990s (particularly in the guise of nationalism, as we shall see) in that they are directed at breaking up the nexus of special interests that Hu and Wang, like other New Left writers, see as protecting the special and often corrupt interests of the economic and political elite. However, the sort of political reform that Hu and Wang call for is quite different from the democratization espoused by liberal writers such as Li Shenzhi and Liu Junning. Whereas Li, Liu, and others focus on the individual – in terms of property rights, protection from the state, and political expression – the emphasis in the writings by Hu and Wang is on "rationalizing" the state. This theme is quite explicit in an article by Hu Angang where he dismisses "carrying out political reform for the sake of political reform," calling instead for "political reform for the sake of accelerating the growth of democracy and promoting social progress."[34] Hoping to avoid the fate of Russia, Hu argues for such reforms as stabilizing the political leadership, promoting continuity of public policy, opening up the policy-making process to greater expertise, reforming the civil service system, and increasing the role of the media in supervising government. It might be said that Hu envisions using democratization, at least in a limited sense of that term, to rationalize and strengthen the state rather than to pursue democratization as a value per se. Indeed, one thing that separates New Left writers from liberals is that liberals emphasize procedural democracy, whereas people like Hu worry that procedural democracy will not achieve social justice ("economic democracy").[35]

The neostatist approach touted by Hu and Wang clearly resonates within the halls of government. Although influence is a notoriously difficult force to measure, there is reason to believe that their advocacy of tax reform played an important role in the reform of 1994. It is not that people in the government, particularly the Ministry of Finance, had not thought of implementing tax reform – indeed, Lou Jiwei was appointed vice-minister of finance largely to draft a reform of the tax system – but that Hu and Wang's report on state capacity packaged the idea in a compelling fashion that helped persuade political elites outside the ministry to accept ideas they had previously rejected. Hu has said that the report was first published in excerpted form by an internal publication of the Xinhua News Agency, *Domestic Trends, First Draft (Guonei*

140

dongtai qingyang) in June 1993. This is a publication directed at provincial- and ministerial-level cadres. The report was subsequently reprinted in the Central Policy Research Office's publication *Internal Information* (*Neibu xinxi*), which is directed at the top leadership, and then, in a longer version, in the *People's Daily*'s internal publication, *Internal Reference Reading* (*Neibu canyue*), which has a much wider circulation. Thus, Hu tried to influence government opinion at different levels by circulating his ideas through various internal publications, and these efforts certainly fed into the government's decision (in the summer of 1993) to revamp the tax system.[36] Certainly the constant attention Hu and Wang have drawn to the problems of regional inequality and political instability have similarly influenced the government's willingness to address such issues, most recently in the decision to develop the west.

In addition to whatever influence Hu and Wang have exerted on specific issues, the neostatist, incremental reform model they advocate appears quite consistent with the views of many government reformers. For instance, in one article, Guo Shuqing – one of China's leading economists, a close advisor to Premier Zhu Rongji, and now Deputy Governor of People's Bank – laid out the case for a strong but rationalized central government. Although he does not cite Hu or Wang's views, his vision is roughly comparable. This particular article was written in the wake of the Asian financial crisis with the intent to defend, and refine, the notion of a strong government after that idea came under fire domestically and internationally in the aftermath of the crisis. Guo makes the case that government functions must be separated from enterprise management but that the "Asian economic miracle" was nevertheless inseparable from a strong government. Guo is strongly market-oriented, but he is no advocate of a laissez-faire approach.[37]

CRITICS OF NEOSTATISM

The work of Hu Angang and Wang Shaoguang has been criticized, explicitly or implicitly, on many grounds. The decline of central government revenues, according to other statistical figures, has not been as serious as they argued, and the amount of extrabudgetary revenues controlled by localities is probably closer to two thirds than to the 80 percent figure they used. Moreover, by focusing not only on revenues but also on the resources controlled by the central government, economist Hu Jiayong of CASS argued that such resources actually amount to 38 percent of GNP, about three times the figure used by Hu and Wang.[38] In addition, they seem to have exaggerated Beijing's loss of control over the localities. In a careful study, Yasheng Huang argued that the center's ability to monitor behavior through the CCP has meant that localities have been successfully controlled despite the localities' interests, which differ from those of the center.[39]

Needless to say, liberal critics view the neostatism of Hu and Wang skeptically. As summarized by the well-known liberal economist Zhang Shuguang of the Economics Institute at CASS, the argument in the state capacity report rests on two assumptions, (1) that the government can play a positive and self-conscious role in the course of the transition and (2) that a strong government is better than a weak one; Zhang describes these as assumptions of "government wisdom" (*zhengfu gaoming lun*) and "state omnipotence" (*guojia wanneng lun*), respectively.[40] Zhang and others have outlined several reasons not to accept these assumptions, reasons that would have been conventional wisdom among reform-minded intellectuals in the 1980s but have come under doubt in the 1990s.

First, critics have questioned the wisdom, benevolence, and efficiency of the central government. For instance, Yang Peixin, an economist at the State Council's Development Research Center and a well-known champion of the enterprise contract system, noted that since 1949 the central government had invested 4 trillion yuan but had created less than 3 trillion yuan of fixed assets. Similarly, from 1989 to 1991, bank loans increased by 750 billion yuan but GNP increased by only 600 billion yuan.[41] Such figures suggested that the government was neither wise nor omnipotent. Dali Yang, a political scientist at the University of Chicago, noted that the concentration of resources was no guarantee of wisdom, as the disaster of the Great Leap Forward and the wasted investment in building the "third front" (the effort to build an industrial base in the hinterland in the 1960s and 1970s) had shown.[42]

Zhang Shuguang has also argued that the bureaucratic interests of many government departments would remain an obstacle to reform. As he noted, these departments were built as part of the old planned economy, and they have always been ambivalent about the growth of the market economy. Given greater resources, they would have no reason to employ them to build enterprises that would accept market competition.[43]

Moreover, the case for governmental efficiency was weak. Even as central government revenues had decreased in relative terms, the size of government and administrative expenses had increased. Yang Peixin stated that administrative expenses in 1978 constituted 4.4 percent of government outlays but by 1990 they had climbed to 9.1 percent. A good place to start would be to reduce the size of government.[44]

Yang Peixin further argued that decentralization and the reduction of government interference in the course of reform had served China well. Guangdong province, once relatively poor, had become the fastest growing province in China because the central government had lowered its tax burden; similarly, TVEs had grown faster and shown more vitality than SOEs because their tax burdens were less. It was important to "pump in water to raise fish" (*fangshui yangyu*) and not to "drain the pond to harvest the fish" (*jieze er yu*).[45]

Moreover, liberal critics questioned (at least privately) the commitment of Hu and Wang to democratic reform, seeing their neostatism as an obstacle, rather than a means, to increasing the role of society in decision making. After all, much of the logic behind their suggestion for bringing the provinces directly into the decision-making process was based on the belief that it would *increase* the bargaining power of the central government. Critics point out that, instead of bargaining with each province separately and often granting concessions to provinces individually, the central government could bring all the provinces together. The views of different provinces would inevitably offset each other, and the central government's bargaining power would actually be enhanced. Just to be sure, Hu and Wang would grant the central government veto power (they say nothing about an override provision).[46]

THE RESPONSE TO HUNTINGTON

Early neoconservative articles tried to explore a path that differed both in economic and political terms from the 1980s discourse of orthodoxy versus reform and centralization versus decentralization; likewise, the revival of interest in national studies and postmodernist critiques tried to carve out a path between "socialism" and "Westernization." This was a question both of political legitimacy – was the Chinese revolution wrong from the very start? – as well as of Chinese identity: did modernization mean Westernization?

Although many of these issues were implicit in much Chinese writing of the early 1990s, it was, ironically, Samuel Huntington's 1993 article in *Foreign Affairs,* "The Clash of Civilizations?", that really jelled the discussion and gave it focus. Of course, Huntington's article (and later book) did not fall on barren ground.[47] In Asia, as the region prospered economically, there was a growing consciousness of "Asian values" and their distinctiveness from – and sometimes opposition to – Western values. The book that heralded the debate over Asian values was Shintaro Ishihara's *The Japan That Can Say No,* published in 1989.[48]

Although Ishihara's book can be seen as the opening shot in this debate, the debate over Asian values accelerated following the end of the Cold War. Barely had the Cold War ended when Francis Fukayama published his controversial 1989 article (and later book), "The End of History."[49] Fukayama argued that, with the disintegration of the Soviet Union and collapse of Marxism–Leninism, the last great ideological debate of modern history had come to a close: the West had won. The post–Cold War world would be unified ideologically under Western neoclassical liberalism.

Not long after Fukayama (a former Foreign Service Officer) pronounced ideological victory, Anthony Lake, National Security Advisor in the first Clinton administration, gave his well-known speech on "democratic enlargement" at the School of Advanced International Studies of Johns Hopkins University. Building on the academic literature on "democratic peace," Lake turned theory into practice, arguing that the world would be a safer place if American policy could help foster democracies around the world.[50] At the same time, as the Cold War came to a close and as images of Tiananmen remained vivid in people's minds, human rights came to have a greater importance in U.S. foreign policy. This was particularly the case when President Bush and National Security Advisor Brent Scowcroft, both schooled in realpolitik, left Washington to be replaced by people with a much more activist approach to human rights, including Anthony Lake, Secretary of State Warren Christopher, and Undersecretary of State for East Asian and Pacific Affairs Winston Lord. President Clinton endorsed this approach not only in his acceptance speech (not "coddl[ing] dictators, from Baghdad to Beijing") but also in his 1993 trip to Japan and South Korea.[51]

For many in Asia, these trends suggested an American triumphalism, even arrogance. Asian critics saw a very different world than Fukayama and other exponents of American triumphalism. The United States had won the Cold War, but it appeared to have expended itself in the effort.[52] Crime rates were high, as were drug use, divorce, pornography, and other indicators of social malaise. The U.S. economy appeared to be on the ropes, as growth rates declined and productivity stagnated. In 1988, the United States went from being the world's largest creditor nation to the world's largest debtor nation.

In contrast, Asia was at that time a study of economic prosperity and social order. Growth rates were high. Books in Western academe began to relate these high growth rates to Asian culture. "Confucian capitalism" became a hot topic, both in Asia and the West.[53] There was constant talk of Asia as the most dynamic region in the world, and there was great confidence that the twenty-first century would be the Pacific century, and particularly the Asian century. China, growing at double-digit rates, shared in this confidence. When the International Monetary Fund (IMF) in 1993 announced that China's economy, when measured in terms of purchasing price parity (PPP), was already the third largest economy in the world and would likely become the largest economy in the world by 2025, pride swelled.[54]

The curious incident of Michael Fay brought these various feelings together. The West loudly objected to the court-decreed caning of Michael Fay, an expatriate accused of vandalism, saying that such corporal punishment was a violation of human rights. Singapore senior minister Lee Kuan Yew relished the moment and lectured the United States. If only the United States would cane a few people, he suggested, U.S. society would not be in such disarray.[55] Soon Malaysian Prime Minister Mohamad Mahathir joined with Shintaro Ishihara to write *The Voice of Asia,*[56] and the debate over Asian values was in full swing. It was into this atmosphere that Huntington launched his article.

Chinese responses to Huntington's article varied, but many took umbrage – seeing the article as a declaration of Western (and specifically American) superiority, or worse as racially tinged. As reviewed by Wang Hui, the editor of *Reading* whose views were discussed in the previous chapter, Huntington's essay reflected a "strong tendency toward Western cultural centrism" that "stimulated cultural nationalism" in China because it led many Chinese intellectuals to think "they were alien to Western cultures."[57]

The young nationalist Wang Xiaodong, writing under his pen name Shi Zhong, was one of those who expressed resentment. Like many contemporary Chinese who have come to view all ideological expressions as a cover for underlying interests, Wang argued that any clash between nations would be based not on civilization but on economic interest. Huntington's article was, Wang believed, an American defense of the status quo and a declaration that the West would not let China into the developed world.[58] In another article, Wang expressed the same thought more bluntly: "I have never believed that the U.S. is really all that concerned with the human rights of the Chinese people .... I also find it hard to believe that the pragmatic American people are willing to spend that much capital to surround us because we believe in Marxism. The reason that the U.S. does not like us is because we are strong; we have the possibility of developing and then could be an obstacle to America's special place in the world."[59] More recently, Wang declared, "I think that Mr. Samuel P. Huntington is a racist, whose 'clash of civilizations' is nothing but a euphemism used instead of the politically incorrect 'clash of races'."[60]

Wang Huning, then about to move to Beijing to work with Jiang Zemin, offered a more subtle critique, one that reflected the cultural concerns taken up in postmodernist critiques. Wang connected Huntington's discussion of culture and cultural conflict to the notion of "soft power" discussed by Joseph Nye and others. Wang agreed with Nye that, with the end of the Cold War, the importance of "hard power" has declined while that of "soft power" has increased – but this did not necessarily make the world a less threatening place.

Cultural arguments, Wang said, often reflected political interests and sometimes expanded into armed conflict (as in Bosnia–Herzegovina). Moreover,
cultural influence was directly related to political and economic strength, so
developed countries were often comfortable talking in terms of an "erosion of
sovereignty" while developing countries found that such "cultural expansionism" often ended up threatening political stability and national sovereignty.
Furthermore, cultural influence was directly related to the construction of international norms and regimes, which were not always in the best interest of
the developing nations. As Wang put it in a passage that suggests his familiar-
ity with postcolonial criticism: "If one nation-state is able to make its power
appear reasonable in the eyes of another people, then its desires will encounter
less resistance. If the culture and ideology of one nation-state is attractive, other
people will voluntarily follow it. If one nation is able to establish international
norms (*guifan*) that are consistent with its domestic society, there is no need for
it to change itself. If one nation-state is able to support an international regime,
and other nation-states are all willing to go through this regime to coordinate
their activities, then it [the first nation-state] has no need to pay the high price
of hard power." Cultural imperialism, in short, is a cheap way of achieving the
goals that states formerly employed hard power to attain.[61]

As Wang Huning's argument suggests, many in China saw Huntington's thesis from the perspective of ongoing discussions of "Orientalism," believing that
there was a need to strengthen Chinese culture in order to meet the challenge of
the clash of civilizations.[62] Others sought to meet this challenge by bolstering
Chinese culture with nationalism. Jiang Yihua, a senior scholar at Fudan University in Shanghai, viewed Huntington's argument through the lens of China's
past: "The bitter history of Asian countries over more than a century shows that
the countries of the West that came to Asia established a bloody colonial ruling
order or semi-colonial ruling order. They never really supported the nations of
Asia to 'enter the West' economically, politically, or culturally.... [W]hat they
brought to Asia was primarily colonial culture...." Jiang viewed Huntington's
argument about the clash of civilizations and his extolling of Western values
as universal values[63] as a continuation of this imperialist past. Having escaped
the "cultural hegemonism" of the West, China would not now accept Western
values as its own.[64]

WANG SHAN AND THE EMERGENCE OF POPULIST NATIONALISM

The previous discussion dealt with the way in which a number of influential
intellectuals responded to China's domestic and international situation in the

146

1990s. Some of these responses, such as the neostatism of Hu Angang and Wang Shaoguang, had a palpable influence on the political system, but most were explorations among an intellectual elite with no direct connection to politics. Nevertheless, as we have suggested, many of these discussions contained a populist element – whether it was Wang Xiaodong's excoriation of the cultural elite who authored and directed *River Elegy,* He Xin's efforts to rally support for a beleaguered government, or the economic democracy touted by Cui Zhiyuan and many others. If populism was in the air, no one had yet tapped this vein to show that their ideas actually had popular support.

That changed in 1994 with the publication of *Looking at China through a Third Eye.* The author turned out to be Wang Shan, a young writer whose persona is reminiscent of that of Wang Shuo, the popular chronicler of the underbelly of urban life. Like Wang Shuo, Wang Shan had already written a first novel, *Tian Shang (Heaven's Elegy),* that depicted a world of hooliganism, incorporating traditional notions that there was a code of honor among that underclass that contrasted favorably with values of their social betters. When an interviewer suggested to Wang that his novels give people the impression that he is a sort of hooligan from the lower classes and that he hates the upper classes, Wang replied that Chinese society has always been divided into an upper class (*shangliu*) and a lower class (*xialiu*); elsewhere he comments that he represents the lower ranks of officialdom.[65]

Born in 1952, Wang was the youngest of those known as *laosanjie,* the three classes (which "graduated" from high school in 1966, 1967, and 1968) who made up the Red Guard generation and were sent to the countryside when Mao had seen enough of the chaos they had generated. Wang went to Shanxi province in 1968, where he labored in the fields for a year before going to work in a coal mine. In 1970, perhaps using his father's connections (his father was a military cadre), Wang joined the PLA, where he served for seven years. In the 1980s, he became director of the Great Wall Social Research Institute (*Changcheng shehui yanjiusuo*). Wang seems to be an unsatisfied and intemperate person; his literary agent noted that Wang switched jobs frequently, and "always inexplicably ended by being fired."[66]

Wang declared that the greatest influences on his thinking were a "sense of responsibility" bequeathed by his father's generation to carry on the task of the revolution and the "heroic thought" (*yingxiong zhuyi sichao*) of tempering oneself through struggle, something he apparently cultivated during the Cultural Revolution.[67] Unlike most of those older than himself, Wang obviously retained a romantic attachment to the Cultural Revolution and to the figure of Mao Zedong, a passion that flared up with Deng's trip to the south in 1992 and the resulting wave of speculation. Wang saw 1992 as a dividing line. Before then, all strata of Chinese society had gained from reform; after that, power and the market merged so that one stratum exploited another.[68] As Wang's friend and literary agent Xu Bing put it, prior to 1992, Wang was a "determined and wildly enthusiastic supporter of reform," but by the spring and summer of that year "his support became rational and conditional."[69]

Wang was not alone in his doubts about the course of reform. We have cited the views of many people who had begun to reconsider the course of reform beginning in the 1990s, but such doubts – even the discussions of the new authoritarianism – were carried out in intellectual and political circles. Wang was not an intellectual, at least not in the sense of belonging to those in government, think tanks, and universities who thought and wrote for each other. Wang was an outsider who claimed few friends in intellectual circles.[70] What Wang Shan did was to make his doubts public by writing what became an instant best seller; in so doing, Wang showed that his doubts were widely shared among the urban population.

The cover of *Looking at China through a Third Eye* identifies one "Luo yi ning ge er" as the author. In the preface, "Luo yi ning ge er" is identified as a German and as Europe's most famous Sinologist. Wang had chosen the name from a dictionary that transliterated foreign names. Germany had the attraction of having produced well-known intellectuals over the years, thus providing an air of *gravitas,* and was also neutral regarding Chinese affairs and hence capable of seeing China's situation "objectively" as a bystander (the implication that "a third eye" was supposed to convey). Attributing authorship to a foreigner may also have permitted the book to be published more easily; it certainly aroused interest and curiosity, much as Joe Klein's attribution of his book *Primary Colors* to "Anonymous" did in the United States. Most important, it attracted buyers and made the book the object of conversation and speculation for months.[71]

What made *Looking at China through a Third Eye* a powerful polemic, however, was its linking of urban anxieties to a systematic critique of the Dengist reforms. Wang strikes hard at urban anxieties by talking in ominous terms about the growing tide of peasants entering the cities. Anyone who flips through Chinese history, Wang declares, will discover that without exception all of China's dynasties have been destroyed by peasants who left the land. They are a "powder keg" and a "living volcano" that have unleashed a wave of criminal activity in the cities and present a serious danger to the political stability of China.[72]

Having raised the specter of peasant violence, Wang unfolds a sympathetic picture of Mao Zedong, contrasting Mao's policies favorably with those of

Deng. As unbelievable as it is, Wang pictures Mao – the person who unleashed the Great Leap Forward and brought about the death of perhaps 30 million Chinese – as the only leader who truly understood the peasants. Wang argues that Mao was basically sympathetic to the peasants, but the task of modernization forced Mao to sacrifice their interests in favor of industrialization. By keeping peasants (described as "lacking in education and full of traditional rebelliousness") "locked docilely" on the land and by "squeezing the peasants' stomachs," Mao was able to pursue industrialization for three decades and was able to turn China into a nuclear power. Had he not done so, says Wang derisively, "today China would look like India."[73] Mao tried to transform the peasants, but after the Great Leap Forward they revealed their "spontaneous capitalist tendencies" and challenged the Party through their laziness, migration, and black markets, confirming Mao's fears that rural society was a "hotbed of spontaneous disease and germs." In the end, Wang suggests, it was the peasants who betrayed Mao and not the other way around, but then "we often find that Chinese simply do not understand or love their leader, Mao Zedong."[74]

Reflecting the same resentment of China's cultural elite as Wang Xiaodong, Wang Shan declares in *A Third Eye* that intellectuals lack the "knowledge, experience, ability, character, and prestige" to participate effectively in government and push forward the democratization of the country.[75] The history of China's various democratic movements, beginning with the Hundred Flowers Movement in 1957, shows that owing to the lack of maturity of China's intellectuals, their struggles have failed to promote the causes for which they strove. In 1957, Wang declares, intellectuals went too far. Mao wanted an "open door" rectification campaign in order to check the unbridled power of the bureaucrats. When accusations were raised against people in the Party, they apologized for their wrongdoing, "but this only whetted the ambitions of intellectuals. Students in Beijing and Shanghai started to leave their campuses. An incident had the possibility of evolving into a destructive riot. Thereupon, Mao could not but take action ...."[76] The intellectuals, like the peasants, were not worthy of Mao. The "tragic history of 1957," Wang writes, proved that "the intellectuals created by China's old culture and civilization ... are born with faults that they cannot overcome. Because of this, they cannot unite with the ruling Party, the state power, and the primary forces that are leading the people forward and thereby bring their great ability to bear."[77]

Wang also casts a sympathetic eye on the Cultural Revolution, particularly on Mao's motivations in initiating it. In striking contrast to the Mao who is known to the West and older intellectuals in China, Wang depicts him as a benevolent, idealistic leader, one even given at times to sentimentalism. Wang

149

describes Mao as having been "like a good and patient family head, thinking of the whole country as a 'large family'." He also declares that "Mao was a god, and people are perhaps only beginning to understand him several years later."[78] Mao's initiation of the Cultural Revolution is depicted as the effort of an idealist to overcome the gap between the common people and officials; his motive was to pre-empt the political crises that certainly would have erupted from such an elitist system by bringing about a nonbureaucratic, classless, and democratic society. The tragedy of Mao was that Chinese society did not have the conditions for such a democratic society and thus his effort failed.[79] But Mao, the author argues, was not wrong in his initial motivation; the mistakes that resulted in tragedy occurred later (and were largely the fault of Jiang Qing and Lin Biao). Indeed, Wang suggests that "people may discover that some ideas from the Cultural Revolution are wise and prescient."[80]

Wang's assessment of Mao is certainly related to (one is tempted to say derived from) his evaluation of contemporary China. *A Third Eye* argues that the reform period eroded faith in Marxism–Leninism, undermined the power and authority of the Party and state, and unleashed a host of social problems – including corruption, crime, economic polarization, and moral decay – that the government, given its weakened authority, is increasingly unable to deal with. Unless something is done to reverse the erosion of state authority, the author maintains, China will find itself beset by political and social turmoil. Ideology is important for Wang. He declares that "[a] society without faith is in danger"[81] and argues that the Dengist reforms have progressively eroded Maoist ideology until there is nothing left to inspire people and unify the nation:[82]

> As soon as one problem is solved, another emerges. As soon as the traditional ideology of Mao Zedong's idealism begins to be broken, then the government's defense line must retreat step by step. Local governments continuously extend their hands asking for new "policies" and the central government has no choice but to compromise in the face of solving new problems. China's economic structural reform was really created in this way. Now, when we look back, what is left of Mao's inheritance? How much is left? Deng Xiaoping has repeatedly said that the four cardinal principles must be upheld, but how much has really been upheld?

For all of Wang Shan's disdain of officialdom and intellectuals (whom he accuses of being destructive), he is clearly in favor of autocracy. In an interview, writer Liu Zhifeng says, "[y]ou hint that China needs a god like Mao Zedong, a great idol"; Wang replies, "[y]es, but I can't easily say this." Liu continues:

"My understanding is that you are saying that China needs a period of rule by man, of elite rule, and cannot very quickly institute rule by law." Wang's response: "Yes, elite rule. Rule by law is unreliable."[83]

Wang's desire for elite rule is rooted in his passion for stability. For all of his expressed sympathy for the Cultural Revolution, Wang declares that he wants China to "improve" (*gailiang*) rather than "reform" (*gaige*) for fear that reform will be too destabilizing.[84] As he puts it: "What I fear most is that as soon as revolutionary thought or theories are imported into China they will stimulate the division of strata, which has already started, and bring about a destructive revolution. China needs stability."[85] In order to enhance stability and stop the decline in morals in society, Wang unabashedly favors raising high the banner of communism, "so that it becomes the banner flying above our heads and becomes our common faith (*xinyang*) and religion (*zongjiao*)."[86]

Wang's diagnosis of China's social ills and his hope that the CCP could provide stability in a period of transition is related to an unabashed nationalism. Wang makes clear his belief that the student demonstrations of spring 1989 were encouraged and supported (if not instigated) by the United States and were aimed at overthrowing the CCP because America feared China's nuclear power.[87] Like other nationalists, he asserts not only that the United States is in moral and social decline but also that the cure to the ills generated by an "economic mechanism flooded with liberalism" could only lie in the East.[88]

STRATEGY AND MANAGEMENT

In late 1993, a new journal called *Strategy and Management* (*Zhanlüe yu guanli*) started publication and quickly became a forum for new and often critical ideas, including nationalism and populism. Even the physical appearance of *Strategy and Management* suggested a journal that differed significantly from the hundreds of academic journals normally circulating in China. It is printed on far better paper than the average journal, indicating its substantial financial backing – reputedly contributed by a wealthy overseas Chinese from Thailand but also suggesting its support from the military. The "honorary director" was former PLA Chief of Staff Xiao Ke, the director was former Secretariat member Gu Mu, and the "senior advisors" included such luminaries as retired general Zhang Aiping, former *People's Daily* editor-in-chief Qin Chuan, former State Economic Commission head Yuan Baohua, and former Secretariat member Yan Mingfu.[89] The editor of *Strategy and Management* was Qin Chaoying, son of the former editor-in-chief of *People's Daily,* Qin Chuan, but the editorial direction came primarily from Yang Ping and Wang Xiaodong. As noted in Chapter 3, Yang Ping was the chief drafter of "Realistic Responses" in 1991 and had served as an editor of *China Youth Daily,* one of the most popular papers in the country. Yang Ping was interested in exploring various nationalist and neoconservative ideas as a way for China to overcome what he and many others saw as the problems generated by the reforms of the 1980s. As "Realistic Responses" and the editorial board of *Strategy and Management* suggested, this was a group of youth who were well connected with higher-ups in the Party but who were also frustrated by what they regarded as the lack of new ideas and forceful leadership of the Party. The different perspective of this group stemmed in part from generational differences and in part from their self-identification with the common people. Yang Ping and Wang Xiaodong brought to their editorial direction a strong sense of nationalism, a desire to see a strong state that expressed that nationalism, and a sense of populism that made them sometimes quite critical of the existing government. Although many outside observers label them "neoconservatives," they reject that label and instead see themselves as "true liberals" or as part of the New Left (*xin zuopai*).

The inaugural issue of *Strategy and Management* carried several articles that indicated its editorial direction. Xiao Gongqin, whose ideas were discussed in Chapter 3, examined such dilemmas of Chinese modernization as the need for centralized authority and the demand to expand popular participation (a frequent concern in his writings),[90] while Wang Xiaodong offered the critique of Samuel Huntington's "Clash of Civilizations?" article discussed previously.

Although by 1993 there were many articles that expressed nationalistic sentiments, few journals took on the topic of nationalism directly and openly. *Strategy and Management* did just that in a symposium in the June 1994 issue. The articles were not particularly inflammatory – certainly much less so than Wang Shan's book *Looking at China through a Third Eye,* published later the same year – but they did raise some important issues.[91] For instance, Pi Mingyong (from the Academy of Military Sciences) argued that nationalism had been a difficult issue in twentieth-century China because it was necessarily compromised. The "great nationalism" of the Han Chinese conflicted with the "small nationalism" of the minority nationalities, Pi wrote, while the antitraditionalism of the nationalistic May Fourth Movement denigrated the history of the very people it hoped to lift up. Therefore, the Chinese government had always adopted an ambiguous policy that tried to use the strengths of nationalism without incurring its weaknesses.[92] Yin Baoyun (from Beijing University) argued that nationalism was a vital component of economic development but that many Third-World countries had encountered difficulties because they emphasized culturalism, racism, or localism, neglecting the pride and progressive spirit of nationalism. Korea's Park Chung Hee provided a positive example of how nationalism could be used to bolster economic development.[93]

Another major theme in the pages of *Strategy and Management* was populism. Like nationalism, populism was not something that was widely discussed in the open press in the early 1990s. Thus, a symposium on populism in late 1994 gave high-profile attention to this important topic. Sun Liping, a professor in the Sociology Department of Beijing University, made the point that much of Maoist rhetoric and practice was populist. The rhetorical status given to peasants and workers, the egalitarian distribution system, the effort to eliminate income differences across regions, the commune movement during the Great Leap Forward, and the criticism of Soviet "revisionism" and of "bourgeois rights" during the Cultural Revolution all reflected populist values. So even though the political system was hierarchical and authoritarian, populism was very much a part of the CCP's tradition.[94] Hu Weixi (of Qinghua University) pushed this analysis back further, noting that the "national essence" movement (*guocui yundong*), the anarchist movement, and the rural reconstruction movement in the first half of the twentieth century – despite all their differences – shared a populist orientation.[95]

In addition to noting the historical importance of populism in modern China, both Sun and Hu related its appearance to the social strains caused by development, factors apparent not only in early twentieth-century China but also in contemporary China. Thus, Sun argued that different social groups have been affected differently by reform, and that those who have lost out (at least relatively) in recent years tend toward populism. Economic development therefore created a group of relatively wealthy people with the result that cadres (particularly lower-level cadres) – who used to have a special status because of their political position – found themselves relatively impoverished and resentful. Workers in state-owned enterprises have also found their wages lagging behind those of other sectors and have certainly lost their social status as "masters." Some intellectuals have also felt that their social status and income have fallen; in addition, they have been indignant about the corruption they see around them. They hence became critical of the political elite and sympathetic to populism.[96] Shifting social statuses provided uneasiness and corruption bred resentment, so people juxtaposed the presumed purity of the revolution with the corruption of reform; because corruption was to some degree linked to the elite, resentment took the form of populism.[97] Hu Weixi added that postmodernist currents in the West, through their criticism of capitalism and appeals to study Eastern culture, unintentionally provided a catalyst for populist thought in China.[98]

Both Sun Liping and Hu Weixi seemed to view the development of populist thought with some concern.[99] Wang Xiaodong's article in the same issue of *Strategy and Management* reflected less ambivalence, recognizing the dangers of populism but nevertheless seeing populism as an important and potent critique of elitism. Wang noted that some very influential "mainstream" theories want to push reform in complete disregard of social justice, and he argued that a "smart" (*jingming*) politician would certainly not disregard the rich populist tradition in China. Thus, he argued for a "balance" between populism and elitism – but one that leans toward the social fairness inherent in populist doctrines.[100]

CHINA CAN SAY NO

The growing sense of popular nationalism reflected in the publication of *Looking at China through a Third Eye* and the emergence of *Strategy and Management* was confirmed with a vengeance by the 1996 publication of *China Can Say No*. Whereas *A Third Eye* focused primarily on domestic social and political issues with a nationalistic introduction, *China Can Say No* was an unabashed outpouring of nationalistic feeling with little attention to domestic issues. Hastily written and published, the five young authors were taking advantage of the anti-American sentiment that had welled up in the wake of the 1995–96 Taiwan Straits crisis and the dispatch of two American carrier task forces to the area. In writing a nationalistic best seller, the authors of *China Can Say No* demonstrated that the same broadening of mass culture that had previously been evident in popular literature, television, and the entertainment industry was also available for political mobilization.

China Can Say No was striking not just because of its highly emotional tone but also because the authors all claimed to have been strongly influenced by the United States, only to have become disillusioned in the 1990s. They cited U.S. efforts to block China's bid to host the 2000 Olympics, the *Yin He* incident, opposition to China's GATT/WTO bid, the Taiwan issue (especially Lee Teng-hui's visit to the U.S.), American support for Tibet, and alleged CIA activity in China to account for their changed attitudes.[101] They had come to realize, they claimed, that the United States was not the bastion of idealism that it claimed to be; "human rights" was merely a facade behind which America pursued its national interests. In fact, far from championing ideals in the world, the United States was an arrogant, narcissistic, hegemonic power that acted as a world policeman; now it was doing everything in its power to keep China from emerging as a powerful and wealthy country.[102]

There is no doubting the support for publishing *China Can Say No* within government circles: Yu Quanyu, then the very conservative deputy head of China's Human Rights Commission and a frequent contributor to China's left-wing journals, endorsed the book in an afterword. But it is equally evident, and perhaps more important, that there was a mass audience for such works.

Although many intellectuals pointed out that the book was shallow, poorly written, and overly emotional, it is also apparent that many read it and perhaps even enjoyed the venting of the frustration that they shared (though perhaps not to the same degree). The book quickly sold almost two million copies. The authors soon followed with a sequel,[103] and imitators sprouted up "like bamboo shoots after a spring rain."[104] Within government circles, it appears that there was at first a sense that someone had finally expressed their frustrations with the United States. One reason was that many government officials share – even if on a more sophisticated level – the authors' view that U.S. actions are guided by national interest, that concern with human rights is a smoke screen for opposing China, and that U.S. policy is based on containment and/or subversion. Moreover, government officials had endured years of abuse at the hands of U.S. columnists. "Let the United States taste some of its own medicine" seems to have been a fairly common sentiment.

That anti-American sentiments were widespread at the time is supported not only by sales figures but also by survey research. Public opinion on foreign policy questions is a politically sensitive topic, and few surveys are allowed (or allowed to be published). One exception was the well-known survey done by Wang Xiaodong, Fang Ning, and others at *China Youth Daily,* which has been conducting investigations of youth attitudes since the mid-1990s.[105] Taking advantage of the fiftieth anniversary of the end of the war against Japan, *China Youth Daily* conducted a large-scale public opinion poll in May of 1995; it found that 87.1 percent of respondents believed the United States was the country "least friendly" to China, while 57.2 percent indicated that the United States was the country toward which they felt most negative. Reflecting cynicism about American motives, 85.4 percent believed that the United States engaged in the Gulf War "out of its own interests."[106] A concluding essay argued that the nationalism reflected in the survey showed that China "still has hope." Setting the results of the survey against recent discussions of globalization, the author (or authors) declared – in the best realist tradition – that the world was still divided into nation-states; the dividing line separating nation-states was far stronger than any other, including (with reference to Huntington) culture. However, the article concluded that one division did not fall neatly into the realist paradigm: that between the "haves" and the "have-nots." The West, the article explained, is guided by self-interest; it fears both that the rest of the world is too poor, which might induce those in poorer nations to immigrate to the West, and that the rest of the world is too prosperous, which would "threaten their [the West's] superiority." Those in the "have-not" camp, the article asserted, "love our camp, love our China." China should have no illusions about the West.[107]

China Can Say No was widely popular and influential. Reviewing the results of a survey of reading habits, the researchers concluded: "It is worth paying attention to the great influence on readers of the thinly veiled (*lugu*) discussion of nationalist sentiment (*minzu zhuyi qingxu*) with regard to international relations in this popular literature"; they also noted that *China Can Say No* "unexpectedly" (*juran*) was the most influential book in the post-1993 period.[108] It is important to observe another side to *China Can Say No* that was apparent to Chinese readers but has been largely ignored in the United States: the populism of the book had a distinctly antigovernment tone to it as well. The authors charged that the Chinese government had been naive and soft in its dealings with the United States, that it should be more forthright in just saying "no," and that the government was neither confident enough nor competent enough – it was too wrapped up in the past and insufficiently bold in engineering China's modernization.[109] Even more than the nationalism expressed in the pages of *Strategy and Management, China Can Say No* had a populist edge that was highly skeptical of the government. Government officials may have welcomed an expression of nationalism, but they also realized that it was something that could be turned against them, as it had been so many times in the twentieth century.

Part III

ELITE POLITICS AND POPULAR NATIONALISM

6

Jiang Zemin's Rise to Power

THE Introduction addressed the issue of the state and intellectuals in broad terms; we are now in a position to consider the issue more specifically. As we saw in the first two chapters, elite politics in the immediate aftermath of Tiananmen was an inside game. This was a period in which a relatively small number of political elites sharply contested the basic issues of the day: the definition (in terms of policy) of reform and opening up, and the relative balance of power between Deng Xiaoping and like-minded reformers on the one hand and Chen Yun and ideological and economic conservatives on the other. Intellectuals had an extremely limited role in this period. Economists could and did advise the government to "increase the weight of reform," but a fundamental re-evaluation of the importance of the market economy had to wait for Deng Xiaoping's trip to the south in 1992 and the subsequent convocation of the Fourteenth Party Congress.

If intellectuals were excluded from meaningful political participation in this period, they nevertheless began a painful process of re-evaluating the course of reform, what had led to the tragedy of Tiananmen, and the role of intellectuals in contemporary China. As a result, a very different intellectual atmosphere began to emerge in the 1990s. This new intellectual discourse was largely independent of politics, a genuinely societal discourse. However, unlike the discourse that grew up in the late 1980s whose participants came to confront the government, many intellectuals in the 1990s found themselves implicitly or explicitly more supportive of the government than they or their counterparts had been only a few years before. The prospect of governmental collapse and social chaos, the object lesson provided by the economic decline in Eastern Europe and the subsequent disintegration of the Soviet Union, a newfound respect for the complexity of reform and state building, and (especially after 1993) a new sense of nationalism – as well as the costs of continuing opposition – inclined many intellectuals to be more tolerant and even supportive of government efforts.

Disillusionment with radical reform (indeed with radicalism in general), consternation with the inequalities that reform had brought to China, and a growing frustration with American triumphalism – not to mention American actions – supported new efforts to rethink the course of reform. Could there be a model of reform that preserved China's identity, avoided the economic and political inequalities associated with capitalism, and yet developed the economy? As we have seen, much of this reflection was rooted in discussions of the new authoritarianism in the 1980s, and found expression in many forms: the neo-conservatism of Wang Huning, Xiao Gongqin, Chen Yuan, and He Xin; the postmodernism of Wang Hui and Cui Zhiyuan; the neostatism of Hu Angang and Wang Shaoguang; and the populist nationalism of Wang Shan, Wang Xiao-dong, and the authors of *China Can Say No*.

This new atmosphere tended to push democratic activists to the margins of Chinese intellectual and social life. Whereas Western commentators continued to view the image of the lone person standing in front of a column of tanks as emblematic of the aspirations of the Chinese people, more and more Chinese saw that person as symbolizing the excessive romanticism of the 1980s reform movement. A new sobriety came to the fore, and the economic progress and social stability of the early and mid-1990s seemed to vindicate a new authoritarian or neoconservative approach to reform – especially in view of the problems the Russian Republic continued to experience.

Although the more conservative intellectual atmosphere associated with neo-conservatism, the New Left, and nationalism developed largely independently of government direction (though the government certainly permitted the development of such discourse), government officials – particularly from the mid-1990s onward – frequently shared many, though not all, of the attitudes of such intellectuals. This was, after all, a government that believed it had to forge ahead with economic reform without questioning the official judgment on Tiananmen, a government that needed to deal with many of the social, economic, and political problems that had given rise to the more conservative intellectual atmosphere in the first place: growing regional inequality, income polarization, central–provincial relations, corruption, internal migration, crime, tense Sino–U.S. relations, and so on. To the extent that there was a common interest in problem solving, intellectuals could, by the mid-1990s, take up roles as advisors. The roles of Hu Angang and Wang Shaoguang are illustrative in this regard.

The interests of critical intellectuals and mainstream government officials, however, diverged on at least two major issues. First, the government continued to back marketizing reforms, a growing role for the private sector, and increasing integration into the global economic order. Whether because of the semireformed nature of the system or the specific interests of the people involved, these reforms often contributed to the corruption, abuse of power, and income inequality that made so many intellectuals skeptical of capitalist solutions. Even as the government pushed forward with what most outside observers believed to be necessary, if painful, reforms, intellectuals decried the social injustices created.

Second, although the government shared and encouraged the nationalism of many intellectuals, it did not share the populism. Populism, as we have noted, was inevitably directed against the government elite, and as the critical perspectives of postmodernist intellectuals blended with the popular nationalism of people like Wang Xiaodong, a powerful critique emerged of a weak and corrupt government selling out the Chinese people in the interests of the government and international corporations. This was a critique that mostly festered in intellectual circles, but it could on occasion – most notably, following the U.S. bombing of the Chinese Embassy in Belgrade – burst into full view.

Increasingly, the Chinese government has been forced to take this critical public opinion into account – not only because of the mobilizing potential inherent in it but also because there are political leaders and interests that support these views. Thus, intellectual critique plays into "oppositional politics." The result is that the government has increasingly had to engage its critics in the public arena. This is not (or at least not yet) the long–hoped-for emergence of a "public sphere" in China, but it does suggest that the days of government pronouncements and media "education" of public opinion have passed. Not only is there now a more obvious dialogue between state and society, but the scope of this dialogue has widened significantly. Only a few years ago, no public discussion of foreign policy was allowed. Wang Shan's *Looking at China through a Third Eye* smashed that taboo, and now books and journals are filled with critiques of official policy. It is only natural – given the role that concern with globalization played in stimulating the discussions of postmodernism examined in Chapter 4 – that China's participation in the WTO has become a major point of intellectual dissension.

We will examine in this and the next chapter some of the ways in which intellectual concerns have intersected with elite politics. Here, we turn our attention back to high politics and particularly to the process through which Jiang Zemin consolidated his authority. It will be recalled that, in looking at the period immediately following Tiananmen, Jiang Zemin was not much of a factor; although general secretary, the main fight was taking place well above his head. To the extent that he did speak out, he was extremely cautious – and thus incurred the wrath of Deng Xiaoping. By 1994, however, the situation had changed significantly. Deng's trip to the south had set off a new round of rapid economic growth and reform, while Zhu Rongji's appointment as vice-premier had placed a solid reformer in charge of the economy, effectively eclipsing Premier Li Peng. Moreover, the actuarial tables were beginning to have an important impact on elite politics. Jiang's closest political supporter, former president Li Xiannian, died in June 1992, followed soon thereafter by the Party's most authoritative ideologue, Hu Qiaomu, in September 1992. Chen Yun was apparently quite ill in 1994 and finally died in April 1995. Deng Xiaoping's health was also failing; when he was shown on television watching fireworks during the October 1 National Day celebration in 1995, the Chinese public was shocked to see an old man staring out blankly. Everyone knew the end could not be far away. Thus, by 1994, it was apparent that a political transition of enormous importance was unfolding.

THE FOURTH PLENUM: EMERGENCE OF THE "THIRD GENERATION"

The Fourth Plenary Session of the Fourteenth Central Committee convened in Beijing on September 25–28, 1994. The session was devoted to issues of Party building, particularly "democratic centralism." Previously, the plenum had been scheduled to discuss the economy as well; however, in what may well have been his last intervention in politics, Deng suggested that economic issues be dropped from the agenda.[1] It was not that there were no economic issues worth discussing. On the contrary, the economy took a serious turn for the worse in 1994. In the spring, the NPC had approved a commitment to keep inflation under 10 percent (down somewhat from the 13 percent registered in 1993). By the summer, it was obvious that the goal could not be attained, and in August the NPC Standing Committee announced that inflation would be kept under 15 percent. The year would end with a yearly inflation rate of 21.7 percent.[2]

If inflation was disturbing, the performance of the state-owned economy was even more so. By September, some 44 percent of SOEs were losing money, "triangular debts" had ballooned to 400 billion yuan, and about 80 percent of SOE income went to debt service.[3] In mid-September, the State Statistical Bureau issued a report in which it said that China's economy was on the verge of entering the "red zone," indicating severe trouble. This was only the third time such a report had been issued; previous reports had come in the summer of 1988 and the spring of 1993.[4]

The decision to focus the plenum on democratic centralism thus reflected Deng Xiaoping's declining health and a decision to declare openly the passing of leadership to a new generation, and particularly to Jiang Zemin. Deng and other top leaders were most worried about three interrelated problems: the authority of the CCP vis-à-vis society, the authority of the center vis-à-vis the localities, and the authority of Jiang Zemin vis-à-vis his colleagues in the leadership. All three problems revolved around the question of whether Jiang could become the "core" of the Party in reality as well as name. The term *core* can perhaps best be understood as that combination of informal and formal authority that makes a leader the final arbiter of Party issues – the ability, as the Chinese put it, to "strike the table" (*pai banzi*) and end discussion. Five years after Deng had made Jiang general secretary and declared that he was the "core" of the Party, Jiang still lacked that authority.

The Fourth Plenum was a major victory for Jiang, the point at which it can be said that Jiang began to come into his own as a political leader. The *People's Daily* editorial hailing the close of the plenum stated that "the second-generation central leading collective has been successfully relieved by its third-generation central leading collective" – a point reiterated by Li Peng during his November trip to Korea and again by Jiang Zemin a few days later during his trip to Malaysia.[5] The plenum adopted the "Decision on Some Major Issues on Strengthening Party Building," which on the one hand excoriated negative trends such as corruption and weakness of grass-roots Party organizations and, on the other hand, urged renewed attention to democratic centralism – emphasizing the subordination of lower levels to higher levels, the part to the whole, and everything to the Party center. As the decision put it, "there must be a firm central leading body ... and there must be a leading core in this leading group." And that core, the plenum reiterated, was Jiang Zemin.[6]

Moreover, Jiang's effective power was enhanced when three of his protégés were promoted to the center. Huang Ju, mayor of Shanghai, was promoted to the Politburo; while Wu Bangguo, Party secretary of Shanghai and already a member of the Politburo, and Jiang Chunyun, Party secretary of Shandong province, were added to the Party Secretariat. The promotion of Wu Bangguo and Jiang Chunyun served not only to shore up Jiang Zemin's personal support at the center but also apparently to check the authority of Zhu Rongji, a potential rival. With the economy performing poorly in 1994, Zhu began to come under fire from both the right and the left. Leftists criticized efforts to "privatize" the economy, and Zhu lashed out at liberal economists who urged him to undertake more radical reforms.[7] Jiang began to parcel out bits of Zhu's portfolio. Wu Bangguo was named deputy head of the Central Finance and Economic Leading Group (replacing Li Peng) and thus would share leadership of that critical body with Zhu, under the general supervision of Jiang, who remained head of the group. More importantly, Wu was placed in charge of the reform of state-owned enterprises, which was designated as the focus of economic reform in 1995. It is not surprising that the personal relationship between Wu Bangguo and Zhu Rongji in the following years was frosty at best.[8] At the same time, Jiang Chunyun was given the task of overseeing agriculture, another task for which Zhu Rongji had previously been responsible.

Although the plenum decision stressed the presumably conservative theme of democratic centralism, it sounded several "liberal" themes that had been associated with NPC chairman Qiao Shi but would later – at the Fifteenth Party Congress in 1997 – be taken over by Jiang Zemin. For instance, the plenum declared that democratic centralism and "system construction" were necessary so that the Party's policies "will not change with a change in leaders or with a change in their ideas and their focus of attention."[9] Previously, when Qiao Shi had taken over as chairman of the NPC, he had declared that "democracy must be institutionalized and codified into laws so that this system and its laws will not change with a change in leadership, nor with changes in [individual leaders'] viewpoints and attention."[10] Moreover, the decision called for inner-Party democracy, declaring that "[i]f there is no democracy, there will be no socialism, nor socialist modernization."[11]

The sounding of such themes is no doubt partly attributable to the drafting process in which different views within the Party needed to be balanced against each other. But it also suggests that, even as he was making a bid for personal power, Jiang was conscious of both a demand and a need to stress democratization and institutionalization. Deng Xiaoping had sounded these themes in his justly famous 1980 speech "On the Reform of the Party and State Leadership System," but Deng's own status as a revolutionary elder, the repeated conflicts over policy, and doubtless also Deng's reflexive resort to personal decision making prevented implementation of his ideas.[12] As a member of the postrevolutionary generation, Jiang could never possess Deng's personal authority; he would have to find ways to build institutions even as he augmented his personal power.

Year-end economic meetings seemed at a loss for how to deal with the problems afflicting the economy. An August 26 communiqué from the State Statistical Bureau had summed up the results achieved over the previous year of tightening macroeconomic control; it concluded that measures "dealt only with symptoms and not with the causes" of inflation and SOE inefficiency.[13] Nevertheless, the Central Economic Work Conference that met November 28 to December 1 called for controlling inflation and "deepening" the reform of state-owned enterprises.[14] As Premier Li Peng put it: "Without solid state-owned enterprises, there will be no socialist China."[15] Hence, reform in 1995 concentrated on the selection of a hundred state-owned enterprises for pilot projects in the creation of a modern "corporate" form – as if China had not already carried out hundreds of pilot projects over the past decade and more. At the same time, leaders vowed to control inflation, though they promised not to repeat the "hard landing" of the 1988–91 austerity program.

FIGHTING CORRUPTION

Even as Jiang tried to reinforce his personal strength through the strategic promotion of protégés, to rein in centrifugal tendencies by re-emphasizing democratic centralism, and to steer a course of "stability and unity" by curbing inflation and slowing the pace of economic reform, he also made a dramatic bid to win public support by finally swatting some tigers in the ongoing campaign against corruption. Public anger at Party corruption had fed the 1989 protest movement as well as the subsequent "Mao craze" that surfaced in late 1989 and the early 1990s,[16] but corruption had been difficult to tackle because of the political clout protecting some of the worst offenders. Hu Yaobang discovered this in 1986 when his hard-hitting campaign against corruption aroused the anger of Party elders and contributed to his own downfall the following January.[17]

The Party had launched a campaign against corruption in the immediate aftermath of Tiananmen, but that had faded away like its predecessors. Finally, in the summer of 1993 and amid evidence that corruption was spreading uncontrollably, the Party launched another campaign. For the first year of this campaign, it seemed to go pretty much as its predecessors had – catching many flies but few tigers.[18] In the winter of 1994–95, however, the campaign shifted into high gear. The first major casualty was Yan Jianhong, the wife of former Guizhou provincial Party secretary Liu Zhengwei, who was executed in January for taking advantage of her connections in order to embezzle and misappropriate millions of yuan.[19]

Then, in February 1995, Zhou Beifang was arrested. Zhou, the head of Shougang (Capital Iron and Steel) International in Hong Kong, is the son of Zhou Guanwu, who was then not only head of the model enterprise Shougang but was well connected to such senior leaders as Wan Li, Peng Zhen, and perhaps Deng Xiaoping himself. It will be recalled that Deng visited Shougang in May 1992 as part of his campaign to reinstitute his vision of reform. The day after Zhou Beifang was arrested, the elder Zhou retired as head of Shougang. In addition, Deng Xiaoping's son, Deng Zhifang (a manager with Shougang International), was apparently detained and questioned with regard to the case, though no charges were filed against him.[20]

At the same time, an ongoing investigation into corruption in Beijing Municipality apparently resulted in the detention of some sixty cadres in the city, including the secretaries of Party chief Chen Xitong and mayor Li Qiyan. Then, in early April, Vice-Mayor Wang Baosen, who had been implicated by the investigation, committed suicide. The upheaval in the city came to a climax in late April when CCP secretary Chen Xitong, a member of the Politburo and ally of Deng Xiaoping, was removed from office and subsequently placed under investigation. At the Party's Fifth Plenary Session in September 1995, Chen was officially removed as a member of the Politburo and in 1998 was sentenced to sixteen years in jail, though he was later released on medical parole.[21]

With the removal of Chen Xitong, it seemed apparent that the effort to strengthen "democratic centralism," the campaign against corruption, and the power struggle among the leadership had come together. Chen had clearly disdained Jiang, and his removal was critical to the consolidation of Jiang's power, but Jiang had invoked the campaign against corruption rather than the older tactic of ideological deviance to rid himself of Chen. In a single stroke, Jiang Zemin moved against one of the most entrenched local leaders in the country, made a bid for popular support in the campaign against corruption, and acted against powerful people who might oppose him in the future – including the Deng family and Party elder Wan Li (Wan was a longtime supporter of Shougang and, as a former vice-mayor of Beijing, had close ties to the city's leadership).

The ouster and investigation of Chen Xitong reflected old-style politics, as one powerful politician defeated another and increased his hold on power, but it was also part of Jiang's popular campaign against corruption and was used to burnish the leader's reputation with the public. It was additionally a stroke, even if a selective one, in a continuing effort to move toward the rule of law in China. Jiang hardly had the power of his predecessors Mao and Deng; he had to invoke general rules in order to move against personal political antagonists. In this, the resolution of the Fourth Plenum appears to have played a significant role. That resolution declared: "The principle of everybody being equal before discipline should be upheld and those Party members who violate discipline should be investigated and dealt with severely."[22] It is not known whether this and other strictures were written into the resolution with the Chen Xitong case in mind.

One other aspect of the Chen Xitong case should be mentioned, and that is Chen's role in Tiananmen. Chen and then–Beijing Party secretary Li Ximing had played a very active role in urging the Party to adopt a hardline stance in the face of popular demonstrations, apparently writing reports that were biased and inflammatory. As a result, they were widely disliked in Beijing. Li Ximing had been forced to step down following Deng Xiaoping's trip to the south, during which Deng had specifically named Li as a "leftist."[23] Now, Chen was forced to step down because of corruption. It seems that in removing Chen, Jiang was indirectly addressing the still angry citizens of Beijing – but doing so in a way that did not call for a direct reversal of the verdict on Tiananmen.

Jiang's ouster of Chen Xitong was his most significant move on the chessboard of elite politics since the 1992 removal of Yang Baibing, and the first that could be attributed to Jiang alone. Chen's arrest hardly brought consensus within the political elite, for the same interests and currents that had clashed in the years following Tiananmen remained. These divergent interests were reflected both in the Party leadership and in those that Jiang gathered around him for policy advice. Within Jiang's own entourage were (and are) conservative officials such as Teng Wensheng (Deng Liqun's protégé), who heads the Policy Research Office of the Central Committee, and Ding Guan'gen (the conservative head of the Propaganda Department), whom Jiang continues to employ despite his being widely disliked within the Party, not to mention among intellectuals. At the same time, there are more "liberal" advisors, such as former Shanghai mayor and all-round political mentor Wang Daohan. Wang has played a critical role in helping Jiang navigate the hidden shoals of elite politics, has shaped much of Jiang's approach to foreign affairs, and has been invaluable as a liaison with the intellectual community. There was also Liu Ji, Jiang's close friend from Shanghai who served as vice-president of CASS from 1993 to 1998, then played an active though much lower-profile role in Beijing, and finally was exiled back to Shanghai to take up a deanship in an MBA program.[24] In between these conservative and liberal advisors, there are a number of people who have worked to further Jiang's interests bureaucratically. The most important of these is Zeng Qinghong, who served as head of the Central Committee's General Office from 1993 to 1998 and then moved over to head the important Organization Department. Zeng was promoted to be an alternate member of the Politburo at the Fifteenth Party Congress in 1997, and may well one day emerge as leader of China in his own right (though this looks less likely as this book goes to press than it did a few years ago).[25]

In the course of the next few years, Jiang tried to navigate between the conflicting demands of the "left" and "right," and the tensions between these poles were sometimes reflected in friction within the group around Jiang. As we shall see, Jiang's response was to try to carve out a "middle course" that would allow him to maneuver between conflicting pressures while not becoming overly tied to any particular interest. But first he had to deal with pressures from the Old Left.

As Jiang moved to consolidate power at the Fourth Plenum, the question was: Which way would Jiang lead China? From 1989 until 1992, Jiang had steered a cautious path, one that no doubt gave conservatives cause to believe that he was "one of them." In 1992, Jiang had then switched gears, as he certainly had to, by endorsing Deng's talks during his southern tour and supporting the Fourteenth Party Congress report that strongly endorsed Deng Xiaoping's reform line and warned against the danger on the left. Following the Fourteenth Party Congress, however, Jiang shifted back toward the center; he showed no inclination to allow the critiques of leftism appearing in the wake of Deng's southern sojourn to continue. This shift back to the center appears to have been part of a broad compromise between different forces in the Party. Deng won a major endorsement of his policies and significant personnel victories. But Deng stopped short of removing leftists from a number of major positions.

In the wake of the Fourteenth Party Congress, Jiang struck a course that might be broadly considered neoconservative, albeit without the explicit nationalistic or populist appeals that some neoconservatives called for. The ideological atmosphere that grew up in the wake of Tiananmen probably facilitated Jiang's policy direction, just as Jiang's cautious political direction encouraged a more conservative intellectual atmosphere. Although Jiang tolerated the de facto privatization of much economic activity in the wake of Deng's southern trip and Zhu Rongji's efforts to squeeze inflation out of the economy, his statements remained ideologically cautious or conservative. Moreover, although Jiang's power had increased, he was not in a position to alienate powerful figures in the Party – and many of those figures were on the left. Thus, conservatives seem to have calculated that a well-aimed critique of the effects of the Dengist program would either convince or force Jiang to identify himself with leftist causes.

In August 1994, leftists convened a meeting in Xiangshan, northwest of Beijing. Attended by such people as Deng Liqun, Xu Weicheng, Shao Huaze, Wang Renzhi, He Jingzhi, Li Ximing, Gao Di, and Yuan Mu, the meeting reportedly declared that the collapse of socialism in Eastern Europe and the former Soviet Union was due to "revisionism," the old Maoist term for heterodox understandings of Marxism–Leninism. Deng Liqun allegedly went so far as to suggest that Deng's views were themselves revisionist: "Deng Xiaoping's theories must be tested in practice to show whether they are correct or wrong. Any attempt to advocate using Comrade Deng Xiaoping's theories to negate or replace Marxism as the guiding principle for revolution and construction in China is idealist

168

and goes against the 'Communist Manifesto.' No doctrine or theory, now or in the future, can replace Marxist truth and science."[26]

In September, more or less the same cast of characters convened a meeting in Shijiazhuang, the capital of Hebei province. Speeches were delivered on such themes as "Revisionism and Right-Deviationist Thinking Are the Traitors of Marxism," "The Line We Are Pushing Now Is One Which Practices Capitalism under the Leadership of the Communist Party," "The Turmoil of 1989 Was the Product of the Party's Right-Deviationist Line," and "The Damage Done to the Country by the Pro-U.S. Line."[27]

Leftist criticism accelerated in early 1995 when a sharply worded document entitled "Several Factors Influencing China's National Security" was anonymously forwarded to the Central Committee and circulated internally. Although no name was attached to the document, it was reportedly written by a researcher at CASS and endorsed by conservative ideologue Deng Liqun. The article, which became known as the first "10,000 character manifesto" (in reference to its length and political character), warned that the proportion of state-owned enterprises in China's aggregate industrial output value had fallen from 76 percent in 1980 to 48.3 percent in June 1994, that there were already 328,000 registered private enterprises with over five million employees and 100 billion yuan of capital, and that a "new bourgeoisie" had already taken shape as a class in itself.[28] As if this were not enough, the document warned that the nature of the Party was changing as more and more technically trained specialists were promoted to leadership positions, that the sovereignty of the country was being undermined by increasing economic dependence on the West, and that "bourgeois liberal" thinking was once again on the rise and linking up with private entrepreneurs to form a threat to the Party. Although the document explicitly or implicitly questioned the whole reform enterprise since the Third Plenum of 1978, it reserved special venom for Deng Xiaoping's 1992 trip to Shenzhen. Not only did it state that bourgeois liberalization has gained the upper hand "since 1992," it also argued that bourgeois liberalization had "spread unchecked under the 'anti-left' signboard" – an apparent reference to Deng's statement during his trip to Shenzhen that the left was the "main danger."

In the late summer or early fall of 1995, as tensions in the Taiwan Straits mounted, a second "10,000 character manifesto" was circulated. Entitled "A Preliminary Exploration of the Shape of China's Domestic and Foreign National Security in the Next Ten or Twenty Years and the Primary Threats to It," this second document maintained that China faced a hostile international environment made up of "monopoly capitalists" who view China as an enemy and that domestically China was undergoing a number of social changes that were threatening its national security and social stability.[29] Unlike the first manifesto, which concentrated on domestic trends, this second document focused on the reasons for the disintegration of the Soviet Union and the collapse of socialism in Eastern Europe – issues that had been central in the 1991–92 period but had since calmed down in the wake of the Fourteenth Party Congress and the efforts to rebuild diplomatic ties with the new Russia. This second manifesto argued that the threat of "peaceful evolution" was the critical issue and that China's reliance on the international economy had weakened China's "national" (domestic) industries, thus making China more vulnerable to Western pressures. The document went on to warn that the ideological confusion in the Party – particularly the belief that it is not necessary to determine whether a given policy is "capitalist" or "socialist," an agnostic approach that derived directly from Deng's trip to the south – might lead to the appearance of a Gorbachev-type leader within the CCP in the next ten to twenty years, though presumably the author was concerned about a much shorter time frame.[30]

SOCIOECONOMIC CHANGES

This resurgence of leftist criticism, which had receded in the period following the Fourteenth Party Congress in 1992, reflected the tensions generated by the rapid socioeconomic changes that occurred after Deng's trip to the south, just as did the various postmodernist critiques considered in Chapter 4. Deng's criticism of leftism and his call for faster economic growth not only brought the usual expansion of investment but also stimulated, for the first time, a lively and speculative real estate market. In 1992, some 73 billion yuan was invested in real estate, 117 percent more than the previous year.[31] By the end of the year, there were over 12,000 real estate companies, a 2.4-fold increase over the year before. These companies leased some 3,000 pieces of land with a total area of 22,000 hectares, marking an 11-fold increase over 1991. In addition, 428,886 million square meters of housing were sold, a 40 percent increase over the previous year.[32] At the same time, local areas continued to open up "developmental zones" in the hope of attracting foreign capital and taking advantage of loopholes in the financial regulations. By the end of 1992, there were said to be some 8,000 developmental zones.[33]

According to He Qinglian, the crusading economic journalist who published a best seller in 1998 entitled *The Pitfalls of Modernization,* Deng's southern journey prompted the formation of hundreds of "joint stock companies." In Jiangsu province alone, over 200 such enterprises were established in the 18 months following Deng's trip, and in Hebei province the number of joint stock enterprises jumped from a mere 23 at the beginning of 1992 to 133 a year later.[34] He Qinglian argued that the local enthusiasm for forming such enterprises resulted from local officials and enterprise managers who saw the joint stock system as a way to drain off state-owned assets for their own benefit.[35] State-owned assets were not only lost to domestic enterprises; joint ventures shared the bounty as well. Already by 1992, she argued, some 46 billion yuan had been lost to joint ventures.[36]

He Qinglian dubbed the selling of land (most of which had previously been an unvalued asset) as China's "enclosure movement," a reference to the seventeenth-century English movement of the same name. According to He, the boom in the real estate market enriched those with connections at the expense of the common people, obstructed the formation of a fair competitive mechanism, and fostered rampant corruption. Such real estate speculation drove up land prices and put housing out of reach of most people – and caused much resentment.[37]

One problem of the booming real estate market was that it was fueled by a speculative fever that created a bubble economy that could, as one researcher put it, "vanish without warning."[38] Much of the money invested came from inland units using money allocated for grain purchases, giving the peasants IOUs instead. According to one report, at least 57 billion yuan was diverted in early 1993 through interbank loans to the coastal areas, where it was used to speculate in real estate and the stock market. As a well-known researcher in the State Council's Development Research Center put it: "Local authorities and banks are ripping off billions of yuan to fund real estate projects. That's why they have no money to pay the peasants."[39] Thus, the speculation in coastal real estate exacerbated tensions in the countryside even as it fueled the growing gap between the coast and the hinterland.

The Maoist period had exerted great efforts to equalize regional differences by large transfer payments to the hinterland and through massive and unwise investments in the "third front" military industries that were built in the hinterland in case the United States or the Soviet Union invaded.[40] The Dengist era reversed these policies by stopping large-scale investments in the third front and by curtailing transfer payments, thus allowing China's "natural economy" to reassert itself. The natural tendency for the east coast – where human talent, technology, communications, and transportation are disproportionately concentrated – to move ahead was obscured at first both by the rural reforms, which increased the incomes of the large numbers of farmers who live inland, and by the slow start of urban reform, particularly in Shanghai (where large numbers of SOEs were concentrated). After the mid-1980s, however, rural incomes began to stagnate, the massive investments in inland areas were curtailed, and TVEs along the east coast began to play an increasingly important role in the economy. In 1992, as just noted, much money flowed to the east coast from inland areas in the hopes of higher returns, thus fueling the speculative bubble. At the same time, foreign investment began growing by a large amount. Seemingly all of a sudden, the east coast began to move ahead quickly, and the gap between the coast and the hinterland began to widen noticeably.[41]

Much of the gap that developed between regions and among citizens was due to the explosive growth of the private economy in this period. Figures on the size of China's private sector are notoriously difficult to pin down because of the propensity of private entrepreneurs to claim to be collectives or to underreport the size of their business. Nevertheless, even if one looks only at the official figures, it is apparent that China has experienced very rapid growth in this sector in recent years. One might date the growth of a significant private sector from 1987, when the Thirteenth Party Congress declared that the private sector should be "permitted to exist," and from the revision of the state constitution in March 1988 to legalize the conduct of private business. In 1989, however, following Tiananmen and the subsequent torrent of articles criticizing "privatization," the number of private enterprises fell 15 percent from 90,581 to 76,581; of these, 8,000 ceased operation and 4,000 declared they were "individual entrepreneurs" (the other 2,000 are not accounted for).[42]

Despite this inauspicious start to the new decade, the private sector soon experienced a boom far exceeding anything it had seen in the 1980s. As in so many other things, the turning point was Deng Xiaoping's trip to the south in 1992 and the subsequent decision of the Fourteenth Party Congress to permit the simultaneous development of different forms of ownership. As can be seen from Table 2, the number of registered private enterprises more than doubled between 1991 (before Deng's trip) and 1993 (after the Fourteenth Party Congress), and the amount of registered capital soared from about 12 billion yuan to over 68 billion yuan – more than a 5-fold increase.

These figures clearly understate – by a considerable margin – the size of China's private sector. For instance, the Hebei Industrial and Commercial Bureau estimated that only about half of its private enterprises had registered, and the author of a CASS investigative report argues that there were probably about 220,000 "hidden" private enterprises in China in 1994.[43] Chen Xiaoping of the All-China Industrial and Commercial Federation Research Office reported data suggesting that some 83 percent of China's TVEs are in reality private enterprises, and he argues that over time they will cast off their "red hats" and operate openly as private enterprises. Apparently incorporating such data, Chen

172

Table 2. *Growth of Registered Private Enterprises, 1989–98*

Year	Number	Employees	Registered Capital	Retail Sales
1989	90,581	1.60 million	8.4 billion yuan	3.4 billion yuan
1990	98,141	1.70 million	9.5 billion yuan	4.3 billion yuan
1991	107,843	1.84 million	12.3 billion yuan	5.7 billion yuan
1992	139,633	2.32 million	22.1 billion yuan	9.1 billion yuan
1993	237,919	3.73 million	68.1 billion yuan	19.0 billion yuan
1994	432,240	6.48 million	144.8 billion yuan	51.3 billion yuan
1995	654,531	9.56 million	262.2 billion yuan	100.6 billion yuan
1996	819,252	11.70 million	375.2 billion yuan	145.9 billion yuan
1997	960,726	13.50 million	514.0 billion yuan	185.5 billion yuan
1998	1,200,978	17.10 million	719.8 billion yuan	305.9 billion yuan

Source: Zhang Houyi and Ming Lizhi (Eds.), *Zhongguo siying qiye fazhan baogao*, pp. 33–9.

suggested that, by the turn of the century, there would be over 2 million private enterprises in China employing nearly 17 million people – an estimate that proved close to the mark (see Table 2).[44]

The rapid expansion of private enterprise, real estate speculation, and stock transactions that followed Deng Xiaoping's 1992 journey to the south were paralleled by an equally rapid growth of foreign investment in China. Direct foreign investment more than doubled, from $4.6 billion to $11.3 billion, between 1991 and 1992; it then doubled again, to $27.8 billion, in 1993.[45] By the summer of 1996, as elite tensions remained high because of the Taiwan Straits crisis and domestic criticism of reform, a new wave of criticism – this one focusing on the impact of foreign investment – began in the pages of *Economic Daily* (*Jingji ribao*), the country's most authoritative economic paper, which is supervised by the State Council. On June 20, *Economic Daily* ran a commentator article introducing a series of fifteen articles that in the coming days would take an unusually critical look at the impact of foreign capital on Chinese enterprises. The commentator article argued that the role of foreign investment in China's economy was growing rapidly: imported capital then accounted for about 20 percent of all investment in fixed assets in China, foreign-invested enterprises (*sanzi qiye*) accounted for 39 percent of China's exports, and foreign trade equaled some 40 percent of domestic production; all this suggested a high degree of dependence. Opening up to the outside world was good, the commentator said, "but looking across the various countries of the world, [we see] that opening up definitely cannot be without certain principles and certain limits." It is important to "pay attention to protecting national industries."[46] As an accompanying report on joint ventures in China's beer industry asked, "Must Chinese beer [companies] form so many joint ventures? How much longer can Chinese-produced beer last?"[47]

The nationalist tone of the articles was evident in a description of the refusal of Yanjing beer to form a joint venture. This was clearly not an economic decision but a patriotic one. As Li Fucheng (general manager of the Yanjing Beer Enterprise Group) put it, "would I let others eat me up?... Creating our own labels, developing national industries is our historical mission."[48] Even the head of the "Five Star" beer company, which had produced beer served at state banquets but had later been forced to form a joint venture, declared that it had done so only because poor management had left it no other option. He expressed great respect for Li Fucheng for refusing to yield to economic pressures, pressures that were no doubt mitigated by the fact that Yanjing held 70 percent of the Beijing beer market.[49]

Other articles in the series discussed the difficulties facing Chinese brand names,[50] how the United States, Japan, and France had protected their markets while their economies were growing,[51] and how a well-known Shanghai cutlery business had refused foreign offers to form a joint venture.[52] A letter to the editor, featured on the front page, declared that the series in *Economic Daily* was doing "a great thing to protect [China's] national industries. There should have been this type of discussion long ago!"[53]

The articles in *Economic Daily* were undertaken at the paper's own initiative but with the intention of appealing to Li Peng, who headed the State Council to which the paper was subordinate. Feeling that the assault on China's policy of opening to the outside could not go unrefuted, economic reformers – including Zhu Rongji – urged *People's Daily* to issue an authoritative rebuttal.[54] Thus, on July 16, about a month after *Economic Daily* launched its series of columns, *People's Daily* published a major commentary implicitly refuting the series. The placement of the *People's Daily* commentary in the upper left-hand "lead article" space of the front page, endorsed by an "editor's note," conveyed the sense of importance that *People's Daily* attached to this rebuttal.[55]

According to the commentary, the import of foreign capital and the formation of joint ventures meant not only an infusion of capital but also an upgrading of technology and management skills. It cited the example of the Shanghai Automobile Manufacturing Factory, which formed a joint venture with Volkswagen to produce the Santana. Now, the local content of the Santana had already reached 90 percent and China's automobile technology had increased several grades. This had led the way to the formation of other joint ventures in the automobile industry and a general upgrading of China's competitiveness in this area. Although importing foreign capital could create problems, including fraudulent joint ventures and the "hollowing out" of some industries, China should not "give up eating for fear of choking." The problems could be managed as China learned to handle such joint ventures better and as China's domestic industries became more competitive.[56]

The obvious – and unusual – public disagreement between *Economic Daily* and *People's Daily* suggests high-level leadership disputes regarding the issue of foreign capital, disputes that would burst into public view three years later when the Chinese leadership finally decided to make the commitments necessary to reach agreement with the United States and other trading partners over China's accession to the World Trade Organization (see Chapter 7). The dispute in the pages of these two leading dailies clearly reflected the intersection of ideological concerns (as expressed in the various "10,000 character" manifestos and other documents), societal concerns (as expressed by the economic nationalism of various enterprises), and elite politics (as reflected in the differing opinions of the two papers). The incident further confirmed the economic and social bases of contemporary Chinese nationalism and the differing responses of the Chinese leadership to international economic forces and the social changes in China.

These dramatic socioeconomic changes have had the effect of producing a *nouveau riche* class. In the mid-1980s, there was fevered talk in the Chinese press, which turned out to be exaggerated, of the emergence of "ten-thousand-yuan households" (*wanyuanhu*) – an almost unimaginable amount of income in a period in which the average rural resident earned only about 350 yuan per year. A decade or so later, there were at least one million households with annual incomes exceeding one million yuan. This was an enormous change with profound social, psychological, and political implications. In many ways, of course, this was a long overdue and healthy change that seemingly marked the appearance of a middle class, albeit one that was still quite small in terms of China's population, or even its urban population. Nevertheless, the new middle class, including the much more prosperous *nouveau riche,* drove the new consumerism of the 1990s and so changed the nature and role of culture in Chinese society by commercializing it and diversifying it.

The seamy side of this story is that those who did the best in this new economy – and some did very well indeed – almost always seemed to have strong political connections. Sometimes they were bureaucrats who tired of the office routine and jumped into the sea of business but retained their connections to colleagues who could offer all-important approvals or access to scarce resources.

175

Sometimes they were family members of officials still in office. Sometimes they were enterprise heads who used their positions to siphon off large amounts of state-owned assets to private firms that they controlled directly or indirectly. Often they were the offspring of high cadres who used their family connections to amass large sums of money. In other words, corruption – massive corruption – was a major part of the story of income redistribution in the 1990s.

A recent study calls this *nouveau riche* group the "never-left-out class" (*bu luokong jieji*) because every time Chinese society entered a new round of adjustment in which resources were reallocated, this group has benefited the most. The same study argues that this group possesses "comprehensive" (*zongtixing*) capital resources, meaning that it is able to mobilize its multidimensional economic and political contacts to monopolize the best opportunities.[57] This is the same group of people that He Qinglian described when she argued that, through the "marketization of politics," officials – or those with close relations to officials – have directed millions of dollars worth of assets into private hands, bringing about a form of "primitive socialist accumulation" that rivals anything Marx and Engels observed about "primitive capitalist accumulation." The result, He argued, has been income inequality surpassing that in either Japan or the United States (keeping in mind that China had a much more equal distribution of income than either of those countries less than a decade before), the rise of secret societies, and mass resentment. China, she argued, seems to be heading not toward liberal democracy and capitalism but toward a "government and mafia alliance."[58]

These socioeconomic trends quickly became a source of popular discontent, and political and intellectual leaders from across the spectrum – the left, postmodernists, neostatists, populist nationalists, and liberals – all responded with diagnoses and prescriptions. The leftist articles (the "10,000 character manifestos") cited previously were clearly intended to exert pressure on Jiang primarily from within elite circles. Although foreign commentators rarely take leftist pronouncements seriously, the evidence strongly suggests that at various times the left has been an important force in elite politics. Even if it has not been able to set the political agenda, it has been able to obstruct the formulation and implementation of reforms. This is in part because the left positions itself as the upholder of Marxist orthodoxy and thus is able to accuse reformers of "deviating" from Marxism. Even after two decades of reform, such charges still have an impact because the Party cannot abandon Marxism without giving up all claims to legitimacy. It should be noted that many leftists come out of the propaganda system and hence are well versed in the language of Marxism–Leninism. As expert symbol manipulators, they can constrain the actions of the leadership. The left further derives influence from the age and long-term service of many of its leaders. As Party elders, they exert an influence out of proportion to their numbers. It should also be noted that the left champions the interests of many members at lower levels, people who oppose reform because they fear it will hurt their interests. So the left is not devoid of a certain mass base; to the extent that it can tap into the fears of workers facing layoffs and a decline in their social status, it can extend that mass base to certain sectors of the population. Thus, after circulating the first 10,000-character manifesto, leftists went to the northeast – which was experiencing wide-scale layoffs – and called meetings in factories to explain the content of the article.[59] This pushed the bounds of acceptable political behavior and was soon curtailed. But the threat to Jiang Zemin was real.

THE FIFTH PLENUM: TRYING TO SHAPE AN AGENDA

When the Fourteenth Central Committee convened its Fifth Plenum on September 25–28, 1996, there were two items at the top of the agenda. The first was the Ninth Five-Year Plan that was to be formally approved by the Fourth session of the Eighth NPC meeting the following spring. As the leadership of the CCP was clearly aware, the inauguration of a new plan presented them with an opportunity to lay out an agenda for where this "third generation" of leadership intended to take China. In other words, if the Fourth Plenary Session the preceding year was marked by political succession, the Fifth Plenum was defined by the effort to lay out, if only in preliminary terms, a program that would define the new generation as distinct from its predecessors.

It has often been remarked that Mao's era was defined by the concentration of power and Deng's by its dispersion; Mao's concentration of power is said to have brought to an end a period of domestic disorder and international war while Deng's devolution of authority unleashed the economic energy that brought a new level of prosperity to the country. The problem of the Jiang Zemin era, as the discussions on neostatism showed, is finding a way that combines centralization and decentralization – or, more precisely, building viable institutions without stifling economic growth.

This is not an easy task, and it is no wonder that Jiang and his colleagues are frequently charged with a lack of "vision." It is difficult to inspire a population through the construction of a tax system or efforts to deal with the social and political problems engendered by corruption, income inequality, regional differences, and so forth. It is also difficult to cope with the society's obvious lack of political belief and the cynicism and self-interested behavior generated

177

thereby. The options of a full-scale Maoist revival or a wholehearted embrace of liberal democracy were obviously unacceptable to the leadership. There is no wonder that the efforts of Jiang would sound flat.

As might be expected, the explanation of the proposal that Li Peng gave to the plenum split the differences among interests and presented a program that was as acceptable as it was vague. The crux of the proposal lay in its affirmation of the critical role played by a limited number of large-scale state-owned enterprises; these 1,000 enterprises, which accounted for over 70 percent of the profits and tax payments of all state-owned enterprises, would be strongly supported by the state and would embody the principle of "taking the publicly owned economy as the main component and the state-owned economy as the guiding factor."[60] Smaller state-owned enterprises were given permission to proceed "more freely" with regard to developing new forms of organization and ownership. The tertiary economy was encouraged to develop freely. What was left vague, however, was an explanation of *how* large-scale SOEs were to be reformed successfully given that similar efforts over the preceding fifteen years had not been impressive, as well as – and perhaps more importantly – how smaller-scale industries should proceed to reshape themselves.

Lurking behind such vague formulations were deep debates about the size and role of state-owned industries and how quickly, and to what degree, the private economy would be allowed to develop. Conservative economists, such as Yang Jianbai, insisted that "socialism absolutely cannot be constructed on an economic foundation of private ownership."[61] Liberal economists, such as Cao Siyuan, best known as the "father" of China's bankruptcy law, enraged conservatives by saying that China's publicly owned economy (that is, SOEs) should not constitute more than 15 percent of the overall economy.[62]

The second issue that dominated the agenda was political leadership. Jiang was trying to consolidate his authority but was obviously still facing considerable difficulty. The left had raised the issue of political direction by circulating the 10,000-character manifestos; the right, then led by NPC Chairman Qiao Shi, was challenging Jiang by emphasizing law and democracy (of the inner-Party sort) and by ignoring calls to support Jiang as the "core." At the Fifth Plenum, Jiang clearly tacked to the left, at least in ideological terms, by emphasizing the need to "talk politics," an admonition that seemed to include ideological considerations in the formulation of policy but also emphasized the need for Party discipline.[63] As Jiang told the plenum:[64]

I also want to underscore one issue here. Our senior cadres – especially provincial party committee secretaries, provincial governors, ministers,

Central Committee members, and members of the CCP Central Committee Politburo – must pay attention to politics. By politics, I mean political
direction, political stand, political viewpoints, political discipline, political
perception, and political sensitivity .... Can we afford not to pay attention
to politics, or can we afford to lower our guard and stop fighting when hostile forces in the West want to "Westernize" (*xihua*) and "divide" (*fenhua*)
us, and impose their "democracy" and "freedom" on us; and when Lee
Teng-hui is bent on promoting "Taiwan independence."

This frank statement suggests the difficulty Jiang Zemin was having in securing the compliance of many of his colleagues as well as Jiang's need to play
the nationalistic card in his warnings of foreign (primarily American) efforts to
"Westernize" and "divide" China.

There was, of course, a danger in Jiang's stress on "talking politics" – namely,
that the "left" is far better than any other political element in talking politics.
For instance, shortly after Jiang raised the slogan of "talking politics," the
People's Daily ran a pseudonymous article implying that reform had gone off
course and that the most important task at the present was to defend the central
authorities.[65] Lost in the emphasis on "politics" and centralization was a sense
of how reform is supposed to proceed.

CARVING OUT A MIDDLE PATH

Following the Fifth Plenum, in late 1995 and early 1996, Jiang made a series
of internal speeches that tried to distinguish his own program from those of
his critics on both the left and the right. Jiang called for drawing a line between Marxism and anti-Marxism in seven areas: between socialist democracy
and Western parliamentary democracy, between developing a diverse economy
with a predominant public sector and privatization, between studying what is
advanced in the West and fawning on the West, and so forth. These distinctions were trumpeted in an important series of commentator articles carried by
the PLA newspaper *Jiefangjun bao* between April 1 and May 6, 1996.

A major purpose of these articles was to warn against rightist tendencies.
In this sense they were consistent with the conservative tendency in post-
Tiananmen political commentary, and their conservative tone may explain their
appearance in the PLA newspaper rather than in *People's Daily*. An editorial
note accompanying the first of these eight articles stated that, "[i]n the course
of opening to the outside world and economic structural reform, some trends
of social thought have inevitably affected the troops, and the corrosive effect
on cadres and troops of various sorts of corrupt thinking and culture should

not be underestimated." That first article discussed drawing a line between "socialist democracy" and "Western parliamentary democracy," decrying the latter but nonetheless calling for new efforts to gradually perfect the former. "Democracy," the commentary stated in its opening line, "is one of the fundamental goals for which our Party has always struggled."[66]

Other articles, however, were more openly critical of the left, even as they defended Party policy against charges of rightism. For instance, in calling for patriotism in the context of opening to the outside world, one article stated – in an implicit but clear reference to Deng Liqun's well-known comment – that "some comrades even believe that every new bit (*fen*) of foreign investment that is brought in is another bit of capitalism."[67] At least two of the commentaries highlighted the thesis that China was in the "primary stage of socialism," a thesis that would become central at the Fifteenth Party Congress in 1997.[68] The most interesting of the commentaries was the final one, which more strongly than its predecessors called for opposing "dogmatism" and "vulgar" Marxism. While Marxism must be upheld, it declared, "without being developed, Marxism would lose its vitality and energy." It was therefore necessary to "break through dogmatic interpretations of Marxism and erroneous viewpoints that are attributed to Marxism, and break through those judgments and conclusions that practice has already proven to be wrong and that are not appropriate to the new circumstances brought about by change."[69]

The most systematic effort to define a middle course and respond to the criticisms of the left came when Xing Bensi, vice-president of the Central Party School, published a long article in *People's Daily*. Apparently angered by the silence with which the *People's Daily* greeted his speeches – a silence induced perhaps by the inability of top leaders to agree on how to respond – Jiang arranged for the publication of Xing's article.[70]

In trying to define what constituted "real" Marxism (and thus refute the left that positioned itself as defender of the faith), Xing argued that a lot had changed since the birth of Marx 150 years ago. Although "some" of the "fundamental principles" (*jiben yuanli*) of Marxism are still applicable, he said, "indeed a considerable portion of the principles" of Marxism have changed. Xing claimed that there are parts of Marxism that contain universal truth and are still applicable, parts that need to be supplemented, and also parts that are "completely unsuitable for use, which should not be continued and upheld in the present day."[71] Thus, according to Xing: "The criterion for determining the border dividing Marxism and anti-Marxism has to rest on developed Marxism; in present day China the 'only correct' criterion for distinguishing Marxism and anti-Marxism is the 'theory of socialism with Chinese characteristics established by Deng Xiaoping' – most importantly upholding the 'one cen-ter [economic construction] and two basic points' [the four cardinal principles and emancipating the mind]." Xing thus juxtaposed "Deng Xiaoping theory" against leftist thought and referred explicitly to the first 10,000-character man-ifesto when he criticized those who declared that reform had brought about a "new bourgeoisie."

At the same time, Xing defined a "right" that was just as anti-Marxist as the left. Xing cited several manifestations of rightism, including "privatization" and revisionist interpretations of Chinese history that implied that China had taken the wrong road in pursuing the revolutionary path and that it was now nec-essary to say "farewell to revolution." This was a reference to the well-known book (discussed in Chapter 3) by prominent philosopher Li Zehou and lead-ing literary critic Liu Zaifu. Although Xing's criticism of Li and Liu's book illustrated the need for the Party to respond to intellectual discussions, Xing's motive here seems to have been to set up a "right" to juxtapose to the "left" of the manifestos. By doing so, Xing could define a "middle course" for Jiang. Xing's criticism of *Farewell to Revolution* also served the purpose of warn-ing liberal thinkers to hold their peace as Jiang turned his primary attention to warding off the left.[72]

What Xing Bensi's long article in *Renmin ribao* did was to begin staking out a defensible middle ground in China's political spectrum. In trying to de-fine a middle course, Jiang seemed at once to be taking a leaf from history and trying to sidestep his most serious political dilemma. Chinese politics since Tiananmen, as in many crisis situations, tended to be defined by polarities: one was either for "upholding socialism" or for "bourgeois liberalization." Tak-ing heed of the fate of his predecessors, Hu Yaobang and Zhao Ziyang, Jiang spent much of his first six years making sure that no one could accuse him of being "lax" on bourgeois liberalization. Indeed, it was this proclivity for caution, if not conservatism, that roused Deng's ire in 1992. But cautiousness implied impotence. Without differentiating himself from the left, Jiang had neither the ability to tackle the serious problems that plagued the economy nor the freedom to define a "line" of his own. In short, cautiousness meant pas-sivity; Jiang was general secretary, but it was the left that defined the limits to his actions.

In contrast, Deng had defined himself and had been able to carry out re-form by carving out a "middle course." Indeed, Deng secured his authority in the post–Cultural Revolution context by abandoning the "struggle *between two lines*" in favor of a "struggle *on two fronts*" (that is, both left and right).[73] At least in some readings of history, Mao had done the same thing in his battles against "rightist opportunism" (represented by Chen Duxiu) and "leftism" (represented by Wang Ming).[74] As Chinese politics had polarized in the late 1980s, it had been increasingly difficult to prevent them from reverting back to a struggle between two lines, as indeed the harsh criticism of Zhao Ziyang in the wake of Tiananmen suggested that, to a certain extent, it had. Now, after six years as general secretary and after being able slowly to build up his personal authority, Jiang began his attempt to define a new center.

Carving out a middle course, however, is not a simple matter. It needs to be articulated and defended against critics on both the left and the right. Although Xing's article was a step in this direction, Jiang was not yet prepared to confront directly the disputes wracking the Party. In the spring of 1996, Jiang was clearly tacking to the right, endorsing a new round of reform. In May, Jiang met with the enterprise heads and political leaders from seven provinces, telling them that reform had reached an "extremely critical moment."[75] This was Jiang's strongest affirmation of reform in the period since he took over as general secretary.[76] Nevertheless, by fall, he was again charting a conservative ideological direction.

SIXTH PLENUM: BUILDING SPIRITUAL CIVILIZATION

When the Sixth Plenary Session of the Fourteenth Central Committee convened on October 7–10, 1996, it adopted a 14,000-character decision entitled, "Resolution of the CCP Central Committee Concerning Several Important Issues on Strengthening the Building of Socialist Spiritual Civilization." In many ways, this resolution seems designed to respond to and defend Jiang from charges that the economic reforms he was presiding over – and those measures he was contemplating – would lead to bourgeois liberalization and privatization. The result was a tortuous document; the committee process by which it was drafted is visible in nearly every paragraph.

The plenum resolution defended reform, but it also warned that "[a]t no time should we achieve short-term economic growth at the expense of spiritual civilization."[77] This was a phrase authored by Teng Wensheng, the protégé of Deng Liqun's whom Jiang had brought over to head the Policy Research Office and, no doubt, to assure conservatives that their concerns would be heard.[78] Indeed, the document came perilously close to giving equal value to economic development and spiritual civilization, as leftists had long urged. It declared: "Economic development as the central link must be grasped firmly and unswervingly. But failure in the promotion of ethical and cultural progress will lead to damage to material progress and even change the nature of society."[79]

The Sixth Plenum resolution was a disappointment to many intellectuals as well as to some of Jiang's own policy advisors. People compared it unfavorably with the resolution on building spiritual civilization that had been adopted a decade earlier under Hu Yaobang's auspices.[80] In language reminiscent of Mao Zedong's "Yenan Forum on Literature and Art," the 1996 document called on writers and artists to "immerse themselves among the masses" and to "earnestly and seriously consider what social effects (*shehui xiaoguo*) their works may produce." Similarly, it called for strengthening control over press and publishing circles and for keeping the propaganda front and public opinion "firmly" in the hands of "those comrades who are loyal to Marxism, Leninism, and Mao Zedong Thought."[81]

The plenum resolution argued that ideological vigilance is necessary because reform has allowed social morality and loyalty to decline, as indeed the left wing of the Party had been arguing. Thus, the document stated that "[t]he standard of moral conduct has been lowered in some spheres, and the practices of worshipping money, seeking pleasure, and individualism have grown," and that "a number of people have a weak concept of the state, and doubt and waver over the future of socialism." It also urged people to "carry forward the cream of our traditional culture, prevent and eliminate the spread of cultural garbage, [and] resist the conspiracy by hostile forces to 'Westernize' and 'divide' our country."[82]

In short, despite Jiang's efforts over the preceding months to carve out a viable middle ground, the Sixth Plenum communiqué ignored these themes. In fact, it does not mention "drawing a line" between Marxism and anti-Marxism; there is neither criticism of dogmatic interpretations of Marxism nor any effort, such as in Xing Bensi's article, to define what constitutes "true" Marxism in the contemporary world. The conservative, cautious tone of the resolution reflected the tense atmosphere at the top of the Party in the months preceding Deng's death.

REVIVING REFORM

Although Jiang chose caution in the fall of 1996, he and his advisors were clearly exploring alternative approaches at the same time. Jiang's 1995–96 talks on distinguishing Marxism from anti-Marxism marked an initial effort, but in the fall of 1996 – almost at the very time that the Sixth Plenum was convening to consider the resolution on building spiritual civilization – a volume was published that showed a very different side of Jiang's thinking. This effort to define Jiang's program in more positive and systematic terms became visible with the October 1996 publication of *Heart-to-Heart Talks with the General Secretary.*

Fourteen young scholars, mostly based at the Chinese Academy of Social Sciences, wrote the book (others participated in discussions about its content), which was an extended gloss on Jiang's 1995 speech to the Fifth Plenum on twelve major problems facing China. Although Jiang's speech had been a reasonable and considered look at the difficulties facing China (drawing comparison to Mao's famous "Ten Great Relationships" speech), there had been little follow-up in policy terms. Indeed, the speech was so well balanced that the policy implications of it were not immediately clear, and the speech soon dropped from public view. A year later, these young intellectuals tried to flesh out Jiang's proposals, dropping some of the balance from the original speech and developing a number of proposals that actually did have implications for the direction in which China was to develop.

The most eye-catching feature of the volume – apart from the picture of Jiang on the cover – was the preface and endorsement by Liu Ji, vice-president of CASS. Despite his background in natural science (he is a 1958 graduate of Qinghua University), Liu took up social science and emerged as a strong voice for reform in the 1980s. A frequent contributor to the reformist paper *World Economic Herald,* in 1982 Liu wrote an article entitled "Making the Decision-Making Process More Scientific," which was said to have been a major influence on Wan Li's 1986 speech, "Making the Decision-Making Process More Democratic and Scientific Is an Important Topic in Political Structural Reform."[83] After Jiang Zemin went to Shanghai in the mid-1980s, he became very close to Liu Ji, elevating Liu to deputy head of the municipal propaganda department. It was in this capacity that Liu was named to head the work group that took over the *World Economic Herald* after Jiang decided to close the controversial paper. Liu's role in this episode certainly exacerbated his relations with many reform-minded intellectuals, but it demonstrated his personal loyalty to Jiang.[84] In 1993, Jiang transferred Liu to Beijing, appointing him as vice-president of CASS.

As vice-president of the Chinese Academy of Social Sciences, one of Liu's jobs was to cultivate a new corps of intellectuals who could provide policy advice for Jiang. This was not an easy task, given the mutual suspicions separating the intellectual community from the political leadership in the years following Tiananmen and the ideological taboos that continued to restrict intellectual discussions – taboos that were personified in CASS by the leadership of Wang Renzhi and Teng Teng, both staunch conservatives. *Heart-to-Heart Talks with the General Secretary* was the most visible manifestation to date of Liu's efforts to bridge this gap and to begin improving the intellectual atmosphere.[85]

The decision to bring together a number of young intellectuals to write *Heart-to-Heart Talks with the General Secretary* was a self-conscious effort to rebut leftist criticisms made in the first and second "10,000 character manifestos" as well as the rising tide of nationalism. It was well recognized that such trends would, if not refuted, severely constrain Jiang Zemin's range of policy choices and his effective power. The rapid improvement in Sino–U.S. relations since March 1996 – fostered by exchanges between Liu Huaqiu, head of the Foreign Affairs Office of the State Council, and Anthony Lake, President Clinton's National Security Advisor – clearly facilitated this effort to respond to critics; Secretary of State Warren Christopher was due in Beijing in November, only weeks after the publication of *Heart-to-Heart Talks,* to finalize plans for Jiang Zemin and President Clinton to exchange summits.[86]

Perhaps the single most notable feature of *Heart-to-Heart Talks with the General Secretary* was its no-holds-barred defense of reform; the title of the second chapter put it as directly as Deng Xiaoping ever had: "Reform, Reform, Reform: There Is No Other Road for China." Recognizing that many problems had accompanied the development of reform, the authors – consistent with the idea of trying to carve out a middle course – argued that it was wrong to reject continued reform either by adopting all-out Westernization or by pulling back and adopting conservative policies. Their attention, however, was focused on the latter concern. Joining ongoing debates about the cause of socialism's collapse in the former Soviet Union, the authors placed the blame on Brezhnev and not on Gorbachev, as China's leftists were wont to do. Brezhnev-type leaders easily appear in difficult circumstances, the authors argued, but the result of Brezhnev was not eighteen years of "stability" but eighteen years of stagnation. The lesson to be drawn from the experience of Brezhnev is that, without reform, there will indeed be instability.[87] Those who advocate retreat whenever reform faces major difficulties, the authors wrote, always say that they are protecting socialism, but in the end they cause great losses to socialism.

Responding to the debate over the large influx of foreign funds, which we saw reflected in the public disagreement between *People's Daily* and *Economic Daily,* the book wholeheartedly endorsed opening to the outside world. Closing the door, it noted, was not really an option. Despite the increasingly fierce competition (between nations and within nations) as multinational corporations increasingly became a part of domestic economies, China had no choice but to face up to this competition. This choice required self-confidence, the adoption of favorable government policies (which were not specified, but protectionism was rejected as not very effective), and the retreat of government from enterprise operations.[88]

Heart-to-Heart Talks, like *The Critical Moment* that soon followed, also reinterpreted the relationship between China's Confucian tradition and socialism.
It drew an analogy to a tree, arguing that China's traditional culture can be
understood as the roots, Marxism–Leninism as the trunk, and the outstanding
parts of various cultures from around the world as the branches. It should be
noted that this analogy stood the orthodox CCP understanding of history on
its head. Whereas the CCP had traditionally rooted itself in the May Fourth
rejection of China's Confucian heritage, the tree analogy envisioned contemporary Marxism as growing out of Confucianism. Although this imagery drew
harsh criticism from the left wing of the Party, it was perfectly consistent with
what the Party had been trying to do over the past several years: somehow
"square the circle" connecting China's traditional history and its modern revolution so that the latter can be viewed as a continuation, rather than a refutation,
of the former.[89]

Heart-to-Heart Talks was deliberately written as a response to leftist criticisms of reform, to refute the growing tide of nationalism, and to set out a more
positive agenda for Jiang Zemin.[90] As with trial balloons in American politics,
the book was both identifiable with Jiang Zemin (given Liu Ji's role) and yet had
a certain plausible deniability. *Heart-to-Heart Talks* anticipated the publication
of a new series of books under the sponsorship of Liu Ji, called *Contemporary
China's Problems,* that would eventually include more than twenty titles. The
publication of these books, some of which will be discussed here, marked a
fascinating attempt by a group of Jiang's advisors – sometimes referred to as
the "enlightened" (*kaiming*) group within the leadership – to set out what they
believed were the main problems facing China and to raise possible solutions.
This book series was in many ways analogous to the books and articles written
in the 1980s by members of Hu Yaobang's intellectual elite and Zhao Ziyang's
think tanks, but whereas those writings more clearly directed their policy advice
upward to the leadership, these books engaged an emerging sphere of public
opinion, refuting those they disagreed with and building support for views they
favored. On the one hand, they reflected the greater role intellectuals play in
policy formation in contemporary China; on the other hand, they suggested the
increasing need to respond to, refute, and encourage views growing up independently among the intelligentsia and the broader public.

The left reacted quickly and strongly to the expression of these more liberal
views. For instance, in August 1996, Yuan Mu – the conservative ideologue
who achieved fame, and infamy, as the public defender of the government
in the days after Tiananmen in his role as spokesman of the State Council –
gave a long speech at the national "Theoretical Symposium on the Question

of Consolidating and Strengthening the Class Foundation of the Ruling Party."
Yuan was clearly exercised by trends he had seen in theoretical discussions, in
policy decisions, and in the attitudes of many Party members. He was anxious
to emphasize the distinction Deng had drawn in 1989 between two types of reform, one that upheld the four cardinal principles and the other that "restored
capitalism": the former was correct, whereas the latter is what had led to the
collapse of socialism in Eastern Europe and the Soviet Union. Yuan lambasted
liberal economists who refused to preface the term "market economy" with the
all-important modifier "socialist" and who called for reducing the percentage
of the state-owned economy to 20 or even 15 percent (an obvious reference
to Cao Siyuan). Decrying trends toward privatization, Yuan declared bluntly:
"Without state-owned enterprises and without public ownership of the means
of production, there is no socialism." Yuan was also concerned about keeping private entrepreneurs out of the Party organization. As he said, the Party
has repeatedly declared that private entrepreneurs, because they are capitalists
engaged in exploitation, are not permitted to enter the Party. Nevertheless, he
said, local Party organizations ignore this injunction.[91]

The leftist assault continued even as Deng Xiaoping lay dying. The left-
ist journal *Mainstream* (*Zhongliu*) published a long critique of *Heart-to-Heart
Talks* by one Feng Baoxing (apparently a pseudonym). Feng mockingly derided
Heart-to-Heart Talks, saying that the authors' desire to "modernize" Marxism
meant diluting it as an ideological weapon for directing class struggle and also
meant turning Marxism into nothing more substantive than a new version of
Chiang Kai-shek's "New Life Movement" – the vapid conservative movement
Chiang had sponsored in the 1930s in an attempt to instill a diluted Confucian morality.[92] Feng also criticized *Heart-to-Heart Talks* for putting out a
"revisionist" interpretation of Deng Xiaoping's thinking (diluting Deng's admonition that socialism means "eliminating exploitation and avoiding polarization"), for arguing that individualism is compatible with Marxism, for desiring
to mix Chinese culture with Western culture, and for advocating greater integration into the world economy. "If we do as the authors propose," Feng wrote,
"our policy of opening up to the outside world will inevitably be led onto the
wrong road, our economy will lose its independence, and we will be thrown into
the embrace of the 'great unity' of international monopoly capital."[93] Referring
to Liu Ji's endorsement of the book, Feng wrote, "I don't understand why this
book, which includes viewpoints directly opposite of our Party's consistent
proposals, directly opposite the resolution of the Sixth Plenum, and directly
opposite the general secretary's proposals regarding establishing socialist spiritual civilization, would receive such high praise from this leading comrade."[94]

At almost the same time, a third 10,000-character manifesto was circulated. Entitled "Several Theoretical and Policy Issues on Upholding the Dominant Position of Public Ownership," this article was written by the editorial office of the conservative journal *Contemporary Trends* and published in the fourth issue of 1996. This manifesto zeroed in on the ownership issue and particularly on the policy of "grasping the large and letting go of the small" that had been adopted in 1995. Citing Jiang Zemin's 1996 statement that China should "always maintain the dominant position of the public sector," the manifesto argued that "dominance" cannot be redefined to mean that the state could simply hold a predominant share of assets within the national economy. The manifesto went on to argue that, if small enterprises were privatized (the intention of the policy), then "the immense majority of the working class will become wage workers, and class polarization will become a general phenomenon."[95] The manifesto also took issue with the proposal that the state sector of the economy be reduced to around 20 percent, as well as with the notion that ownership does not determine economic development. It argued further against the proposition that the state should remove itself from competitive industries and adopt a role of supporting infrastructure and certain basic industries. As the manifesto put it, "people who uphold this view actually want the state to bear all the losses so that different types of capital can make their earnings." Doing so, the manifesto declared, would end up making the state-owned economy into one that is "mainly in the service of foreign capital."[96]

Perhaps the most interesting of the manifestos published at that time, though not generally counted as one of the 10,000-character manifestos, was one titled "Reform and Economic Man." This essay reflected the thinking of the New Left more than the Old Left, but it showed the overlap that had emerged between the two groups. The point of the essay was that any reform – whether in China, Eastern Europe, or the former Soviet Union – takes the concept of "economic man" (as conceived by Adam Smith) as central, and that the concept of "economic man" is fundamentally contradictory to the collectivism that is central to the socialist ethos. Indeed, the author argued that the richest villages in contemporary China, such as Henan's Nanjie Village, are all run as collectives with a leader acting wholeheartedly in the public interest.[97] The introduction of individualism, based on the concept of economic man, is not the solution to problems in socialism but on the contrary can only exacerbate those problems. Thus, the article argued, the more the notion of economic man has been introduced in state-owned enterprises, the worse they have done, and the more individualism has come to be accepted by society, the more social problems have developed.[98] Putting the issue in apocalyptic terms, the author declared that, if reform guided by the concept of economic man was not "decisively" (*guoduan*) turned around and the collectivist concept restored, then everything for which the Party had struggled for seventy years would be lost.[99]

TROUBLE FROM THE RIGHT

At the same time that Jiang felt pressured from the left, he was also being buffeted from the right. By the mid-1990s, Qiao Shi, then the third-ranked member of the Politburo Standing Committee and head of the NPC, had established himself as the standard-bearer of the liberal wing of the Party. When Qiao took over as head of the NPC in March 1993, he was stripped of his other positions as secretary of the powerful Central Political and Legal Committee and president of the Central Party School. But Qiao apparently continued to have much influence in the security apparatus in which he had built his career. Ren Jianxin, who replaced Qiao as head of the Central Political and Legal Committee, had been promoted by Qiao, and Wei Jianxing, who had become secretary of the Central Discipline Inspection Commission (CDIC) and subsequently replaced Chen Xitong as Beijing Party secretary (before being replaced in turn by Jia Qinglin), had strong ties to Qiao.[100] Meanwhile, Qiao turned the NPC into a base of support, much as Peng Zhen (who headed that body from 1983 to 1988) had used it as a base from which to oppose reform.

Qiao, who ranked higher than Jiang Zemin in the Shanghai underground in the late 1940s, frequently challenged Jiang by being out in front of him on reform issues. As noted earlier, he beat the drums for Deng's reform campaign in the spring of 1992 long before Jiang Zemin came out in support of it. In January 1995, even as Jiang Zemin was stressing democratic centralism and the role of the core, Qiao chose to stress political reform and democratization.[101] At the same time, Qiao stepped up the pace of legislation and incorporated greater expertise into its formulation; he also gave greater weight to provincial initiative and to the speed of economic reform than did Jiang Zemin or Li Peng.[102]

Aiding Qiao in this effort was Tian Jiyun, the Politburo member whose withering criticism of leftism in April 1992 may have cost him a seat on the Politburo Standing Committee. During the March 1995 session of the NPC, Tian listened sympathetically to Guangdong delegates, who complained that China's rulers were not allowing the NPC to function as the "highest administrative organ" as called for by the constitution. The day after this raucous meeting, 36 percent of NPC delegates either abstained or voted against Jiang Chunyun, Jiang Zemin's handpicked nominee as vice-premier. Never before had China's legislature registered such a large protest.

Elite Politics in an Era of Globalization and Nationalism

B ETWEEN the Fourth Plenum in 1994 and the Fifteenth Party Congress
in 1997, "public opinion" played a limited but not insignificant role. As
discussed in Part II, the intellectual atmosphere became considerably more conservative and nationalistic in this period, which helped the government preserve
the social stability that it prized so highly. Moreover, there was greater interaction between government and intellectual circles as each tried to influence the
other (a trend that coexisted with its opposite, as some intellectuals oriented
their activities toward society – ignoring the government – while others withdrew into scholarly endeavors or developed new critiques of government). We
have seen how intellectuals such as Hu Angang and Wang Shaoguang influenced government policy, at least to some extent, on such issues as tax reform
and regional disparities, and how the government tried to organize and solicit
new, but acceptable, ideas through such books as *Heart-to-Heart Talks with the
General Secretary*. We have also seen how the Old Left tried to influence both
elite politics and public opinion through the various 10,000-character manifestos. There were also clear connections between elements of the elite and
expressions of nationalistic opinion, whether through journals such as *Strategy
and Management* or books such as *China Can Say No*.

These conflicting trends of elite and popular opinion reached a new level of
intensity in 1997 as Jiang tried to put his imprint on the post-Deng era, only to
face another powerful wave of nationalism that grew up around the issues of
China's entry into the WTO and, more importantly, the tragic bombing of the
Chinese Embassy in Belgrade. As one century yielded to the next, nationalism, corruption, globalization, elite conflict, and new intellectual controversies
suggested an important reshaping of the Chinese polity.

DENG'S DEATH AND JIANG'S MOVE TO CONSOLIDATE POWER

Facing challenges from the left and right, one might think that Jiang hoped
Deng Xiaoping would survive long enough to see Jiang through the critical

Fifteenth Party Congress. Indeed, on the eve of Deng's death, the left circulated the fourth 10,000-character manifesto.[1] Despite this challenge, Deng's passing in February 1997 proved a blessing for the general secretary. Because Deng's demise was long anticipated and activities surrounding the events occurred with orchestrated smoothness, its impact has been obscured. Stability and continuity seemed to be the order of the day, but – in his eulogy at Deng's funeral – Jiang dropped a hint that he had something more than mere continuity in mind. Jiang quoted Deng as saying (when he returned to power in the late 1970s) that there are two possible attitudes: "One is to act as a bureaucrat, the other is to work."[2] It seemed a risky quote for Jiang to cite, given his reputation for caution. But Jiang was using Deng's words to make his own personal declaration – that he, too, was determined to "work."

Jiang's intimation of important changes to come was perhaps as much a reflection of the dilemmas facing the Party as it was of personal ambition. As Deng entered his final decline, the Party fought vigorously over his legacy; with Deng's passing the Party would have to make choices. The first and arguably most critical point of decision came in March, when a draft of Jiang's report to the Fifteenth Party Congress was circulated among officials for comment. Reportedly it met with a barrage of criticism from the left. Jiang either had to water down his proposals extensively or break with the left, something he had refrained from doing in the years since his arrival in Beijing. Indeed, Jiang had drawn much support from the left wing of the Party in his early years. As late as 1996, Jiang had reached out to the left with his statement in the Sixth Plenum resolution cited previously that "spiritual civilization would not be sacrificed to material civilization."

However, the political situation had changed notably since Jiang had arrived in the capital. Many conservative Party elders – including Li Xiannian, Hu Qiaomu, Wang Renzhong, and Chen Yun – had died. Such generational change did not end opposition to more thoroughgoing reform, as there seemed to be a limitless supply of central officials whose careers and interests are tied to the preservation of the old state-run economy, but it certainly weakened political resistance at the highest reaches of the Party. What is more, the mounting problems of state-owned enterprises were becoming increasingly difficult to deny. In 1996, for the first time, subsidies to SOEs actually outweighed their contributions to the state budget. Leftists, for all their ability to obstruct reform, had never been able to present a viable alternative; Li Peng's efforts in the wake of Tiananmen had been their last, best hope.

Given the possibilities presented by the changed political landscape, the crisis facing the economy, and Jiang's own need to put his stamp on the post-Deng era, Jiang went to the Central Party School in late May to give the most important political speech of his career. In a thinly veiled jab at the left, Jiang declared that "[t]here is no way out if we study Marxism in isolation and separate and set it against vivid development in real life." In the unpublicized portion of the speech, Jiang reportedly went further, explicitly criticizing the left and laying out his rationale for reform of the ownership structure.[3] Deng had raised the slogan "guard against the right, but guard primarily against the left" in his 1992 trip to the south, but it had been largely dropped from the official media (except for inclusion in formal Party resolutions) following the Fourteenth Party Congress later that year. Now Jiang was reviving it and identifying himself with Deng's reforms. For a leader often criticized as bland, cautious, and technocratic, Jiang was beginning to reveal a degree of boldness previously visible only in his deft maneuvers against political enemies.

Although Jiang had previewed some of his major themes in his speech to the Central Party School, it was not until the Fifteenth Party Congress convened in Beijing on September 12–18 that the full scope of Jiang's program and his personnel arrangements for carrying it out were unveiled. The theme of the congress, as Jiang's report declared, was to "hold high the banner of Deng Xiaoping theory," and Deng Xiaoping theory was subsequently incorporated into both the Party and state constitutions. Jiang had evidently considered a variety of ideological themes in his efforts to consolidate his own authority; it certainly would have been more satisfying to enunciate a doctrine that could reasonably have been considered "Jiang Zemin theory" rather than to tie his fortunes to the "theory" of the deceased Deng. Praising Deng, however, had two distinct virtues: no one could openly disagree; and, the more Deng was praised, the more the leftists who looked to Mao's legacy were disparaged. Jiang's report, then, was a highly authoritative response to the 10,000-character manifestos and other expressions of leftist discontent. Thus, Jiang declared in his report to the congress that Deng Xiaoping theory "breaks with outmoded conventions on the basis of new practice" and that "[d]iscussing Marxism without regard to our actual situation and development of the times is misleading."[4]

This effort to break with leftist interpretations of Marxism–Leninism was also apparent in Jiang's unexpected decision to feature the thesis that China is in the "primary stage of socialism," an argument that had been developed by then–General Secretary Zhao Ziyang at the Thirteenth Party Congress in 1987 in order to justify further reform but then quietly dropped after 1989. Jiang revived the thesis in 1997 to legitimize reforming SOEs through the widespread adoption of the shareholding system, a theme anticipated in *Heart-to-Heart Talks with the General Secretary* and Liu Ji's writings.[5] "The shareholding system," Jiang declared, "can be used both under capitalism and socialism." Large and medium-sized state-owned enterprises would be reorganized into "standard corporations" with "clear ownership" that would be genuinely independent of government control. The largest of them (frequently proposed as some 500–1,000 SOEs) would be reorganized into large enterprise groups that were to function like *chaebol,* while smaller enterprises could be reorganized, merged, leased, contracted out, or sold off – a policy known as "grasp the large and let go of the small" (*zhuada fangxiao*).[6] Jiang also called for the development of diverse forms of ownership, a formulation that would permit the continued rapid development of the private economy. Together these reforms would allow room for a massive restructuring of the Chinese economy in the years ahead.

One of the most interesting aspects of Jiang's report to the congress was that even as he touted Deng's reputation and legacy, he hinted that he himself would push that legacy forward, which he has tried to do in the years since. Jiang cited Deng's 1978 battle with Party Chairman Hua Guofeng's "two whatevers" ("whatever decisions Chairman Mao made, we resolutely support; whatever instructions Chairman Mao made, we will steadfastly abide by") as a period of "emancipating the mind"; he said Deng's 1992 trip to the south was a second such period. Intimating that he would continue this process, Jiang called for an "emancipation of the mind in the new period."[7] Conservative Premier Li Peng, of all people, made this implication clear when he reiterated to a group of delegates that the present was the third of three periods of emancipating the mind.[8] This theme would be picked up and expanded upon in the months that followed during the limited political opening that became known as the "Beijing spring."

The other news that caught the Western headlines was that Qiao Shi had been dropped from the Central Committee. Qiao, as noted before, had repeatedly challenged Jiang Zemin's authority by calling for greater attention to law and by ignoring Jiang's call to rally around the "core" of the Party (i.e., Jiang). Qiao certainly presented a political problem for Jiang, and Jiang responded by lining up support for Qiao's ouster. Although Jiang apparently surprised Qiao by calling for all those over age 70 to step down (only to have Party elder Bo Yibo say that the rule should not apply to Jiang himself), the real work had been done behind the scenes. Qiao supporters Wan Li and Yang Shangkun reportedly sat mute through the meeting, realizing that they had been out-maneuvered.[9]

Many interpreted Qiao's removal as a pulling back from the liberal themes that he had touted, but in fact Qiao's ouster facilitated Jiang's move to the "right." With Qiao in place, any movement to relax political control and emphasize the rule of law would have been taken advantage of by Qiao to increase

Table 3. *Leadership of the Chinese Communist Party
following the 15th Party Congress*

Politburo Standing Committee

Jiang Zemin (age 71)	Hu Jintao (55)
Li Peng (69)	Wei Jianxing (66)
Zhu Rongji (69)	Li Lanqing (65)
Li Ruihuan (64)	

Politburo – Other Full Members

Ding Guan'gen (64)	Qian Qichen (69)
Huang Ju (59)	Chi Haotian (68)
Jia Qinglin (57)	Wen Jiabao (55)
Jiang Chunyun (67)	Wu Bangguo (56)
Li Changchun (53)	Wu Guanzheng (59)
Li Tieying (61)	Xie Fei (64)*
Luo Gan (62)	Zhang Wannian (69)
Tian Jiyun (68)	

Secretariat

Hu Jintao (55)	Wen Jiabao (55)
Ding Guan'gen (64)	Zhang Wannian (69)
Luo Gan (62)	Zeng Qinghong (58)
Wei Jianxing (66)	

* Died October 1999.

the role of the National People's Congress at Jiang's expense. By getting rid of Qiao, Jiang was free to adopt much of Qiao's program.

In his report to the Party congress, Jiang devoted considerable space to political and legal reform; he stated: "Without democracy, there can be no socialism and no socialist modernization." Although Jiang stopped well short of endorsing anything resembling Western-style democracy, his repeated use of the word "democracy" (some 32 times) prompted hopes of greater opening up. More important for many listeners was his use of the term "rule of law" instead of the standard formula "rule by law."[10] This formulation seemed to presage a new era in institution building and an acceptance of limitations on the arbitrary use of power.

Personnel arrangements made at the congress (see Table 3) supported the fresh image Jiang was cultivating, while the removal of many older personnel enhanced Jiang's ability to control the Party. Overall, 60 percent of the 193 people selected as full members of the latest Central Committee were new.

The current Central Committee is younger, better educated, and more professionally capable than any of its predecessors. Military representation on the Central Committee also declined from five years previous and, more importantly, no PLA representatives now sit on the powerful Politburo Standing Committee. This, combined with Jiang's call to reduce military staffing by 500,000 – with 100,000 to be shorn from the officer corps – marks a clear effort to make China's military smaller, better equipped, more professional, and less political.[11]

One aspect of the Fifteenth Party Congress that is particularly illuminating in terms of institutionalization is the way Li Peng was handled. Having served two terms as premier, Li was constitutionally barred from continuing in office, but no Party head or premier had ever left office voluntarily. The obvious friction between the newly instituted formal rules and the long-standing informal rules was clearly a delicate issue, especially given Li's role in Tiananmen. His complete removal from office would have been viewed as a repudiation of the crackdown, and there would no doubt have been new calls to "reverse the verdict" on the Tiananmen demonstrations. Such a possibility was actually suggested by a letter – calling for such a reappraisal – that Zhao Ziyang sent to the Central Committee on the eve of the Fifteenth Party Congress.[12] Several scenarios for dealing with Li Peng were bruited during the summer, but in the end Jiang decided to give Qiao Shi's NPC position to Li but allow Li to retain the number-two ranking on the Politburo Standing Committee. Qiao Shi was angered by his dismissal (though apparently able to secure the appointment of some of his followers as a price), and Zhu Rongji was similarly upset by not being named as the second-ranking member of the Politburo Standing Committee (the usual ranking of the premier, which Zhu was slated to become the following spring). Nevertheless, Jiang was able to move Li to a distinctly less powerful position without a major political upheaval, an apparently skillful effort to blend informal and formal politics.

In short, the Fifteenth Party Congress was an important milestone in the Party's development: the first time power had passed fully from the revolutionary generation to a postrevolutionary generation. Moreover, it had done so smoothly. Jiang had survived from an improbable beginning to become "core" of the Party in reality. As important as securing personal power was, Jiang was not – and could not become – the sort of pre-eminent leader Deng had been. Jiang lacked the revolutionary legitimacy, the authority within the military and other key Party components, and perhaps the personality to dominate the Party the way Deng had. Although intensely conscious of his role as Party leader and hence sensitive to perceived slights, Jiang was nevertheless a consensus builder.

He preferred to meet challenges by maneuvering rather than by confrontation. And he realized that both his own personal authority and the legitimacy of the Party required greater attention to institution building. Thus, whether ousting political threats like Chen Xitong and Qiao Shi, diminishing the political clout of the PLA, or laying out a program for reform, Jiang sought to base his legitimacy in institutional procedure. The transformation to a more authoritarian and less Leninist political system was underway. But such transformations are delicate at best. Jiang hoped for tranquility to solidify his own rule and create a more stable political system. Such tranquility would prove elusive.

BEIJING SPRING

As Jiang moved to secure power, promote his scheme for enterprise reform, and create a better atmosphere for Sino–U.S. relations, he began to allow greater space for political expression, at least among intellectuals.[13] In the summer of 1997, the press was filled with reform-minded articles as the Party prepared public opinion for the upcoming congress and intellectuals tried to push the limits of acceptable discussion. Proposals for the establishment of a "socialist market economy," soon to be endorsed by the congress, appeared regularly; more sensitive was that some intellectuals again began raising demands for political reform. After several years of relative quiescence, liberal thought was making itself heard in broader circles.

The first to openly raise the issue of political reform was Shang Dewen, then a 65-year-old economics professor at Beijing University. In August 1997, he penned a letter to Jiang Zemin in which he said the disjuncture between economic reform and political reform was causing "contradictions, frictions, and conflict." He then proceeded to outline a program of democratization, including direct election of the presidency and checks and balances among three branches of government, that might take a quarter century to implement – but needed to be inaugurated immediately.[14] A gentle person, Shang's letter was extremely circumspect but also unmistakable in its demand for democratization. His initial letter was followed up by two similar appeals.[15]

Shortly after the Fifteenth Party Congress, Jiang Zemin visited the United States and was apparently very pleased by his trip. Lower levels soon got the message that relations with the United States were to be improved, and Chinese television broadcast a movie depicting the role of the Flying Tigers and Sino–American cooperation in the Second World War. Many Chinese learned for the first time about General Claire Lee Chennault and how his ragtag group of fighter pilots had prevented Japanese bombing of cities such as Kunming.

Another sign was the improvement in the treatment that authoritative Chinese media accorded the United States.

China's intellectuals, as Shang Dewen's inaugural letter suggests, were quick to sense the changing mood and pick up the themes articulated at the Party congress. In November (two months after the congress), Fang Jue, then a 44-year-old former deputy director of the planning commission of Fuzhou city, distributed a statement calling for political reform. Fang, who had previously been a researcher in the Institute of Politics at CASS and later had left government to go into business in 1995, called for multiparty democracy, direct elections of legislative bodies at all levels, the acceptance of international economic and political norms, respect for human rights, and an improvement in China's international relations, especially with the United States and Japan. It was the most direct and farthest-ranging proposal for political reform since Tiananmen – and Fang remained free until the crackdown on democratic activists a year later.[16]

In December, Hu Jiwei, the crusading former editor-in-chief of *People's Daily,* published a series of articles calling for political reform in a major Hong Kong daily. Scathing in its criticism of Deng Xiaoping and his handling of the June 4 incident, Hu decried the fact that Zhao Ziyang had been under house arrest and "deprived of his minimal rights as a Party member and citizen" ever since. Hu asked pointedly, "[o]ne can well imagine that if a ruling Party can wantonly deprive its leaders of their minimal human rights, is it not more difficult for this Party to respect the human rights of dissidents in general?"[17]

In March the journal *Methods* (*Fangfa*), whose editorial board was stocked with liberal intellectuals, ran a series of articles that would have been risky only a short time before. Picking up Jiang Zemin's call for "rule of law" and political reform at the Fifteenth Party Congress, China's liberal intelligentsia tried to push for greater political reform. Zhang Ximing, a young journalist at CASS who had been involved in the writing of *Heart-to-Heart Talks with the General Secretary,* opened by calling for a press law (something that had been widely discussed in the 1980s before being abandoned after Tiananmen) that would protect freedom of the press.[18] Ma Licheng, a journalist in the editorial department of *People's Daily* who would soon become famous for coauthoring a controversial book called *Crossed Swords,* followed with a short article arguing that press supervision of public authority would benefit, not detract from, social order. Press supervision, Ma said in adapting a line from Deng Xiaoping, "could be used by capitalism, and could be used as well by socialism."[19] Liu Junning, the political theorist at CASS whose ideas were discussed in Chapters 4 and 5, argued that political reform should start by protecting individual

197

property rights. Historian Lei Yi argued that, with the task of national independence accomplished by the 1949 revolution and with the people's livelihood basically guaranteed by the economic reforms, it was time to move on to the third of Sun Yat-sen's three principles: democracy.[20]

In May, Liu Junning put out a rapidly edited book entitled *Beijing University's Tradition and Modern China* that took advantage of the approaching centennial anniversary of Beijing University to emphasize the liberal tradition in China. A preface by Li Shenzhi noted the central role that Beijing University has played in the introduction and development of liberalism in China – from Yan Fu, the translator of Adam Smith and Montesquieu; to Cai Yuanpei, the chancellor during the May Fourth Movement who insisted on academic freedom; to Chen Yinke, the historian persecuted for his unwillingness to yield to political power; to Ma Yinchu, the economist who argued in the 1950s for birth control. It was with the introduction of liberalism to China via Beijing University that China began to "go toward the world, go toward modernization, and go toward globalization."[21]

In striking contrast to the mood of only a couple of years before – when *China Can Say No* topped the best-seller list and spawned a whole cottage industry of imitators – books depicting the United States in a more favorable light began to appear on the market. One notable work was *China Will Not Be "Mr. No"* by Shen Jiru, a senior intellectual in the Institute of World Economics and Politics at CASS, which was published in the *China's Contemporary Problems* book series under the general editorship of Liu Ji. Like *Heart-to-Heart Talks,* Shen's book joined the long-standing debate over causes of the Soviet Union's collapse. Whereas the earlier book had concentrated on domestic causes, Shen extended the argument to international relations by arguing that it had been the steadfast refusal of Soviet leaders to cooperate with other countries and open up their country (which had earned Soviet Foreign Minister Andrei Gromyko the nickname of "Mr. No") that had brought about its demise. In opposition to conservatives' argument that it was reform that led to collapse, Shen and others argued that it was the *lack* of reform that brought about the failure of socialism in the Soviet Union and Eastern Europe.[22]

Like *Heart-to-Heart Talks,* the publication of Shen's book was tacit recognition that public opinion had become important, even in the realm of foreign policy. In the face of nationalistic books like *China Can Say No,* reformers within the government needed to publicly justify the policy of rapprochement that Jiang was pursuing vis-à-vis the United States. An even more outstanding instance of using public opinion both to justify accelerating reform and to advance policy battles within the upper reaches of the Party was the publication of *Crossed Swords,* easily the most controversial book of the spring.

Written by Ma Licheng of the theoretical department of *People's Daily* and *People's Daily* senior reporter Ling Zhijun, the book starts by tracing the history of the emergence of the Dengist reforms – particularly the opening up of intellectual freedom – against the opposition of Mao's successor, Hua Guofeng, and goes on to link this early period of relaxation to the heated debates surrounding Deng Xiaoping's trip to the south in 1992. Finally, and most controversially, the book details the sharp political debates of 1995–97, specifically the efforts of the Old Left to hamstring reform through the circulation of the 10,000-character manifestos. Ignoring certain historical realities, particularly that much of Deng's animus in his 1992 trip was directed against Jiang Zemin, the book portrays Jiang as inheriting and pushing forward the "emancipation of the mind" begun in 1978.[23]

Crossed Swords was even more controversial than other works published during the spring because, like Shen Jiru's book, it was included in the *China's Contemporary Problems* series and because it publicly criticized the leftist manifestos, which had been widely circulated but not published (except for the one in *Mainstream*). Despite Liu Ji's close relationship with Jiang Zemin, it was apparent that the publication of *Crossed Swords* was part of the ongoing conduct of "court politics" surrounding the Party leader rather than a direct reflection of his views. In an effort to conciliate (or at least mediate among) different wings of the Party, Jiang had surrounded himself with a variety of advisors, ranging from the conservative Teng Wensheng to the neoconservative Wang Huning to the more liberal Liu Ji. Inevitably there were controversies among such people, and the personal animosities among some of them were quite deep. For instance, Wang Renzhi, the former head of the Propaganda Department who was forced to step down (following Deng's trip to the south) and take a position as Party secretary of CASS, was angry about the publication of *Heart-to-Heart Talks* and quarreled on more than one occasion with Liu Ji, then a vice-president of CASS.[24] This may well have made Liu even more willing to allow the publication of *Crossed Swords.* In any event, it was clear that the publication of *Crossed Swords* set off a political maelstrom. Ding Guan'gen, the conservative head of the Propaganda Department who is widely disliked by intellectuals, quickly condemned the book. Wang Renzhi was predictably outraged, as was conservative elder Song Ping. Leftists, who were angered by the *Crossed Swords* wholesale criticism of them, organized a meeting in April to attack the book, to which they invited Communist ideologues from Russia (provoking liberals to mock the gathering as one of the "Communist

International"). Eventually, the editors of the conservative journal *Mainstream,* which had published one of the 10,000-character manifestos, took the authors of *Crossed Swords* to court, charging copyright violation. The court eventually dismissed the charges, but not without some dramatic political theater.[25]

On the liberal side of the spectrum, Party elder Wan Li pre-empted efforts to ban the book by meeting privately with the authors (though news of the meeting was quickly leaked to the Hong Kong press). Wan sharply criticized the 10,000-character manifestos and told Ma and Ling, "[h]ow can one have reform without crossing swords?... If swords aren't crossed enough, there will not be enough reform." Finally, Jiang Zemin's closest political advisor Zeng Qinghong and his political mentor Wang Daohan stepped in and urged a Solomonic decision: *Crossed Swords* should be neither criticized nor praised; both leftist and rightist opinions could be aired. This decision, endorsed by Jiang, allowed the continued circulation of the book.[26]

With this clash of criticism and countercriticism swirling around him, Jiang decided to go to Beijing University on May 4 to participate in the university's centennial ceremonies. Jiang made this decision on his own and against the counsel of some of his advisors; they feared that the trip would be too controversial and perhaps even stir up a new student movement. Beijing University has been the fount of liberal thinking in modern China and, more specifically, the leading force in the 1989 Tiananmen demonstrations. Wang Dan, the student leader released to the United States in April 1998, was a Beijing University student.

Critics have argued that Jiang's visit to Beijing University paid too much attention to patriotism and the university's role in the development of the CCP (the cofounders of the party, Li Dazhao and Chen Duxiu, were both Beijing University faculty). Nevertheless, what seems important was Jiang's personal gesture in reaching out to intellectuals. According to some professors at the school, the president's visit was highly successful. Jiang spent a whole morning there, addressing faculty in French, English, Russian, and Japanese (which he said he would speak better if he had not been forced to learn it under the Japanese occupation) and exchanging couplets of Tang poetry with students.[27]

Jiang's visit to Beijing University appears to have been part of a strategy to assuage the anger left by Tiananmen without formally revising the Party's judgment on that event. Like the removal of the Yang brothers from the military in 1992, the ouster of the widely disliked Beijing Party secretary Chen Xitong in 1995, the various campaigns against corruption, and the easing of Li Peng out of the premiership, Jiang's visit to Beijing University was an important gesture that tried to put Tiananmen behind him and reach out to the intellectual community at the same time.

In the year since Deng Xiaoping's death, Jiang had been remarkably successful in putting his own mark on Chinese politics. He had rejected pressure exerted by the Old Left, had opened up the intellectual and political atmosphere modestly but significantly, and had dealt skillfully with personnel issues at the Fifteenth Party Congress. These moves were necessary if Jiang was going to handle successfully the paramount issue of the day, economic reform.

The biggest problem was that of the state-owned enterprises. In some ways, China had sidestepped the problem of SOEs in the 1980s and early 1990s as the TVE sector grew dramatically. The SOE sector, however, did not fade away. In some ways, it actually increased in importance as the number of workers employed by SOEs rose by 40 million between 1978 and 1994.[28] Despite the decreasing importance of SOEs in the overall economy, they continued to dominate important sectors, particularly heavy industry, and their failure to reform was increasingly a drag on economic growth. By the late 1990s, it was apparent that SOE reform could not be avoided.[29]

One of the central obstacles in SOE reform had always been the relationship between the enterprises and the state. It was not only that the enterprises sought help from their supervising administrators but also that the various ministries had an incentive to support even weak SOEs and to encourage production even if it was not economically efficient. Unless the apron strings that bound SOEs to state ministries could be severed, there was no way that SOEs, however their ownership structure might be changed, could truly make their way in the market economy. This issue cut to the heart of the debates about socialism and also involved major interests in Chinese society. Ministries had no real desire to force their subordinate industries onto the market, just as industries had no incentive to compete when administrative support was available.

Furthermore, there was the question of how and to what extent China's economy should be linked to the international economy. Since China had begun to open its doors in the late 1970s, its trade with the outside world had expanded rapidly. In the mid-1990s, in an effort to increase foreign investment, China had relaxed its rules on foreign ownership. This had brought a huge increase in the amount of foreign funds invested, but it had also stimulated economic nationalism in response. Should the rules on foreign investment be relaxed even further? If they were not, would foreign enterprises continue to invest large sums in the Chinese economy? Without the pressures of foreign investment, how could enterprises behind a wall of protection be expected to reform? Such questions were, of course, linked to China's bid to join the WTO – to what extent should China compromise in order to join the world trade body?

This last question was closely related to China's international relations. China's isolation following Tiananmen put the government under a great deal of pressure. China initially concentrated its efforts on Asia and managed to gain diplomatic recognition from Indonesia and Singapore, from which China had long been estranged. At the same time, it was able to persuade Saudi Arabia to extend diplomatic relations, followed by South Africa. Such diplomatic successes put Taiwan under greater pressure but did little to normalize China's relations with the United States. Indeed, there is reason to believe that conservatives in China had scant interest in improving relations with the United States, at least past a certain point. Tension with the leading capitalist nation in the world had the effect of legitimizing continued efforts to oppose "bourgeois liberalization" at home and to delegitimize the private economy.

Coming into his own as a political leader, Jiang Zemin recognized the importance of improving relations with the United States for both domestic reform and his own legitimacy. Gaining China's international acceptance as one of the great powers of the world would diminish the lingering effects of post-Tiananmen isolation; it would also realize the century-old desire of Chinese patriots to no longer be treated as a second-rate power but instead to be regarded as an equal in world affairs. This was an issue of status that would clearly enhance Jiang Zemin's political prestige, but it was also an economic issue with profound implications for domestic reform.

In March 1998, the Ninth Session of the NPC formally named Zhu Rongji premier, replacing Li Peng. Luo Gan, secretary general of the State Council, presented a proposal for a massive restructuring of the government. Pointing to the costs of bloated administration, to the demands posed by the reform of state-owned enterprises, and to the challenges presented by the Asian financial crisis, he outlined a sweeping plan to reduce the number of government ministries from 40 to 29. Although Jiang had called for administrative restructuring at the Fifteenth Party Congress the previous fall and Luo Gan had presented the plan to the NPC, this was clearly Zhu's program.

Ironically, considering the harsh criticism to which he would be subjected a year later, Zhu was easily the most popular politician in China in the spring of 1998. His declaration at a post-NPC news conference that "[n]o matter whether there is a mine field ahead of me or whether there is a deep ravine in front of me, I will bravely forge ahead, will not turn my back, and will do my best until my last breath" seized the public imagination.[30] When asked if the recent political demonstrations that brought down the Suharto government in Indonesia could spread to China in a new expression of "people power," Chinese repeatedly responded: "Not with Zhu Rongji as premier." Zhu had won himself and China a honeymoon period.[31]

The plan to reorganize the government marked the biggest readjustment of the government–enterprise relationship since the beginning of reform. Combined with the "grasping the large and letting go of the small" policy adopted in 1995, the elimination of so many of China's line ministries opened up the possibility of a radical retreat of the government from the economy. The idea appears to have been to centralize the supervision of a limited number (500–1,000) of large enterprise groups in the State Economic and Trade Commission (SETC). Zhu established a number of inspection groups, each headed by a person of vice-ministerial rank, that were to keep tabs on the enterprise groups and report directly back to the SETC. Because they were no longer ministerially based, they were expected to provide the government with more objective information on the state of industry. At the same time, numerous enterprises at the local level were reorganized as shareholding enterprises or simply sold off.

The impact of the South Korean model on this reorganization plan was apparent. Just as the Korean economy was dominated by a small number of large-scale *chaebol,* so too would a relatively small number of enterprise groups dominate the Chinese economy. Moreover, just as management of the Korean economy was highly centralized, the Chinese plan eliminated the multiplicity of bureaucratic interests, centralizing control in the SETC. Finally, just as small-scale enterprise was left to the market in Korea, so the central state would retreat from ownership and management of most industry in China. Private enterprise would be given room to expand; indeed, the government hoped it would expand rapidly because the pressure of unemployment was perhaps the most serious problem China faced. Not only would people laid off from state-owned enterprises need to find new jobs, there was still a large number of underemployed people in the rural areas – frequently estimated to be at least 150 million – who needed to switch to nonagricultural employment. Only private enterprise, with its small investment of capital and labor-intensive production, could hope to provide sufficient employment.

Along with the plan to reorganize government and streamline industry, there was also an intent to wed the Chinese economy more closely to the global economy. It was at this time – in the spring of 1998, as details of President Clinton's forthcoming trip to China were being planned – that China expressed renewed interest in joining the World Trade Organization (WTO). China had first applied to join the trade body, then known as the General Agreement on Trade and Tariffs (GATT), in 1986 but negotiations to complete China's entry were interrupted by Tiananmen.[32] There was a period of renewed interest and possibility in 1994, prior to the formal establishment of the WTO at the beginning of 1995, but by then the bar to admission had been raised significantly. This was not simply a matter of political bias against China (though, given the image of China in the U.S., tougher conditions were certainly needed to convince a skeptical Congress); primarily it reflected a new image of China as a potential economic juggernaut that might overwhelm the United States with cheap exports. In any case, Chinese negotiators were not yet willing to make the sort of commitments that would secure their entry, so the opportunity passed. Trade negotiations were suspended during the tensions in the Taiwan Straits following President Lee Teng-hui's visit to Cornell University, and it was only after Sino–U.S. relations improved in the wake of that incident that serious trade negotiations could be resumed.

Jiang Zemin had long been a supporter of China's entry into the WTO, as a way both of tying China's economy more closely to the world's and of demonstrating his ability to enhance China's status as a world power. However, many bureaucracies in China feared the impact of joining the trade organization, and Li Peng had effectively blocked serious negotiations.[33] But by the spring of 1998, the time was ripe to reopen negotiations. Sino–U.S. relations were significantly improved, deflating opposition on nationalist grounds, and Li Peng was stepping down as premier. Thus, on March 8, Jiang Zemin stated: "We have to gain a complete and correct understanding of the issue of economic 'globalization' and properly deal with it. Economic globalization is an objective trend of world economic development, from which none can escape and in which everyone has to participate."[34] The direction in which Jiang hoped to move the country was quite apparent.

NATIONALISM, ELITE POLITICS, AND THE WTO

Given the economic nationalism in 1995, the precarious economic situation facing China in 1996–98, and the concern with its economic security and potential vulnerability to the Asian financial crisis, it is almost surprising that China continued to express interest in the WTO.[35] Whereas the period following Tiananmen had been marked by a new suspicion of the outside world and a resurgence of nativist thinking, the WTO challenged China to engage – and be engaged by – the world in the best cosmopolitan tradition. In the 1980s this thinking came naturally, if somewhat naively; in the 1990s China's sophistication regarding the outside world had leaped ahead, but cosmopolitan thinking was under fire in many circles. In terms of elite politics, this posture of "half-in, half-out" of the world was highlighted by both rhetoric and conflict. In 1989, Jiang Zemin had stressed the difference between "socialist" reform and opening up versus "capitalist" reform and opening up; in 1991, he had stressed the danger of "peaceful evolution." Jiang had only slowly relaxed his concern with being accused, like his predecessors, of being "lax on bourgeois liberalization," and he was quick to retreat if domestic stability seemed threatened. Aside from (or perhaps lurking behind) such ideological concerns were very different interests, both political and economic. A certain degree of international tension was good for those who liked to raise the nationalist banner; it also provided a good excuse to continue to protect the interests of enterprises and bureaucracies that were threatened by international competition. Conversely, other enterprises and bureaucracies benefited from opening up internationally. To a degree, policy oscillations reflected these competing interests.

As we have seen in looking at the sub-elite level, the enlightenment project and globalization had come under considerable criticism by many intellectuals in the 1990s. Lurking behind much of this criticism, as with similar criticism in the West, was a deep-seated suspicion of multinational firms and capitalism. But whereas such criticisms in the West tend to be fueled more by concerns with the environment and labor standards, in China they are fueled by nationalism – the fear that China will be entrapped by global capital and by U.S. "hegemony" in particular. This is the point at which the nationalistic concerns of the postmodernist intellectual elite slide very easily into the rawer, more populist nationalism typified by *China Can Say No.*

China's proposed entrance into the WTO thus struck an uneasy balance between the desire of Chinese leaders to demonstrate China's "great power" status and to further economic development by joining the international economy on one side, and, on the other, the protectionist instincts of some regions and bureaucracies, the ideological and political concerns that such integration might prove socially disruptive, the concerns of postmodernist intellectuals, and the populist nationalism of a large segment of the public.

Following China's failed bid to become an inaugural member of the WTO, the 1995–96 Taiwan Straits crisis further delayed negotiations. Nevertheless, the very seriousness of that crisis prompted new efforts to improve relations. As a result, Jiang Zemin traveled to the United States in October 1997, the first Chinese president to do so since Li Xiannian visited in 1986, and President

Clinton returned the visit by going to China in June 1998 – the first presidential visit since President Bush's ill-fated trip in February 1989. As the relationship warmed, discussions on China's accession to the WTO were renewed. In the months leading up to President Clinton's visit, China evinced considerable interest in joining the WTO, but U.S. negotiators were convinced that China was still hoping for a "political pass" – that is, an agreement allowing them into the WTO out of consideration for Sino–U.S. relations rather than an offer requiring serious economic commitments.

There were clearly domestic political factors in China that were blocking progress toward a WTO agreement in this period. Jiang Zemin's support for China's entry into the GATT/WTO can be traced back to the 1993–94 period. China's efforts to join the WTO were coordinated by Vice-Premier Li Lanqing, who was known to be close to Jiang (as well as to Li Peng) and enjoyed a reputation as a strong supporter of China's bid. But Li Lanqing's efforts were constrained by Li Peng, who continued to serve as premier until March 1998. Li Peng opposed China's efforts to join the WTO – at least on terms that came close to being "commercially viable" – on both foreign policy and protectionist grounds. Li has always been a major voice within the Chinese government against close ties with the United States. Not only did he move slowly and reluctantly in the period following Tiananmen to improve bilateral relations (e.g., by ending martial law and allowing astrophysicist Fang Lizhi to leave the U.S. Embassy for exile), he also used his position as head of the Foreign Affairs Leadership Small Group to undercut efforts by the Ministry of Foreign Affairs to improve Sino–U.S. relations.[36] Given the division of labor on the Politburo Standing Committee, it was easy for Li to set a tone on foreign policy that made it difficult for Jiang Zemin to improve relations. At the same time, as premier and as a product of ministerial culture, Li consistently supported the interests of China's bureaucracy – making him a popular figure within influential circles. Indeed, one could argue that Li's greatest (negative) effect on China's government was his willingness to let things drift. Lacking vision and unwilling to ride roughshod over inefficient bureaucrats, Li allowed China's SOEs to become ever more inefficient and eventually to threaten the solvency of the banking system.

In March 1998, Zhu Rongji replaced Li Peng as premier. At first, this seemed to make little difference. Zhu focused primarily on domestic reform, particularly the plight of SOEs, and seems to have worried that international competition would make his task harder, not easier. There may also have been an element of bureaucratic competition involved. Zhu is clearly someone who is very possessive of his power as premier, and he moved vigorously to centralize control over the economy in his office. As we have seen, he quickly elevated the SETC above other bureaucratic interests; he also undercut the authority of the various vice-premiers – including Li Lanqing, who had good relations with both Jiang Zemin and Li Peng and had been touted as a possible candidate for premier.

In any event, the opportunity to move forward on the WTO issue in the run-up to President Clinton's visit to China was missed. It was only in the fall of 1998 that the issue moved back onto the agenda, and it seems to have done so largely at the initiative of the American government. At the time, a number of issues were once again roiling the bilateral relationship: China was cracking down on the China Democracy Party; there were reports of illegal contributions to the Democratic Party; and, most sensational of all, Congressman Christopher Cox began investigating allegations that China had engaged in extensive nuclear spying. Indeed, it was startling that within six months of Clinton's highly successful trip to China, Sino–U.S. relations were once again caught in a downward spiral. The WTO was seen as an issue that could provide ballast to the relationship. It would recognize China's full membership in the global economy, remove the annual ritual of renewing China's MFN status, and underscore important interests that the two nations have in common.

According to Chinese sources, President Clinton wrote Jiang Zemin a letter on November 6, 1998, expressing hope that the WTO issue could be resolved in the first quarter of 1999. On February 8, 1999, Clinton is said to have written a second letter to Jiang Zemin stating that he hoped that WTO negotiations could be concluded during Premier Zhu Rongji's visit to the United States. A third letter, on February 12, expressed hope that a package deal could be reached.[37]

By January 1999, the Chinese position on the WTO had changed enough that Premier Zhu was able to tell Alan Greenspan, chairman of the U.S. Federal Reserve, that China was prepared to offer substantial concessions. Nevertheless, a clear-cut leadership decision on concessions was apparently made only in February, after receipt of President Clinton's letters. Sometime in the latter part of the month there seems to have been an enlarged Politburo meeting that approved broad-gauged concessions in an effort to achieve WTO membership. All major bureaucracies would have been represented at such a meeting and would have had an opportunity to present their views – although the expression of those views would have been constrained by the obvious support of the top leadership, and particularly of Jiang Zemin, for joining the WTO.

To argue that there had been, at least formally, full bureaucratic consultation does not mean that there was consensus. Indeed, although support for China's entry into the WTO appears to have grown over the preceding years, the same divisions that had plagued China's previous efforts continued to exist. The difference now was that Jiang Zemin's own resolve seems to have grown and the reorganization of the government in spring 1998 had enhanced Zhu Rongji's leverage. Zhu's own support for China's entry into the WTO apparently increased over the preceding months. From Zhu's perspective, China's economy faced three major problems. First, in the wake of the Asian financial crisis, China's exports were suffering. With the Chinese economy entering a period of deflation, a weakening of exports would have serious adverse consequences for the country's overall economic performance. Second, foreign investment in China was beginning to slow, and entry into the WTO and permanent MFN status were seen as ways to reassure investors. Third, and most important, foreign competition was widely seen as a means to force otherwise reluctant SOEs to carry out painful restructurings. Protectionism was beginning to cost China plenty as SOEs, supported by bureaucratic interests and high tariffs, continued their inefficient ways. Zhu wanted to carry out a restructuring plan that would force the more efficient industries to become competitive on the world market, thus becoming pillars of a leaner state-owned economy, and simultaneously force less efficient industries to be sold off or shut down.

Even as Zhu prepared for his departure to the United States, however, opposition came from an unexpected source. On March 24, 1999, frustrated by its inability to persuade Serbian leader Milosović to accept the Ramboulait agreement, NATO began to bomb targets in Serbia. Originally intended as a short campaign to intimidate Milosović into compliance, it encountered unexpectedly stiff resistance, including the expulsion of many Kosovars from their homeland, and thus had to be extended – ultimately for 78 days until Milosović capitulated. Because the Yugoslav campaign was initially seen as a purely local issue of limited duration, there appears to have been no consideration of the campaign's effects on other countries, particularly Russia and China. Yet this impact soon proved to be tremendous.

For years, the thrust of U.S. policy vis-à-vis China across a whole range of issues – including trade, human rights, and arms control – was to accept "international norms." There were, or so the line went, certain universally accepted norms that were embodied in various conventions and treaties; China, if it wanted to be accepted as a full member of the international community, would have to accept those norms and "play by the rules." Doing so would assure it equal treatment, a chance to "sit at the table" and influence the future evolution of rules governing the international system. It was a powerful appeal, backed as it was by positive incentives for compliance and penalties for noncompliance. It even appealed to many in China who both desired China to be recognized as a great power and hoped that China would fully join the international system.

However, the issue of bombing Serbia to protect the rights of Kosovars was never taken to the United Nations Security Council. American officials were probably correct when they claimed that doing so would have been ineffective and that the Chinese government would use such a forum to constrain U.S. actions; nevertheless, unilateral NATO action touched the deepest fears of many Chinese officials. It seemed that the United States and NATO could join in any action, at any time and any place, without international consultation. Moreover, the NATO meeting in May declared that the organization's mission would include "out of area" concerns, yet "out of area" was not defined.[38] Worse, from the Chinese government's perspective, was the NATO declaration that "human rights" transcended "sovereign rights." Chinese officials immediately began envisioning the use of U.S. and/or NATO forces in or around China itself – North Korea, Taiwan, Xinjiang, and Tibet were the places most frequently named. Even had there never been a bombing of the Chinese Embassy in Belgrade, there would have been long-term consequences of the NATO actions in Yugoslavia.

Because of such concerns over U.S. actions in Serbia, conservatives in China suggested that Zhu Rongji's trip to the United States be postponed. But these suggestions were overruled, indicating the weight that Jiang Zemin put on Sino–U.S. relations and the WTO issue.

Most of the negotiating on the WTO issue had taken place in Beijing in March, and a deal appeared pretty much complete. On the eve of Zhu's departure, however, President Clinton met with his advisors over the weekend of April 4–5. His foreign policy advisors – National Security Advisor Samuel Berger and Secretary of State Madeline Albright, along with United States Trade Representative (USTR) Charlene Barshefsky – favored clinching a deal that was better for American business than any had dared hope only a few months earlier. However, Clinton's domestic advisors – Treasury Secretary Robert Rubin, National Economic Council head Gene Sperling, and domestic political advisor John Podesta – argued that if there were no guaranteed protections for labor unions and industries that compete directly with their Chinese counterparts then Congress would vote to kill the deal, and that would be worse for U.S.–China relations than no agreement at all. President Clinton sided with his domestic advisors and requested that the USTR go back to the negotiating table to ask for both extended protection for textiles and added assurances against large-scale increases in imports.[39]

Thus it was that, when Zhu Rongji's plane touched down on April 6, the stage was set for one of the most conspicuous foreign policy failures of recent years. Perhaps more than any other part of the agreement, Chinese negotiators found it difficult to accept the U.S. demand that the Multi-Fiber Agreement, designed to protect the U.S. textile industry from Chinese and other foreign competition, be extended an additional five years beyond its scheduled phase-out date.[40] To offer the far-ranging concessions envisioned by the Chinese proposal and then yield to a demand for U.S. protectionism was a difficult proposition for Chinese negotiators to take back to their own government (eventually, they did accept a four-year extension).

On the morning of April 7, President Clinton declared that it would be an "inexplicable mistake" to walk away from a good agreement with China. Then, in a $2\frac{1}{2}$-hour meeting with Premier Zhu at the White House that evening, he did exactly that. Although an agricultural agreement was quickly signed the next morning, Zhu was sent back to China almost empty-handed.[41]

Shortly after President Clinton turned his back on the WTO deal, details of China's concessions appeared in a 17-page document posted on the USTR website. The decision to post such details – without informing the Chinese – apparently came from the White House. Oddly, White House officials did not feel that the U.S. business community had been vocal enough in supporting China's accession. This unilateral posting was a breach of faith that was insulting to the Chinese side, and it quickly compounded the political difficulties of those Chinese in favor of WTO membership.

First of all, posting the concessions was widely seen in China as a way to publicly hold the government's feet to the fire, an action bound to evoke a hostile response. Second, the posting apparently gave many officials in China their first full look at the proposed trade package, or at least at the provisions to which Zhu had agreed. Third, the U.S. posting allowed public opinion to play a role in China. Large enterprises and provinces that would be affected by China's entry began to calculate the impact on themselves; many students and intellectuals thought that China had offered too high a price. With the posting, the Chinese government lost control of the flow of information.[42]

The reaction in China to the failed WTO agreement and to the publication of details was both strong and immediate. Wu Jichuan, Minister of Information Industries (which includes telecommunications), reportedly tendered his resignation (which was not accepted).[43] Wu's apparent resignation offer and his subsequent actions, particularly his curious announcement on September 13 that it was illegal for foreign firms to buy into China's Internet business (something that was already happening), indicates the ferocity of high-level opposition.[44]

Wu Jichuan himself has a reputation as a mild-mannered person – not the sort to defy his boss, particularly one with a reputation for a bad temper like Zhu Rongji. The fact that Wu played such a public role in the domestic controversy indicates that he had strong political backing, backing that could only have come from former premier Li Peng. It also indicates that criticism of Zhu was immediate and harsh.

Thus, there had already been a strong reaction in China when, on the morning of May 8, news was received that the United States had bombed the Chinese Embassy in Belgrade. Beijing's initial reaction was one of shock and confusion. There were clearly expressions of outrage within the Chinese government, but it appears that the top leadership quickly came to the conclusion that the bombing was either accidental, as the United States claimed, or that it reflected a low-level conspiracy within the depths of some bureaucracy and not government policy. But the bombing came on the heels of many events that were seen as "anti-China": accusations of illegal campaign contributions and nuclear spying, new denunciations of China's human rights record in the wake of arrests of democracy activists, the bombing campaign in Serbia, and now the failure to reach an agreement on the WTO. Nationalistic sentiment within the government reached a new peak, and there was real and deep anger among the broader population, especially students.

In the wake of the WTO failure and the embassy bombing, Zhu Rongji was abused mercilessly by public opinion. Articles on the Internet and student demonstrators labeled him a "traitor" (*maiguozei*) following the embassy bombing. At the same time, some old cadres were heard to mutter that the government's readiness to accept globalization was like Wang Jingwei's willingness to serve as head of Japan's puppet government in occupied China during World War II. Others called Zhu Rongji's compromises in Washington the "new 21 demands selling out the country" – a reference to Japan's infamous demands of 1915 that sought to reduce China to a colony.

Jiang Zemin's own position was very delicate. Within the government, Jiang was widely seen as "soft" on the United States and as a strong advocate of WTO membership. There were rumblings that the real "traitor" was not Zhu Rongji but rather Jiang Zemin. In the face of this rising tide of hostility, Jiang Zemin told an internal meeting that China had waited thirteen years to join the WTO (GATT) and it could wait another thirteen years.[45] But Jiang and other top leaders also recognized the importance of the U.S. relationship: without the trade benefits it provides, developing the economy would be impossible to continue; and without a reasonably good political relationship, many resources would have to be devoted to building up the military. Thus, the relationship was considered just too valuable to sacrifice to the emotion of the moment. Jiang therefore had to preserve the U.S. relationship as well as demonstrate to his critics his toughness.

This dual need was quickly reflected in the divided messages sent by the *People's Daily*. On the one hand, Jiang Zemin's public statements and the authoritative editorials issued by the *People's Daily* underscored continuity in policy even while expressing outrage over the bombing. For instance, in Jiang's May 13 speech welcoming the return of embassy staff from Yugoslavia, he reiterated that China "must continue to unswervingly take economic construction as the central task."[46] A series of editorials in *People's Daily* emphasized that policy would not change and concluded with the declaration that China wants to "develop amity and cooperation with developed countries in the West, including the United States."[47] On June 12, Vice Prime Minister Qian Qichen declared, "China does not want confrontation with the United States."[48]

At the same time, *People's Daily* also published a series of very harsh articles signed "observer" (*guanchajia*). Such observer articles are published rarely, which indicates their importance, but they are not as authoritative as editorials, which are approved by the top leadership. Observer articles thus express views that are highly important but that do not carry the endorsement of the Party and so cannot be said to reflect official policy. A pair of critical "observer" articles published in *People's Daily* on May 16 and May 27 suggested deep anti-U.S. sentiment.[49] These articles were followed by a particularly strident observer article on June 22, which pushed rhetoric well beyond the bounds of diplomatic discourse by comparing – at length – the United States to Nazi Germany.[50]

Rather than express a point of view different from that of Jiang Zemin, these articles were intended to show the military and other critics that his government could be just as harsh on the United States as they were. These articles, which were evidently approved by Ding Guan'gen, head of the Propaganda Department, suggest the degree of threat that Jiang felt in the immediate aftermath of the embassy bombing. This interpretation jibes with reports of Jiang adopting harsh rhetoric in internal meetings – saying, for instance, that U.S. imperialism will not die (*wangwozhixin busi,* an evocative expression used by Mao Zedong) and calling for "biding time while nurturing grievances" (*woxin changtan*).[51]

Given the delicacy of Jiang's position and the genuine anger felt in student circles, the Party quickly made the decision to channel public opinion by providing buses for students to go into the embassy district from the universities in the Haidian district (in northwestern Beijing). Students got off the buses and walked past the U.S. ambassador's residence, throwing stones as they went, and then on to the embassy building and chancellery – throwing more bricks, stones, ink bottles, and occasionally feces. It was certainly better, from the Party's point of view, to have such public anger directed at the United States than to have students throw stones at Zhongnanhai (the compound in which the leadership lives), which they certainly would have done had the Party's reaction been perceived as weak. That this explosion of anti-American anger came a month before the tenth anniversary of the Tiananmen crackdown was certainly a plus from the Party's point of view.

The reaction in China was extraordinary because it was the first time since 1949 that elite politics, bureaucratic interests, intellectual opinion, and broader (but still urban) public opinion came together to oppose the official position on an important foreign policy issue. Indeed, more than any other issues, China's proposed membership in the WTO and the reaction to the embassy bombing demonstrate the coming together – at least temporarily – of elite politics and public opinion. Without understanding the change in political atmosphere and public opinion described in the previous chapters, neither the actions of the government nor those of the students in the spring of 1999 makes sense.

At the elite level, Li Peng clearly used Zhu's trip to the United States and the nationalistic reaction to the embassy bombing to try to reduce Zhu's influence – and perhaps that of Jiang Zemin as well. Li was particularly antagonistic to Zhu, not only because their policy positions differed on many issues but also because Zhu, in his investigation of corruption in Zhanjiang (Guangdong province), had exposed the role of Li's wife, Zhu Lin.[52] Now it was payback time.

At a Politburo meeting in May, Li Peng, knowing the pressure Jiang was under, feigned support for Jiang in order to undercut Zhu. Li reportedly expressed his complete support for Jiang Zemin and then turned to Zhu Rongji and leveled three criticisms. First, Li accused Zhu of not respecting Jiang Zemin as the core. According to Li, Zhu had set himself up as a separate center, focusing on the economy and not reporting back or asking for instructions from the center (which would include both Jiang and Li, who is ranked second on the Politburo). Zhu, Li said, did not listen to his subordinates either. Second, Li alleged that Zhu had misspoken in the United States. Zhu's claim that he did not want to come to the United States but was asked to come by Jiang was similar to what Zhao Ziyang had done in 1989 when he said Deng Xiaoping was the man in charge, that is, redirect blame onto the Party core – in this case, Jiang. Third, Li was critical of Zhu for pursuing too many reforms too quickly. Many of these reforms were good, Li asserted, but they cannot all be done at once or pushed too quickly. Cutting the bureaucracy had hurt lots of good cadres, just as housing and medical reforms had hurt the common people (*laobaixing*), causing them to bear heavy financial burdens.[53]

Jiang offered support for Li's assessment, as did Vice-Premier Li Lanqing. Finding himself in a humiliating and untenable position, Zhu offered his resignation. Jiang reportedly turned to Zhu and asked how he could say such a thing – did he not have any regard for the overall situation? When Zhu used his sore back as an excuse, Jiang suggested he spend some time in Hangzhou recuperating. Zhu went to Hangzhou in June; when he came back, he found that his portfolios had been parceled out to various vice-premiers: Wu Bangguo had taken over policy for SOE reform, Li Lanqing for trade, and Wen Jiabao for agriculture and finance.[54] The statement by Taiwan President Lee Teng-hui on July 9 that characterized cross-straits relations as "special state-to-state" relations caused another upsurge of nationalism in government circles, making Zhu's position even more difficult. Finally, when the leadership met in their annual meeting at the seaside resort of Beidaihe in July, Li Peng launched an open assault on Zhu's management of the economy. By the end of the summer, Zhu was severely weakened, and there were many rumors circulating that he would either resign or be forced out of office.[55]

This extremely tense situation within the highest leadership was not unrelated to dissatisfaction in the military. Like other large organizations in China, the military is not uniform in its opinion on reform issues, but there is certainly a strong nationalistic current within a significant portion of it. The statements on telecommunications by Wu Jichuan (cited earlier) probably had the support of the military, which is concerned about the implications of communications for military security. Moreover, as we have suggested, some discontent was directed against Jiang Zemin in the wake of the embassy bombing; after all, Jiang had been slow to express opposition to the U.S. bombing in Yugoslavia, had supported Zhu Rongji's trip to the United States, and had supported China's entry into the WTO. To some, it seemed that Jiang was simply too naive about the U.S. threat. Jiang had to deflect and conciliate such opinions: first by demonstrating that he had not been taken in by the United States, and second by increasing the size of the PLA's budget.[56]

POSTMODERNIST CRITICS AND THE WTO

The WTO issue, more than any other, brings together the different concerns of this book. As we have seen, it was an issue of bureaucratic and elite politics. With the deepening of economic reform, the improvement of Sino–U.S. relations, and the replacement of Li Peng with Zhu Rongji as premier, bureaucratic resistance was muted and elite opposition finessed. However, the failure of the WTO agreement in April – and especially the bombing of the Chinese

214

Embassy in May – reraised all the old issues and embroiled the WTO issue in the most important rift in elite politics since the death of Deng. Because it affected real interests throughout the country, because it was a direct expression of the globalization that had been at the center of intellectual discussions since 1992, and because – with the bombing of the embassy – it engaged the nationalistic emotions that had built up in the course of the 1990s, the WTO became an issue that engaged public opinion like none other since Tiananmen. The merging of popular concerns over globalization, sovereignty, and national identity with elite struggles over power and the course of reform gave the WTO opposition a scope and power that left Zhu Rongji vulnerable, put Jiang Zemin on the defensive, and threatened to end China's bid for admission. Restarting negotiations and reaching a last-minute agreement in mid-November was a difficult and fragile process; it could easily have gone awry.

Recalling the discussion in Chapter 4 of postmodernist critics and liberals and how their different responses to globalization marked one of the fundamental points separating these very different schools of thought, it is not surprising that postmodernists (the New Left) almost uniformly opposed China's entry into the WTO (at least on the terms being offered), while liberals came down in support of it. At the same time, the issue of nationalism – exacerbated greatly by the bombing of the Chinese Embassy – sharply divided the postmodernist critics from the liberals. Postmodernists, not to mention those already identified as populists, took a strongly nationalistic stance, while liberals worried openly and deeply about the impact of a rising nationalism.

Postmodernist commentary was led by Gan Yang, who quickly criticized Zhu Rongji and the Chinese leadership for focusing too much on gaining entry to the WTO during Zhu's trip to the United States, thus giving away their negotiating advantage. This effort, Gan said, reflected the "pro-U.S., pro-West" (*qinMei qinxifang*) stance of the Chinese leadership. Regarding Zhu's comment that he allowed the United States to vent its anger (*xiaoxiaoqi*), Gan said: "Unless China collapses and becomes like present-day Russia, Americans will always have anger. This sort of deep-rooted anger cannot be vented (*xiaobuliao*)."[57]

Similarly, Cui Zhiyuan (whose views were also discussed in Chapter 4) argued that the benefits of joining the WTO at this time were uncertain but the costs very real. For example, he argued that WTO membership, by protecting the intellectual property rights of the United States and other advanced capitalist nations, would hurt the development of China's high-tech sector. His argument was based on the need to protect infant industries from foreign competition; if China agreed to the provisions on trade-related property rights, China's high-tech industries would not have time to develop. Cui also argued that the WTO provisions (as summarized in the outline of Chinese commitments that the USTR posted in April 1999) would force China's financial markets open, preventing China from using capital controls to protect itself from events like the Asian financial crisis. Moreover, as with many other young intellectuals, there is more than a whiff of nationalism in his thinking. He quotes former UN Secretary General Boutros Boutros-Ghali, a person who had more than a few disagreements with the U.S. government, as stating that "[t]he U.S. sees hardly any need for diplomacy; power is enough. Only weak nations need diplomacy."[58]

Similarly, in a fairly typical expression of New Left opinion regarding international capital and the WTO, a Beijing-based scholar argued that the only reason the United States had changed its mind and had become eager for China to join the WTO was because the U.S. strategy of globalization had encountered difficulties in 1998 (Japan unilaterally announced economic aid for countries hurt by the Asian financial crisis, Hong Kong interfered in its stock market and fought off international speculators, Malaysia announced capital controls, and so forth) and because China had announced a policy of expanding domestic demand, thus threatening to pull away from the international economic order.[59] Clearly this scholar saw the WTO as part of a broader web of institutions designed to enhance the control of Western capitalist states, particularly the United States, over the developing world. As he wrote:[60]

> The U.S. controls the regulations that have been formulated by the international economic organizations; all are designed to accord with the interests and needs of the institutional model of the strong capitalist states. As soon as China joins the WTO, the U.S. can at any time find an excuse to interfere in, sanction, and intimidate our country into accepting so-called "international norms" that do not accord with our national characteristics. And to help the multinational companies to control China's industrial and financial lifelines, it [the U.S.] will usurp our economic sovereignty and force us to carry out suicidal reforms just as it has in Latin America, Russia, Southeast Asia, and elsewhere.

Another fairly typical expression of this line of thinking returned to the issue of globalization. According to the authors, "globalization is really Americanization and incorporation into multinational corporations." Its purpose is to force governments around the world to take orders from the "multinational corporations and international financial chieftains who control the world's economy" and from the "IMF, World Bank, WTO, UN, and other organs controlled by the U.S. government and Federal Reserve Bank" – all of which is to serve the interests of the United States.[61] The same authors warned that entering the

216

WTO presented a greater risk than any other reform undertaken by China, that it could destabilize society, and that "as soon as China enters the WTO, the U.S. will be able to find an excuse at any time to interfere in our country and sanction us."[62]

In contrast, liberals were far more welcoming of the WTO, as they had been of globalization in the debates earlier in the decade. For instance, Liu Junning argued that China's accession to the WTO will force a separation between politics and economics, increase the transparency of policy making, increase pressure to implement rule of law, and undermine the structural basis of corruption. In short, "China's entry into the WTO implies that China will start to formally (*zhengshi*) integrate itself into the world capitalist economic and political system, the basic characteristics of which are market economics and democratic politics."[63]

IMPACT OF THE EMBASSY BOMBING

The gulf between the New Left and liberals was already quite great before the Chinese Embassy in Belgrade was bombed; with the explosion of nationalistic emotion following that event, the rhetoric became more heated and more personal – and the gap between the two sides less bridgeable. We have already noted the public condemnations many made of Zhu Rongji (and the more private questions raised about Jiang Zemin), but soon the Internet and later the bookstores were filled with expressions of nationalism.

Liberals were concerned about this new outburst of nationalism. The most interesting expression of concern came from Xiao Gongqin, the intellectual who had embraced neoconservatism more openly than any other. As noted in Chapter 3, Xiao – consistent with his original neoauthoritarian approach – had always hoped to use the power of the state to bring about a liberal, democratic polity; this approach distinguished him from other neoconservatives, postmodernists, and nationalists. In that quest, he had seen nationalism as a positive force, something that could rally people and provide stability during a difficult transition period. In 1999, however, Xiao was taken aback by the emotion displayed by students marching on the U.S. Embassy, and he came to believe that nationalism could quickly and easily become irrational and that "opportunists" could easily fish in troubled waters. As he pointed out, the greatest danger of such emotional discourse was that it could easily exclude more rational ideas. As he put it: "Any insufficiently radical or insufficiently extreme voices could be attacked and suppressed as 'capitulationism,' 'assisting the enemy,' 'fifth columnist,' or 'traitor.'"[64]

Wang Xiaodong wrote a short but heated response, reflecting the deepening gap between different positions on the ideological spectrum. "No matter how others hit us," Wang asked, "would it be better for us to very 'understandingly' respond without anger?"[65] Wang quickly wrote a number of articles, which were brought together with some of his earlier writings to form the first book of a new wave of nationalistic writings, *China's Road under the Shadow of Globalization.*

Wang co-authored this book with (among others) Fang Ning, a professor at Capital Normal University with whom Wang Xiaodong had previously collaborated in the famous 1995 survey conducted by *China Youth News,* and Song Qiang, the lead writer of *China Can Say No.* Like that earlier volume, *China's Road* was endorsed by Yu Quanyu, the former deputy head of China's Human Rights Commission (under the equally conservative Zhu Muzhi), who has allied himself with leftist causes in recent years. According to Yu, "[t]he attack of America's bombs brought a conclusion to the debate among our intellectuals in recent years; who is right and who is wrong is now clear to all."[66] Yu also touted *China's Road* as the third major expression of nationalism after *China Can Say No* and *Behind the Demonization of China*; like the other works, *China's Road* quickly hit the best-seller list. This self-professed genealogy is interesting because in previous years Wang Xiaodong had kept his distance from the authors of *China Can Say No,* believing them shallow and extreme, as well as from such Old Leftists as Yu Quanyu. Perhaps his removal from *Strategy and Management* in 1998 made him more willing to associate himself with these people, but perhaps also the impact of the bombing had caused different groups to coalesce.

Wang, who contributed the bulk of the book, gives his most extended expression of nationalism. He takes every opportunity to denigrate and mock the political and intellectual elite of China, especially so-called liberals. He depicts them as lapdogs, saying they "support the U.S., support everything about the U.S.," whereas the reality is that the interests of China and the United States clash.[67] The United States, fearing China's growing strength, simply will not let China join the world; indeed, it has made clear its intention of using NATO to control the world in the twenty-first century.[68] Against this unsentimental view of power politics, Wang sees China's elite as selling out the interests of China for their own selfish purposes. The foreign policy elite have long cherished excessively high hopes for Sino–U.S. relations,[69] Wang writes, but in fact the United States simply does not care about Sino–U.S. relations, the United States pursues its own interests selfishly, and it is simply laughable to believe that Americans have a higher sense of morality.[70] Like Wang Shan in

Looking at China through a Third Eye, Wang Xiaodong laments the lack of spirit (*yanggang zhi qi*) among Chinese leaders and intellectuals.[71] The Serbs, through their stubborn resistance to the overwhelming force of NATO, demonstrated that they – unlike many in China – still have self-respect.[72] According to Wang, India's elite shows more panache than China's (a reference to India's defying Western norms by conducting a nuclear test).[73]

Wang's contempt for China's intellectual and political elite explains much of his self-announced democratic thought. Wang declares that he wants to see China democratized and that he favors "one man, one vote." But clearly Wang believes that the Chinese people, given a chance, would throw the pro-American (*qinMei*) foreign policy elite out and reject the liberal intelligentsia. As he puts it, "[w]ithout individual rights, the people will not believe that they are the masters of the nation, will not exert themselves on behalf of the nation, and will have no way to stop the ruling clique (*shangceng jituan*) from selling out the country for its own self interest."[74] Nationalism is driving Wang's "liberalism"; the commitment to democracy is secondary.

Whereas Wang Xiaodong rarely invokes the language of postmodernism or even Marxism (he is too focused on national power to care much about Marxist theory), his primary coauthor Fang Ning wallows in the vocabulary of dependency theory, showing how the postmodernist critique that developed in the 1990s has merged, in less capable hands, with crude nationalism. According to Fang, colonialism was replaced following the Second World War by neocolonialism – the use of foreign capital to bind and exploit the Third World. But neocolonialism was losing its grip as some nations escaped dependency and others carried out revolutions. Thus, the world was moving toward postcolonialism (*houzhiminzhuyi*), which requires more military force to shore up the position of the Western "core" nations.[75] The U.S. actions in Iraq and Yugoslavia, Fang declared, reflected this logic.

Although Fang's combination of postmodernist critique and nationalism was published at a time of considerable emotional stress, the vocabulary he resorted to was, by the mid- to late-1990s, fairly common and not restricted to isolated academics. We saw in Chapter 5 that Wang Huning, in his critique of Huntington, accepted the notion that cultural influence was inherently related to political domination: "If the culture and ideology of one nation-state is attractive, other people will voluntarily follow it."[76] Similarly, an article in the normally reform-minded journal *Democracy and Legality* (*Minzhu yu fazhi*) declared that "[f]oreign goods and foreign culture have made China 'modern' but have also caused our great and proud country, with its thousands of years of civilized history, to sense the sorrow of gradually losing its ego."[77]

219

The left-wing journal *Mainstream* proved that it could decry cultural trends as well as any American conservative when it said:[78]

> we also find a good deal of the patina of colonial culture [in China]. All kinds of Japanese and Western "noxious substances" are poisoning our children; disco and rock 'n' roll deafen our ears; the autobiography of Michael Jackson, the king of rock 'n' roll, has been printed in three or four translated versions; and that obscene and foul-smelling autobiography entitled *Sex* by the rock 'n' roll star Madonna, who has been called "the most shameless hussy of the century," has also been published.

The Party's official journal *Seeking Truth,* which tends to be conservative but nevertheless represents a mainstream government point of view, has likewise published articles denouncing Western "cultural imperialism." For instance, one article lamented U.S. cultural dominance (U.S. movies, it said, accounted for only 6–7 percent of world production but over half of total projection time) and claimed that the reason "international monopoly capital groups" promoted colonial culture was to turn those living in the Third World "into slaves without their knowing it." With such a slave mentality would come economic and political domination.[79]

Shortly after the embassy bombing, Fang Li, a bureau chief in the Policy Research Office of the Central Committee (of which Wang Huning is deputy head), published an article in the Central Party School's internal journal *Theoretical Trends* (*Lilun dongtai*) arguing that the "cultural diplomacy" of the United States had become a very important tool for "dividing" (*fenhua*) and "Westernizing" (*xihua*) socialist countries. In trade negotiations the United States tries anything it can to induce other nations, "especially developing nations," to open their cultural markets. The result, Fang concluded, was that "whether from a macro-perspective or a micro-perspective, the United States' cultural expansion is bound tightly with its economic expansion, so that in the course of economic exchange it [cultural expansion] can achieve the effect of 'politics in command' (*zhengzhi guashuai*)."[80]

Conclusion

BY the fall of 1999, there was palpable tension both within the political elite and among intellectuals. The sharp exchange between Wang Xiaodong and Xiao Gongqin, cited at the end of Chapter 7, was all too typical of the relations among disputants, especially those who were identified as liberals and postmodernists (the New Left). The range of opinion among intellectuals was greater than at any time in post-1949 China, but it would be more accurate to say that public opinion was fragmented than to say it had pluralized. If one part of "civil society" is civility, China had not yet reached it. Globalization, including the collapse of socialism in Eastern Europe and the Soviet Union, had provided the context for the deepening disputes between postmodernists and liberals; the WTO and the sometimes acrimonious negotiations that accompanied China's quest for accession made globalization a very real issue for intellectuals, enterprises, and bureaucrats alike. Moreover, the embassy bombing heightened emotions behind a nationalism that had been building in the context of American criticism of China, American triumphalism, and the Taiwan Straits crisis. As postmodernists and nationalists became more emotional, liberals worried openly that nationalism would once again bury hopes for democracy.

The political elite was no less divided than the intelligentsia, as suggested by the criticism of Zhu Rongji and by Jiang Zemin's delicate position vis-à-vis the military and other conservatives. These divisions were exacerbated by maneuvering that was already underway by the latter part of 1999 for the Sixteenth Party Congress – which was not scheduled to convene until the fall of 2002. At the Fifteenth Party Congress in 1997, Jiang Zemin had apparently pledged to remain as general secretary for only one more five-year term,[1] but his desire to stay on as "paramount leader" and to put his stamp on China was palpable. One clear indication came on October 1, 1999, when the country celebrated the fiftieth anniversary of the establishment of the PRC with a well-orchestrated parade that featured a huge portrait of Jiang Zemin following similarly large portraits of Mao Zedong and Deng Xiaoping – implying that Jiang was of equal stature to those two giants of CCP history.

Most intellectuals and many political leaders have declined to give Jiang that sort of respect, and Jiang appears very sensitive to slights to his leadership. After a decade as general secretary, he seems to continue to suffer from comparisons to Hua Guofeng, the ill-fated successor to Mao Zedong who yielded power to Deng Xiaoping only two years after Mao's death. Thus, Jiang was infuriated when he read a statement penned by Li Shenzhi, the aging conscience of Chinese liberalism, at the time of the National Day celebrations. By the late 1990s, Li was increasingly frustrated by the lack of political reform, the continuing conservative intellectual atmosphere, and the rise of nationalism. Having known Mao, Zhou Enlai, and Deng Xiaoping, perhaps Li could not help but think of Jiang as a mediocrity; he worried that China had entered a period of stagnation like that associated with Soviet leader Brezhnev. In any event, on the night of October 1, Li sat down and wrote a deeply moving reflection, a *crie de coeur,* on the fifty years of the PRC. Li recalled the optimism and pride that surrounded the first National Day celebration he had attended on October 1, 1949; Hu Feng's famous poem "Time Has Now Begun" captured that sense of infinite possibility. Of course, a few years later, Hu Feng was charged with leading an "anti-Party, counterrevolutionary clique," and Li himself missed the following two decennial celebrations because he was in labor camp as a "rightist." With reference to the extravagant celebration that was held in 1999, Li wrote: "The state seems to be thriving. It is said that at least 100 billion yuan were spent in preparations for celebrating National Day, all for showy purposes. Hitler is dead, and Stalin is no longer around. There should be few countries in the world that would seek such a grandiose spectacle. Maybe I am a bit old fashioned, but I suppose only a man like Kim Jong-il of Korea would have that kind of enthusiasm ...."[2]

Li went on to criticize the June 4 suppression and the unwillingness of the authorities to open up the archives on that and other events. "The cost," Li said, "is the national loss of memory and the loss of the ability to think logically among the people." He wrote dismissively of the Party general secretary: "Jiang Zemin has worn the mantle of the reign and consolidated his powers for over a decade. Although he has not contributed a bit to the founding of the People's Republic of China, he now has an iron grip on the throne, if merely because of the natural law that 'people grow old.'" Li then pleaded for Jiang to gain political merit by embarking on political reform:[3]

I have noticed that Jiang Zemin also likes to use Sun Yat-sen's words, "The currents of the world are vast and mighty; those who follow them flourish, while those who go against them perish." The problem is seeing clearly the currents of the world. Globalization is the current of the world, market economics is the current of the world, democratic politics is the current of the world, and increasing human rights is the current of the world. Those who follow these currents will flourish, and those who go against them will perish.

Zhu Rongji criticized Li by name in an internal meeting, and Jiang would respond angrily in due course, but first Jiang had to resolve the most important issue facing him and China: whether or not to accept a WTO agreement with the United States. Chinese negotiators tried hard to induce their American counterparts to accept a significant compromise that would make the agreement more acceptable to the Chinese leadership. But USTR head Charlene Barshefsky and National Economic Council director Gene Sperling, sent to Beijing on November 8 by President Clinton, refused to compromise – something that would have certainly killed prospects for passage of permanent normal trade relations in Congress. Three times the U.S. delegation packed their bags and threatened to leave Beijing. Sperling exploded in anger and Barshefsky demanded to see Zhu Rongji. The premier intervened in the talks, meeting with Barshefsky and Sperling on Saturday the 13th and then again on Monday the 15th. The logjam was broken.[4]

It had been a long and difficult summer and fall for Jiang Zemin. Clinton had urged renewing WTO negotiations when the two leaders met at the Association of Southeast Asian Nations (ASEAN) meeting in Auckland (New Zealand) in late August, but Jiang had been cool. He did send Ministry of Foreign Trade and Economic Cooperation head Shi Guangsheng to Washington in September, but Shi's purpose was more to lay out the differences separating the two countries than to find a way to bridge the gap. China's top trade negotiator, Long Yongtu, did not even accompany Shi, and the talks – originally scheduled for two days – lasted only about two hours. It was not until Jiang had made it through the Fourth Plenum in September and the National Day celebration on October 1 that he became more receptive, when President Clinton called him on October 16.[5] Any indication that he was actually eager to resume negotiations would have subjected him to all the old charges of being pro-American, which is why Jiang had to wait for Clinton's call. But it is just as true that Jiang understood the importance of gaining entrance to the WTO for reforming the economy and projecting China as one of the major powers in the world. Jiang may well have considered the possibility of jettisoning Zhu Rongji, but Jiang's wife (Wang Yeping) supported Zhu. During the summer when Zhu seemed under attack from every direction, Wang had a talk with Zhu in which she urged him to struggle on.[6] Wang supported Zhu not only because she recognized his abilities but also because she realized he was no threat to Jiang. In contrast, Li Peng, who had offered his complete support for Jiang, was a real threat, for Li had the backing of a whole group of leftists. Whether because of his wife's influence or because he reached the same conclusions on his own, Jiang – after keeping Zhu dangling for most of the summer and fall – once again made common cause with his embattled premier.

The U.S. negotiators were certainly correct in suspecting that there were those on the Chinese side who were willing to let the frustrating negotiations fizzle out. When the Politburo Standing Committee finally voted on the agreement, Li Peng was the lone dissenter as the other six members lined up in support. Formal votes of the Politburo Standing Committee are rare; open opposition to the head of the Party even rarer.[7]

The signing of the accession agreement on November 15 brought to a relative conclusion the acrimony within government circles that had surrounded the WTO issue since the spring. The agreement seemed to demonstrate Jiang's ability to manage the political and social tensions unleashed by Zhu's failure in Washington, as well as the subsequent bombing of the Chinese Embassy, and still bring about the policy outcome he desired. But even at this moment of political triumph, a scandal was unfolding that would challenge Jiang's political skills to the hilt.

On April 20, 1999, a task force was set up under the leadership of Liu Liying, daughter of Party veteran Liu Bocheng and deputy secretary of the Central Discipline Inspection Commission (CDIC), to investigate a case of corruption in Xiamen, a Fujian port that lies directly across from Taiwan. Liu was supported strongly by her superior, Wei Jianxing, the protégé of Qiao Shi who was granted the post as head of the Party watchdog organization in exchange for Qiao's stepping down at the Fifteenth Party Congress. Liu had previously headed the investigations into Chen Xitong's corruption and the Zhanjiang (Guangdong) smuggling case in 1998, which had resulted in death sentences for six people and jail terms for twenty-five others.[8]

Liu dispatched a thousand investigators to Xiamen, but finding evidence proved difficult. It turned out that the local state security bureau was tapping the phones of the investigation team and tipping off people who were under suspicion; those who were questioned refused to provide information. Liu turned to Zhu Rongji for high-level support in breaking the case, and Zhu reported the matter to Jiang Zemin. Zhu told Jiang that the case involved a massive smuggling of automobiles, telecommunications equipment, oil, and other commodities. Over $140 million of Nokia telecommunications equipment were said to be involved,[9] and, incredibly, one third of the 42 million barrels of oil believed to be smuggled into China each year was controlled by the Xiamen ring, enough to force the Daqing oil field to shut down in the face of falling oil prices.[10] Jiang backed Zhu enthusiastically, telling Zhu he had Jiang's full support in rooting out the corruption. It was a decision Jiang would soon regret.[11] Besides Wei Jianxing and Zhu Rongji, Hu Jintao played a major role because Zhu asked him to participate in the case.

In August, some 300 investigators were dispatched to Xiamen, where they took over the Jinyan Hotel. The investigation focused on Lai Changxing, a Fujian native who had immigrated to Hong Kong in 1990. After setting up several businesses in Hong Kong, Lai returned to Fujian in the mid-1990s and established the Fairwell (Yuan Hua) Company, which engaged in widespread smuggling operations. Lai was a well-known figure in Xiamen and elsewhere. He built a replica of the Forbidden City about 70 kilometers outside of Xiamen as a tourist attraction and movie set; he also paid $4 million for the local soccer team and hired a well-known coach to turn it into a winner. He ran a private club known as the Red Mansion, where he allegedly entertained the well-connected in luxurious and decadent style. He was in the process of building the Yuan Hua International Center and the Yuan Hua International Hotel when the scandal broke.[12]

Lai was apparently lavish with his bribes. According to knowledgeable observers, Lai presented over 100 Mercedes-Benz cars to high-level cadres in Beijing. The scope of his network and extent of the corruption in Xiamen is suggested by some of those arrested: Li Jizhou, the vice-minister of the Public Security Ministry; Zhuang Rushun, deputy chief of the Public Security Bureau of Fujian; Yang Qianxian, chief of Xiamen customs; Chen Yaoqing, chief of police in Xiamen; and Lan Fu, a deputy mayor of Xiamen. Altogether, more than 200 local officials were arrested. Lai Changxing himself was tipped off to his imminent arrest, allegedly by Zhuang Rushun, allowing Lai to flee to Canada (from which China is attempting to extradite him). Altogether, the case was said to involve over $10 billion worth of smuggled goods.[13]

The Xiamen case was only one of several high-profile instances of corruption that have come to light in recent years.[14] What made the case politically explosive, however, was not its size but those who appear to have been involved, directly or indirectly. One was Lin Youfang, wife of Beijing Party secretary and Politburo member Jia Qinglin. Jia was a close protégé of Jiang Zemin; they had known each other since the 1960s. Jiang had brought Jia to Beijing from Fujian (where he had served as Party secretary from 1993 to 1995) to replace Wei Jianxing, who had filled in briefly after Chen Xitong was removed from office in 1995. Jia was clearly slated to move up to the Politburo Standing Committee at the Sixteenth Party Congress and was a possible candidate to replace Zhu Rongji as premier – perhaps even earlier, if Zhu had to step down.

On December 24, Zhu met with Jia and told him to divorce his wife immediately to avoid further involvement in the corruption scandal. On January 14, Jiang Zemin gave a major address to the Fourth Plenary Session of the CDIC and declared, with reference to corruption, that "[n]o matter who it is, no matter how high the post, those who deserve punishment will be punished. There will be no leniency."[15] In a reference that could have been (but apparently was not) tailor-made for the Jia Qinglin case, Jiang warned that "leading cadres must do a good job of controlling their spouses and children."[16] He then added: "Intercession on behalf of cadres who are under investigation for involvement in irregularities is prohibited, let alone providing cover and shielding them."[17] Having said that, Jiang proceeded to do exactly what he had warned others not to do. On January 20, the *Wall Street Journal* reported that Lin Youfang had been detained for questioning – the first time the suggestion that the scandal reached all the way to the Politburo had been reported in the West[18] – but on January 24, Jiang Zemin suddenly appeared with Jia Qinglin to take a tour of Beijing's high-tech district, Zhongguancun. On January 26, the chief government spokesman declared that Lin Youfang had not been detained for questioning and had not been divorced from Jia Qinglin. The same evening, Lin Youfang made an unprecedented appearance on Phoenix television, a Hong Kong–owned station whose primary viewership – some 30 million – reside in China, to declare that she and Jia Qinglin were "very happy" together and that she had never heard of Lai Changxing. It was an extraordinary effort to defend Jia Qinglin and prevent the case from threatening Jiang Zemin.[19] In fact, the reports that Jia and Lin had divorced at Zhu Rongji's request were true, and Lin's assertion that she had never heard of Lai was simply not credible given Lai's very high-profile life in Xiamen. Jiang had, despite his promise to Zhu Rongji and his declaration to the CDIC, decided to limit the damage by declaring that no one above the vice-ministerial level should be investigated.[20] Despite Jiang's public defense of Jia, which allowed him to retain his positions for the time being and limited the damage to Jiang, the possibility of Jia continuing in office after the Sixteenth Party Congress – much less being promoted – seemed remote. By exposing Jia's situation, Zhu had eliminated a rival and reinserted himself back into leadership politics in a very forceful way.[21]

Although Jia Qinglin was the highest-ranked person publicly associated with the scandal, others were also involved. Rumors have persisted that the family of Liu Huaqing, vice-chairman of the Central Military Commission and member of the Politburo Standing Committee who stepped down from both posts at the Fifteenth Party Congress, was involved. Similar rumors plagued Chi Haotian, the current Minister of Defense and member of the Politburo. Lai Changxing reportedly had an inscription from Chi prominently displayed in his office.[22] Politburo member and Vice-Premier Wen Jiabao was apparently also tainted through the involvement of his son-in-law. In short, the scandal threatened to engulf a considerable fraction of the political elite of China.

In his January 14 speech to the CDIC, Jiang had warned that problems within the Party were sufficiently serious that they could, if not checked, destroy it.[23] Indeed, besides the increasingly serious problems of corruption within the Party, the numbers of unemployed were growing, the democratization of Asia was continuing, the legitimacy of socialism continued to wane, and entry into the WTO – although desired by China – presented both a political and economic challenge. It is no wonder, then, that the Party rolled out new campaigns to combat corruption and tighten control over ideology.

Li Shenzhi's National Day *crie de coeur* was only the boldest of many challenges to the Party's control over national memory and legitimacy. In his January talk Jiang had said, perhaps in reference to Li's essay (among others), that "some Party members and cadres are openly expressing opposition in newspapers, books, and speeches to the Party line and general and specific policies" and – with apparent reference to Tiananmen – "to the historical conclusions and decisions that the central authorities have already made on major political issues."[24] Worried that the political situation might get out of hand, Jiang resolved to tighten control over publishing.

In an unpublicized speech in January, Jiang declared: "I do not believe that our Party cannot manage well publishing houses; I do not believe that our Party cannot manage well book numbers."[25] A meeting of publishing heads in March disseminated Jiang's remarks and further cracked down on publishing. Publishing had faced numerous political difficulties since the embassy bombing the previous year, but now another 15–20 houses were suspended, reorganized, or closed. Some editors were jailed.[26] Indeed, the crackdown on editors reflected a new stage in the evolution of the Party's ongoing struggle with the publishing industry. In the past, criticism of an author was enough to turn him or her into a nonperson; the censorship system worked, for the most part. By the 1990s, however, in an effort to make money, publishing houses were increasingly selling book numbers (without which books cannot legally be published) to agents who would promise to bring in popular works.[27] With the increasing importance of the market, criticism was no longer the kiss of death; in fact, it could bring notoriety and sales, just as it often does in the West. But even Party censors must have been taken aback when Wei Hui, the young author whose *Shanghai Baby* (*Shanghai baobei*) pushed sexual frankness and youthful jaundice to new lengths, celebrated the banning of her book with a party to which she invited, among many others, foreign reporters.[28] The only targets left for the Party to go after were publishing houses and editors.

At the same time that Jiang tightened controls on publishing, he initiated a crackdown on intellectuals. As Jiang's January speech to the CDIC suggested, he was worried that liberal intellectuals were getting out of hand; Li Shenzhi is taken by many to be the spiritual leader of liberal intellectuals, and Jiang feared that Li's reflections would launch a new upsurge of liberal criticisms of the Party. (One should not forget the personal reasons – Jiang no doubt resented Li's belief that he was without political accomplishment.) The crackdown started when a student in the law department at Beijing University wrote a letter to Jiang Zemin complaining that the political theorist Liu Junning had completely ignored Marxism in a talk about Karl Popper, the philosopher whose work *The Open Society and Its Enemies* is a direct assault on Communist and authoritarian political systems, at an independent bookstore near the Beijing University campus. The student's letter was published in excerpted form and without naming Liu in *Enlightenment Daily* on March 29, but then was published in full, including Liu's name, in the leftist journal *Mainstream*.[29] Jiang wrote a note on the student's letter, telling Hu Jintao to handle the case. Hu subsequently sent a note to the Chinese Academy of Social Sciences, saying that such un-Marxist thinkers should not be allowed to stay at CASS, and Liu was subsequently forced to leave.

Liu was not the only one criticized. Li Shenzhi was criticized, and eventually a delegation from CASS visited him at his home and "educated" him. Mao Yushi, a liberal economist (and former secretary to Hu Yaobang) who was working at an independent economic think tank named Unirule, was also singled out for criticism, as was Fan Gang, a liberal but moderate economist at the private National Economic Research Institute who sometimes advises Zhu Rongji. The targets of criticism indicated the areas of Jiang Zemin's concern. Liu Junning and Li Shenzhi were criticized to signal opposition to "bourgeois liberalization" (that is to say, democracy), while Mao Yushi and Fan Gang were criticized to signal opposition to "privatization." Criticizing bourgeois liberalization was intended to appeal to conservative elders, who continue to play a role on leadership issues, while criticizing privatization was intended to check Zhu Rongji, whose exposure of Jia Qinglin was an embarrassment to Jiang.

In April, Li Peng – apparently frustrated by his failure to stop China's accession into the WTO, embarrassed by the exposure of his wife's corruption, and angry that Jiang was unlikely to allow him a second term as head of the NPC – endorsed for the first time the three leftist journals (*Mainstream, Quest for Truth,* and *Contemporary Thought*). The only part of Li's endorsement that appeared publicly was praise for an article in the relatively obscure journal *Quest for Truth* by conservative ideologue Yu Quanyu.[30] The article by Yu was a harsh attack on privatization, and Li's endorsement amounted to an attack on the policies of Jiang Zemin and Zhu Rongji. Between Zhu's pursuit of the Xiamen corruption case (following his own near demise) and Li Peng's open endorsement of the Old Left, one could say that leadership politics were anything but stable as China entered the new millennium.

It is into this context that one must put Jiang's latest initiative, the so-called "three representatives" campaign. In late February of 2000, Jiang Zemin traveled to Guangdong province where he inspected high-tech industries in the Shenzhen SEZ and elsewhere. After listening to reports on the ongoing "three stresses" (*sanjiang*) campaign, the rectification effort Jiang launched in 1998 to strengthen his political control, Jiang gave a speech in which he introduced new and potentially important ideological theses. Jiang claimed that, in summing up the Party's history, one could conclude that it had always represented the most advanced productive forces, the most advanced culture, and the fundamental interests of the broad masses of the Chinese people. This formulation, summed up as the "three representatives" (*sange daibiao*), is the sort of ideological exposition that makes Americans' eyes glaze over. It shouldn't. In summing up the Party's history in this fashion, Jiang managed to avoid saying anything about upholding the Four Cardinal Principles. Obviously, he was not dropping such prohibitions, but there was a palpable shift in emphasis.

Jiang's call for representing advanced culture left room for opposition to bourgeois liberalization and upholding socialist values, but Jiang also stressed – as he had in recent years – absorbing the "fine cultural achievements of foreign countries" and the "fine cultural traditions of the Chinese nation." The influence of the discussions on culture contained in such books as *Heart-to-Heart Talks with the General Secretary* and *The Critical Moment* (discussed in Chapter 6) was apparent. Jiang's demand to represent the development of "advanced social productive forces" certainly justified the further adjustment of the Chinese economy in the wake of the WTO agreement, a move ratified by the Party's Fifth Plenum in October 2000 (which also endorsed the "three representatives").[31] Zheng Bijian, vice-president of the Central Party School and one of the primary theoreticians of the Party, made clear in his explication of the "three representatives" that Jiang's remarks were intended to meet the demands of globalization and international competition, particularly the rapid development of science and technology. Zheng said that the Party had "seen clearly" that the domestic and international environment in which the Party found itself was undergoing "broad and profound changes" and that the Party needed to change to meet those challenges. The Party needed to maintain ideological unity and organizational integrity in the face of a diversifying society.[32]

From Zheng's remarks, it is apparent that the Party needed to explain how it, as a workers' party, could allow millions of workers to be laid off. Zheng Bijian argues that, inevitably, some productive forces that are no longer in the forefront need to be weeded out and workers let off. "But this does not mean that the Chinese working class has lost its advanced nature, much less that the working class is no longer the foundation of the CCP. Exactly the opposite. In the course of contemporary China's strategic adjustment of its socioeconomic structure and particularly its industrial structure, the overall quality and superiority of the Chinese working class is being raised to a new level." Zheng talks about the role of intellectuals, particularly those who understand high technology, as part of the working class and about the need to remake the working class.[33] Whereas Dengist doctrine made intellectuals a part of the working class, Jiang seems to be coming close to saying that intellectuals are the most advanced part of the working class. Perhaps borrowing a page from Bill Clinton and Tony Blair, Jiang seems to be trying to declare himself a new Communist.

From a theoretical point of view, the most interesting of Jiang's three representatives is his call for the Party to represent the fundamental interests of the broad masses of the Chinese people. This formulation leaves room for ambiguity, but it moves away from traditional notions of the Communist Party representing the vanguard of the working class and toward the notion that it represents the interests of all the people. The notion of an "all people's party" has long been an anathema to Marxist doctrine in China, but Jiang's formulation clearly edges in that direction, as both proponents and detractors of the "three representatives" note. It is a formulation that leaves the door open for political reform (in particular, voting might demonstrate that individual Party leaders really did "represent" the people). There are people in the Party studying the issue of whether (and, if so, how) to make political reform a major part of the Sixteenth Party Congress in 2002. Jiang's formulation does not guarantee that the CCP will move in this direction, but it does open up that possibility.

A decade after going into a protective shell, decrying the threat from "peaceful evolution," and wheeling out an arsenal of already outdated ideological formulas to defend the reimposition of conservative policies, China has largely dropped the rhetoric associated with the Old Left and is clearly joining the world. But doing so – and the terms on which it joins the world – have been controversial at both the elite and popular levels. As we have seen, neoconservatism and later neostatism defended the role of a strong state during a period of political transition, while nationalism and the intellectual critique of globalization generated by postmodernist critics resisted the embrace of the international economy and world political order. At times of international conflict – such as the failure of China's Olympic bid, the 1995–96 Taiwan Straits crisis, and especially the May 1999 bombing of the Chinese Embassy – such intellectual critiques resonated strongly with popular nationalism. Global capital also generated economic nationalism, as enterprises and bureaucracies tried to defend their vested interests.

So far, however, economic and political trends have overwhelmed these urges to keep the world at arm's length. As China's top WTO negotiator Long Yongtu commented, China's gradual willingness to accept the far-reaching commitments necessary for accession to the world trade group paralleled the deepening of China's domestic reforms. The acceptance of the term "market economy" (even if modified by the term "socialist") at the Fifteenth Party Congress in 1997 was a major step forward; the old planned economy was giving ground in the face of the ever-expanding nonstate and foreign-invested sectors.[34] Increasingly, there was an economic and political constituency pulling for China's further integration into the world economy. And nationalism, in the cosmopolitan sense, could be a force for economic integration as well as a force resisting it. Joining the WTO clearly appealed to the sense of many (and particularly of Jiang Zemin) that doing so would mark China's coming of age as a major economic power. These were the forces that propelled Jiang to send Zhu Rongji to the United States in April 1999.

The failure of Zhu's trip, compounded shortly thereafter by the embassy bombing, threw open all the old questions and threatened to reverse the relatively smooth political transition that Jiang was engineering. For a while, nationalism, Old Left ideology, and bureaucratic interest combined with nearly unstoppable force. The delicate balance among different leadership interests that Jiang had contrived over the previous years was thrown wildly out of whack, as Li Peng tried to bring down Zhu Rongji, as Jiang considered his options should Zhu fall, and as Zhu counterattacked through his investigation of the Xiamen and other corruption cases, undermining both Li and Jiang. Charging one's opponents (or their close followers) with corruption – a charge that seems increasingly true of most officials – had become the weapon of choice for political maneuver. Perhaps this is an improvement over the old technique of charging one's rivals with ideological deviance or laxity, but it nevertheless highlights the continued fragility of political relations at the top level.

At the same time, "public opinion" – in the form of books, articles, Internet notices, speeches, and, in May 1999, demonstrations – was fully engaged by the issues of globalization and nationalism. But it was deeply divided. As we have seen, the division between the postmodernists/New Left and the liberals was driven to an extreme when postmodernists attacked liberals as lackeys of the United States and liberals returned the compliment by accusing the New Left of being fascist (or at least abetting fascism).[35] Most illustrative of the polarization and passion that had grown up among intellectuals was the position of Xiao Gongqin, a person of liberal desires who was intellectually persuaded that neoauthoritarianism/neoconservatism was the best way to realize those desires. His warning against extreme nationalism is one of the most important writings to come out in recent years.

Jiang's efforts in early 2000 to stabilize the political situation and shore up his own political standing – by cracking down on publishing houses, criticizing liberal intellectuals, continuing to root out the unexpectedly tenacious Falun Gong movement, and trying to establish himself as a politician with vision through his "three representatives" campaign – reflected the very complex political and social situation that China faced at the beginning of the new century. Public opinion was no longer something that could be ignored. Both postmodernist and liberal intellectuals were – each in their different ways – harshly critical of the corruption, inequality, and abuse of power that has permeated the political economy of China. Cracking down on publishing houses was perhaps a backhanded way of acknowledging that publishing and public opinion had, a decade after their harsh suppression in the wake of Tiananmen, once again become forces in Chinese public life – indeed, more important than they had been a decade ago. The effort to transform Party ideology through the "three representatives" campaign was similarly an acknowledgment of the profound changes Chinese society had experienced in the previous decade as well as recognition that more orthodox interpretations of Marxism, even in attenuated form, no longer had any force in Chinese society. Whether or not Jiang can take the route that he seemed to leave open – that of carrying out political reform to make the Party better represent the interests of the "broad masses" of the Chinese people – remains to be seen.

Epilogue

In the decade following the Tiananmen crisis, reform in China continued, however unevenly, to move forward. The inability of conservatives to fashion a viable economic policy during this period meant that the political leadership was forced not only to turn once again to economic reform but also to accelerate its reforms, allowing the private economy to expand rapidly, encouraging state-owned enterprises to issue shares, and attracting unprecedented levels of foreign investment. Deng Xiaoping's trip to the south in 1992 and the passing from the scene of such Party elders as the conservative economic policy specialist Chen Yun and Jiang Zemin's primary political supporter Li Xiannian (also a conservative) provided new room for economic reformers, while the mounting difficulties of the state-owned sector (made more pressing by the prospect of China's entry into the World Trade Organization) increased pressures to take increasingly bold steps in reforming the economy. The result was that the government largely ignored the rising tide of social criticism from the New Left that pointed to growing inter- and intraregional inequalities and that questioned China's commitment to globalization. Even as the government benefited to some extent from increased nationalist sentiment, it ignored calls to say "no" to the United States and to the global economy. In the area of political reform, growing commercialization accelerated the state's retreat from society, while reformers began to redefine the role of the state and to experiment with village elections (which began in 1988 and have now spread, however imperfectly, to most of China's 900,000 villages).

The bombing of the Chinese Embassy in Belgrade in May 1999 and the subsequent outpouring of nationalist sentiment threatened to a certain extent the delicate balance that had kept reform moving forward. Leadership tensions were exposed in that crisis and again in various large-scale corruption cases. The shadow of the Sixteenth Party Congress, scheduled for the fall of 2002, loomed over these various conflicts. In the fall of 2000, it was widely expected that Jiang Zemin's protégé Zeng Qinghong would be promoted from alternate status on the Politburo to full membership in that body. That move would have

Epilogue

prepared the way for Zeng to be promoted to the Politburo Standing Committee at the Sixteenth Party Congress, thus allowing Jiang Zemin, who is expected to retire then as general secretary, to continue to exercise a great deal of political influence from behind the scenes. However, Zeng's promotion never occurred; several members of the Politburo Standing Committee successfully opposed Jiang's plans, opening new questions about the political succession and heightening tensions within the leadership.

Shortly thereafter, in December 2000, Xu Junping – a senior colonel in the People's Liberation Army who had served as head of the Americas Bureau at the Foreign Affairs Office of the Central Military Commission – defected to the United States. Then *The Tiananmen Papers,* purporting to be official documents chronicling the leadership's decision to crack down on student protestors in 1989, were published: first in an English volume in January; and then, in April, in a two-volume Chinese edition. In late January, adherents of the banned Falun Gong sect set themselves on fire in Tiananmen Square, perhaps in response to urgings from Li Hongzhi (the group's spiritual leader) to resist the government's ongoing crackdown. This series of challenges appears to be related – though precisely how is uncertain – to the detention in early 2001 of several ethnic Chinese scholars who have either permanent resident status or citizenship in the United States.

These events were deeply troubling for China's leadership, already beset by internal conflict. At least some people in security and foreign policy circles seem to believe that the United States had a hand in these events, perhaps trying to use the Falun Gong and the release of *The Tiananmen Papers* to destabilize or bring down the Chinese government. This anxiety was not allayed by statements coming from the newly installed Bush administration. The new administration sought to downgrade relations with China, describing China as a "strategic competitor" (rather than "strategic partner" as President Clinton had said), building stronger ties with Japan and other countries in the region, strengthening the American commitment to Taiwan, and embarking on a National Missile Defense system (which China sees as directed toward itself).

It was in this atmosphere that on April 1, 2001, a Chinese F-8 fighter collided with an American EP-3 surveillance plane off the coast of Hainan island in the South China Sea. Emotions ran extremely high in both countries as the twenty-four American crew members were kept on Hainan for eleven days while diplomats worked out a solution. The Chinese government and citizenry blamed the incident – erroneously, it appears – on the movements of the American plane and the government demanded an apology, while many Americans saw the incident as an expression of an increasingly assertive and militaristic

China. Internet chat rooms in both countries were filled with overheated nationalist and sometimes racist sentiment.

This book goes to press shortly after the crew has been released but while the American aircraft remains on Hainan, so it is difficult to assess the long-term impact of this incident. Perhaps it will turn out to be a blip on the screen; after all, the Sino–U.S. relationship is a multidimensional one involving large economic benefits (bilateral trade in 2000 totaled $125 billion) as well as overlapping political interests and cultural ties. However, reassessment of the relationship's value appears to be going on in both Washington and Beijing. If the result is continued friction, then the nationalist sentiments whose growth and evolution have been detailed in the previous pages will no doubt be strengthened, making political reform more difficult.

In short, the international atmosphere will continue to interact with domestic socioeconomic and intellectual trends to shape China's response to its own needs and its external environment. How this will affect the restructuring of the political leadership at the Sixteenth Party Congress – and how those changes, in turn, will shape China's efforts to deal with its domestic pressures and international challenges – will affect not only the lives of one fifth of the world's population but perhaps also the peace and stability of the Western Pacific.

Notes

INTRODUCTION

1. Steven Lee Myers, "Chinese Embassy Bombing."
2. Liu Yiqing, "Na chengshi zuo jiaoyi"; Erik Eckholm, "After an Attack, Chinese Won't Print Expatriate's Novel."
3. Richard Bernstein and Ross H. Munro, *The Coming Conflict with China.*
4. Alastair Iain Johnston and Robert S. Ross (Eds.), *Engaging China*; Elizabeth Economy and Michel Oksenberg (Eds.), *China Joins the World.*
5. On the pessimistic side lie Edward Friedman, *National Identity and Democratic Prospects in Socialist China,* and James Miles, *The Legacy of Tiananmen.* For a survey of potential outcomes, see Richard Baum, "China After Deng: Ten Scenarios in Search of Reality."
6. "Destructive Engagement."
7. Robert Kagan, "What China Knows That We Don't." See also Robert Kagan, "The Canary in the Chinese Coal Mine" and "China: The End of Engagement."
8. Patrick Tyler, *A Great Wall.*
9. "Clinton's China Syndrome."
10. Andrew Nathan and Perry Link (Eds.) and Zhang Liang (Comp.), *The Tiananmen Papers.* On the Blue Team, see Steven Mufson and Robert G. Kaiser, " 'Blue Team' Draws a Hard Line on Beijing." In this vein is Bill Gertz, *The China Threat.* Donald Rumsfeld, President Bush's Secretary of Defense, oversaw the 1998 Rumsfeld Report, which identified China's missiles as a possible threat to the United States. See Paul H. B. Godwin and Evan S. Medeiros, "China, America, and Missile Defense," p. 287.
11. Ezra Vogel (Ed.), *Living with China*; James Shinn (Ed.), *Weaving the Net.*
12. Tang Tsou, "Prolegomenon to the Study of Informal Groups in CCP Politics," p. 99.
13. Zou Dang [Tsou Tang], *Ershi shiji Zhongguo zhengzhi,* p. 244.
14. Giovanni Sartori, *Parties and Party Systems.*
15. Juan J. Linz and Alfred Stepan, *Problems of Democratic Transition and Consolidation,* p. 16.
16. Ibid., p. 26 (italics in original).
17. The phrase is from Juan J. Linz and Alfred Stepan, "Toward Consolidated Democracies."
18. Jose Guilherme Merquior, quoted in Merilee S. Grindle, "The Good Government Imperative," p. 3.

19. Mary E. Hilderbrand and Merilee S. Grindle, "Building Sustainable Capacity in the Public Sector."
20. World Bank, *The State in a Changing World.*
21. Stephen Holmes, "Cultural Legacies or State Collapse?"
22. Linz and Stepan, "Toward Consolidated Democracies"; Linz and Stepan, *Problems of Democratic Transition and Consolidation.*
23. Minxin Pei has argued that China's approach of concentrating first on economic reform will allow China to transform itself politically; see his book entitled *From Reform to Revolution.*
24. Guillermo O'Donnell and Philippe C. Schmitter, *Transitions from Authoritarian Rule.*
25. Joseph Fewsmith, "The Impact of Reform on Elite Politics."
26. Deng Xiaoping, "On the Reform of the System of Party and State Leadership," p. 316.
27. For instance, the 1983 publication of Deng's selected works preceded the adoption of the critical Decision on Economic Structural Reform.
28. Melanie Manion, *Retirement of Revolutionary Cadres in China.*
29. Hong Yung Lee, *From Revolutionary Cadres to Party Technocrats in Socialist China.* See also Hong Yung Lee, "China's New Bureaucracy?"
30. Yasheng Huang, *Inflation and Investment Controls in China.*
31. Barry Naughton, *Growing Out of the Plan.*
32. Nicholas Lardy, *Foreign Trade and Economic Reform in China, 1978–1990.*
33. Murray Scot Tanner, *The Politics of Lawmaking in China*; Stanley Lubman, *Bird in a Cage.*
34. Adam Przeworski, *Democracy and the Market*; Adam Przeworski et al., *Sustainable Democracy.*
35. Tang Tsou, "The Tiananmen Tragedy."
36. Vera Schwarcz, *The Chinese Enlightenment.*
37. Deng Xiaoping, "Speech at the Opening Ceremony of the National Conference on Science," p. 113.
38. Mao Tse-tung [Mao Zedong], "The Yenan Forum on Literature and Art."
39. X. L. Ding, *The Decline of Communism in China.*
40. The best discussion of these trends is Chen Fong-ching and Jin Guantao, *From Youthful Manuscripts to River Elegy.*
41. Xu Jilin, *Ling yizhong qimeng,* pp. 8–15.
42. The best compendium of intellectual debates in the 1990s is Zhang Ming and Li Shitao (Eds.), *Zhishi fenzi lichang.*
43. Merle Goldman, *Sowing the Seeds of Democracy in China.*
44. Joseph Fewsmith, *Dilemmas of Reform.*
45. Carol Lee Hamrin and Timothy Cheek (Eds.), *China's Establishment Intellectuals.*
46. Chen Fong-ching and Jin Guantao, *From Youthful Manuscripts to River Elegy.*
47. The important changes that have taken place as a result of generational change are explored in Cheng Li, *China's Leaders.*
48. There are exceptions to this generalization, as many intellectuals have become much more specialized than before – a trend that reflects an important change in the intellectual community. The government can and does tap the expertise of intellectuals

at universities and think tanks, but such advice tends to be issue-specific rather than the broader advocacy of policy orientation that dominated in the 1980s. This trend toward expertise suggests a maturation in both the government and the intellectual community.

49. Joseph Fewsmith and Stanley Rosen, "The Domestic Context of Chinese Foreign Policy."
50. One exception to this generalization is that economists could report and analyze the failings of the economy in this period, thus influencing the debate.
51. Stanley Rosen, "Youth and Social Change in the PRC."
52. I have no direct knowledge of whether the students at Beijing University were told to raise the somewhat hostile questions that they did. I have been told that, when Secretary of State Warren Christopher visited Fudan University and government officials wanted to get a point across, every student in the audience had been given the same question to ask if called on first.
53. I do not want to portray the government as open-minded and "liberal" or suggest that all intellectuals line up on the side of nationalism. As we will see in later chapters, there is a significant community of liberal intellectuals that has experienced considerable government pressure, particularly in early 2000. I refer here to the growth of nationalism and opposition to the WTO because these attitudes are in such striking contrast to those prevailing a decade ago.

CHAPTER 1

1. In the reform period, different conceptions of the scope, pace, and goal of reform grew up around Chen Yun on the one hand and Deng Xiaoping on the other. Although Chen never challenged Deng's "core" status directly, he and his colleagues did develop a systematic critique of Deng's approach to reform. This critique was used to try to limit reform. The conservative critique of reform became the basis for criticizing a whole series of policies, and implicitly Deng's leadership, in the post-Tiananmen period. It thus seems appropriate to refer to this struggle as a "line" struggle, even if it remained implicit. For a discussion of the conflict between Chen and Deng, see Joseph Fewsmith, *Dilemmas of Reform.*
2. Deng Xiaoping, "Zai jiejian shoudu jieyan budui junyishang ganbu shi de jianghua," p. 302.
3. Tang Tsou, "Chinese Politics at the Top."
4. Stuart R. Schram, "General Introduction," p. xix.
5. Deng, "Zai jiejian shoudu jieyan budui junyishang ganbu shi de jianghua."
6. Ibid.
7. Deng Xiaoping, "Zucheng yige shixing gaige de you xiwang de ling dao jiti." According to *The Tiananmen Papers* (p. 262), Deng first proposed Tianjin Party Secretary Li Ruihuan to be general secretary.
8. Deng Xiaoping, ibid. The full text of Deng's remarks is reportedly far more scathing than the passages included in Deng's selected works.
9. Nathan, Link, and Zhang, *The Tiananmen Papers,* p. 262.
10. Bruce Gilley, *Tiger on the Brink,* pp. 3–23; Yang Zhongmei, *Jiang Zemin zhuan,* pp. 45–59.

11. Gilley, *Tiger on the Brink,* pp. 37–62; Yang, *Jiang Zemin zhuan,* pp. 70–90.
12. Gilley, *Tiger on the Brink,* pp. 64–98; Yang, *Jiang Zemin zhuan,* pp. 106–18, 145–59.
13. Richard Baum, *Burying Mao,* pp. 251–5.
14. Gao Xin, *Jiang Zemin de muliao,* p. 207.
15. Nathan, Link, and Zhang, *The Tiananmen Papers,* p. 135.
16. Gao Xin, *Jiang Zemin de muliao,* pp. 210–11.
17. Ibid., pp. 211–12.
18. One can draw distinctions between Zhao and Deng, but the similarities predominate. Overall, Zhao appears to have been closer to Deng on most issues than Hu Yaobang. Although Zhao was more open-minded than Deng in his response to the Tiananmen demonstrations, Zhao was hardly a liberal. After all, it was Zhao who sponsored discussions on the "new authoritarianism." The Thirteenth Party Congress, which clearly bears Zhao's imprint, was strongly supported by Deng. On economic issues, Deng was in some sense the more radical, or at least the more impatient, as suggested by his 1988 advocacy of rapid price reform. Certainly in the eyes of their critics, the similarities were far greater than the differences.
19. Tang Tsou, "Political Change and Reform."
20. Nathan, Link, and Zhang, *The Tiananmen Papers,* pp. 184–93; author interviews.
21. Author interview.
22. "Zhongguo gongchandang disanjie zhongyang weiyuanhui disice quanti huiyi gongbao," p. 544.
23. Chen Xitong, "Report on Checking the Turmoil and Quelling the Counter-Revolutionary Rebellion," p. 29.
24. Ibid., p. 21.
25. "Li Peng's Life-Taking Report Lays Blame on Zhao Ziyang," pp. 21, 22, 23.
26. "Full text" of speech delivered by Zhao Ziyang, pp. 17, 18, 19.
27. Ibid., p. 17.
28. "Zhongguo gongchandang disanjie zhongyang weiyuanhui disice quanti huiyi gongbao," pp. 543–6.
29. Xinhua News Service, in Foreign Broadcast Information Service, *China Daily Report* (hereafter FBIS-CHI), July 12, 1989, p. 25.
30. Tseng Pin, "Party Struggle Exposed by Senior Statesmen Themselves"; see also *Wen wei po,* July 24, 1989.
31. *Ta kung pao,* July 22, 1989, trans. FBIS-CHI, July 24, 1989.
32. Jiang Zemin, "Zai qingzhu Zhonghua renmin gongheguo chengli sishi zhounian dahuishang de jianghua," p. 618.
33. Deng Xiaoping, "Zucheng yige shixing gaige de you xiwang de lingdao jiti," p. 297.
34. Zhao Ziyang, "Further Emancipate the Mind and Further Liberate the Productive Forces."
35. Song Ping, "Zai quanguo zuzhi buzhang huiyi shang de jianghua," pp. 568–9, 574; emphasis added. Contrast Song's emphasis on political loyalty with Li Ruihuan's statement that, "[i]n assessing a leading cadre, his accomplishments in government are primary." See *Nanfang ribao,* October 28, 1989, trans. FBIS-CHI, November 6, 1989, p. 22.

36. Lo Ping and Li Tzu-ching, "Chen Yun Raises Six Points of View to Criticize Deng Xiaoping."

37. "More than Seventy Writers and Artists Attend a Forum to Study the Spirit of the Fourth Plenary Session."

38. Gong Yantao, "The Essence of 'Transformation' Is to Abolish Ideological and Political Work"; Yao Fan, "How Comrade Zhao Ziyang Weakened the Party's Ideological and Political Work"; Liu Shi, "The Purpose of 'Transformation' Is to Pave the Way for Capitalism."

39. Dong Jinguan, "The Main Characteristics of Class Struggle at the Present Stage," p. 44.

40. AFP, April 30, 1987, in FBIS-CHI, May 4, 1987, p. G2.

41. The sense of Zhao's speech was conveyed by two *People's Daily* editorials: "Deepen the Struggle against Bourgeois Liberalization" and "We Must Not Only Persevere in Reform and Opening Up but Also Speed Them Up." The speech was subsequently published on June 15, 1987. On the drafting, see Guoguang Wu, " 'Documentary Politics'."

42. *People's Daily* restored language that had been deleted when the speech was originally published in 1983. For a comparison, see FBIS-CHI, July 7, 1987, p. K22.

43. Baum, *Burying Mao,* p. 319.

44. Deng Xiaoping, "Disandai lingdao jiti de dangwu zhiji," p. 312.

45. See, for instance, Beijing television service, August 24, 1989, trans. FBIS-CHI, August 25, 1989, pp. 15–16.

46. "Li Ruihuan Meets with Hong Kong Journalists."

47. Deng Xiaoping, "Disandai lingdao jiti de dangwu zhiji."

48. "Zhonggong Zhongyang, Guowuyuan guanyu jinqi zuo jijian qunzhong guanxin de shi de jueding," pp. 555–7.

49. Deng apparently first used this phrase in his October 31, 1989, talk with Richard Nixon. See Deng Xiaoping, "Jiesu yanjun de ZhongMei guanxi yao you Meiguo caiqu zhudong," p. 331.

50. Deng Xiaoping, "Women you xinxin ba Zhongguo de shiqing zuode genghao," p. 327.

51. *Renmin ribao,* September 22, 1989.

52. "Decision of the Central Committee of the Communist Party of China on Reform of the Economic Structure."

53. Fewsmith, *Dilemmas of Reform,* pp. 133–5.

54. Deng Xiaoping, "Zai jiejian shoudu jieyan budui junyishang ganbu shi de jianghua," p. 306.

55. Fewsmith, *Dilemmas of Reform,* chapter 3.

56. Baum, *Burying Mao,* p. 294.

57. "Zhonggong Zhongyang guanyu jinyibu zhili zhengdun he shenhua gaige de jueding (zhaiyao)."

58. Jiang Zemin, "Zai dang de shisanjie wuzhong quanhui shangde jianghua," p. 711.

59. Some within the Party argued that the implementation of reform in Eastern Europe had led to the collapse of communism there, while others argued that communism collapsed because the planned economy had continued to prevail in those countries. Wu Jinglian, *Jihua jingji haishi shichang jingji,* p. 41.

60. Wang Renzhi, "Guanyu fandui zichan jieji ziyouhua." See also the harsh speech Wang delivered to *Qiushi* staffers in August, "Lilun gongzuo mianlin de xin qingkuang he dangqian de zhuyao renwu."

61. Yi Ren, "Zhuozhuo huiyi de qianqian houhou."

62. *Hong Kong Standard,* December 18, 1989, in FBIS-CHI, December 20, 1989, p. 22; *Ching chi tao pao* 50, December 18, 1989, trans. FBIS-CHI, December 20, 1989, pp. 22–3.

63. *Ching chi tao pao,* ibid.

64. *Jinrong shibao,* January 30, 1990, trans. FBIS-CHI, February 14, 1990, pp. 24–5.

65. See Ma Hong, "Have a Correct Understanding of the Economic Situation"; Zhang Zhuoyuan, "Promoting Economic Rectification by Deepening Reform"; Li Chengrui, "Some Thoughts on Sustained, Steady, and Coordinated Development"; and Wang Jiye, "Several Questions on Achieving Overall Balance and Restructuring."

66. Li Peng, "Wei woguo zhengzhi jingji he shehui de jinyibu wending fazhan er fendou."

67. Barry Naughton, *Growing Out of the Plan,* p. 275.

68. Ibid., p. 281 and p. 347, note 2.

69. Ibid., pp. 284–5.

70. Ho Te-hsu, "China Has Crossed the Nadir of the Valley but Is Still Climbing Up from the Trough."

71. Wu Jinglian, *Jihua jingji haishi shichang jingji,* pp. 12–13.

72. Ibid., p. 14. Wu does not specify which leaders raised this issue.

73. Ibid., p. 25; see also "Yi gaige cu wending zai wending zhong fazhan."

74. Xinhua, July 24, 1988, in FBIS-CHI, July 25, 1988, pp. 42–3.

75. Shen Liren and Dai Yuanchen, "Woguo 'zhuhou jingji' de xingcheng ji qi biduan he genyuan."

76. For an influential study of this issue, which will be discussed in Chapter 5, see Hu Angang and Wang Shaoguang, *Jiaqiang zhongyang zhengfu zai shichang jingji zhuanxing zhong de zhudao zuoyong.*

77. *Jingji daobao,* November 5, 1990, as cited in Willy Lam, *China after Deng Xiaoping,* p. 56.

78. Baum, *Burying Mao,* pp. 326–8.

79. A third reason to support higher growth rates was that a greater percentage of the growth would necessarily occur outside the scope of the plan and thus limit the ability of such conservative bureaucratic organs as the SPC to restrict reform.

80. Gao Xin and He Pin, *Zhu Rongji zhuan,* p. 212.

81. Deng Xiaoping, "Disandai lingdao jiti de dangwu zhiji," p. 310.

82. Deng Xiaoping, "Jiesu yanjun de ZhongMei guanxi yao you Meiguo caiqu zhudong," p. 331.

83. Harry Harding, *The Fragile Relationship,* p. 236.

84. Jiang Zemin, "Zai qingzhu Zhonghua renmin gongheguo chengli sishi zhounian dahuishang de jianghua," p. 631.

85. Deng Xiaoping, "Jiesu yanjun de ZhongMei guanxi yao you Meiguo caiqu zhudong," p. 332.

86. Harding, *The Fragile Relationship,* p. 254.

87. Beijing radio, December 1, 1990.

CHAPTER 2

1. Lo Ping, "Report on Deng Xiaoping's Behind-the-Scenes Activities."
2. Guangdong radio, November 27, 1990, trans. FBIS-CHI, November 29, 1990, pp. 36–7.
3. Deng Xiaoping, "Shicha Shanghai shi de tanhua," p. 364.
4. Wei Yung-cheng, "Reveal the Mystery of Huangfu Ping," p. 19.
5. Jiang Zemin, "Zai dang de shisanjie qizhong quanhui bimushi de jianghua."
6. "Zhongguo gongchandang dishisanjie zhongyang weiyuanhui diqice quanti huiyi gongbao"; emphasis added.
7. Cited in Liu Pi, "Deng Xiaoping Launches 'Northern Expedition' to Emancipate Mind."
8. The four commentaries were published on February 15, March 2, March 22, and April 12, 1991. The writers of the Huangfu Ping articles were Zhou Ruijin, Ling He, and Shi Zhihong. See Wei Yung-cheng, "Reveal the Mystery of Huangfu Ping." According to Gao Xin and He Pin, the galleys of each article were personally approved by Deng's daughter, Deng Nan (see *Zhu Rongji zhuan,* p. 218).
9. Huangfu Ping, "The Consciousness of Expanding Opening Needs to Be Strengthened."
10. Huangfu Ping, "Reform and Opening Require a Large Number of Cadres with Both Morals and Talents."
11. Huangfu Ping, "The Consciousness of Expanding Opening Needs to Be Strengthened."
12. In making this argument, Lin was paraphrasing, no doubt deliberately, the argument made thirteen years earlier by Hu Qiaomu in his famous 1978 report to the State Council, "Act in Accordance with Economic Laws, Step Up the Four Modernizations." Lin Ruo, "Dui fazhan shehui zhuyi shangpin jingji de jidian renshi."
13. Tan Shaowen, "Emancipate the Mind, Seek Truth from Facts, Be United as One, and Do Solid Work."
14. Cheng Weigao, "Further Emancipate the Mind and Renew the Concept, and Accelerate the Pace of Reform and Development."
15. "Increase Weight of Reform, Promote Economic Development: Speech Delivered by Wu Guanzheng at the Provincial Structural Reform Work Conference."
16. Luo Xiaolu, "Chen Xitong tan jiefang sixiang." See also Sun Yushan, "Chen Xitong Points Out at a Municipal Supervision Work Conference That Supervision Departments Should Emancipate Their Minds in Carrying Out Work."
17. Chen Chien-ping, "China Stresses Modernization of Science and Technology."
18. Xinhua, April 23, 1991, in FBIS-CHI, April 24, 1991, pp. 18–19.
19. "March toward the New Scientific and Technological Revolution."
20. However, this acknowledgment did not stop Jiang from saying in his Party Day (July 1) speech that men, not weapons, were the most important thing in war. See Jiang Zemin, "Zai qingzhu Zhongguo gongchandang chengli qishi zhounian dahuishang de jianghua."
21. Gao Xin and He Pin, *Zhu Rongji zhuan,* pp. 70–2.
22. Ibid., p. 170.
23. Ibid., pp. 173–8.

24. Interenterprise (triangular) debts were debts that accrued between suppliers, producers, and buyers. These debts accrued as enterprises sent – in accordance with mandatory plans – materials or finished products to others but received little or no payment in return.
25. The Leading Group for the Resolution of Triangular Debt was established in March 1990 with Zou Jiahua in charge. At that time, triangular debt amounted to over 100 billion yuan (up from 32 billion yuan in 1988). Despite a State Council circular setting a four-month deadline for the clearing of such debt and despite state expenditures of about 160 billion yuan, enterprise indebtedness by the end of 1990 was nearing 150 billion yuan. *China Daily,* July 6, 1991.
26. Gao Xin and He Pin, *Zhu Rongji zhuan,* pp. 242–56.
27. Zhu Rongji, "Summarize Experiences in Clearing Debt Defaults and Preventing New Defaults to Ensure Sound Development of the National Economy."
28. Defiance of Li Ruihuan's leadership of ideological work was evident not only from the speeches of such leaders as Wang Renzhi and Song Ping and from Gao Di's management of the *People's Daily,* but also from such specific comments as Wang Renzhi's December 1989 claim that the campaign against pornography, championed by Li, "certainly cannot replace opposing bourgeois liberalization." See *"Deng Xiaoping lun wenyi* yantaohui zaijing juxing."
29. *Renmin ribao,* January 18, 1991, trans. FBIS-CHI, January 22, 1991, p. 18.
30. Chen Yuan, "Wo guo jingji de shenceng wenti he xuanze (gangyao)"; Joseph Fewsmith, "Neoconservatism and the End of the Dengist Era"; Gao Xin and He Pin, *Zhonggong "taizidang,"* pp. 97–124.
31. Xinhua, May 15, 1991, in FBIS-CHI, May 17, 1991, p. 22. Although there is no obvious difference in meaning between this aphorism and Deng's favorite slogan, "seek truth from facts," Chen always used his own phraseology and never reiterated Deng's slogan.
32. Liu Pi, "Deng Xiaoping Launches 'Northern Expedition' to Emancipate Mind"; Lam, *China after Deng Xiaoping,* p. 434, note 35.
33. "Why Must We Unremittingly Oppose Bourgeois Liberalization?"
34. It should be noted that by mid- to late April, just as the *People's Daily* was reprinting the *Contemporary Trends* article, Gorbachev was once again turning toward radical reform – which also scared conservatives into taking a harder line. Though it seems inconsistent, it can be argued that Chinese conservatives reacted to both a tightening up and a political relaxation in the Soviet Union by calling for ideological orthodoxy in China. In the former they would see confirmation of the need to prevent reform from getting out of control, and in the latter they would see a hostile foreign environment that would necessitate a reassertion of socialist values at home.
35. Jiang Zemin, "Zai qingzhu Zhongguo gongchandang chengli qishi zhounian dahuishang de jianghua," pp. 1647, 1640, 1646, 1639, and 1638.
36. "Build Up a Great Wall of Steel against Peaceful Evolution."
37. Qin Si, "Wenyiwen 'xingshe haishi xingzi'."
38. Yu Xinyan, "Preface to *Practice and Future of Contemporary Socialism.*"
39. Xinjiang television, August 24, 1991, trans. FBIS-CHI, August 27, 1991, pp. 28–9; Wang Youfu, "Wang Zhen Inspects Xinjiang."

40. See, for instance, Xinjiang television, August 21, 1991, trans. FBIS-CHI, August 22, 1991, p. 20. The *People's Daily* account of Wang's trip deleted most of Wang's harshest language, including his vow to "fight to the death."
41. *South China Morning Post,* August 26, 1991.
42. *South China Morning Post,* September 4, 1991; Baum, *Burying Mao,* p. 333. Note *Wen wei po's* reference to Yeltsin as a "dangerous" person in its examination of the abortive coup. See Cheng Jo-lin, "Short but Strange Coup."
43. Sun Hong, "Anecdotes about Deng Xiaoping's Political Career and Family Life."
44. Ho Yuen, "CCP's 'Five Adherences' and 'Five Oppositions' to Prevent Peaceful Evolution."
45. Both statements were released by Xinhua on September 1, 1991, the first at 0723 GMT and the second at 1456 GMT. See FBIS-CHI, September 2, 1991.
46. In the early 1980s, the editor-in-chief was the highest ranking official of the *People's Daily.* In the wake of the 1983 campaign against spiritual pollution, a separate post of director was created to allow Hu Jiwei, criticized during that campaign, to take up a "second-line" position. Nevertheless, as director, Hu was able to exercise considerable influence over the paper, as evidenced by the selection of the open-minded Qin Chuan as editor-in-chief to replace Hu in that position. Thus, well before Tiananmen the position of director had become the effective head of the *People's Daily,* although the distinction between director and editor-in-chief continued. After the Tiananmen crackdown, Gao Di was named director (replacing Qian Liren), and Shao Huaze became editor-in-chief (replacing Tan Wenrui). In December 1992, Shao replaced Gao as director, and Fan Jingyi became editor-in-chief.
47. Gao Xin and He Pin, *Zhu Rongji zhuan,* pp. 231–2.
48. Guoguang Wu, "'Documentary Politics'."
49. Chen Yeping, "Have Both Political Integrity, Ability, Stress Political Ability: On Criterion for Selecting Cadres."
50. Cited in Baum, *Burying Mao,* p. 334.
51. Yang Shangkun, "Zai jinian Xinhai geming bashi zhounian dahuishang de jianghua."
52. See "Resolution of the Central Committee of the Communist Party of China on the Guiding Principles for Building a Socialist Society with Advanced Culture and Ideology."
53. Yang Shangkun, "Zai jinian Xinhai geming bashi zhounian dahuishang de jianghua."
54. Quoted in Gao Xin and He Pin, *Zhu Rongji zhuan,* p. 232.
55. Ching Wen, "Abnormal Atmosphere in *Renmin ribao*"; Deng Liqun, "Have Correct Understanding of Contradictions in Socialist Society."
56. Lo Ping and Li Tzu-ching, "Chen Yun Raises Six Points of View to Criticize Deng Xiaoping."
57. *South China Morning Post,* January 1, 1992, in FBIS-CHI, January 2, 1992, p. 25; Baum, *Burying Mao,* p. 336.
58. *Tangtai* 14, May 15, 1992, pp. 21–2, trans. FBIS-CHI, May 21, 1992, pp. 18–20.
59. Deng Xiaoping, "Zai Wuchang, Shenzhen, Zhuhai, Shanghai dengdi de tanhua yaodian," p. 372.
60. Ibid., p. 377.
61. Ibid., pp. 370–83.
62. "Deng Xiaoping's Visit to Special Zones Shows China Is More Open."

63. Beijing television, May 16, 1989, trans. FBIS-CHI, May 16, 1989, p. 28; *Renmin ribao,* May 17, 1989, trans. FBIS-CHI, May 17, 1989, p. 16.
64. Suisheng Zhao, "Deng Xiaoping's Southern Tour," p. 751.
65. The first three of these are translated in FBIS-CHI, February 24, 1992, pp. 27–30. A report on the fourth appears in FBIS-CHI, February 26, 1992, p. 16, and the fifth and sixth are translated in FBIS-CHI, March 2, 1992, pp. 33–4. The seventh is translated in FBIS-CHI, March 4, 1992, p. 19, and the eighth in FBIS-CHI, March 10, 1992, p. 16.
66. "Adhere Better to Taking Economic Construction as the Center."
67. "Be More Daring in Carrying Out Reform."
68. Fang Sheng, "Opening Up to the Outside World and Making Use of Capitalism."
69. *South China Morning Post,* May 11, 1992, in FBIS-CHI, May 11, 1992, pp. 16–17.
70. Zhao, "Deng Xiaoping's Southern Tour," p. 754.
71. *Ming pao,* March 7, 1992, trans. FBIS-CHI, March 9, 1992, pp. 26–7.
72. Ling Hsueh-chun, "Wang Zhen and Li Xiannian Set Themselves Up against Deng."
73. Ching Wen, "Abnormal Atmosphere in *Renmin ribao,*" p. 21.
74. Xinhua, March 11, 1992; Baum, *Burying Mao,* p. 347.
75. Jen Hui-wen, "Political Bureau Argues over 'Preventing Leftism'."
76. Zhao, "Deng Xiaoping's Southern Tour," p. 752.
77. *Renmin ribao,* March 31, 1992. The article had originally appeared in the *Shenzhen tequ bao (Shenzhen Special Economic Zone Daily)* on March 26. By merely reprinting the article, the *People's Daily* demonstrated its desire to keep an arm's length from the content.
78. Jen Hui-wen, "Political Bureau Argues over 'Preventing Leftism'."
79. Xinhua, March 23, 1992. Note that the *Jiefangjun bao* editorial hailing the close of the NPC prominently played the theme of "protecting and escorting" reform. See "Make Fresh Contributions on 'Protecting and Escorting' Reform, Opening Up, and Economic Development."
80. The first group of PLA leaders visited Shenzhen in late February, and the fourth group visited Shenzhen in early June. See *Wen wei po,* April 16, 1992, p. 2, trans. FBIS-CHI, April 16, 1992, p. 38; Xinhua, May 19, 1992, in FBIS-CHI, May 21, 1992, pp. 31–2; *Xinwanbao,* June 11, 1992, p. 2, trans. FBIS-CHI, June 16, 1992, pp. 32–3. On *Jiefangjun bao's* support for reform, see Shi Bonian and Liu Fang, "Unswervingly Implement the Party's Basic Line"; He Yijun, Jiang Bin, and Wang Jianwei, "Speed Up Pace of Reform, Opening Up"; and Lan Zhongping, "Why Do We Say That Special Economic Zones Are Socialist Rather than Capitalist in Nature?"
81. Yueh Shan, "Central Advisory Commission Submits Letter to CCP Central Committee Opposing 'Rightist' Tendency."
82. Yuan Mu, "Firmly, Accurately, and Comprehensively Implement the Party's Basic Line."
83. Leng Rong, "To Realize Lofty Aspirations and Great Ideals of the Chinese Nation." See also *Xinbao,* May 4, 1992, trans. FBIS-CHI, May 4, 1992, pp. 19–21.
84. Lin Wu, "Deng's Faction Unmasks Face of 'Ultraleftists'."
85. Xinhua, April 22, 1992, in FBIS-CHI, April 23, 1992, pp. 11–12.
86. Gong Yuzhi, "Emancipate Our Minds, Liberate Productive Forces." See also Lu Yu-shan, "Chen Yun Responds to Document No. 2."

87. *South China Morning Post,* May 7, 1992, in FBIS-CHI, May 7, 1992, pp. 22–3; "Summary of Tian Jiyun's Speech Before Party School"; Baum, *Burying Mao,* p. 353.
88. Jen Hui-wen, "There Is Something behind Chen Yun's Declaration of His Position."
89. Xinhua, May 1, 1992, in FBIS-CHI, May 1, 1992, pp. 18–19.
90. Deng's comments were reported by Hong Kong media in May but were not publicized by PRC media until early July, when Shanghai's *Jiefang ribao* finally broke the long silence. See *Ming pao,* May 28, 1992, trans. FBIS-CHI, May 28, 1992, p. 15; *South China Morning Post,* May 28, 1992, in FBIS-CHI, May 28, 1992, p. 15; and AFP, July 7, 1992. The following month, Deng followed up his trip to Shougang with a trip to the northeast. See *South China Morning Post,* June 24, 1992.
91. Yen Shen-tsun, "Deng Xiaoping's Talk during His Inspection of Shoudu Iron and Steel Complex."
92. Xinhua, June 14, 1992, in FBIS-CHI, June 15, 1992, pp. 23–6.
93. See "New Stage of China's Reform and Opening to the Outside World."
94. Hsia Yu, "Beijing's Intense Popular Interest in CPC Document No. 4"; "The CCP Issues Document No. 4."
95. *Lishi de chaoliu* bianweihui (Ed.), *Lishi de chaoliu.*
96. Lu Ming-sheng, "Inside Story of How *Historical Trends* Was Banned."
97. *Ming pao,* June 15, 1992, trans. FBIS-CHI, June 15, 1992, pp. 26–7.
98. See Zhao Shilin (Ed.), *Fang "zuo" beiwanglu;* Wen Jin (Ed.), *Zhongguo "zuo" huo;* and Yuan Yongsong and Wang Junwei (Eds.), *Zuoqing ershinian.*
99. *South China Morning Post,* June 24, 1992. See also Meng Lin, "Deng Liqun Reaffirms Disapproval of Phrase 'Deng Xiaoping Thought'."
100. Baum, *Burying Mao,* p. 334.
101. "Political Report" to the Fourteenth Party Congress. Quotes taken from pages 25 and 24, respectively.
102. Ibid., p. 29.
103. Joseph Fewsmith, "Reform, Resistance, and the Politics of Succession," pp. 8–11.
104. Former Politburo Standing Committee member Hu Qili, purged for his support of Zhao during the 1989 demonstrations, was appointed vice-minister of the Ministry of the Machine-Building and Electronics Industry. Yan Mingfu, former member of the Secretariat and head of the Party's United Front Work Department, was appointed a vice-minister of Civil Affairs. A third Zhao associate, Rui Xingwen, was named vice-minister of the SPC at the same time. Xinhua, June 1, 1991, in FBIS-CHI, June 4, 1991, p. 30.
105. On Hu Jintao, see Cheng Li, *China's Leaders.* For Hu's relations with Song Ping and Zhao Ziyang, I have relied on a number of interviews.
106. Quoted in Lam, *China after Deng Xiaoping,* p. 171.
107. Gao Xin, *Jiang Zemin quanli zhi lu,* pp. 58–80.
108. He Po-shih, "The Army Reshuffle Was Carried Out to Pacify the Leftist Faction."
109. Lo Ping, "Blowing of the 'Left' Wind, and the Four-Horse Carriage."
110. Cheng Te-lin, "Yao Yilin Launches Attack against Zhu Rongji, Tian Jiyun"; Jen Hui-wen, "Deng Xiaoping Urges Conservatives Not to Make a Fuss"; Chen Chienping, "Zhu Rongji Urges Paying Attention to Negative Effects of Reform."

111. Xinhua, December 27, 1992, in FBIS-CHI, December 28, 1992, pp. 34–6.
112. China Central Television, January 22, 1993, trans. FBIS-CHI, January 22, 1993, pp. 20–1.
113. Xinhua, March 7, 1993, in FBIS-CHI, March 8, 1993, pp. 13–14.
114. "Major Revisions to the Government Work Report."

CHAPTER 3

1. Wu Jiaxiang, "Xin quanwei zhuyi shuping."
2. Ibid., p. 4. Yu Guanghua, "Xin quanwei zhuyi de shehui jichu ji huanxiang."
3. Author interview.
4. Gu Xin, "Xin quanwei zhuyi de lilun kunjing," p. 46.
5. Zhang Bingjiu, "Jingji tizhi gaige he zhengzhi tizhi gaige de jincheng yu xietiao."
6. "Deng Xiaoping on Neoauthoritarianism"; Stanley Rosen and Gary Zou, "The Road to Modernization in China Debated."
7. Chen Yizi, Wang Xiaoqiang, and Li Jun, "The Deep-Seated Questions and the Strategic Choice China's Reform Faces."
8. Dai Qing, "From Lin Zexu to Jiang Jingguo."
9. On the debates in this period, see Mark Petracca and Mong Xiong, "The Concept of Chinese Neo-Authoritarianism"; Liu Jun and Li Lin (Eds.), *Xinquanwei zhuyi*; and Qi Mo (Ed.), *Xinquanwei zhuyi*.
10. On Yu's background, see Merle Goldman, *Sowing the Seeds of Democracy,* pp. 70–1. Most of the liberal critics of the new authoritarianism were related in some fashion to Hu's intellectual network, while most of the advocates of the new authoritarianism (at least in Beijing) were tied in some fashion to Zhao Ziyang. This debate therefore reflected the deepening divisions among reformers in the late 1980s.
11. Yu Haocheng, "Zhongguo xuyao xin quanwei zhuyi ma?"
12. Ding Xueliang, *Gongchanzhuyihou yu Zhongguo*, p. xxii.
13. John McMillan and Barry Naughton, "How to Reform a Planned Economy"; Chen Kang, Gray Jefferson, and Inderjit Singh, "Lessons from China's Economic Reform."
14. Sheng Hong, "Zhongguo de guodu jingjixue," p. 4.
15. Sheng Hong, "A Survey of the Research on the Transitional Process of Market-Oriented Reform in China," p. 10.
16. Ibid., p. 13.
17. Sheng Hong, "Zhongguo de guodu jingjixue," p. 5.
18. Ibid.
19. Lin Yifu, Cai Fang, and Li Zhou, "On the Gradual-Advance Style of Economic Reform in China"; see also Sheng Hong, "Cong jihua junheng dao shichang junheng." Fan Gang takes an opposing point of view in "Liangzhong gaige chengben yu liangzhong gaige fangshi."
20. Sheng Hong, "A Survey of the Research on the Transitional Process of Market-Oriented Reform in China," p. 11.
21. Yu Yingshi, "Zhongguo jindai sixiangshi zhongde jijin yu baoshou," p. 139.
22. Yu Yingshi, "Zailun Zhongguo xiandai sixiang zhongde jijin yu baoshou," p. 146.

23. Li Zehou and Liu Zaifu, *Gaobie geming.*
24. Shen Liren and Dai Yuanchen, "Woguo 'zhuhou jingji' de xingcheng jiqi biduan he genyuan."
25. Gao Xin and He Pin, *Zhonggong "taizidang,"* pp. 112–13.
26. Chen Yuan, "Wo guo jingji de shenceng wenti he xuanze (gangyao)," pp. 18–19.
27. Ibid., p. 19.
28. Ibid., p. 20.
29. Ibid., p. 23.
30. Chen Yuan, "Several Questions on Methods and Theory Regarding Studies in Economic Operations in China," pp. 40–1.
31. Gao Xin, *Jiang Zemin de muliao,* pp. 284–6.
32. Wang Huning, "Zhongguo zhengzhi tizhi gaige de beijing yu qianjing," pp. 5–6.
33. Ibid., p. 10. See also Wang Huning, "Chuji jieduan yu zhengzhi tizhi gaige"; Wang Huning, "Juece gongneng de shehuihua ji qi tiaojian"; and Wang Huning, "Zhiwei fenlei yu ganbu guanli tizhi."
34. Wang Huning, "Zhongguo zhengzhi tizhi gaige de beijing yu qianjing," p. 10.
35. Wang Huning, "Lun minzhu zhengzhi jianshe," p. 34.
36. Ibid., p. 36.
37. Wang Huning, "Zhongguo bianhua zhong de zhongyang he difang zhengfu de guanxi: Zhengzhi de hanyi," p. 4.
38. Ibid., p. 7. For a positive interpretation of these trends, see Jean Oi, *Rural China Takes Off.*
39. Wang Huning, "Zhongguo bianhua zhong de zhongyang he difang zhengfu de guanxi: Zhengzhi de hanyi," p. 8.
40. Samuel Huntington, *Political Order in Changing Societies.*
41. Wang Huning, "Shehui ziyuan zongliang yu shehui tiaokong: Zhongguo yiyi," p. 11. See also Wang Huning, "Jifen pingheng: Zhongyang yu difang de xietong guanxi."
42. Wang Huning, "Zhongguo zhengzhi – Xingzheng tizhi gaige de jingji fenxi."
43. Ibid., p. 139.
44. Ibid., p. 140.
45. See the biographical note in Xiao Gongqin, *Xiao Gongqin ji.*
46. Benjamin Schwartz, *In Search of Wealth and Power.*
47. Xiao Gongqin, " 'Yan Fu beilun' yu jindai xinbaoshou zhuyi biange guan," p. 32.
48. Ibid., p. 35.
49. Ibid.
50. Xiao Gongqin, "Wuxu bianfa de zai fanxing," p. 20. See also Xiao's full-length treatment, *Weijizhong de biange.*
51. Gu Xin and David Kelly, "New Conservatism," p. 221.
52. For a discussion of Chinese nationalism see Fewsmith and Rosen, "The Domestic Context of Chinese Foreign Policy."
53. He Xin, "Dangqian Zhongguo neiwai xingshi fenxi ji ruogan zhengce jianyi (zhaiyao)," p. 1.
54. As He wrote: "At present there is no other country more desirous of replacing a declining U.S. as global hegemon than Japan." See He Xin, "Lun Zhongguo xiandaihua de guoji huanjing yu waijiao zhanlüe," p. 9.

55. He Xin, "Dangqian Zhongguo neiwai xingshi fenxi ji ruogan zhengce jianyi (zhai-yao)," pp. 2–3.
56. He Xin, "Lun Zhongguo xiandaihua de guoji huanjing yu waijiao zhanlüe," p. 14.
57. Nevertheless, in a 1990 interview with Japanese economist Yabuki Susumu, He said that "during the next 10–20 years the entire capitalist world economic system will experience the most profound and serious overall crisis since the dawn of history." See "Current World Economic Situation" (I), p. 11.
58. He Xin, "Lun ZhongMeiRi guanxi de zhanlüe beijing yu duice," pp. 40–2.
59. Ibid., pp. 45–6.
60. Ibid., p. 32.
61. Ibid., p. 31.
62. Ibid., p. 47.
63. Ibid., p. 34.
64. Ibid., pp. 35–6.
65. He Xin, "Wo xiang nimen de liangzhi huhuan," p. 481. In an interesting case of mirror-image thinking, He insisted that ideology played no role in U.S. foreign policy; the United States saw the world in terms of a zero-sum game (*nisi wohuo* – literally, "you die, I live"). See He Xin, "Lun Zhongguo xiandaihua de guoji huanjing yu waijiao zhanlüe," p. 18; He Xin, "Dangdai shijie jingji xingshi fenxi," p. 57; and He Xin, "Wo xiang nimen liangzhi huhuan," p. 495.
66. He Xin, "Wo xiang nimen liangzhi huhuan," pp. 484, 494.
67. He Xin, "Lun ZhongMeiRi guanxi de zhanlüe beijing yu duice," p. 40.
68. He Xin, "Dui woguo shinian gaige de fansi," p. 402.
69. Ibid., p. 403.
70. He Xin, "Aiguo de Qu Yuan yu ruguo de 'He Shang'."
71. "Current World Economic Situation" (III), p. 12.
72. He Xin, "Aiguo de Qu Yuan yu ruguo de 'He Shang'," pp. 406–7. See also He Xin, "Wode kunhuo yu youlu," pp. 427–8.
73. He Xin, "Tan dangdai ziben zhuyi," p. 70.
74. He Xin, "Lun woguo jingji gaige zhidao lilun de shiwu," p. 508.
75. Ibid., p. 503. See also He Xin, "Dangqian jingji xingshi pinglun (zhi yi)," p. 544; He Xin, "Lun woguo jingji gaige zhidao lilun de shiwu," p. 506; and He Xin, "Woguo duiwai kaifang zhanlüe de yizhong shexiang," p. 83.
76. See Li Zehou, *Zhongguo xiandai sixiangshi lun*; and Vera Schwarcz's masterful study, *The Chinese Enlightenment*.
77. Quoted in Meng Fanhua, *Zhongshen kuanghuan*, p. 10.
78. Su Xiaokang and Wang Luxiang, *He Shang (River Elegy)*.
79. Cited in Jing Wang, *High Culture Fever*, p. 123; emphasis in original. See also Frederic Wakeman, "All the Rage in China."
80. Jing Wang, *High Culture Fever*.
81. Chen Fong-ching and Jin Guantao, *From Youthful Manuscripts to River Elegy*. Perhaps the word "cosmopolitanism" does not convey the complexity of China's emotional response to the outside world. As Jing Wang commented, "Chinese [enlightenment] intellectuals [are] at once proud of and hostile toward their own cultural and national heritage, while defiant toward and subservient to the imported Western culture at the same time." See Jing Wang, *High Culture Fever*, p. 124.

82. Yi jia yan [pseud.], " 'He Shang' xuanyangle shenma?" It quickly became known that this article was by Wang Zhen. An "editor's note" prefacing the article states that Zhao Ziyang had refused to run the article.
83. He Xin, " 'He Shang' de piping."
84. Wang Xiaodong [Shi Zhong], "Zhongguo de minzu zhuyi he Zhongguo de weilai."
85. Wang Xiaodong and Qiu Tiancao, "Jiqing de yinying: Ping dianshi xiliepian 'He shang'."
86. Wang Xiaodong [Shi Zhong], "Zhongguo de minzu zhuyi he Zhongguo de weilai."
87. Gu Xin and David Kelly, "New Conservatism."
88. Ibid., p. 231.
89. Ling Zhen, "Zugepai de xingdong xinhao"; author interviews.
90. *China Youth Daily* Ideology and Theory Department, "Realistic Responses and Strategic Options for China after the Soviet Upheaval," pp. 18–19.
91. Ibid., p. 29.
92. Ibid., p. 20.
93. Ibid., p. 22.
94. Ibid., p. 27.
95. Ibid., pp. 23–4.

CHAPTER 4

1. The use of the term "third way" to describe these intellectual efforts should not be confused with the articulation of a liberal "third way" (or "third force") in China in the 1930s and 1940s. See Carson Chang, *The Third Force in China.*
2. Geremie R. Barmé, *In the Red,* especially chapters 6, 8, and 9.
3. Yunxiang Yan, "The Politics of Consumerism in Chinese Society."
4. Actually, this change can be dated from the late 1980s, when inflation eroded the incomes of many people; this trend contributed to the resentments that were displayed so clearly in Tiananmen Square in spring 1989. Li Ping, *Zhongguo xiayibu zenyang zou,* pp. 67–70.
5. Ibid.
6. Jianying Zha, *China Pop,* pp. 38–9.
7. Ibid., p. 38.
8. Ibid., p. 46.
9. Meng Fanhua, *Zhongshen kuanghuan.*
10. Jia Pingwa, *Fei du*; Jianying Zha, *China Pop,* pp. 129–64.
11. Quoted in Barmé, *In the Red,* p. 184.
12. Xu Jilin, *Ling yizhong qimeng,* p. 10.
13. Wang Hui, "Dangdai Zhongguo de sixiang zhuangkuang yu xiandaixing wenti," p. 134.
14. Xu Jilin, *Ling yizhong qimeng,* p. 15.
15. There is no question, as Perry Link points out, that the normally ham-handed propaganda machine performed brilliantly in building up popular expectations and then allowing the United States to take the fall for the subsequent disappointment. Nevertheless, it would be wrong to see the changed popular perceptions as simply the product of government manipulation. This was a period in which many statements

perceived as hostile to China (not just to the Chinese government) were made. It was also followed up by the ill-advised decision to stop and inspect the *Milky Way,* a Chinese ship that was incorrectly thought to be carrying precursor chemicals for the manufacture of chemical weapons. See Perry Link, "The Old Man's New China."

16. Wang Shuo, *Playing for Thrills*; Wang Shuo, *Please Don't Call Me Human.* On Wang Shuo, see Geremie R. Barmé, "The Apotheosis of the *Liumang,*" in Barmé, *In the Red,* pp. 62–144.

17. "Wang Shuo zibai"; Xu Jilin, *Ling yizhong qimeng,* p. 264; Barmé, *In the Red,* pp. 298–301.

18. Wang Xiaoming, "Kuangyeshang de feixu," p. 1.

19. Ding Xueliang, "Dangdai Zhongguo de daode kongbai."

20. Min Lin, *The Search for Modernity,* p. 147; Liu Xiaofeng, *Geti xinyang yu wenhua lilun.*

21. See, for instance, Jiang Qing, *Gongyangxue yinlun.*

22. Chen Fong-ching and Jin Guantao, *From Youthful Manuscripts to River Elegy,* pp. 129–57.

23. Wang Hui, "Dangdai Zhongguo de sixiang zhuangkuang yu xiandaixing wenti," p. 134.

24. Peter L. Berger and Hsin-Huang Michael Hsiao (Eds.), *The Search for an East Asian Development Model.*

25. Ji Xianlin, "Dongxifang wenhua de zhuanzhedian."

26. Ji Xianlin, " 'Tianren heyi' fang neng chengjiu renlei"; Ji Xianlin, " 'Tianren heyi' xinjie."

27. Hua Jinzhong, "Guoxue, zai Yanyuan you qiaoran xingqi."

28. Sheng Hong, "Zhongguo xianqin zhexue he xiandai zhidu zhuyi."

29. Sheng Hong, "Shenma shi wenming," p. 91.

30. Sheng Hong, "Cong minzu zhuyi dao tianxia zhuyi."

31. Yue Daiyun, "Shijie wenhua duihua zhongde Zhongguo xiandai baoshou zhuyi"; Yue Daiyun and Carolyn Wakeman, *To the Storm.*

32. Notable exceptions are Charlotte Furth (Ed.), *The Limits of Change,* and Guy Alitto, *The Last Confucian.*

33. Axel Schneider, "Bridging the Gap."

34. Ibid.

35. Lu Jiandong, *Chen Yinke de zuihou ershi nian.*

36. Schneider, "Bridging the Gap." The "Chen Yinke phenomenon" was followed quickly by intense interest in Gu Zhun, a scholar of classical Greek civilization. See Xu Jilin, *Ling yizhong qimeng,* p. 265.

37. This and the following two paragraphs are drawn from my article, "Historical Echoes and Chinese Politics: Can China Leave the Twentieth Century Behind?"

38. Li Zehou, *Zhongguo xiandai sixiangshi lun*; Vera Schwarcz, *The Chinese Enlightenment.* See also Woei Lien Chong (Ed.), *Li Zehou.*

39. Wang Ruoshui's *Wei rendao zhuyi bianhu* is the classic work in this regard.

40. Yan Jiaqi was one of the first and best-known advocates of instituting a civil service system. See Yan Jiaqi, *Toward a Democratic China.*

41. Wu Jinglian was probably the best known of the early advocates, but there were many others. See Fewsmith, *Dilemmas of Reform.*

42. Gan Yang edited a famous series of translations under the general title *Culture: China and the World*. See Chen Fong-ching and Jin Guantao, *From Youthful Manuscripts to River Elegy*, pp. 159–85.
43. Su Shaozhi was an early and consistent advocate of democratization. See Su Shaozhi (Ed.), *Marxism in China*; see also Su's memoirs, *Shinian fengyu*.
44. Wang notes that conceptions of democracy were restricted to reform programs designed by the highest levels and that they neglected political participation. There is some truth in his criticism – Chinese intellectuals have generally been wary of the lesser-educated rural population – but it is also true that they were working in an environment in which even limited "formalistic" democracy (as Wang calls it) marked progress. Wang's criticism appears in "Dangdai Zhongguo de sixiang zhuangkuang yu xiandaixing wenti."
45. Wang Hui, ibid., pp. 16 and 8.
46. Ibid., p. 20.
47. In Chinese, the common term is *houxue* ("post-studies"), and those who employ these methodologies are sometimes referred to as "post-ists"; see Ben Xu, *Disenchanted Democracy*. But this term is likely to be confusing to many American readers, so the more understandable (if somewhat less accurate) term "postmodernists" is used instead.
48. Wang Hui, "Dangdai Zhongguo de sixiang zhuangkuang yu xiandaixing wenti," p. 2.
49. Suisheng Zhao, *In Search of a Right Place?*, p. 13.
50. The introduction of postmodernism is usually dated from the lectures given by Fredric Jameson at Beijing University in the mid-1980s. Many of Jameson's works have since been translated into Chinese and have become virtually required reading for Chinese intellectuals, particularly those in literary criticism. Despite the introduction of postmodernist thought in the mid-1980s, it was only with the Tiananmen incident and the subsequent changes in Chinese society that postmodernism really caught on. See "Bianzhe qianyan" (Editors' introduction) in Wang Hui and Yu Guoliang (Eds.), *90 niandai de "houxue" lunzheng*; Edward Said, *Orientalism*; Edward Said, *Culture and Imperialism*; Michel Foucault, *The Order of Things*; and Fredric Jameson, *The Cultural Turn*. For a useful introduction, see Perry Anderson, *The Origins of Postmodernism*.
51. In his later article "Zaitan Sayide," Zhang ties this influence directly to John King Fairbank and his students. The theme that Western views of China have changed from idealizing it to condemning it as Western colonialism developed has become widespread in recent years. In a review of the book series *Xifang shiyeli de Zhongguo xingxiang* (The Image of China in Western Eyes) edited by Huang Xingtao and Yang Nianqun, the liberal scholar Qin Hui argues that Western images of China vary according to profession and interest rather than historical period. Thus, business people take a more optimistic view of China whereas "missionaries" (including contemporary human rights advocates) take a more negative view. See Qin Hui, "Bainian zhuanhuan – 'Shangren' yu 'jiaoshi' de Zhongguoguan."
52. Zhang Kuan, "OuMeiren yanzhong de 'feiwo zulei'," pp. 7 and 9. This sort of attack on Zhang Yimou and others has become a staple in criticism of "colonial culture" in recent years. For instance, the leftist journal *Mainstream* declared, "Zhang Yimou,

Chen Kaige, and their ilk make use of the textual form of 'pop culture' – cinema – to offer the barbarous and ugly aspects of our nation's former-day habits and customs to the West so as to gratify the hegemonic 'the West-is-the-center' mentality and to seek postcolonial rewards." See Cheng Zhi'ang, "Beware of So-Called Popular Culture," p. 52. The convergence of views between a postmodernist literary critic like Zhang Kuan and an Old Leftist journal like *Zhongliu* exemplifies why liberal intellectuals consider postmodernists the "New Left" and see the New Left as working in tandem with the Old Left.

53. Zhang Kuan, "Wenhua xinzhimin de keneng," p. 20.
54. Zhang Kuan, "Zaiyan Sayide," p. 12; see also Zhang Kuan, "Wenhua xinzhimin de keneng."
55. Zhang Kuan, "Sayide de 'dongfang zhuyi' yu xifang de hanxue yanjiu," p. 37.
56. Qian Jun, "Saiyide tan wenhua," pp. 14–15. See also Liu Kang, "Quanqiuhua 'peilun' yu xiandaixing 'qitu'."
57. Liu Kang, "Quanqiuhua yu Zhongguo xiandaihua de butong xuanze."
58. Zhang Fa, Zhang Yiwu, and Wang Yichuan, "Cong 'xiandaixing' dao 'Zhonghua-xing'," pp. 18–19.
59. Zhang Yiwu, "Chanshi 'Zhongguo' de jiaolu."
60. Fei Hsiao-t'ung, *Peasant Life in China.*
61. Quoted in Yongnian Zheng, *Discovering Chinese Nationalism in China,* p. 57.
62. Gan Yang, " 'Jiangcun jingji' zairenshi." See also Wang Ying, "Xin jiti zhuyi yu Zhongguo tese de shichang jingji." For a recent article on the nativization of political science, see Wang Shaoguang, " 'Jiegui' haishi 'nalai'."
63. Wang Hui, "Dangdai Zhongguo de sixiang zhuangkuang yu xiandaixing wenti," pp. 20–2.
64. Ibid., p. 10.
65. Wang Hui, "Guanyu xiandaixing wenti dawen," p. 24.
66. Wang Hui, "Dangdai Zhongguo de sixiang zhuangkuang yu xiandaixing wenti," p. 20.
67. Wang Hui, "Guanyu xiandaixing wenti dawen," pp. 28–9.
68. Wang Hui, "Dangdai Zhongguo de sixiang zhuangkuang yu xiandaixing wenti," p. 18.
69. Although generational differences are important, one must be careful not to assume that generalizations are universals. The Red Guard generation (often called *laosanjie*), drawing on their experience in the countryside during the Cultural Revolution, contributed greatly to the implementation of rural reform and the breakup of the communes. Nevertheless, even friends who worked together on the early rural reforms have diverged over the years: some have tried to tackle the problems remaining in the rural areas by pursuing further property rights reform – essentially privatization – while others have advocated a type of return to socialism. The problem that these and other scholars have faced in dealing with the countryside is essentially one of public goods. The communes provided public goods (e.g., welfare and health care) to rural residents, and their breakup left a vacuum that has not been effectively filled to date. Deng Yingtao, Deng Liqun's son, was a prominent participant in the rural reforms in the 1980s, but in the 1990s he has embraced socialist solutions; he has also worked closely with Cui Zhiyuan in this regard. See Cui

Zhiyuan, Deng Yingtao, and Miao Zhuang, *Nanjiecun.* Nevertheless, in general, young scholars of Cui's generation seem more inclined to embrace "collectivist" solutions than do those who are older.

70. Cui Zhiyuan, "Zailun zhidu chuangxin yu di'erci sixiang jiefang," p. 26.

71. Cui Zhiyuan, "Angang xianfa yu houfute zhuyi." Interestingly enough, even such a liberal official as Hu Ping (head of the Special Zones Office of the State Council) referred favorably to the Angang Constitution in a speech defending the Special Economic Zones. See Hu Ping, "Special Zone Construction and Opening to the Outside," p. 25.

72. Cui Zhiyuan, "Zhidu chuangxin yu di'erci sixiang jiefang," p. 2.

73. Francis Fukayama, *The End of History and the Last Man.* This book is an elaboration of his controversial article entitled "The End of History?". Criticism of Fukayama plays a central role in Zhang Yiwu's thinking. See Zhang Yiwu, "Miandui quanqiuhua de tiaozhan."

74. Cui Zhiyuan, "Zhidu chuangxin yu di'erci sixiang jiefang," p. 2.

75. John Roemer (Ed.), *Property Relations, Incentives, and Welfare*; Roberto Mangabeira Unger, *Democratic Experimentalism.*

76. Zhang Weiying has been particluarly forceful in this regard. See *Qiye de qiyejia.*

77. See in particular Cui Zhiyuan, "Zhidu chuangxin yu di'erci sixiang jiefang." In his article "Meiguo ershiji zhou gongsifa biange de lilun beijing," Cui argues that the recognition of stakeholder rights marks an important change in the understanding of the property rights of shareholders. For a refutation by liberal economist Zhang Weiying, see "Suoyouzhi, zhili jiegou ji weituo."

78. Cui Zhiyuan, "Zhidu chuangxin yu di'erci sixiang jiefang," p. 10. It should be noted that critical legal studies have played an important role in the ongoing development of legal thinking, but they are hardly as widely accepted within legal circles as Cui's footnotes might lead one to believe. See Nicholas Mercuro and Steven G. Medema, *Economics and the Law.*

79. Cui Zhiyuan, "Zailun zhidu chuangxin yu di'erci sixiang jiefang," p. 26.

80. Jin Longde, "Zhongyuan dadi de yimian hongqi."

81. Although Deng Yingtao is the son of Deng Liqun, he does not share his father's orthodox understandings of Marxism–Leninism. In the 1980s, Deng Yingtao was one of the core members of the Rural Development Group, which played an important role in the development of the Household Responsibility System. He also wrote some of the most creative academic articles exploring various aspects of reform. In the 1990s, however, it appears that he – like many of those described in this section – has become convinced that China cannot follow the Western route of development and has devoted himself to exploring a uniquely Chinese path. On the role of the Rural Development Group, see Fewsmith, *Dilemmas of Reform*, pp. 34–41. For Deng Yingtao's economic thinking in the 1980s, see *Deng Yingtao ji.* In the 1990s, Deng joined the neoconservatives. See Deng Yingtao, *Xin fazhan fangshi yu Zhongguo de weilai.*

82. Deng Yingtao, Cui Zhiyuan, and Miao Zhuang, *Nanjiecun,* p. 10. For hagiographic accounts of Nanjie Village, see Chen Xianyi and Chen Ruiyao, *Zhongguo youge Nanjiecun,* and Zhao Guoliang and Cui Jianlin (Eds.), *Lixiang zhi guang.*

83. Deng Yingtao, Cui Zhiyuan, and Miao Zhuang, *Nanjiecun,* p. 18.

84. Ibid., p. 4. This had led to much criticism in China that Nanjie maintains its prosperity, and its collectivism, by exploiting outsiders. It is certainly true that only the 3,000 native villagers are entitled to share in the revenue streams (as opposed to the wages) generated by the village enterprises. This raises one of the most interesting and difficult issues in contemporary China (explored by Dorothy Solinger in *Contesting Citizenship in Urban China*) – namely, the citizenship rights of internal migrants.

85. Deng Yingtao, Cui Zhiyuan, and Miao Zhuang, *Nanjiecun,* pp. 95–109.

86. Cui often cites the work of Joseph E. Stiglitz, who has been a leading critic of the standard neoclassical model; see, for instance, his *Whither Socialism.*

87. In this sense, Cui's work is very different from those who look to China's Confucian heritage for solutions to its present problems. It should be noted that there is an important but unarticulated argument going on between those of the New Left and at least some of their critics about the value of the Chinese revolution. Although those of the New Left reject both the mass mobilizations of the Maoist era and the rigid, bureaucratic apparatus associated with the planned economy, they nevertheless see the revolution as overwhelmingly positive. For instance, in their discussion of state capacity, Hu Angang and Wang Shaoguang note the very rapid increase in state capacity following the revolution and argue that "such an accomplishment was indeed rare in the annals of the world" [*Wang Shaoguang Proposal (I),* p. 47]. Liberals and traditionalists, while willing to work within the framework bequeathed by the revolution, seem much less enamored of the revolution itself.

88. Li Rui, *Li Rui fan "zuo" wenxuan.*

89. Hu Jiwei, *Cong Hua Guofeng xiatai dao Hu Yaobang xiatai.*

90. Wang Ruoshui, *Hu Yaobang xiatai de beijing.*

91. On Li's background, see A. Doak Barnett, *The Making of Foreign Policy in China,* pp. 88–9, 129.

92. Li Shenzhi, "Bian tongyi, hedongxi," p. 822.

93. Li Shenzhi, "Zhongguo chuantong wenhuazhong jiwu minzhu yewu kexue."

94. Li Shenzhi, "Chongxin dianran qimeng de huoju," p. 2.

95. Ibid., p. 5.

96. Ibid., p. 6.

97. Li Shenzhi, "Quanqiuhua yu Zhongguo wenhua."

98. Li Shenzhi, "Ershiyi shiji de yousi"; Zbigniew K. Brzezinski, *Out of Control.*

99. Li Shenzhi, "Shuliang youshixia de kongju."

100. See, for instance, Li Shenzhi, "Zhongguo zhexue de jingshen."

101. Li Shenzhi, "Quanqiuhua yu Zhongguo wenhua," p. 7.

102. Li Shenzhi, "Guanyu wenhua wenti de yixie sikao," p. 1132.

103. Li Shenzhi, "Zhongguo yingqu shenmayang de fengfan?", p. 955.

104. The story goes on that Zhang Fei was soft-hearted and failed to kill Guan Yu's pregnant wife. When Guan Yu's son, Guan Suo, was born and grew up, he went to find his father and demand that he recognize him as his son. When Guan Yu refused, Guan Suo angrily declared that he would surrender to Cao Cao and raise an army to capture Guan Yu. This story, so contrary to the filial piety that is supposed to imbue Chinese culture from top to bottom, suggested to both Wang Xuetai

and Li that there are contradictory elements in Chinese culture that are rarely acknowledged, much less studied. See Li Shenzhi, "Faxian lingyige Zhongguo," p. 1243.

105. Ibid.
106. Ibid., p. 1247.
107. Ibid., p. 1249.
108. Ibid.
109. Here Li references Perry Link's article, "China's 'Core' Problem."
110. Li Shenzhi, "Quanqiuhua yu Zhongguo wenhua," p. 8.
111. Ibid., p. 9.
112. See, for instance, his observation that the human species had a common starting point and then spread out to the far reaches of the globe but now is coming together again. Li Shenzhi, "Bian tongyi, hedongxi," p. 826.
113. Unfortunately, this term is also pronounced *fazhi,* but the character for *zhi* in this expression differs from the character for *zhi* in the first expression. Whereas the character *zhi* in "rule by law" carries the meaning "control or restrain," that for *zhi* in "rule of law" means "govern," giving the expression a less authoritarian connotation.
114. Li notes that this phrase was coined by Mao Yushi, Hu Yaobang's former secretary (who was speaking at the same conference), but that he (Li) fully endorsed it.
115. Li Shenzhi, "Yeyao tuidong zhengzhi gaige."
116. Li Shenzhi, "Quanqiuhua yu Zhongguo wenhua," p. 5.
117. Liu Junning, "Feng neng jin, yu neng jin, guowang buneng jin!"
118. Liu Junning, "Zhijie minzhu yu jianjie minzhu" and "Quanqiuhua yu minzhuhua."
119. Liu Junning, "Minzu zhuyi simianguan."
120. Immanuel Wallerstein, *The Modern World System.*
121. Cui Zhiyuan, "Lusuo xin lun."
122. "Zhongguo shehui jiegou zhuanxing de zhongjinqi qushi yu yinhuan."
123. Xu, Jilin, "Xunqiu 'disantiao daolu' – guanyu 'ziyouzhuyi' yu 'xinzuopai' de duihua."
124. Zhao Yiheng, " 'Houxue' yu Zhongguo xinbaoshou zhuyi."
125. Xu Ben, "Shenma shi Zhongguo de 'houxin shiqi'?"
126. Zhang Longxi, "Duoyuan shehui zhongde wenhua piping."
127. Lei Yi, "Beijing yu cuowei."
128. Zhang Kuan, "Wenhua xinzhimin de keneng."

CHAPTER 5

1. Joel Migdal, *Strong Societies and Weak States*; John Zysman, *Government, Markets, and Growth.*
2. Zhongguo kexueyuan guoqing fenxi yanjiu xiaozu, *Shengcun yu fazhan.*
3. Author interviews.
4. Hu Angang and Wang Shaoguang, *Jiaqiang zhongyang zhengfu zai shichang jingji zhuanxing zhong de zhudao zuoyong.* (Hereafter cited as *Wang Shaoguang Proposal (I)* or *(II)*.) *Wang Shaoguang Proposal (I),* p. 60. It should be noted that because of the tax reform adopted in 1994, central revenues began to climb. Instead

of being 11.3 percent of GNP in 2000, as Hu and Wang predicted, they were about 14.3 percent. I appreciate Barry Naughton sharing his data with me.

5. Ibid., p. 64. In fact, central revenues as a percentage of GDP reached a low in 1995 and, in part because of the tax reforms implemented in 1994, began to increase thereafter.

6. Ibid., p. 63.

7. Jean Oi, *Rural China Takes Off.*

8. Jean Oi, "Fiscal Reform and the Foundations of Local State Corporatism in China."

9. *Wang Shaoguang Proposal (I),* p. 66.

10. Ibid., p. 24.

11. *Wang Shaoguang Proposal (II),* p. 5

12. *Wang Shaoguang Proposal (I),* pp. 66–7; emphasis in original.

13. Ibid., p. 54; emphasis in original.

14. In addition to Migdal's and Zysman's works cited in note 1, other influential works in this tradition include Frederic C. Deyo (Ed.), *The Political Economy of the New Asian Industrialization*; Gary Gereffi and Donald L. Wyman (Eds.), *Manufacturing Miracles*; Peter Evans, *Embedded Autonomy*; Chalmers Johnson, *MITI and the Japanese Miracle*; and Peter Katzenstein (Ed.), *Between Power and Plenty.*

15. Wu Jinglian, "Guanyu gaige zhanlüe xuanze de ruogan sikao."

16. Dorothy Solinger, *Contesting Citizenship in Urban China.*

17. Deng Xiaoping, "Zai Wuchang, Shenzhen, Zhuhai, Shanghai dengdi de tanhua yaodian," p. 374.

18. For their argument on fairness, see Hu Angang, Wang Shaoguang, and Kang Xiaoguang, *Zhongguo diqu chaju baogao,* pp. 292–303.

19. Ibid., p. 542.

20. Ibid., pp. 312–17, 337.

21. Ibid., pp. 318–25.

22. Ibid., p. 541. See also Wang Shaoguang and Hu Angang, *The Political Economy of Uneven Development.*

23. *Guangming ribao,* October 7, 1994.

24. Cited in Zhu Tao, "A Brief Introduction to the Special Zones Debate," p. 44.

25. Ibid., p. 46.

26. *Xibu dakaifa zhanlüe juece ruogan wenti.*

27. Cheng Li, "Promises and Pitfalls of Reform."

28. Hu Angang, Zhao Tao, and Yao Zengqi, *Guoqing yu juece.*

29. Hu Angang, *Zhongguo jingji bodong baogao,* pp. 15, 420.

30. Ibid., p. 387. One curiosity is the absence of such an expansion of the money supply in the run-up to the National Party Conference of 1985. Although not technically a Party congress, that conference played a very similar role, including selecting a new and younger Central Committee. It was at this time that "third-generation" leaders Jiang Zemin and Li Peng first entered the Central Committee.

31. Ibid., pp. 185–90, 196.

32. Ibid., pp. 213–14.

33. Wang Shaoguang, "The Social and Political Implications of China's WTO Membership."

34. Hu Angang, "Zhizai cujin jingji fazhan de Zhongguo zhengzhi gaige," p. 14.

35. Ibid., p. 9.
36. Hu Angang, "Background to Writing the Report on State Capacity," pp. 15–18.
37. Guo Shuqing, "Zhongguo shichang jingji zhong de zhengfu zuoyong."
38. Hu Jiayong, "Dui zhengfu zhipei ziyuanliang de shizheng fenxi."
39. Yasheng Huang, *Inflation and Investment Controls in China.*
40. Zhang Shuguang, "Zhengfu de caizheng guanxi," p. 167.
41. Yang Dali, "Dui 'binweilun' de jidian fanbo."
42. Ibid.
43. Zhang Shuguang, "Guojia nengli yu zhidu biange he shehui zhuanxing," p. 143.
44. Yang Peixin, "Shenhua gaige de zhongxin shi shenma?"
45. Ibid.
46. *Wang Shaoguang Proposal (II),* pp. 58–9.
47. Samuel Huntington, "The Clash of Civilizations?"; Samuel Huntington, *The Clash of Civilizations.*
48. Shintaro Ishihara, *The Japan That Can Say No.*
49. Francis Fukayama, "The End of History?"; Francis Fukayama, *The End of History and the Last Man.* See also Francis Fukayama, "A Reply to My Critics."
50. Anthony Lake, "From Containment to Engagement."
51. William Jefferson Clinton, "Remarks to Students and Faculty of Waseda University"; William Jefferson Clinton, "Address to the National Assembly of the Republic of Korea."
52. Asian critics approvingly cited Paul Kennedy's *The Rise and Fall of the Great Powers,* which suggested that the United States was engaged in "imperial overreach."
53. Peter L. Berger and Hsin-Huang Michael Hsiao (Eds.), *In Search of an East Asian Development Model.*
54. International Monetary Fund, *World Economic Outlook,* 1993.
55. Alejandro Reyes, "A Caning in Singapore Stirs Up a Fierce Debate about Crime and Punishment."
56. Mohamad Mahathir and Shintaro Ishihara, *The Voice of Asia.*
57. Wang Hui, "Wenhua pipan lilun yu dangdai Zhongguo minzu zhuyi wenti." In conversation, several people expressed to me the same view (albeit more bluntly), saying that Huntington's views "proved" that the West would never admit Asians – and particularly Chinese – as equals.
58. Wang Xiaodong [Shi Zhong], "Weilai de chongtu."
59. Wang Xiaodong [Shi Zhong], "Ping liangzhong butong de gaige guan."
60. Wang Xiaodong [Shi Zhong], "The West in the Eyes of a Chinese Nationalist," p. 20.
61. Wang Huning, "Wenhua guozhang yu wenhua zhuquan," p. 356.
62. Zhang Kuan, "Zaitan Sayide."
63. It should be noted that Huntington denies this. It is not clear whether Jiang misread Huntington or rather (more likely) supplied this interpretation despite Huntington's actual words.
64. Jiang Yihua, "Lun dongya xiandaihua jinchengzhong de xinlixing zhuyi wenhua."
65. Liu Zhifeng, "Disizhi yanjing kan Zhongguo," pp. 302, 304.
66. Xu Bing, "Wang Shan qi ren," p. 61.

67. Liu Zhifeng (Ed.), *Jieshi Zhongguo,* pp. 298–9.
68. Xu Bing, "Wang Shan qi ren," p. 38.
69. Ibid., pp. 50–1.
70. Liu Zhifeng, "Disizhi yanjing kan Zhongguo," p. 303.
71. See Yang Ping, "The Third Eye – Commenting on *Seeing China through a Third Eye*"; Sha Feng, "Ultraleftists within CCP Launch Comeback by Criticizing Five New Rightists"; and Tseng Hui-yen, "*Looking at China with a Third Eye* Reportedly Written by Pan Yue."
72. Wang Shan [Luo yi ning ge er], *Disanzhi yanjing kan Zhongguo,* pp. 28, 62–3.
73. Ibid., pp. 34, 37, 40.
74. Ibid., pp. 39, 40, 45.
75. Ibid., p. 88.
76. Ibid., p. 92.
77. Ibid., pp. 93–4.
78. Ibid., pp. 78, 167.
79. Ibid., pp. 100, 106, 150.
80. Ibid., p. 176.
81. Ibid., p. 211.
82. Ibid., p. 61.
83. Liu Zhifeng, "Disizhi yanjing kan Zhongguo," p. 312.
84. Ibid., p. 316.
85. Ibid., p. 318.
86. Ibid., p. 330.
87. Wang Shan [Lo yi ning ge er], *Disanzhi yanjing kan Zhongguo,* pp. 7–8, 24.
88. Ibid., p. 25.
89. It is not clear whether – and, if so, to what extent – *Strategy and Management* is supported by the military. Some say it does have military backing; others maintain that it does not. In any event, it seems that the journal enjoys substantial editorial freedom and thus has the character of a nonofficial (*minjian*) publication. It was assigned a new editor in the summer of 1998 and became more liberal in orientation. Some say that its nationalism was too far out of line with official policy, triggering the editorial change.
90. Xiao Gongqin, "Qingmo xinzheng yu Zhongguo xiandaihua yanjiu."
91. For instance, Wang Yizhou's article, "Minzu zhuyi gainian de xiandai sikao" (Contemporary reflections on the concept of nationalism) is a solid academic discussion of nationalism without any effort to tout Chinese nationalism.
92. Pi Mingyong, "Zhongguo jindai minzu zhuyi de duozhong jiagou."
93. Yin Baoyun, "Minzu zhuyi yu xiandai jingji fazhan."
94. Sun Liping, "Pingmin zhuyi yu Zhongguo gaige." It should be noted that "populism" can be translated into Chinese several ways; *pingmin zhuyi* ("common people-ism") and *mincui zhuyi* ("people essence-ism") are most common. The former captures the sense of class conflict while the latter invokes a sense of *volk*.
95. Hu Weixi, "Zhongguo jinxiandai de shehui zhuanxing yu mincui zhuyi."
96. Sun Liping, "Pingmin zhuyi yu Zhongguo gaige," p. 8.
97. Ibid., pp. 8–9.
98. Hu Weixi, "Zhongguo jinxiandai de shehui zhuanxing yu mincui zhuyi," p. 27.

99. Another article included in the same issue of *Strategy and Management* expressed even more concern. See Zhang Xiangping, "Qimeng, mincui, daminzhu de lishi fansi." Zhang's article was not only critical of populism but also of the enlightenment, whether in Europe or in China.
100. Wang Xiaodong [Shi Zhong], "Zai pingmin yu jingying zhijian xunqiu pingheng."
101. Song Qiang, Zhang Zangzang, and Qiao Bian, *Zhongguo keyi shuobu,* pp. 36, 62, 71, 77, 143, 147, 186, 243.
102. Song Qiang et al., *Zhongguo keyi shuobu,* pp. 34, 140, 312, 316, 322, 326.
103. Song Qiang et al., *Zhongguo haishi neng shuobu.*
104. See Liu Kang and Li Xiguang, *Yaomo Zhongguo de beihou;* Peng Qian, Yang Mingjie, and Xu Deren, *Zhongguo weishenma shuobu?;* Zhang Xueli, *Zhongguo heyi shuobu;* Li Shuyi and Yong Jianxiong (Eds.), *Ershiyi shiji Zhongguo jueqi;* He Jie, Wang Baoling, and Wang Jianji (Eds.), *Wo xiangxin Zhongguo;* and He Degong, Pu Weizhong, and Jin Yong, *Qingxiang Zhongguo.*
105. See *Zhongguo qingnian bao,* February 1, 1997, for a five-part series on survey research and its uses.
106. *Beijing qingnian bao,* July 14, 1995, p. 8. The United States was not the only target of Chinese popular opprobrium. One survey of Chinese attitudes toward Japan, conducted at the end of 1996, surprised even the surveyors. For example, the word "Japan" "most easily" made 83.9 percent of the youth surveyed think of the Nanjing massacre and made 81.3 percent think of "Japanese denial" and the "war of resistance against Japanese aggression." When asked which Japanese in the twentieth century is most representative of Japan, first place (28.7 percent) went to Tojo Hideki, of World War II fame. When asked to place a label on the Japanese, 56.1 percent chose "cruel" – the most frequently chosen personality trait. See *Zhongguo qingnian bao,* March 18, 1997, trans. FBIS-CHI-97-094, May 16, 1997.
107. "Miandui 'shengtu de yingdi'."
108. See Kang Xiaoguang, Wu Yulun, Liu Dehuan, and Sun Hui, *Zhongguoren dushu toushi,* pp. 52–9.
109. Song et al., *Zhongguo keyi shuobu,* pp. 64, 90, 165.

CHAPTER 6

1. Reportedly, Deng in September instructed that the plenum concentrate on democratic centralism. See Jen Hui-wen, "What Is the 'Bottom Line' of CCP Political Reform?"
2. Ling Zhijun, *Chenfu,* pp. 388–428.
3. *South China Morning Post,* October 27, 1994, p. 11, in FBIS-CHI, October 27, 1994, pp. 52–3.
4. Ling Zhijun, *Chenfu,* p. 416.
5. Hsu Szu-min, "On the Political Situation in Post-Deng China."
6. "Decision of the Central Committee of the Communist Party of China Concerning Some Major Issues on Strengthening Party Building."
7. Zhu said "some people in economists' circles have advocated the role of the invisible hand in guiding the economy [and] blindly worshipped spontaneous forces...."

Zhongguo tongxun she, December 1, 1994, trans. FBIS-CHI, December 2, 1994, pp. 24–5.

8. Author interviews.
9. "Decision of the Central Committee of the Communist Party of China Concerning Some Major Issues on Strengthening Party Building," p. 16.
10. Xinhua, March 31, 1993, in FBIS-CHI, March 31, 1993, p. 34.
11. "Decision of the Central Committee of the Communist Party of China Concerning Some Major Issues on Strengthening Party Building," p. 16.
12. Deng Xiaoping, "On the Reform of the System of Party and State Leadership."
13. Ling Zhijun, *Chenfu,* p. 420.
14. Xinhua, December 1, 1994, in FBIS-CHI, December 2, 1994, pp. 26–8.
15. "Forward: Explosive Economic Growth Raises Warning Signal."
16. Geremie Barmé, *Shades of Mao.*
17. Joseph Fewsmith, *Dilemmas of Reform,* pp. 194–7.
18. The slow pace of the campaign against corruption in 1993 might be due to Deng Xiaoping's apparent statement, during an inspection trip around Beijing on October 31 of that year, that the campaign should not be allowed to undermine the "reform enthusiasm" of cadres and citizens (see *South China Morning Post,* November 30, 1993). This comment makes it all the clearer that Jiang Zemin's stepping up of the campaign in late 1994 really was intended to distance himself from his erstwhile patron – as his actions against Deng protégés would strongly suggest.
19. "Crimes behind the Power."
20. Zhang Weiguo, "Chen Xitong an yu quanli douzheng."
21. "Communiqué of the Fifth Plenary Session of the Fourteenth Central Committee of the CCP."
22. "Decision of the Central Committee of the Communist Party of China Concerning Some Major Issues on Strengthening Party Building."
23. The official version of Deng's talks that are contained in the third volume of his *Selected Works* names no names, but that he identified Li Ximing, Wang Renzhi, Gao Di, and others as "leftists" was widely reported at the time and confirmed by interviews.
24. It should be noted that the influence of Wang Daohan and even more so of Liu Ji appears to have waned in 1999 and 2000.
25. On Zeng, see Gao Xin, *Jiang Zemin de muliao,* pp. 71–196.
26. Lo Ping, "The Anti-Deng Meeting Incident in Hebei."
27. Ibid.
28. In Marxist terminology, "class in itself" indicates a class that has formed sociologically but has not yet articulated a distinct class ideology. When the latter state is reached, Marxists speak of a "class for itself."
29. "Weilai yi, ershinian woguo guojia anquan de neiwai xingshi ji zhuyao weixie de chubu tantao."
30. Ibid., pp. 139, 141, 143. Since Zhu Rongji has often been called a Gorbachev-type figure, the barb was presumably aimed at him.
31. He Qinglian, *Xiandaihua de xianjing,* p. 52.
32. Xinhua, May 21, 1993, in FBIS-CHI, May 21, 1993, pp. 28–9. See also Zhu Jianhong and Jiang Yaping, "Development and Standardization Are Necessary."

33. Xiang Jingquan, "Review and Prospects of China's Economic Development."
34. He Qinglian, *Xiandaihua de xianjing*, p. 23.
35. Ibid., p. 29.
36. Ibid., p. 30.
37. Ibid., p. 65.
38. "Central Authorities Urge Banks to Draw Bank Loans and Stop Promoting the Bubble Economy."
39. *South China Morning Post*, July 4, 1993, in FBIS-CHI, July 7, 1993, p. 33.
40. Barry Naughton, "The Third Front."
41. Barry Naughton, "Causes et conséquences des disparités dans la croissance économique des provinces chinoises."
42. Zhang Xuwu, Li Ding, and Xie Minggan (Eds.), *Zhongguo siying jingji nianjian, 1996*, p. 138.
43. Shi Xiuyin, "Zhongguo xinshiqi siyou qiyezhu jieceng baogao," p. 226.
44. Chen Xiaoping, "Woguo siying jingji de 'bawu' fazhan he 'jiuwu' zoushi yishu."
45. *Zhongguo jingji nianjian, 1995*, p. 766.
46. Commentator, "Dajia lai taolun zhege zhongda keti – Cong pijiu hezi yinqi de sikao."
47. Jiang Po, "Guochan pijiu you biyao gao zhema duo hezi ma?"
48. Jiang Po, " 'Yanjing' wei shenma bu hezi?"
49. Jiang Po and Zheng Po, " 'Wuxing' wei shenma yao hezi?"
50. Jiang Po, "Woguo mingpai mianlin yanjun tiaozhan."
51. Wang Yungui, "Kan RiMeiFa zhengfu ruhe baohu benguo gongye."
52. "Shanghai 'Zhang Xiaochuan' jianchi bumai pinpai."
53. "Zao gai zheyang taolunle."
54. Author interview.
55. Ling Zhijun and Ma Licheng, *Jiao feng*, pp. 282–3.
56. Wu Yan and Gu Zhaonong, "Jiji yinzi mo panghuang."
57. "Zhongguo shehui jiegou zhuanxing de zhongjinqi qushi yu yinhuan."
58. He Qinglian, *Xiandaihua de xianjing*.
59. Author interviews.
60. Li Peng, "Explanations of the Proposal for the Formulation of the Ninth Five-Year Plan and the Long-Term Target for the Year 2010," p. 21.
61. Zhang Wenmin et al. (Eds.), *Zhongguo jingji dalunzhan*, vol. 2, p. 15.
62. Ibid., pp. 107–10.
63. The call to "talk politics" was drawn from a remark Deng had made during an inspection tour of Tianjin. That speech is not included in the three-volume compendium of Deng's selected works, but it is contained in a volume published in conjunction with the Sixth Plenum of the Fourteenth Central Committee. The volume editors acknowledge that the selection is only an excerpt of Deng's remarks and that the title, "Always Talk Politics," had been selected by the editors. See Zhonggong zhongyang wenxuan yanjiushi (Ed.), *Shehui zhuyi jingshen wenming jianshe wenxian xuanbian*.
64. Jiang Zemin, "Leading Cadres Must Pay Attention to Politics."
65. Ren Zhongping, "Wei jingji jianshe he shehui fazhan tigong qiangyouli de zhengzhi baozhang." Ren Zhongping is an abbreviation of *Renmin ribao zhongyao pinglun* (important commentary from *People's Daily*). Such articles are approved by the

Propaganda Department. This one suggested the very conservative atmosphere then prevailing.

66. "Jianchi he fazhan you Zhongguo tese de shehui zhuyi minzhu."
67. "Zai duiwai kaifang zhong hongyang aiguo zhuyi jingshen."
68. "Yongyuan baochi he fayang jianku fendou jingshen" and "Jianchi gongyouzhi de zhuti diwei buneng dongyao."
69. "Makesi zhuyi yongyuan shi women shengli de qizhi."
70. Author interview.
71. Xing Bensi, "Jianchi Makesi zhuyi bu dongyao."
72. Shen Hongpei, "Ershi shijimo gongchan zhuyi dalunzhan," p. 9.
73. Tang Tsou, "Political Change and Reform," p. 222.
74. Xing Bensi, "Emphasis on Study, Politics, and Uprightness as Fine Party Traditions."
75. Xinhua, May 5, 1996, in FBIS-CHI-96-088, May 5, 1996.
76. Ling Zhijun, *Chenfu,* p. 512.
77. "Resolutions of the CPC Central Committee Regarding Important Questions on Promoting Socialist Ethical and Cultural Progress."
78. Gao Xin, *Jiang Zemin de muliao,* pp. 237–76.
79. "Resolutions of the CPC Central Committee Regarding Important Questions on Promoting Socialist Ethical and Cultural Progress."
80. "Resolution of the Central Committee of the Communist Party of China on the Guiding Principles for Building a Socialist Society with Advanced Culture and Ideology."
81. "Resolutions of the CPC Central Committee Regarding Important Questions on Promoting Socialist Ethical and Cultural Progress."
82. Ibid.
83. Liu Ji, "Lun juece kexuehua"; Wan Li, "Juece minzhuhua he kexuehua shi zhengzhi tizhi gaige de yige zhongyao keti"; Gao Xin, *Jiang Zemin de muliao,* pp. 197–233.
84. For Liu's role in this complicated incident see Gao Xin, *Jiang Zemin de muliao,* pp. 208–14.
85. *Heart-to-Heart Talks* was only the first in a series of books. It was followed quickly by a more substantive and systematic effort to discuss the various problems facing China. See Xu Ming (Ed.), *Guanjian shike.* Note that the title, "the critical moment," comes from Jiang Zemin's remark in Shanghai on May 4, 1996.
86. Author interview.
87. Weng Jieming, Zhang Ximing, Zhang Qiang, and Qu Kemin (Eds.), *Yu zongshuji tanxin,* pp. 18–19.
88. Ibid., pp. 16–19.
89. The effort to base contemporary Marxism on Chinese traditional culture is a major thrust of efforts to reinvigorate the Party's legitimacy and give content to an otherwise hollow Marxism. See the chapter on ideology in Xu Ming (Ed.), *Guanjian shike,* pp. 54–83.
90. Author interviews.
91. Yuan Mu, "Zhongguo gongren jieji shi Zhongguo gongchandang bu ke dongyao de jieji jichu," pp. 11 and 5.
92. Feng Baoxing, "Zhe shi yiben shenmayang de zhuzuo?" p. 233.

93. Ibid., p. 239.
94. Ibid.
95. *Dangdai sichao* editorial department, "Guanyu jianchi gongyouzhi zhuti diwei de ruogan lilun he zhengce wenti," p. 58.
96. Ibid., p. 60.
97. Xin Mao, "Gaige yu jingjiren," p. 216.
98. Ibid., pp. 213–14, 221.
99. Ibid., p. 227.
100. Gao Xin and He Pin, "Tightrope Act of Wei Jianxing."
101. Xinhua, January 5, 1995, in FBIS-CHI, January 6, 1995, pp. 11–13.
102. Xinhua, October 13, 1994, in FBIS-CHI, October 20, 1994, pp. 35–7.

CHAPTER 7

1. Wei Ming, "Yijiu jiu'er nian yilai zichan jieji ziyouhua de dongtai he tedian."
2. Jiang Zemin, "Memorial Speech at Deng Xiaoping's Memorial Meeting."
3. Xinhua, May 29, 1997, in FBIS-CHI-97-105, May 29, 1997; author interview.
4. Jiang Zemin, "Text of Political Report by General Secretary Jiang Zemin at the 15th CPC National Congress."
5. Liu Ji (Ed.), *Shehui zhuyi gaige lun,* pp. 190–217.
6. Richard Baum, "The Fifteenth National Party Congress: Jiang Takes Command?"
7. Jiang Zemin, "Text of Political Report by General Secretary Jiang Zemin at the 15th CPC National Congress."
8. Xinhua, September 13, 1997, in FBIS-CHI-97-260, September 17, 1997.
9. Author interviews.
10. Richard Baum, "The Fifteenth National Party Congress: Jiang Takes Command?" In Chinese, "rule by law" is rendered *yifa zhiguo,* the *zhi* meaning "to rule," whereas "rule of law" is phonetically the same but a different character, meaning "system," is used for *zhi.* It is probably a hopeful exaggeration to render the latter phrase "rule of law" since the Chinese phrase carries more a sense of institution-alization than of law having a independent status, as the English phrase suggests. Jiang probably meant to convey a sense of regularization, already a step forward, whereas liberal intellectuals have tried to push the interpretation a step farther. See Li Shenzhi, "Yeyao tuidong zhengzhi gaige."
11. Cheng Li and Lynn White, "The 15th Central Committee of the Chinese Communist Party."
12. Zhao's letter was not circulated to the delegates at the time of the congress, so they had no chance to discuss it. The text is reproduced in *Beijing zhi chun,* no. 54 (November 1997), p. 105.
13. This section is adapted from my article, "Jiang Zemin Takes Command." Permission of *Current History* to use this material is gratefully acknowledged.
14. Shang Dewen, "Guanyu Zhongguo zhengzhi tizhi gaige de ruogan wenti yu jiben duice."
15. Shang Dewen, "Cong eryuan jiegou kan Zhongguo."
16. Fang Jue, "Zhongguo xuyao xinde zhuanbian"; see also Steven Mufson, "Former Chinese Official Advocates Democracy."

17. Hu Jiwei, "If the Party Is Correct, Bad Things Can Be Turned into Good Things; If the Party Is Wrong, Good Things Can Be Turned into Bad Things"; Hu Jiwei, "Despotic Dictatorship Lingers On"; Hu Jiwei, "Given a Good Central Committee, We Will Have a Good Party; Given a Good Party, We Will Have a Good State." The citation is from part three. Shao Huaze, head of *People's Daily,* reportedly went to Hu's house to serve him with a warning that he had violated Party discipline. See Yin Yen, "Hu Jiwei Served with Warning after Releasing Articles Criticizing CCP Autocracy and Exposing Its Errors in June 4 Incident."
18. Zhang Ximing, "Xinwen fazhi yu shehui fazhan."
19. Ma Licheng, "Xinwen jiandu buxing 'zi'."
20. Liu Junning, "Caichanquan de baozhang yu youxian zhengfu"; Lei Yi, "Minzu, minsheng, minquan."
21. Li Shenzhi, "Hongyang Beida de ziyou zhuyi chuantong."
22. Shen Jiru, *Zhongguo bu dang "bu xiansheng."*
23. Ma Licheng and Ling Zhijun, *Jiao feng.*
24. Author interviews.
25. "Zhongliu Loses Lawsuit against 'Jiaofeng'."
26. Zhongguo jushi fenxi zhongxin (Ed.), *Beijing zaochun de jiaofeng,* pp. 27–31. See also the Preface to the Taiwan edition of *Jiaofeng.*
27. Author interviews.
28. Nicholas Lardy, *China's Unfinished Economic Revolution,* p. 3.
29. Edward Steinfeld, *Forging Reform in China.*
30. China Central Television, March 19, 1998, trans. FBIS-CHI-98-078, March 19, 1998.
31. Author interviews.
32. The history of China's GATT/WTO bid is traced in Harold K. Jacobson and Michel Oksenberg, *China's Participation in the IMF, World Bank and GATT*; Susan Shirk, *How China Opened Its Door*; Margaret M. Pearson, "China's Integration into the International Trade and Investment Regime"; and Margaret M. Pearson, "The Case of China's Accession to GATT/WTO."
33. Author interviews.
34. *Renmin ribao,* March 9, 1998, p. 1.
35. This section is adapted from my article "The Impact of the Kosovo Conflict on China's Political Leaders and Prospects for WTO Accession," which was prepared for and published by the National Bureau of Asian Research, Seattle, WA.
36. Li's efforts to hamper relations, even in petty ways, were visible when George Bush, as former president, traveled to China on two occasions, both times asking to see Wan Li, an old friend and tennis partner. Li Peng blocked Bush's request both times, perhaps afraid their conversation would turn to the last time the two had met – in May 1989, as the Tiananmen demonstrations were nearing their climax. Author interviews.
37. Author interviews.
38. "The Defense Capabilities Initiative and NATO's Strategic Concept."
39. Helene Cooper and Bob Davis, "Overruling Some Staff, Clinton Denies Zhu What He Came For."
40. Helene Cooper and Bob Davis, "Barshefsky Drove Hard Bargain, but Lost to Politics."

41. Cooper and Davis, "Overruling Some Staff, Clinton Denies Zhu What He Came For." For a vivid description of President Clinton's meeting with Premier Zhu Rongji, see Steven Mufson and Robert G. Kaiser, "Missed U.S.–China Deal Looms Large."
42. Yong Wang, "China's Accession to WTO."
43. *Shijie ribao,* May 5, 1999; *Wall Street Journal,* May 3, 1999, p. A16.
44. "China Warns off Foreign Investment in Internet."
45. Author interviews.
46. Xinhua, May 13, 1999.
47. "Firmly Implement the Independent Foreign Policy of Peace."
48. Xinhua, June 12, 1999.
49. Observer, "Humanitarianism or Hegemonism?"; Observer, "On the New Development of U.S. Hegemonism."
50. Observer, "We Urge Hegemon Today to Take a Look at the Mirror of History."
51. Author interviews.
52. Author interviews. The Zhanjiang corruption case was at that time the largest of its kind to have come to light. See Wang Chi, Zhao Zhiwen, and Zheng Hongfan, "Trading Power for Money is Not Tolerated by Law."
53. Author interviews.
54. These vice-premiers were originally assigned these portfolios as their areas of responsibility, but, as noted previously, Zhu had centralized all policy in his office. In June, Zhu's authority was reduced and the vice-premiers were given authority in these respective areas.
55. Author interviews.
56. Author interviews.
57. Gan Yang, "Ping Zhu Rongji fangMei de shiwu yu wenti."
58. Cui Zhiyuan, "Jiaru shijie maoyi zuzhi bushi Zhongguo dangwu zhiji."
59. Shao Ren, "Zhongguo: Ruguan buru tao," p. 6.
60. Ibid., p. 14.
61. Di Yinqing and Guan Gang, "Meiguo wei shenma jiyu yu Zhongguo chongkai ruguan tanpan."
62. Di Yinqing and Guan Gang, "Guanjian shi yao zhangwo jingji fazhan de zhudongquan." See also Di Yinqing and Guan Gang, "Ruguan dui Zhongguo changyuan liyi jiujing yiweizhe shenma."
63. Liu Junning, "Zhongguo jiaru WTO de zhengzhi yiyi."
64. Xiao Gongqin, "Jingti jiduan minzu zhuyi." Xiao's whole approach was distinguished by his deep-seated aversion to emotionalism and extremism, which he saw as the root of China's failure to modernize. Thus, in his discussions of the 1898 reform, Xiao blamed Kang Youwei and other reformers for their radicalism, which caused moderates and conservatives to join together in opposition to the reform. In 1999, Xiao saw Wang Xiaodong and other nationalists as displaying the same lack of moderation.
65. Wang Xiaodong [Shi Zhong], posting under "Guanyu Zhongguo minzu zhuyi de taolun (er)."
66. Yu Quanyu, "Qianyan: Women de guojia dayou xiwang," p. 2.
67. Fang Ning, Wang Xiaodong, and Song Qiang (Eds.), *Quanqiuhua yinyingxia de Zhongguo zhilu,* p. 21.

68. Ibid., p. 22.
69. Ibid., pp. 7, 11.
70. Wang states that, contrary to intellectual opinion in China, American opposition to the war in Vietnam did not derive from moral concerns but simply from the fact that the United States was losing the war; ibid., p. 26.
71. Ibid., p. 15.
72. Ibid., p. 147.
73. Ibid., p. 49.
74. Ibid., p. 31. Elsewhere he writes, "in China, 'nationalism' stems from the lower and middle classes, while 'reverse racism', pro-American and pro-Western attitudes, are common in the upper class of dignitaries, many of whom are corrupt officials hated by the people." See Wang Xiaodong, "The West in the Eyes of a Chinese Nationalist," p. 25.
75. Fang Ning, "Ershiyi shiji de liangzhong qushi."
76. Wang Huning, "Wenhua guozhang yu wenhua zhuquan," p. 356.
77. Bai Mu, " 'Foreign Winds' Invade China," p. 59.
78. Cheng Zhi'ang, "Beware of So-Called Popular Culture," p. 51.
79. Liu Runwei, "Zhimin wenhua lun."
80. Fang Li, "Meiguo quanqiu zhanlüe zhong de wenhua kuozhang yu cantuo."

CONCLUSION

1. Richard Baum, "China After Deng." Some sources say that a secret resolution to that effect was passed at the Fifteenth Party Congress. See Ching Cheong, "Scandal Rocks Jiang's Leadership Plans."
2. Li Shenzhi, "Fengyu canghuang wushi nian – Guoqingye duyu."
3. Ibid.
4. David E. Sanger, "The Trade Deal: The Drama."
5. John F. Harris and Michael Laris, " 'Roller Coaster Ride' to an Off-Again, On-Again Trade Pact."
6. Author interviews.
7. Author interviews.
8. James Kynge, "Top Investigator to Probe Smuggling."
9. James Kynge, "Smuggling Row Rocks Chinese Politburo."
10. John Pomfret, "Chinese Tie Leaders to Smuggling"; Ching Cheong, "Big Trouble in Xiamen."
11. Author interviews.
12. Mark O'Neill, "Fairwell to the Smuggler King."
13. "Dirty Linen: Here, There, Everywhere"; John Pomfret, "Chinese Tie Leaders to Smuggling"; and author interviews. There have also been suggestions that Lai was involved in secret work with the Ministry of State Security. See Xiao He, "Yuanhua an he dangjun gaoceng de guanxi."
14. Hu Changqing, former vice-governor of Jiangxi, was executed for corruption in March 2000, and Cheng Kejie, former vice-chairman of the NPC Standing Committee, was executed in September 2000. A major case of corruption in Shantou

came to light in December 2000, and the Shenyang Party leadership was accused in January 2001 of being involved in organized crime.

15. "Jiang Zemin Delivers an Important Speech at the Fourth Plenary Session of the Central Discipline Inspection Commission"; see also "Jiang Must Act Fast."
16. "Speech by Jiang Zemin at the Fourth Plenary Session of the Commission for Discipline Inspection." Note that this is a fuller text of Jiang's speech than that transmitted by Xinhua on January 14 (see note 15). However, there are significant differences between the texts, so one cannot simply cite the fuller text as the more authoritative.
17. "Jiang Zemin Delivers an Important Speech at the Fourth Plenary Session of the Central Discipline Inspection Commission." Note that this sentence does not appear in the version carried by *Dangjian yanjiu* (see note 16).
18. *Wall Street Journal,* January 20, 2000.
19. Mark O'Neill, "Politburo Closes Ranks"; Ma Ling, "Who Starts Rumors about Jia Qinglin's Divorce?"
20. Author interviews.
21. Author interviews.
22. "Dirty Linen: Here, There, Everywhere."
23. "Speech by Jiang Zemin at the Fourth Plenary Session of the Commission for Discipline Inspection."
24. Ibid.
25. As quoted to me by a knowledgeable observer.
26. Author interviews.
27. Orville Schell, *Mandate of Heaven.*
28. Craig R. Smith, "Shanghai Journal."
29. "Yiwei yanjiusheng guanyu gaoxiao sixiang zhandi wenti de laixin"; Zi Yu, "Shei zai zhanling daxuesheng de sixiang zhandi."
30. "Xiangqile 'zai' mai yetian xin butong." The article that Li Peng praised was Yu Quanyu, "Zan dangdai qingnian de 'sixiang jiefang'."
31. "Jiang Zemin zai Guangdong kaocha gongzuo qiangdiao jinmi jiehe xinde lishi tiaojian jiaqiang dangde jianshe shizhong dailing quanmin renmin cujin shengchanli de fazhan"; "Communiqué of the Fifth Plenary Session of the Fifteenth Central Committee of the Communist Party of China."
32. Zheng Bijian, "'Sange daibiao' zhongyao lunshu yu mianxiang ershiyi shiji de Zhongguo gongchandang."
33. Ibid., p. 132.
34. Long Yongtu, "Guanyu jiaru shijie maoyi zuzhi de wenti."
35. Lei Yi, "Jingti faxisi"; Lei Yi, "Yihetuan de beiju."

Bibliography

BOOKS AND ARTICLES

"Adhere Better to Taking Economic Construction as the Center." *Renmin ribao* editorial, February 22, 1992, trans. FBIS-CHI, February 24, 1992, pp. 40–1.

Alitto, Guy. *The Last Confucian: Liang Shu-ming and the Chinese Dilemma of Modernity.* Berkeley: University of California Press, 1979.

Anderson, Perry. *The Origins of Postmodernism.* London: Verso, 1998.

Bai Mu. " 'Foreign Winds' Invade China." In *Minzhu yu fazhi* 6 (March 21, 1996): 8–10, trans. Stanley Rosen (Ed.), *The Contention in China over "Cultural Colonialism,"* (*Chinese Sociology and Anthropology* 31(4): 58–67, Summer 1999).

Barmé, Geremie R. *In the Red: On Contemporary Chinese Culture.* New York: Columbia University Press, 1999.

Barmé, Geremie. *Shades of Mao: The Posthumous Cult of the Great Leader.* Armonk, NY: M.E. Sharpe, 1996.

Barnett, A. Doak. *The Making of Foreign Policy in China: Structure and Process.* Boulder, CO: Westview, 1985.

Baum, Richard. *Burying Mao: Chinese Politics in the Age of Deng Xiaoping.* Princeton, NJ: Princeton University Press, 1994.

Baum, Richard. "China after Deng: Ten Scenarios in Search of Reality." *The China Quarterly* 145 (March 1996): 153–75.

Baum, Richard. "The Fifteenth National Party Congress: Jiang Takes Command?" *The China Quarterly* 153 (March 1998): 141–56.

"Be More Daring in Carrying Out Reform." *Renmin ribao* editorial, February 24, 1992, trans. FBIS-CHI, February 24, 1992, pp. 41–2.

Berger, Peter L., and Hsin-Huang Michael Hsiao (Eds.). *In Search of an East Asian Development Model.* New Brunswick, NJ: Transaction Books, 1988.

Bernstein, Richard, and Ross H. Munro. *The Coming Conflict with China.* New York: Knopf, 1997.

Boutros-Ghali, Boutros. *Unvanquished: A U.S.–U.N. Saga.* New York: Random House, 1999.

Brzezinski, Zbigniew K. *Out of Control: Global Turmoil on the Eve of the Twenty-First Century.* New York: Scribner's, 1993.

"Build Up a Great Wall of Steel against Peaceful Evolution." *Renmin Ribao* commentator, August 16, 1991, trans. FBIS-CHI, August 19, 1991, pp. 27–8.

"Central Authorities Urge Banks to Draw Bank Loans and Stop Promoting the Bubble Economy." *Ta kung pao,* July 1, 1993, trans. FBIS-CHI, July 1, 1993, pp. 31–2.

271

Chang, Carson. *The Third Force in China*. New York: Bookman, 1952.

Chang, Jung. *Wild Swans: Three Daughters of China*. New York: Simon & Schuster, 1991.

Chen Chien-ping. "China Stresses Modernization of Science and Technology." *Wen wei po,* March 12, 1991, p. 1, trans. FBIS-CHI, March 12, 1991, p. 21.

Chen Chien-ping. "Zhu Rongji Urges Paying Attention to Negative Effects of Reform." *Wen hui po,* January 13, 1993, trans. FBIS-CHI, January 15, 1993, pp. 27–8.

Chen Fong-ching and Jin Guantao. *From Youthful Manuscripts to River Elegy: The Chinese Popular Cultural Movement and Political Transformation 1979–1989.* Hong Kong: Chinese University Press, 1997.

Chen Kang, Gary Jefferson, and Inderjit Singh. "Lessons from China's Economic Reform." *Journal of Comparative Economics* 16 (June 1992): 201–25.

Chen Xianyi and Chen Ruiyao. *Zhongguo youge Nanjiecun* [In China, there is a Nanjie village]. Beijing: Jiefangjun wenyi chubanshe, 1999.

Chen Xiaoping. "Woguo siying jingji de 'bawu' fazhan he 'jiuwu' zoushi yishu" [The development of China's private economy during the fifth five-year plan and its trend in the ninth five-year plan]. In Zhang Xuwu et al. (Eds.), *Zhongguo siying jingji nianjian, 1996,* pp. 136–9.

Chen Xitong. "Report on Checking the Turmoil and Quelling the Counter-Revolutionary Rebellion." Xinhua, July 6, 1989, in FBIS-CHI, July 6, 1989, pp. 20–36.

Chen Yeping. "Have Both Political Integrity, Ability, Stress Political Ability: On Criterion for Selecting Cadres." *Renmin ribao,* September 1, 1991, trans. FBIS-CHI, September 6, 1991, pp. 26–31.

Chen Yizi, Wang Xiaoqiang, and Li Jun. "The Deep-Seated Questions and the Strategic Choice China's Reform Faces." In Rosen and Zou (Eds.), "The Chinese Debate on New Authoritarianism (II)," pp. 39–60.

Chen Yuan. "Several Questions on Methods and Theory Regarding Studies in Economic Operations in China." *Jingji yanjiu,* February 1992, pp. 29–37, trans. FBIS-CHI, May 27, 1992, pp. 32–41.

Chen Yuan. "Wo guo jingji de shenceng wenti he xuanze (gangyao)," [China's deep-seated economic problems and choices (outline)]. *Jingji yanjiu* 4 (April 1991): 18–26.

Cheng Jo-lin. "Short But Strange Coup (Part I)." *Wen wei po,* August 23, 1991, trans. FBIS-CHI, August 27, 1991, pp. 8–9.

Cheng Nien. *Life and Death in Shanghai*. New York: Grove Press, 1986.

Cheng Te-lin. "Yao Yilin Launches Attack against Zhu Rongji, Tian Jiyun." *Ching pao* 1, January 5, 1993, pp. 44–5, trans. FBIS-CHI, January 22, 1993, pp. 46–7.

Cheng Weigao. "Further Emancipate the Mind and Renew the Concept, and Accelerate the Pace of Reform and Development." *Hebei ribao,* April 18, 1991, trans. FBIS-CHI, June 7, 1991, pp. 60–8.

Cheng Zhi'ang. "Beware of So-Called Popular Culture." *Zhongliu* 6 (June 1996): 54–8, trans. Stanley Rosen (Ed.), *The Contention in China over "Cultural Colonialism"* (*Chinese Sociology and Anthropology* 31(4): 42–57, Summer 1999).

Cheong, Ching. "Big Trouble in Xiamen." *The Straits Times,* January 30, 2000.

Cheong, Ching. "Scandal Rocks Jiang's Leadership Plans." *The Straits Times,* February 5, 2000, p. 30.

"China Warns off Foreign Investment in Internet." *Financial Times,* September 14, 1999.

China Youth Daily Ideology and Theory Department. "Realistic Responses and Strategic Options for China after the Soviet Upheaval," trans. David Kelly, *Chinese Law and Government* 29 (March/April 1996): 13–31.

Ching Wen. "Abnormal Atmosphere in *Renmin ribao*," *Ching pao* 178, May 5, 1992, pp. 46–7, trans. FBIS-CHI, May 18, 1992, p. 22.

Chong, Woei Lien (Ed.). *Li Zehou* (*Contemporary Chinese Thought* 31, Winter 1999/2000).

Clinton, William Jefferson. "Address to the National Assembly of the Republic of Korea." Retrieved from ⟨www.pub.whitehouse.gov⟩.

Clinton, William Jefferson. "Remarks to Students and Faculty of Waseda University." Retrieved from ⟨www.mofa.go.jp/region/n-america/us/archive/1993/remarks.html⟩.

"Clinton's China Syndrome." *The Weekly Standard,* April 27, 1998, pp. 7–8.

Commentator. "Dajia lai taolun zhege zhongda keti – Cong pijiu hezi yinqi de sikao" [Everybody come discuss this important topic – Thoughts derived from joint ventures in the beer industry]. *Jingji ribao,* June 20, 1996, p. 1.

"Communiqué of the Fifth Plenary Session of the Fifteenth Central Committee of the Communist Party of China." Xinhua, October 11, 2000, in FBIS-CHI-2000-1011, October 11, 2000.

"Communiqué of the Fifth Plenary Session of the Fourteenth Central Committee of the CCP." Xinhua, September 28, 1995, in FBIS-CHI, September 28, 1995, pp. 15–17.

Cooper, Helene, and Bob Davis. "Barshefsky Drove Hard Bargain, but Lost to Politics." *Wall Street Journal,* April 12, 1999, p. 24.

Cooper, Helene, and Bob Davis. "Overruling Some Staff, Clinton Denies Zhu What He Came For." *Wall Street Journal,* April 9, 1999, pp. A1, A6.

"Crimes behind the Power: Analyzing the Serious Crimes Committed by Yan Jianhong." *Renmin ribao,* January 14, 1995, trans. FBIS-CHI, January 24, 1995, pp. 29–31.

Cui Zhiyuan. "Angang xianfa yu houfute zhuyi" [The Angang constitution and post-Fordism]. In Cui Zhiyuan, *Di'erci sixiang jiefang,* pp. 143–56.

Cui Zhiyuan. *Di'erci sixiang jiefang* [The second liberation of thought]. Hong Kong: Oxford University Press, 1997.

Cui Zhiyuan. "Jiaru shijie maoyi zuzhi bushi Zhongguo dangwu zhiji" [Entering the WTO is not an urgent task for China]. In *Zhongguo yu shijie* [China and the World], Internet journal, ⟨www.chinabulletin.com/99/zs9908c.htm#2⟩.

Cui Zhiyuan. "Lusuo xin lun" [A new discussion on Rousseau]. In Han Shuifa (Ed.), *Shehui zhengyi shi ruhe keneng de – Zhengzhi zhexue zai Zhongguo* [How is social justice possible? Political philosophy in China]. Guangzhou chubanshe, 2000.

Cui Zhiyuan. "Meiguo ershijiu zhou gongsifa biange de lilun beijing" [The theoretical background to the change in the company law in twenty-nine American states]. *Jingji yanjiu* 4 (April 1996): 35–40, 60.

Cui Zhiyuan. "Zailun zhidu chuangxin yu di'erci sixiang jiefang" [Again discussing institutional innovation and the second emancipation of thought]. In Cui Zhiyuan, *Di'erci sixiang jiefang,* pp. 21–40.

Cui Zhiyuan. "Zhidu chuangxin yu di'erci sixiang jiefang" [Institutional renovation and the second emancipation of thought]. In Cui Zhiyuan, *Di'erci sixiang jiefang,* pp. 1–19.

Cui Zhiyuan, Deng Yingtao, and Miao Zhuang. *Nanjiecun* [Nanjie village]. Beijing: Dangdai Zhongguo chubanshe, 1996.

"Current World Economic Situation – Chinese Scholar He Xin's Talk with Japanese Professor Yabuki Susumu." *Beijing Review* 33 (1990). Part I (November 19–25): 8–11; Part II (November 26–December 2): 14–19; Part III (December 3–9): 7–14.

Dai Qing. "From Lin Zexu to Jiang Jingguo." In Rosen and Zou (Eds.), "The Chinese Debate on the New Authoritarianism (II)," pp. 61–6.

Dangdai sichao Editorial Department. "Guanyu jianchi gongyouzhi zhuti diwei de ruogan lilun he zhengce wenti" [Several theoretical and policy questions concerning upholding the primary position of public ownership]. *Kaifang* 123 (March 1, 1997): 54–63.

Davis, Deborah S., Richard Kraus, Barry Naughton, and Elizabeth J. Perry (Eds.). *Urban Spaces in Contemporary China*. Cambridge University Press, 1995.

"Decision of the Central Committee of the Communist Party of China Concerning Some Major Issues on Strengthening Party Building." Xinhua, October 6, 1994, in FBIS-CHI, October 6, 1994, pp. 13–22.

"Decision of the Central Committee of the Communist Party of China on Reform of the Economic Structure." Xinhua, October 20, 1984, in FBIS-CHI, October 22, 1984, pp. K1–K9.

"Deepen the Struggle against Bourgeois Liberalization." *Renmin ribao* editorial, May 17, 1987, trans. FBIS-CHI, May 18, 1987, pp. K2–K4.

"The Defense Capabilities Initiative and NATO's Strategic Concept." Sub-Committee on Future Security and Defense Capabilities, ⟨www.nato.int⟩.

Deng Liqun. "Have Correct Understanding of Contradictions in Socialist Society, Grasp Initiative in Handling Contradictions." *Renmin ribao*, October 23, 1991, p. 5, trans. FBIS-CHI, October 29, 1991, pp. 22–9.

Deng Xiaoping. *Deng Xiaoping wenxuan, di san juan* [Selected works of Deng Xiaoping, vol. 3]. Beijing: Renmin chubanshe, 1993.

Deng Xiaoping. "Disandai lingdao jiti de dangwu zhiji" [Urgent tasks of the third generation leadership collective]. In *Deng Xiaoping wenxuan*, vol. 3, pp. 309–14.

Deng Xiaoping. "Jiesu yanjun de ZhongMei guanxi yao you Meiguo caiqu zhudong" [Resolving the serious situation in Sino–U.S. relations requires that the U.S. take the initiative]. In *Deng Xiaoping wenxuan*, vol. 3, pp. 330–3.

Deng Xiaoping. "On the Reform of the System of Party and State Leadership." In *Selected Works of Deng Xiaoping (1975–1982)*, pp. 302–25. Beijing: Foreign Languages Press, 1983.

Deng Xiaoping. "Shicha Shanghai shi de tanhua" [Talks when inspecting Shanghai]. In *Deng Xiaoping wenxuan*, vol. 3, pp. 366–7.

Deng Xiaoping. "Speech at the Opening Ceremony of the National Conference on Science." In *Selected Works of Deng Xiaoping (1975–1982)*, pp. 101–16. Beijing: Foreign Languages Press, 1983.

Deng Xiaoping. "Women you xinxin ba Zhongguo de shiqing zuode genghao" [We are confident that we can do even better in China's affairs]. In *Deng Xiaoping wenxuan*, vol. 3, pp. 324–7.

Deng Xiaoping. "Zai jiejian shoudu jieyan budui junyishang ganbu shi de jianghua" [Talk on receiving martial law cadres at the army level and above in the capital]. In *Deng Xiaoping wenxuan,* vol. 3, pp. 302–8.

Deng Xiaoping. "Zai Wuchang, Shenzhen, Zhuhai, Shanghai dengdi de tanhua yaodian" [Essential points from talks in Wuchang, Shenzhen, Zhuhai, and Shanghai]. In *Deng Xiaoping wenxuan,* vol. 3, pp. 370–83.

Deng Xiaoping. "Zucheng yige shixing gaige de you xiwang de lingdao jiti" [Organizing a reformist, hopeful leadership collective]. In *Deng Xiaoping wenxuan,* vol. 3, pp. 296–301.

"*Deng Xiaoping lun wenyi* yantaohui zaijing juxing" [Discussion meeting on *Deng Xiaoping on literature and art* convened in capital]. *Renmin ribao,* December 23, 1989, pp. 1, 3.

"Deng Xiaoping on Neoauthoritarianism." *Zhongguo tongxun she,* April 7, 1989, trans. FBIS-CHI-89-066, April 7, 1989, p. 15.

"Deng Xiaoping's Visit to Special Zones Shows China Is More Open." *Wen wei po,* January 28, 1992, trans. FBIS-CHI, January 28, 1992, pp. 23–4.

Deng Yingtao. *Deng Yingtao ji* [Collected essays of Deng Yingtao]. Harbin: Heilongjiang chubanshe, 1989.

Deng Yingtao. *Xin fazhan fangshi yu Zhongguo de weilai* [A new model of development and China's future]. Beijing: Zhongxin chubanshe, 1991.

"Destructive Engagement." *The New Republic,* March 10, 1997, p. 9.

Deyo, Frederic C. (Ed.). *The Political Economy of the New Asian Industrialization.* Ithaca, NY: Cornell University Press, 1987.

Di Yinqing and Guan Gang. "Guanjian shi yao zhangwo jingji fazhan de zhudongquan" [What is critical is grasping the initiative in economic development]. *Gaige neican* 11 (May 20, 1999): 35–9.

Di Yinqing and Guan Gang. "Meiguo wei shenma jiyu yu Zhongguo chongkai ruguan tanpan" [Why is the U.S. anxious to reopen negotiations on entering the WTO?]. *Gaige neican* 8 (April 20, 1999): 39–42.

Di Yinqing and Guan Gang. "Ruguan dui Zhongguo changyuan liyi jiujing yiweizhe shenma" [What after all are the implications of entering WTO for China's long-term interests?]. *Gaige neican* 9 (May 5, 1999): 34–8.

Ding, X. L. *The Decline of Communism in China: Legitimacy Crisis, 1977–1989.* Cambridge University Press, 1994.

Ding Xueliang. "Dangdai Zhongguo de daode kongbai" [The moral vacuum in contemporary China]. *Kaifang zazhi* (April 1994): 9–11.

Ding Xueliang. *Gongchanzhuyihou yu Zhongguo* [Post-Communism and China]. Hong Kong: Oxford University Press, 1994.

"Dirty Linen: Here, There, Everywhere." *The Straits Times,* January 30, 2000.

Dong Jinguan. "The Main Characteristics of Class Struggle at the Present Stage." *Guangming ribao,* September 11, 1989, p. 3, trans. FBIS-CHI, September 11, 1989, pp. 41–5.

"East Wind Brings Spring All Around: On-the-Spot Report on Comrade Deng Xiaoping in Shenzhen." *Renmin ribao,* March 31, 1992, trans. FBIS-CHI, April 1, 1992 (suppl.), pp. 7–15.

Eckholm, Erik. "After an Attack, Chinese Won't Print Expatriate's Novel." *New York Times,* June 24, 2000, pp. A17, A22.

Economy, Elizabeth, and Michel Oksenberg (Eds.). *China Joins the World.* New York: Council on Foreign Relations, 1999.

Evans, Peter. *Embedded Autonomy: States and Industrial Transformation.* Princeton, NJ: Princeton University Press, 1995.

Evans, Peter R., Dietrich Rueschemeyer, and Theda Skocpol (Eds.). *Bringing the State Back In.* Cambridge University Press, 1985.

Fan Gang. "Liangzhong gaige chengben yu liangzhong gaige fangshi" [Two reform costs and two reform forms]. *Jingji yanjiu* 1 (1993): 3–15.

Fang Jue. "Zhongguo xuyao xinde zhuanbian" [China needs a new change]. Unpublished letter.

Fang Li. "Meiguo quanqiu zhanlüe zhong de wenhua kuozhang yu cantuo" [Cultural expansion and penetration in America's global strategy]. *Lilun dongtai* [Theoretical Trends] 1446 (June 15, 1999).

Fang Ning. "Ershiyi shiji de liangzhong qushi" [Two trends in the twenty-first century]. In Fang Ning et al. (Eds.), *Quanqiuhua yinyingxia de Zhongguo zhilu,* pp. 230–41.

Fang Ning, Wang Xiaodong, and Song Qiang (Eds.). *Quanqiuhua yinyingxia de Zhongguo zhilu* [China under the shadow of globalization]. Beijing: Shehui kexue chubanshe, 1999.

Fang Sheng. "Opening Up to the Outside World and Making Use of Capitalism." *Renmin ribao,* February 23, 1992, trans. FBIS-CHI, February 24, 1992, pp. 37–9.

Fei Hsiao-t'ung, *Peasant Life in China: A Field Study of Country Life in the Yangtze Valley.* New York: Oxford University Press, 1946.

Feng Baoxing. "Zhe shi yiben shenmayang de zhuzuo?" [What type of work is this?]. In Shi Liaozi (Ed.), *Beijing dixia "wanyanshu,"* pp. 231–40.

Fewsmith, Joseph. *Dilemmas of Reform: Political Conflict and Economic Debate.* Armonk, NY: M.E. Sharpe, 1994.

Fewsmith, Joseph. "Historical Echoes and Chinese Politics: Can China Leave the Twentieth Century Behind?" In Tyrene White (Ed.), *China Briefing, 2000,* pp. 11–48. Armonk, NY: M.E. Sharpe, 2000.

Fewsmith, Joseph. "The Impact of the Kosovo Conflict on China's Political Leaders and Prospects for WTO Accession." National Bureau of Asian Research, Seattle, WA, 1999.

Fewsmith, Joseph. "The Impact of Reform on Elite Politics." In Joseph Fewsmith, *Elite Politics in Contemporary China,* pp. 86–117. Armonk, NY: M.E. Sharpe, 2001.

Fewsmith, Joseph. "Jiang Zemin Takes Command." *Current History* 97 (1998): 250–6.

Fewsmith, Joseph. "Neoconservatism and the End of the Dengist Era." *Asian Survey* 35 (July 1995): 635–51.

Fewsmith, Joseph. "Reform, Resistance, and the Politics of Succession." In William A. Joseph (Ed.), *China Briefing, 1994,* pp. 7–34. New York: The Asia Society, 1994.

Fewsmith, Joseph, and Stanley Rosen. "The Domestic Context of Chinese Foreign Policy: Does 'Public Opinion' Matter?" In David M. Lampton (Ed.), *The Making of Chinese Foreign and Security Policy, 1978–2000,* pp. 151–87. Stanford, CA: Stanford University Press, 2001.

Bibliography

"Firmly Implement the Independent Foreign Policy of Peace." Xinhua, June 2, 1999, in FBIS-CHI-1999-0602, June 2, 1999.

"Forward: Explosive Economic Growth Raises Warning Signal." *Jiushi niandai* 10, October 1, 1993, pp. 58–9, trans. FBIS-CHI, January 11, 1994, pp. 49–50.

Foucault, Michel. *The Order of Things: An Archaeology of the Human Sciences.* New York: Vintage, 1994.

Friedman, Edward. *National Identity and Democratic Prospects in Socialist China.* Armonk, NY: M.E. Sharpe, 1995.

Fukayama, Francis. "The End of History?" *The National Interest* 16 (Summer 1989): 3–18.

Fukayama, Francis. *The End of History and the Last Man.* New York: The Free Press, 1992.

Fukayama, Francis. "A Reply to My Critics." *The National Interest* 18 (Winter 1989): 21–8.

"Full text" of speech delivered by Zhao Ziyang. *Hsin pao,* June 4, 1994, trans. FBIS-CHI, June 7, 1994, pp. 13–20.

Furth, Charlotte (Ed.). *The Limits of Change: Essays on Conservative Alternatives in Republican China.* Cambridge, MA: Harvard University Press, 1976.

"Gaige buneng likai gongyouzhi zhege jichu" [Reform cannot depart from the pillar of public ownership]. *Zhenli de zhuiqiu,* September 1995.

Gan Yang. " 'Jiangcun jingji' zairenshi" [Reunderstanding 'Rural Economy']. *Dushu* (October 1994): 50–7.

Gan Yang. "Ping Zhu Rongji fangMei de shiwu yu wenti" [Critiquing the mistakes and problems of Zhu Rongji's trip to the U.S.]. *Zhongguo yu shijie* [China and the World] 5 (May 1999), available at ⟨www.chinabulletin.com/99/zs9905a.htm⟩.

Gao Xin. *Jiang Zemin de muliao* [Jiang Zemin's counselors]. Hong Kong: Mingjing chubanshe, 1996.

Gao Xin. *Jiang Zemin quanli zhi lu* [Jiang Zemin's road to power]. Hong Kong: Mingjing chubanshe, 1997.

Gao Xin and He Pin. "Tightrope Act of Wei Jianxing." *Tangtai* 23, February 15, 1993, pp. 42–5, trans. FBIS-CHI, February 24, 1993, pp. 24–6.

Gao Xin and He Pin. *Zhonggong "taizidang"* ["Princelings" of the CCP]. Taipei: Shibao wenhua, 1992.

Gao Xin and He Pin. *Zhu Rongji zhuan* [Biography of Zhu Rongji]. Taipei: Xinxinwen, 1993.

Gereffi, Gary, and Donald L. Wyman (Eds.). *Manufacturing Miracles: Paths of Industrialization in Latin America and East Asia.* Princeton, NJ: Princeton University Press, 1990.

Gertz, Bill. *The China Threat: How the People's Republic Targets America.* Washington, DC: Regency Publishing, 2000.

Gilley, Bruce. *Tiger on the Brink: Jiang Zemin and China's New Elite.* Berkeley: University of California Press, 1998.

Godwin, Paul H. B. "Party–Military Relations." In Merle Goldman and Roderick MacFarquhar (Eds.), *The Paradox of China's Post-Mao Reforms,* pp. 76–99. Cambridge, MA: Harvard University Press, 1999.

Godwin, Paul H. B., and Evan S. Medeiros. "China, America, and Missile Defense: Conflicting National Interests." *Current History* 99 (2000): 285–7.

Goldman, Merle. *Sowing the Seeds of Democracy in China.* Cambridge, MA: Harvard University Press, 1994.

Gong Yantao. "The Essence of 'Transformation' Is to Abolish Ideological and Political Work." *Renmin ribao,* August 9, 1989, trans. FBIS-CHI, August 10, 1989, pp. 9–11.

Gong Yuzhi. "Emancipate Our Minds, Liberate Productive Forces – Studying Comrade Deng Xiaoping's Important Talks." *Wenhui bao,* April 15, 1992, trans. FBIS-CHI, April 20, 1992, pp. 25–8.

Grindle, Merilee S. (Ed.). *Getting Good Government: Capacity Building in the Public Sectors of Developing Countries.* Cambridge, MA: Harvard University Press, 1997.

Grindle, Merilee S. "The Good Government Imperative: Human Resources, Organizations, and Institutions." In Merilee S. Grindle (Ed.), *Getting Good Government,* pp. 3–28.

Grindle, Merilee S., and John W. Thomas. *Public Choices and Policy Change.* Baltimore: Johns Hopkins University Press, 1991.

Gu Xin. "Xin quanwei zhuyi de lilun kunjing" [The theoretical dilemmas of new authoritarianism]. *Ming pao* 6 (June 1989): 46–50.

Gu Xin and David Kelly. "New Conservatism: Intermediate Ideology of a 'New Elite'." In David S. G. Goodman and Beverly Hooper (Eds.), *China's Quiet Revolution: New Interactions Between State and Society,* pp. 219–33. Melbourne: Longman Cheshire, 1994.

Guo Shuqing. "Zhongguo shichang jingji zhong de zhengfu zuoyong" [The government's role in China's market economy]. *Gaige* 3 (1999): 48–57, trans. Joseph Fewsmith (Ed.), *The Role of Government in a Period of Economic Reform* (*The Chinese Economy* 32(5): 26–8, September/October 1999).

Hamrin, Carol Lee, and Timothy Cheek (Eds.). *China's Establishment Intellectuals.* Armonk, NY: M.E. Sharpe, 1986.

Harding, Harry. *The Fragile Relationship: The United States and China Since 1972.* Washington, DC: Brookings, 1992.

Harris, John F., and Michael Laris. " 'Roller Coaster Ride' to an Off-Again, On-Again Trade Pact." *Washington Post,* November 16, 1999, p. A26.

He Degong, Pu Weizhong, and Jin Yong. *Qingxiang Zhongguo* [Biased toward China]. Guangzhou: Guangdong renmin chubanshe, 1997.

He Jie, Wang Baoling, and Wang Jianji (Eds.). *Wo xiangxin Zhongguo* [I believe in China]. Beijing: Chengshi chubanshe, 1997.

He Po-shih. "The Army Reshuffle Was Carried Out to Pacify the Leftist Faction: Commentary on the Post-14th Party Congress Political Situation in China." *Tangtai* 21, December 15, 1992, pp. 32–6, trans. FBIS-CHI, January 7, 1993, pp. 15–18.

He Qinglian. *Xiandaihua de xianjing: Dangdai Zhongguo de jingji shehui wenti* [The pitfalls of modernization: The economic and social problems of contemporary China]. Beijing: Jinri Zhongguo chubanshe, 1998.

He Xin. "Aiguo de Qu Yuan yu ruguo de 'He Shang'" [The patriotic Qu Yuan and the national shame 'River Elegy']. *Beijing ribao,* August 26, 1989.

He Xin. "Dangdai shijie jingji xingshi fenxi" [Analysis of the contemporary world's economic situation]. In He Xin, *Zhonghua fuxing yu shijie weilai,* vol. 1, pp. 56–65.

He Xin. "Dangqian jingji xingshi pinglun (zhi yi)" [An evaluation of the current economic situation (part I)]. In He Xin, *Zhonghua fuxing yu shijie weilai,* vol. 2, pp. 542–5.

He Xin. "Dangqian Zhongguo neiwai xingshi fenxi ji ruogan zhengce jianyi (zhaiyao)" [Analysis of the domestic and international situation facing contemporary China and some policy suggestions (outline)]. In He Xin, *Zhonghua fuxing yu shijie weilai,* vol. 1, pp. 1–6.

He Xin. "Dui woguo shinian gaige de fansi" [Reflecting on the ten years of China's reform]. In He Xin, *Zhonghua fuxing yu shijie weilai,* vol. 2, pp. 401–13.

He Xin. " 'He Shang' de piping" [Criticism of 'River Elegy']. In He Xin, *Weiji yu fansi* [Crisis and reflection], vol. 1, pp. 282–99. Beijing: Guoji wenhua chuban gongsi, 1997.

He Xin. "Lun woguo jingji gaige zhidao lilun de shiwu" [The mistakes of guiding theory of China's economic reform]. In He Xin, *Zhonghua fuxing yu shijie weilai,* vol. 2, pp. 503–12.

He Xin. "Lun Zhongguo xiandaihua de guoji huanjing yu waijiao zhanlüe" [The international environment of China's modernization and its diplomatic strategy]. In He Xin, *Zhonghua fuxing yu shijie weilai,* vol. 1, pp. 7–27.

He Xin. "Lun ZhongMeiRi guanxi de zhanlüe beijing yu duice" [On the strategic background of Sino–U.S.–Japanese relations and countermeasures]. In He Xin, *Zhonghua fuxing yu shijie weilai,* vol. 1, pp. 28–47.

He Xin. "Tan dangdai ziben zhuyi" [Contemporary capitalism]. In He Xin, *Zhonghua fuxing yu shijie weilai,* vol. 1, pp. 66–79.

He Xin. "Wo xiang nimen de liangzhi huhuan" [My call to your conscience]. In He Xin, *Zhonghua fuxing yu shijie weilai,* vol. 2, pp. 466–97.

He Xin. "Wode kunhuo yu youlu" [My doubts and fears]. In He Xin, *Zhonghua fuxing yu shijie weilai,* vol. 2, pp. 421–42.

He Xin. "Woguo duiwai kaifang zhanlüe de yizhong shexiang" [A concept for our strategy for opening to the outside world]. In He Xin, *Zhonghua fuxing yu shijie weilai,* vol. 1, pp. 80–5.

He Xin. *Zhonghua fuxing yu shijie weilai* [China's renaissance and the future of the world], 2 vols. Chengdu: Sichuan renmin chubanshe, 1996.

He Yijun, Jiang Bin, and Wang Jianwei. "Speed Up Pace of Reform, Opening Up." *Jiefangjun bao,* March 25, 1992, trans. FBIS-CHI, April 22, 1992, pp. 30–3.

Hilderbrand, Mary E., and Merilee S. Grindle. "Building Sustainable Capacity in the Public Sector: What Can Be Done?" In Merilee S. Grindle (Ed.), *Getting Good Government,* pp. 31–61.

Ho Te-hsu. "China Has Crossed the Nadir of the Valley but Is Still Climbing Up from the Trough – Liu Guoguang Talks about the Current Economic Situation in China." *Jingji daobao* 38/39, October 1, 1990, pp. 12–13, trans. FBIS-CHI, October 12, 1990, pp. 27–30.

Ho Yuen. "CCP's 'Five Adherences' and 'Five Oppositions' to Prevent Peaceful Evolution." *Ming pao,* August 29, 1991, trans. FBIS-CHI, August 29, 1991, pp. 23–5.

Holmes, Stephen. "Cultural Legacies or State Collapse? Probing the Postcommunist Dilemma." In Michael Mandelbaum (Ed.), *PostCommunism: Four Perspectives,* pp. 22–76. New York: Council on Foreign Relations, 1996.

Hsia Yu. "Beijing's Intense Popular Interest in CPC Document No. 4." *Ta kung pao,* June 12, 1992, trans. FBIS-CHI, June 12, 1992, pp. 17–18.

Hsu Szu-min. "On the Political Situation in Post-Deng China." *Ching pao* 210, January 5, 1994, pp. 26–9, trans. FBIS-CHI, January 30, 1994, pp. 13–17.

Hu Angang. "Background to Writing the Report on State Capacity." In Joseph Fewsmith (Ed.), *Hu Angang on China's 1994 Tax Reform* (*The Chinese Economy* 31(4): 5–29, July/August 1998).

Hu Angang. "Zhizai cujin jingji fazhan de Zhongguo zhengzhi gaige" [The aim of political reform in China is to promote economic development]. *Gaige* 3 (1999): 58–64, trans. Joseph Fewsmith (Ed.), *The Role of Government in a Period of Economic Reform* (*The Chinese Economy* 32(5): 5–25, September/October 1999).

Hu Angang. *Zhongguo jingji bodong baogao* [Report on China's economic fluctuations]. Shenyang: Liaoning renmin chubanshe, 1994.

Hu Angang and Wang Shaoguang. *Jiaqiang zhongyang zhengfu zai shichang jingji zhuanxing zhong de zhudao zuoyong: Guanyu Zhongguo guojia nengli de yanjiu baogao* [Strengthen the leading role of the central government in the transition to a market economy: A research report on China's state capacity]. Shenyang: Liaoning renmin chubanshe, 1993. Trans. in Joseph Fewsmith (Ed.), *The Chinese Economy* 28, nos. 3 and 4 (May/June and July/August 1995); cited as *Wang Shaoguang Proposal (I)* and *(II)*.

Hu Angang, Wang Shaoguang, and Kang Xiaoguang. *Zhongguo diqu chaju baogao* [Report on regional inequalities in China]. Shenyang: Liaoning renmin chubanshe, 1995.

Hu Angang, Zhao Tao, and Yao Zengqi. *Guoqing yu juece* [National conditions and policy]. Beijing chubanshe, 1990.

Hu Jiayong. "Dui zhengfu zhipei ziyuanliang de shizheng fenxi" [An empirical analysis of the amount of resources controlled by the government]. *Gaige* 3 (1999): 65–72, trans. Joseph Fewsmith (Ed.), *The Role of Government in a Period of Economic Reform* (*The Chinese Economy* 32(5): 69–93, September/October 1999).

Hu Jiwei. *Cong Hua Guofeng xiatai dao Hu Yaobang xiatai* [From Hua Guofeng's stepping down to Hu Yaobang's stepping down]. Hong Kong: Mingjing chubanshe, 1997.

Hu Jiwei. "Despotic Dictatorship Lingers On – Notes on Studying the Political Report of the 15th Party Congress." *Hsin pao,* December 30, 1997, trans. FBIS-CHI, December 30, 1997.

Hu Jiwei. "Given a Good Central Committee, We Will Have a Good Party; Given a Good Party, We Will Have a Good State – Notes on Studying the Political Report of the 15th Party Congress." *Hsin pao,* December 31, 1997, trans. FBIS-CHI, December 31, 1997.

Hu Jiwei. "If the Party Is Correct, Bad Things Can Be Turned into Good Things; If the Party Is Wrong, Good Things Can Be Turned into Bad Things." *Hsin pao,* December 29, 1997, trans. FBIS-CHI, December 29, 1997.

Hu Ping. "Special Zone Construction and Opening to the Outside." In *Zhonggong zhongyang dangxiao baogao xuan* [Selected reports from the Central Party School], trans. Stanley Rosen (Ed.), *Debates over Special Economic Zones, Income Polarization, and Other Related Issues* (*Chinese Economic Studies* 29(3), May/June 1996).

Hu Qiaomu. "Act in Accordance with Economic Laws, Step Up the Four Modernizations." Xinhua, October 5, 1978, in FBIS-CHI, October 11, 1978, pp. E1–E22.

Hu Weixi. "Zhongguo jinxiandai de shehui zhuanxing yu mincui zhuyi" [Populism and social transformation in modern China]. *Zhanlüe yu guanli* 5 (October 1994): 24–7.

Hua Jinzhong. "Guoxue, zai Yanyuan you qiaoran xingqi" [National studies have appeared quietly again in the Yan garden]. *Renmin ribao,* August 16, 1993, p. 3.

Huang, Yasheng. *Inflation and Investment Controls in China: The Political Economy of Central-Local Relations During the Reform Era.* Cambridge University Press, 1996.

Huangfu Ping. "The Consciousness of Expanding Opening Needs to Be Strengthened." *Jiefang ribao,* March 22, 1991, trans. FBIS-CHI, April 1, 1991, pp. 39–41.

Huangfu Ping. "Reform and Opening Require a Large Number of Cadres with Both Morals and Talents." *Jiefang ribao,* April 12, 1991, trans. FBIS-CHI, April 17, 1991, pp. 61–3.

Huntington, Samuel. "The Clash of Civilizations?" *Foreign Affairs* 72 (Summer 1993): 22–49.

Huntington, Samuel. *The Clash of Civilizations and the Remaking of World Order.* New York: Simon & Schuster, 1996.

Huntington, Samuel P. *Political Order in Changing Societies.* New Haven, CT: Yale University Press, 1968.

"Increase Weight of Reform, Promote Economic Development: Speech Delivered by Wu Guanzheng at the Provincial Structural Reform Work Conference." *Jiangxi ribao,* May 4, 1991, trans. FBIS-CHI, June 12, 1991, pp. 45–9.

International Monetary Fund. *World Economic Outlook.* Washington, DC: IMF, 1993.

Ishihara, Shintaro. *The Japan That Can Say No: Why Japan Will Be First among Equals.* New York: Simon & Schuster, 1989.

Jacobson, Harold K., and Michel Oksenberg. *China's Participation in the IMF, World Bank and GATT: Toward a Global Economic Order.* Ann Arbor: University of Michigan Press, 1991.

Jameson, Fredric. *The Cultural Turn: Selected Writings on the Postmodern, 1983–1998.* London: Verso, 1998.

Jameson, Fredric. *Postmodernism, or, The Cultural Logic of Late Capital.* Durham, NC: Duke University Press, 1991.

Jen Hui-wen. "Deng Xiaoping Urges Conservatives Not to Make a Fuss." *Hsin pao,* January 1, 1993, trans. FBIS-CHI, January 4, 1993, pp. 43–4.

Jen Hui-wen. "Political Bureau Argues over 'Preventing Leftism'." *Hsin pao,* April 14, 1992, p. 6, trans. FBIS-CHI, April 17, 1992, pp. 28–9.

Jen Hui-wen. "There Is Something behind Chen Yun's Declaration of His Position." *Hsin pao,* May 12, 1992, p. 22, trans. FBIS-CHI, May 13, 1992, pp. 21–2.

Jen Hui-wen. "What Is the 'Bottom Line' of CCP Political Reform?" *Hsin pao,* November 4, 1990, p. 30, trans. FBIS-CHI, November 10, 1990, pp. 24–6.

Ji Xianlin. "Dongxifang wenhua de zhuanzhedian" [The turning point between Eastern and Western civilizations]. *Ershiyi shiji* 3 (February 1991): 4–5.

Ji Xianlin. " 'Tianren heyi' fang neng chengjiu renlei" [Humanity can be saved through 'unity of nature and man']. *Dongfang* 1 (1993): 6.

Ji Xianlin. " 'Tianren heyi' xinjie" [A new interpretation of 'unity of man and nature']. *Chuantong wenhua yu xiandaihua* 1 (1993): 9–16.

Jia Pingwa. *Fei du* [Abandoned capital]. Beijing chubanshe, 1993.

"Jianchi gongyouzhi de zhuti diwei buneng dongyao" [The primary position of upholding public ownership must not be shaken]. *Jiefangjun bao,* April 29, 1996, pp. 1, 6.

"Jianchi he fazhan you Zhongguo tese de shehui zhuyi minzhu" [Uphold and develop socialist democracy with Chinese characteristics]. *Jiefangjun bao,* April 1, 1996, pp. 1, 4.

"Jiang Must Act Fast." *The Straits Times,* February 5, 2000, p. 30.

Jiang Po. "Guochan pijiu you biyao gao zhema duo hezi ma?" [Must Chinese beer form this many joint ventures?]. *Jingji ribao,* June 20, 1996, p. 1.

Jiang Po. "Woguo mingpai mianlin yanjun tiaozhan" [Chinese famous brands are facing a serious challenge]. *Jingji ribao,* July 10, 1996, pp. 1, 3.

Jiang Po. " 'Yanjing' wei shenma bu hezi?" [Why doesn't 'Yanjing' form a joint venture?]. *Jingji ribao,* July 2, 1996, p. 1.

Jiang Po and Zheng Po. " 'Wuxing' wei shenma yao hezi?" [Why did 'Five Star' form a joint venture?]. *Jingji ribao,* July 2, 1996, p. 1.

Jiang Qing. *Gongyangxue yinlun* [An introduction to the study of the Gongyang commentary]. Shenyang: Liaoning jiaoyu chubanshe, 1997.

Jiang Yihua. "Lun dongya xiandaihua jinchengzhong de xinlixing zhuyi wenhua" [On the new rationalist culture Asia [developed] in the course of modernization]. *Shanghai wenhua* 4 (1994); reprinted in Wang Jisi (Ed.), *Wenming yu guoji zhengzhi*, pp. 259–80.

Jiang Zemin. "Leading Cadres Must Pay Attention to Politics." Excerpted from Jiang Zemin's speech to the Fifth Plenum of the Fourteenth Central Committee by Xinhua, January 17, 1996, in FBIS-CHI, January 17, 1996.

Jiang Zemin. "Memorial Speech at Deng Xiaoping's Memorial Meeting." *Beijing Review* 40 (March 10–16, 1997): 14–22.

Jiang Zemin. "Text of Political Report by General Secretary Jiang Zemin at the 15th CPC National Congress." Beijing television service, September 12, 1997, trans. FBIS-CHI-97-255, September 12, 1997.

Jiang Zemin, "Zai dang de shisanjie qizhong quanhui bimushi de jianghua" [Address to the closing session of the seventh plenary session of the thirteenth CCP Central Committee]. In *Shisanda yilai*, vol. 2, pp. 1427–36.

Jiang Zemin. "Zai dang de shisanjie wuzhong quanhui shangde jianghua" [Address to the fifth plenary session of the thirteenth CCP Central Committee]. In *Shisanda yilai*, vol. 2, pp. 709–20.

Jiang Zemin. "Zai qingzhu Zhongguo gongchandang chengli qishi zhounian dahuishang de jianghua" [Talk celebrating the 70th anniversary of the founding of the CCP]. In *Shisanda yilai*, vol. 3, pp. 1627–60.

Jiang Zemin. "Zai qingzhu Zhonghua renmin gongheguo chengli sishi zhounian dahui shang de jianghua" [Talk celebrating the 40th anniversary of the establishment of the PRC]. In *Shisanda yilai*, vol. 2, pp. 609–35.

Bibliography

"Jiang Zemin Delivers an Important Speech at the Fourth Plenary Session of the Central Discipline Inspection Commission." Xinhua, January 14, 2000, in FBIS-CHI-2000-0115, January 15, 2000.

"Jiang Zemin zai Guangdong kaocha gongzuo qiangdiao jinmi jiehe xinde lishi tiaojian jiaqiang dangde jianshe shizhong dailing quanmin renmin cujin shengchanli de fazhan" [Inspecting work in Guangdong, Jiang Zemin emphasized firmly integrating the new historical conditions, strengthening Party building, and continuously leading the whole people to speed development of productive forces]. In *Shenru xuexi "sange daibiao" quanmian luoshi "sange daibiao"* [Study deeply the "three representatives"; comprehensively implement the "three representatives"], pp. 1–8. Beijing: Xuexi chubanshe, 2000.

Jiefang wenxuan (1978–1998) [Essays of liberated [thought] – 1978–1998)], 2 vols. Beijing: Jingji ribao chubanshe, 1998.

Jin Longde. "Zhongyuan dadi de yimian hongqi – Henan Linyingxian Nanjie fangwen jishi" [A bright red flag in the land of middle China – A true report of Nanjie, Linying county, Henan]. *Dangdai sichao* 3 (March 1994): 2–10.

Johnson, Chalmers. *MITI and the Japanese Miracle: The Growth of Industrial Policy, 1925–1975.* Stanford, CA: Stanford University Press, 1982.

Johnston, Alastair Iain, and Robert S. Ross (Eds.). *Engaging China.* London: Routledge, 1999.

Kagan, Robert. "The Canary in the Chinese Coal Mine." *Weekly Standard,* June 30, 1997, pp. 23–6.

Kagan, Robert. "China: The End of Engagement." *Weekly Standard,* November 10, 1997, pp. 20–2.

Kagan, Robert. "What China Knows That We Don't: The Case for a New Strategy of Containment." *Weekly Standard,* January 20, 1997, pp. 22–5.

Kang Xiaoguang, Wu Yulun, Liu Dehuan, and Sun Hui. *Zhongguoren dushu toushi: 1978–1998 dazhong dushu shenghuo bianqian diaocha* [A perspective on the reading habits of the Chinese: An investigation of the changes in the reading habits of the masses from 1978–1998]. Nanning: Guangxi jiaoyu chubanshe, 1998.

Katzenstein, Peter (Ed.). *Between Power and Plenty.* Madison: University of Wisconsin Press, 1978.

Kennedy, Paul M. *The Rise and Fall of the Great Powers: Economic Change and Military Conflict from 1500 to 2000.* New York: Random House, 1987.

Kynge, James. "Smuggling Row Rocks Chinese Politburo." *Financial Times,* January 22, 2000, p. 7.

Kynge, James. "Top Investigator to Probe Smuggling." *Financial Times,* January 24, 2000, p. 4.

Lake, Anthony. "From Containment to Engagement." Address at the School of Advanced International Studies, Washington, DC, September 23, 1993.

Lam, Willy Wo-lap. *China after Deng Xiaoping: The Power Struggle in Beijing Since Tiananmen.* Hong Kong: PA Professional Consultants, 1995.

Lam, Willy Wo-lap. *The Era of Jiang Zemin.* New York: Prentice-Hall, 1999.

Lan Zhongping, "Why Do We Say That Special Economic Zones Are Socialist Rather than Capitalist in Nature?" *Jiefangjun bao,* May 22, 1992, trans. FBIS-CHI, June 11, 1992, pp. 25–6.

283

Lardy, Nicholas R. *China's Unfinished Economic Revolution*. Washington, DC: Brookings, 1998.

Lardy, Nicholas. *Foreign Trade and Economic Reform in China, 1978–1990*. Cambridge University Press, 1992.

Lee, Hong Yung. "China's New Bureaucracy?" In Arthur Lewis Rosenbaum (Ed.), *State and Society in China: The Consequences of Reform*. Boulder, CO: Westview, 1992.

Lee, Hong Yung. *From Revolutionary Cadres to Party Technocrats in Socialist China*. Berkeley: University of California Press, 1991.

Lei Yi. "Beijing yu cuowei" [Background and reversed positions]. *Dushu* (April 1995): 16–20.

Lei Yi. "Jingti faxisi" [Beware of fascism]. Unpublished manuscript.

Lei Yi. "Minzu, minsheng, minquan" [Nationalism, people's livelihood, and democracy]. *Fangfa* 3 (1998): 13–14.

Lei Yi. "Yihetuan de beiju" [The tragedy of the Boxers]. *Daxuesheng* (August 1999): 24–5.

Lei Yi. "Zhongguo xiandaihua de 'huaxia zhongxinguan' yu 'minzu zhuyi'" ['Sinocentrism' and 'nationalism' in China's modernization]. *Zuojia shuzhai* 3 (March 1999): 163–7.

Leng Rong. "To Realize Lofty Aspirations and Great Ideals of the Chinese Nation – Studying Comrade Deng Xiaoping's Ideas Concerning Strategic Goals for China's Modernization and Development." *Renmin ribao*, April 27, 1992, trans. FBIS-CHI, April 28, 1992, pp. 17–23.

Li, Cheng. *China's Leaders: The New Generation*. Lanham, MD: Rowman & Littlefield, 2001.

Li, Cheng. "Promises and Pitfalls of Reform: New Thinking in Post-Deng China." In Tyrene White (Ed.), *China Briefing 2000: The Continuing Transformation*, pp. 123–58. Armonk, NY: M.E. Sharpe, 2000.

Li, Cheng, and Lynn White. "The 15th Central Committee of the Chinese Communist Party: Full-Fledged Technocratic Leadership with Partial Control by Jiang Zemin." *Asian Survey* 38 (April 1988): 231–64.

Li Chengrui. "Some Thoughts on Sustained, Steady, and Coordinated Development." *Renmin ribao*, November 20, 1989, trans. FBIS-CHI, December 12, 1989, pp. 32–4.

Li Peng. "Explanations of the Proposal for the Formulation of the Ninth Five-Year Plan and the Long-Term Target for the Year 2010." Xinhua, October 5, 1995, in FBIS-CHI, October 6, 1995, pp. 17–28.

Li Peng. "Wei woguo zhengzhi jingji he shehui de jinyibu wending fazhan er fendou" [Struggle to take another step for the stable development of China's politics, economics, and society]. In *Shisanda yilai*, vol. 2, pp. 948–94.

"Li Peng's Life-Taking Report Lays Blame on Zhao Ziyang." *Tungfang jihpao*, July 16, 1989, p. 3, trans. FBIS-CHI, July 18, 1989, pp. 16–23.

Li Ping. *Zhongguo xiayibu zenyang zou* [How will China take its next step?]. Hong Kong: Mingjing chubanshe, 1998.

Li Rui. *Li Rui fan "zuo" wenxuan* [Li Rui's essays opposing the "left"]. Beijing: Zhongyang bianyi chubanshe, 1998.

"Li Ruihuan Meets with Hong Kong Journalists." *Ta kung pao,* September 20, 1989, trans. FBIS-CHI, September 20, 1989, pp. 10–12.

Li Shenzhi. "Bian tongyi, hedongxi" [Differentiating what is the same and what is different; synthesizing East and West]. *Ershiyi shiji* (1993); reprinted in *Jiefang wenxuan,* vol. 2, pp. 818–29.

Li Shenzhi. "Chongxin dianran qimeng de huoju – Jinian 'wusi' bashi zhounian" [Relight the torch of enlightenment – Commemorating the eightieth anniversary of 'May Fourth']. *Dangdai Zhongguo yanjiu* 3 (September 1999): 2–15.

Li Shenzhi. "Ershiyi shiji de yousi" [Worries about the twenty-first century]. *Dushu* (April 1996); reprinted in *Jiefang wenxuan,* vol. 2, pp. 934–43.

Li Shenzhi. "Faxian lingyige Zhongguo" [Discovering another China]. Reprinted in *Jiefang wenxuan,* vol. 2, pp. 1242–54.

Li Shenzhi. "Fengyu canghuang wushi nian – Guoqingye duyu" [Fifty years of storms and clouds – Solitary words on the evening of national day]. Unpublished manuscript.

Li Shenzhi. "Guanyu wenhua wenti de yixie sikao" [Some thoughts about the question of culture]. *Tianjin shehui kexue* (1998); reprinted in *Jiefang wenxuan,* vol. 2, pp. 1125–35.

Li Shenzhi. "Hongyang Beida de ziyou zhuyi chuantong" [Extol Beijing University's tradition of liberalism]. Preface to Liu Junning (Ed.), *Beida chuantong yu jindai Zhongguo,* pp. 1–5.

Li Shenzhi. "Quanqiuhua yu Zhongguo wenhua" [Globalization and China's culture]. *Taipingyang xuebao* 2 (December 1994): 3.

Li Shenzhi. "Shuliang youshixia de kongju – Ping Hengtingdun disanpian guanyu wenming chongtu de wenzhang" [Under the fear of numerical superiority – Critiquing Huntington's third essay on the clash of civilizations]. *Taipingyang xuebao* 2 (1997): 3–7.

Li Shenzhi. "Yeyao tuidong zhengzhi gaige." *Gaige* 1 (1998); reprinted in *Jiefang wenxuan,* vol. 2, pp. 1002–5.

Li Shenzhi. "Zhongguo chuantong wenhuazhong jiwu minzhu yewu kexue" [There is no democracy or science in China's traditional culture]. *Zhongguo jingji shibao* (1998); reprinted in *Jiefang wenxuan,* vol. 2, pp. 1118–24.

Li Shenzhi. "Zhongguo yingqu shenmayang de fengfan?" [What sort of attitude should China adopt?]. *Xiandai chuanbo* (1997); reprinted in *Jiefang wenxuan,* vol. 2, pp. 952–7.

Li Shenzhi. "Zhongguo zhexue de jingshen" [The spirit of Chinese philosophy]. *Chuantong wenhua yu xiandaihua* 2 (1993); reprinted in *Jiefang wenxuan,* vol. 2, pp. 805–17.

Li Shuyi and Yong Jianxiong (Eds.). *Ershiyi shiji Zhongguo jueqi* [The rise of China in the twenty-first century]. Beijing: Zhonggong zhongyang dangxiao chubanshe, 1997.

Li Zehou. *Zhongguo xiandai sixiangshi lun* [History of contemporary Chinese thought]. Beijing: Dongfang chubanshe, 1987.

Li Zehou and Liu Zaifu. *Gaobie geming* [Farewell to revolution]. Hong Kong: Cosmos Books, 1996.

Lin, Min. *The Search for Modernity: Chinese Intellectuals and Cultural Discourse in the Post-Mao Era,* with Maria Galikowski. New York: St. Martin's, 1999.

Lin Ruo. "Dui fazhan shehui zhuyi shangpin jingji de jidian renshi" [Some points of understanding regarding the development of the socialist commodity economy]. *Renmin ribao,* March 1, 1999, p. 5.

Lin Wu. "Deng's Faction Unmasks Face of 'Ultraleftists'." *Zhengming* 175, May 1, 1992, pp. 17–18, trans. FBIS-CHI, May 12, 1992, pp. 27–8.

Lin Yifu, Cai Fang, and Li Zhou. "On the Gradual-Advance Style of Economic Reform in China." *Jingji yanjiu* 9 (1993), trans. *Chinese Economic Studies* 26 (November/December 1995): 5–39.

Ling Hsueh-chun. "Wang Zhen and Li Xiannian Set Themselves Up against Deng." *Zhengming* 175, May 1, 1992, pp. 14–15, trans. FBIS-CHI, May 12, 1992, p. 26.

Ling Zhen. "Zugepai de xingdong xinhao" [Signs that the faction to form a cabinet is acting]. *Kaifang* (October 1994): 20–3.

Ling Zhijun. *Chenfu: Zhongguo jingji gaige beiwanglu (1989–1997)* [Turmoil: A record of China's economic reform (1989–1997)]. Shanghai: Dongfang chuban zhongxin, 1998.

Link, Perry. "China's 'Core' Problem." *Daedalus* 122 (Spring 1993): 189–206.

Link, Perry. "The Old Man's New China." *New York Review of Books* 41 (June 9, 1994): 31–6.

Linz, Juan J., and Alfred Stepan. *Problems of Democratic Transition and Consolidation: Southern Europe, South America, and Post-Communist Europe.* Baltimore: Johns Hopkins University Press, 1996.

Linz, Juan J., and Alfred Stepan. "Toward Consolidated Democracies." In Larry Diamond et al. (Eds.), *Consolidating the Third Wave Democracies: Themes and Perspectives,* pp. 14–33. Baltimore: Johns Hopkins University Press, 1997.

Lishi de chaoliu bianweihui (Ed.). *Lishi de chaoliu: Xuexi Deng Xiaoping nanxun zhongyao jianghua fudao cailiao* [Historical trends: Supplementary materials for the study of Deng Xiaoping's important talks during his southern tour]. Beijing: Zhongguo renmin daxue chubanshe, 1992.

Liu Binyan and Perry Link. "A Great Leap Backward?" *New York Review of Books* 45 (October 8, 1998): 19–23.

Liu Ji. "Lun juece kexuehua" [On making decision making scientific]. *Zhongguo shehui kexue zazhi* 3 (1982): 3–25.

Liu Ji (Ed.). *Shehui zhuyi gaige lun* [On the reform of socialism]. Shanghai: Renmin chubanshe, 1997.

Liu Jun and Li Lin (Eds.). *Xinquanwei zhuyi: Dui gaige lilun gangling de zhenglun* [New authoritarianism: Debates on the principles of reform theory]. Beijing: Jingjixueyuan chubanshe, 1989.

Liu Junning (Ed.). *Beida chuantong yu jindai Zhongguo* [Beijing University and Modern China]. Beijing: Zhongguo renshi chubanshe, 1998.

Liu Junning. "Caichanquan de baozhang yu youxian zhengfu – Cong zhengfu de zongzhi kan zhengti gaige" [Guaranteeing property rights and limited government – Looking at political reform from the commitments of government]. *Fangfa* 3 (1998): 11–13.

Liu Junning. "Feng neng jin, yu neng jin, guowang buneng jin!" [The wind and rain can enter, but the king may not!]. In Liu Junning, *Gonghe, minzhu, xianzheng,* pp. 38–62.

Liu Junning. *Gonghe, minzhu, xianzheng: Ziyou zhuyi sixiang yanjiu* [Republicanism, democracy, and constitutionalism: Studies in liberal thought]. Shanghai: Sanlian shudian, 1998.

Liu Junning. "Minzu zhuyi simianguan" [Viewing nationalism from four perspectives]. In Liu Junning, *Gonghe, minzhu, xianzheng,* pp. 250–9.

Liu Junning. "Quanqiuhua yu minzhuhua" [Globalization and democratization]. In Liu Junning, *Gonghe, minzhu, xianzheng,* pp. 243–9.

Liu Junning. "Zhijie minzhu yu jianjie minzhu" [Direct democracy and indirect democracy]. In Liu Junning, *Gonghe, minzhu, xianzheng,* pp. 199–215.

Liu Junning. "Zhongguo jiaru WTO de zhengzhi yiyi" [The political meaning of China's entry into the WTO]. *Duowei xinwen wang* (November 16, 1999), ⟨www.chinesenewsnet.com⟩.

Liu Kang. "Quanqiuhua 'peilun' yu xiandaixing 'qitu' " [The 'paradox' of globalization and modernity's 'wrong roads']. *Dushu* (July 1995): 98–105.

Liu Kang. "Quanqiuhua yu Zhongguo xiandaihua de butong xuanze" [Globalization and the different choices of China's modernization]. *Ershiyi shiji* 37 (October 1996); reprinted in Wang Hui and Yu Guoliang (Eds.), *90 niandai de "houxue" lunzheng,* pp. 31–42.

Liu Kang and Li Xiguang. *Yaomo Zhongguo de beihou* [Behind the demonization of China]. Beijing: Zhongguo shehui kexue chubanshe, 1996.

Liu Pi. "Deng Xiaoping Launches 'Northern Expedition' to Emancipate Mind; Beijing, Shanghai, and Other Provinces and Municipalities 'Respond' by Opening Wider to the Outside World." *Ching pao* 166, May 10, 1991, trans. FBIS-CHI, May 6, 1991, pp. 26–9.

Liu Runwei. "Zhimin wenhua lun" [On colonial culture]. *Qiushi* 5 (March 1, 1996): 26–33.

Liu Shi. "The Purpose of 'Transformation' Is to Pave the Way for Capitalism – On Comrade Zhao Ziyang's Erroneous Guiding Ideology for Ideological and Political Work among Staff Members and Workers." *Gongren ribao,* September 5, 1989, p. 1, trans. FBIS-CHI, September 5, 1989, pp. 30–2.

Liu Xiaofeng. *Geti xinyang yu wenhua lilun* [Individual belief and cultural theory]. Chengdu: Sichuan chubanshe, 1997.

Liu Yiqing. "Na chengshi zuo jiaoyi" [Trading away the truth]. *Zhonghua dushu bao,* June 14, 2000.

Liu Zhifeng. "Disizhi yanjing kan Zhongguo – Wang Shan fangtanlu" [Looking at China through a fourth eye – Interview with Wang Shan]. In Liu Zhifeng (Ed.), *Jieshi Zhongguo,* pp. 293–343.

Liu Zhifeng (Ed.). *Jieshi Zhongguo: "Disanzhi yanjing kan Zhongguo" pipan* [Explaining China: Criticism of "Looking at China through a Third Eye"]. Beijing: Jingji ribao chubanshe, 1998.

Lo Ping. "The Anti-Deng Meeting Incident in Hebei." *Zhengming* 205, November 1, 1994, pp. 9–14, trans. FBIS-CHI, November 17, 1994, pp. 16–18.

Lo Ping. "Blowing of the 'Left' Wind, and the Four-Horse Carriage." *Zhengming* 183, January 1, 1993, pp. 6–8, trans. FBIS-CHI, January 7, 1993, pp. 12–14.

Lo Ping. "Report on Deng Xiaoping's Behind-the-Scenes Activities." *Zhengming* 159, January 1, 1991, trans. FBIS-CHI, December 31, 1990, pp. 20–1.

Lo Ping and Li Tzu-ching. "Chen Yun Raises Six Points of View to Criticize Deng Xiaoping." *Zhengming* 171, January 1, 1992, pp. 18–19, trans. FBIS-CHI, January 3, 1992, pp. 22–3.

Long Yongtu. "Guanyu jiaru shijie maoyi zuzhi de wenti" [On the question of our joining the World Trade Organization]. *Zhonggong zhongyang dangxiao baogaoxuan* 11, July 22, 1998, pp. 1–6, trans. Joseph Fewsmith (Ed.), *China and the WTO, Part I* (*The Chinese Economy* 33(1): 5–52, January/February 2000).

Lu Jiandong. *Chen Yinke de zuihou ershi nian* [The last twenty years of Chen Yinke]. Beijing: Sanlian, 1995.

Lu Ming-sheng. "Inside Story of How *Historical Trends* Was Banned." *Zhengming* 177, July 1, 1992, pp. 33–4, trans. FBIS-CHI, July 7, 1992, pp. 19–21.

Lu Yu-shan. "Chen Yun Responds to Document No. 2." *Tangtai* 14, May 15, 1992, pp. 21–2, trans. FBIS-CHI, May 21, 1992, pp. 18–20.

Lubman, Stanley. *Bird in a Cage: Legal Reform in China after Mao*. Stanford, CA: Stanford University Press, 1999.

Luo Xiaolu. "Chen Xitong tan jiefang sixiang" [Chen Xitong talks about liberating thought]. *Banyuetan* 6 (March 25, 1991): 16–18.

Luo yi ning ge er. *See* Wang Shan.

Ma Hong. "Have a Correct Understanding of the Economic Situation, Continue to Do a Good Job in Economic Improvement and Rectification." *Renmin ribao,* November 17, 1989, trans. FBIS-CHI, December 5, 1989, pp. 37–9.

Ma Licheng. "Xinwen jiandu buxing 'zi'" [Press supervision is not 'capitalist']. *Fangfa* 3 (1998): 6–7.

Ma Licheng and Ling Zhijun. *Jiao feng: Dangdai Zhongguo sance sixiang jiefang shilu* [Crossed swords: A true account of the three emancipations of thought in contemporary China]. Beijing: Jinri Zhongguo chubanshe, 1998.

Ma Ling. "Who Starts Rumors about Jia Qinglin's Divorce?" *Ta kung pao,* January 27, 2000, trans. FBIS-CHI-2000-0127, January 27, 2000.

Mahathir, Mohamad, and Shintaro Ishihara. *The Voice of Asia: Two Leaders Discuss the Coming Century*. Tokyo: Kodansha, 1995.

"Major Revisions to the Government Work Report." *Wen wei po,* March 16, 1993, p. 3, trans. FBIS-CHI, March 16, 1993, pp. 23–4.

"Make Fresh Contributions on 'Protecting and Escorting' Reform, Opening up, and Economic Development – Warmly Congratulating Conclusion of the Fifth Sessions of the Seventh National People's Congress and Seventh Chinese People's Political Consultative Conference." *Jiefangjun bao,* April 4, 1992, trans. FBIS-CHI, April 21, 1992, pp. 36–7.

"Makesi zhuyi yongyuan shi women shengli de qizhi" [Marxism is our victorious banner forever]. *Jiefangjun bao,* May 6, 1996, pp. 1, 6.

Manion, Melanie. *Retirement of Revolutionary Cadres in China: Public Policies, Social Norms, Private Interests*. Princeton, NJ: Princeton University Press, 1993.

Mao Zedong. "The Yenan Forum on Literature and Art." In *The Selected Works of Mao Tse-tung,* vol. 3, pp. 69–98. Peking: Foreign Languages Press, 1967.

"March toward the New Scientific and Technological Revolution." Xinhua, May 2, 1991, in FBIS-CHI, May 3, 1991, pp. 23–6.

McMillan, John, and Barry Naughton. "How to Reform a Planned Economy: Lessons from China." *Oxford Review of Economic Policy* 8 (1992): 130–43.

Meng Fanhua. *Zhongshen kuanghuan – Dangdai Zhongguo de wenhua chongtu wenti* [Bacchanalia of culture – The clash of cultures in contemporary China]. Beijing: Jinri Zhongguo chubanshe, 1997.

Meng Lin. "Deng Liqun Reaffirms Disapproval of Phrase 'Deng Xiaoping Thought'." *Ching pao* 180, July 5, 1992, p. 42, trans. FBIS-CHI, July 6, 1992, pp. 28–9.

Mercuro, Nicholas, and Steven G. Medema. *Economics and the Law.* Princeton, NJ: Princeton University Press, 1997.

"Miandui 'shengtu de yingdi' – Yu women de qingnian jiaoliu" [Facing 'the camp of the saints' – An exchange with our youth]. *Beijing qingnian bao,* August 11, 1995, p. 8.

Migdal, Joel. *Strong Societies and Weak States.* Princeton, NJ: Princeton University Press, 1988.

Miles, James. *The Legacy of Tiananmen: China in Disarray.* Ann Arbor: University of Michigan Press, 1996.

"More than Seventy Writers and Artists Attend a Forum to Study the Spirit of the Fourth Plenary Session." *Renmin ribao,* July 13, 1989, p. 2, trans. FBIS-CHI, July 24, 1989, pp. 26–7.

Mufson, Steven. "Former Chinese Official Advocates Democracy." *Washington Post,* January 12, 1998, p. A3.

Mufson, Steven, and Robert G. Kaiser. " 'Blue Team' Draws a Hard Line on Beijing: Action on Hill Reflects Informal Group's Clout." *Washington Post,* February 22, 2000, p. A1.

Mufson, Steven, and Robert G. Kaiser. "Missed U.S.–China Deal Looms Large." *Washington Post,* November 10, 1999, p. A1.

Myers, Steven Lee. "Chinese Embassy Bombing: A Wide Net of Blame." *New York Times,* April 17, 2000, pp. A1, A10.

Nathan, Andrew, Perry Link (Eds.), and Zhang Liang (Comp.). *The Tiananmen Papers: The Chinese Leaderships' Decision to Use Force Against Their Own People – In Their Own Words.* New York: Public Affairs, 2001.

Naughton, Barry. "Causes et conséquences des disparités dans la croissance économique des provinces chinoises" [Causes and consequences of differential economic growth of Chinese provinces]. *Revue d'Économie du Développement* 1999 (Juin): 33–70.

Naughton, Barry. *Growing Out of the Plan: Chinese Economic Reform, 1978–1993.* Cambridge University Press, 1995.

Naughton, Barry. "The Third Front: Defence Industrialization in the Chinese Interior." *China Quarterly* 115 (1988): 351–61.

"New Stage of China's Reform and Opening to the Outside World." *Renmin ribao* editorial, June 9, 1992, trans. FBIS-CHI, June 9, 1992, pp. 17–18.

Observer. "Humanitarianism or Hegemonism?" Xinhua, May 16, 1999, in FBIS-CHI, May 16, 1999.

Observer. "On the New Development of U.S. Hegemonism." *Renmin ribao,* May 27, 1999, trans. in FBIS-CHI, May 27, 1999.

Observer. "We Urge Hegemon Today to Take a Look at the Mirror of History." *Renmin ribao,* June 22, 1999, trans. in FBIS-CHI-1999-0622, June 22, 1999.

O'Donnell, Guillermo, and Philippe C. Schmitter. *Transitions from Authoritarian Rule: Tentative Conclusions about Uncertain Democracies.* Baltimore: Johns Hopkins University Press, 1986.

Oi, Jean. "Fiscal Reform and the Foundations of Local State Corporatism in China." *World Politics* 45 (October 1992): 99–126.

Oi, Jean. *Rural China Takes Off: Institutional Foundations of Economic Reform.* Berkeley: University of California Press, 1999.

O'Neill, Mark. "Fairwell to the Smuggler King." *South China Morning Post,* January 25, 2000.

O'Neill, Mark. "Politburo Closes Ranks." *South China Morning Post,* January 29, 2000, p. 17.

Pearson, Margaret M. "The Case of China's Accession to GATT/WTO." In David M. Lampton, *The Making of Chinese Foreign and Security Policy in the Era of Reform, 1978–2000,* pp. 337–70. Stanford, CA: Stanford University Press, 2001.

Pearson, Margaret M. "China's Integration into the International Trade and Investment Regime." In Elizabeth Economy and Michel Oksenberg (Eds.), *China Joins the World,* pp. 161–205.

Pei, Minxin. *From Reform to Revolution: The Demise of Communism in China and the Soviet Union.* Cambridge, MA: Harvard University Press, 1994.

Peng Qian, Yang Mingjie, and Xu Deren. *Zhongguo weishenma shuobu?* [Why does China say no?]. Beijing: Xinshijie chubanshe, 1996.

Petracca, Mark P., and Mong Xiong. "The Concept of Chinese NeoAuthoritarianism." *Asian Survey* (November 1990): 1099–1117.

Pi Mingyong. "Zhongguo jindai minzu zhuyi de duozhong jiagou" [The multiple frameworks of modern Chinese nationalism]. *Zhanlüe yu guanli* 3 (June 1994): 22–5.

"Political Report" to the Fourteenth Party Congress. Beijing television service, October 12, 1992, trans. FBIS-CHI, October 13, 1992, pp. 23–43.

Pomfret, John. "Chinese Tie Leaders to Smuggling; Party, Military Chiefs Among Suspects." *Washington Post,* January 22, 2000, p. A1.

Przeworski, Adam. *Democracy and the Market: Political and Economic Reforms in Eastern Europe and Latin America.* Cambridge University Press, 1991.

Przeworski, Adam, et al. *Sustainable Democracy.* Cambridge University Press, 1995.

Qi Mo (Ed.). *Xinquanwei zhuyi: Dui Zhongguo dalu weilai mingyun de lunzheng* [New authoritarianism: Debates on the fate of the Chinese mainland]. Taipei: Tangshan chubanshe, 1991.

Qian Jun. "Saiyide tan wenhua" [Said on culture]. *Dushu* (September 1993): 10–17.

Qin Hui. "Bainian zhuanhuan – 'Shangren' yu 'jiaoshi' de Zhongguoguan" [Hundred years' transformation – 'Merchants' and 'missionaries' views of China]. In Qin Hui, *Wenti yu zhuyi: Qin Hui wenxuan* [Problems and isms: Essays by Qin Hui], pp. 3–7. Changchun: Changchun chubanshe, 1999.

Qin Si. "Wenyiwen 'xingshe haishi xingzi'" [Asking whether this is 'capitalist or socialist']. *Guangming ribao,* August 7, 1991, p. 3.

Ren Zhongping. "Wei jingji jianshe he shehui fazhan tigong qiangyouli de zhengzhi baozhang" [A powerful political guarantee for economic construction and social development]. *Renmin ribao,* April 1, 1996, pp. 1, 3.

"Resolution of the Central Committee of the Communist Party of China on the Guiding Principles for Building a Socialist Society with Advanced Culture and Ideology." Xinhua, September 28, 1986, in FBIS-CHI, September 29, 1986, pp. K2–K13.

"Resolutions of the CPC Central Committee Regarding Important Questions on Promoting Socialist Ethical and Cultural Progress." *Beijing Review* 39 (November 4–10, 1996): 20–31.

Reyes, Alejandro. "A Caning in Singapore Stirs Up a Fierce Debate about Crime and Punishment." *Asiaweek,* May 25, 1994.

Roemer, John (Ed.). *Property Relations, Incentives, and Welfare.* New York: St. Martin's, 1996.

Rosen, Stanley. "Youth and Social Change in the PRC." In Ramon H. Myers (Ed.), *Two Societies in Opposition: The Republic of China and the People's Republic of China after Forty Years,* pp. 288–315. Stanford, CA: Hoover Institution Press, 1990.

Rosen, Stanley, and Gary Zou (Eds.). "The Chinese Debate on the New Authoritarianism (I), (II), (III), (IV)." *Chinese Sociology and Anthropology* (Winter 1990, Spring 1991, Summer 1991, and Fall 1991).

Rosen, Stanley, and Gary Zou. "The Road to Modernization in China Debated: The Origins, Development and Decline of Neoauthoritarianism and Direct Democracy Schools." Unpublished manuscript.

Said, Edward. *Culture and Imperialism.* New York: Knopf, 1993.

Said, Edward. *Orientalism.* New York: Pantheon, 1978.

Sanger, David E. "The Trade Deal: The Drama." *New York Times,* November 16, 1999, p. A14.

Sartori, Giovanni. *Parties and Party Systems: A Framework for Analysis.* Cambridge University Press, 1976.

Schell, Orville. *Mandate of Heaven: The Legacy of Tiananmen Square and the Next Generation of Leaders.* New York: Simon & Schuster, 1994.

Schneider, Axel. "Bridging the Gap: Attempts at Constructing a 'New' Historical-Cultural Identity in the PRC." Unpublished manuscript.

Schram, Stuart R. "General Introduction." In *Mao's Road to Power: Revolutionary Writings 1912–1949* (vol. 1: The Pre-Marxist Period, 1912–1920), pp. xv–xx. Armonk, NY: M.E. Sharpe, 1992.

Schwarcz, Vera. *The Chinese Enlightenment: Intellectuals and the Legacy of the May Fourth Movement of 1919.* Berkeley: University of California Press, 1986.

Schwartz, Benjamin. *In Search of Wealth and Power: Yen Fu and the West.* Cambridge, MA: Harvard University Press, 1964.

Sha Feng. "Ultraleftists within CCP Launch Comeback by Criticizing Five New Rightists." *Ming pao,* August 20, 1994, p. A2, trans. FBIS-CHI, August 22, 1994, pp. 17–18.

Shang Dewen. "Cong eryuan jiegou kan Zhongguo" [Viewing China from the perspective of a dual structure]. Unpublished letter.

Shang Dewen. "Guanyu Zhongguo zhengzhi tizhi gaige de ruogan wenti yu jiben duice" [Several questions about and fundamental measures for China's political structural reform]. Unpublished letter.

"Shanghai 'Zhang Xiaochuan' jianchi bumai pinpai" [Shanghai's 'Zhang Xiaochuan' adamantly refuses to sell its brand name]. *Jingji ribao,* July 26, 1996, p. 1.

Shao Ren. "Zhongguo: Ruguan buru tao" [China: Joining the WTO without falling into the trap]. *Tianya* 3 (May 1999): 4–15, 90.

Shen Hongpei. "Ershi shijimo gongchan zhuyi dalunzhan" [A great Communist debate at the end of the twentieth century]. Introduction to Shi Liaozi (Ed.), *Beijng dixia "wanyanshu,"* pp. 1–24.

Shen Jiru. *Zhongguo bu dang "bu xiansheng"* [China should not be "Mr. No"]. Beijing: Jinri Zhongguo chubanshe, 1998.

Shen Liren and Dai Yuanchen. "Woguo 'zhuhou jingji' de xingcheng ji qi biduan he genyuan" [The emergence of China's 'feudal lord' economy: Its harm and resolution]. *Jingji yanjiu* 3 (March 1990): 12–19, 67.

Sheng Hong. "Cong jihua junheng dao shichang junheng" [From planned equilibrium to market equilibrium]. In *Sheng Hong ji,* pp. 464–80.

Sheng Hong. "Cong minzu zhuyi dao tianxia zhuyi" [From nationalism to universalism]. *Zhanlüe yu guanli* 1 (1996): 14–19.

Sheng Hong. *Sheng Hong ji* [Collected essays of Sheng Hong]. Harbin: Heilongjiang jiaoyu chubanshe, 1996.

Sheng Hong. "Shenma shi wenming" [What is civilization?]. *Zhanlüe yu guanli* 5 (1995): 88–98.

Sheng Hong. "A Survey of the Research on the Transitional Process of Market-Oriented Reform in China." In Joseph Fewsmith (Ed.), *Reflections on the Economic Reform Process (II)* (*Chinese Economic Studies* 29(2): 5–38, March/April 1996).

Sheng Hong. "Zhongguo de guodu jingjixue" [China's transitional economics]. In Sheng Hong (Ed.), *Zhongguo guodu jingjixue* [China's transitional economics]. Shanghai renmin chubanshe, 1994.

Sheng Hong. "Zhongguo xianqin zhexue he xiandai zhidu zhuyi" [China's pre-Qin philosophy and contemporary institutionalism]. In *Sheng Hong ji,* pp. 230–54.

Shi Bonian and Liu Fang. "Unswervingly Implement the Party's Basic Line." *Jiefangjun bao,* March 18, 1992, trans. FBIS-CHI, April 15, 1992, pp. 44–7.

Shi Liaozi (Ed.). *Beijing dixia "wanyanshu"* [Beijing's underground "ten thousand character manifestos"]. Hong Kong: Mingjing chubanshe, 1997.

Shi Xiuyin. "Zhongguo xinshiqi siyou qiyezhu jieceng baogao" [Report on the private entrepreneurial stratum in China in the new period]. In Li Peilin (Ed.), *Zhongguo xinshiqi jieji jieceng baogao* [Reports on classes and strata of China in the new period], pp. 221–91. Shenyang: Liaoning renmin chubanshe, 1995.

Shi Zhong. *See* Wang Xiaodong.

Shinn, James (Ed.). *Weaving the Net: Conditional Engagement with China.* New York: Council on Foreign Relations, 1996.

Shirk, Susan. *How China Opened Its Door: The Political Success of the PRC's Foreign Trade and Investment Reforms.* Washington, DC: Brookings, 1994.

Shisanda yilai zhongyao wenxuan bian [Selected important documents since the Thirteenth Party Congress], 3 volumes. Beijing: Renmin chubanshe, 1991, 1991, and 1993.

Smith, Craig R. "Shanghai Journal; Sex, Lust, Drugs: Her Novel's Too Much for China." *New York Times,* May 11, 2000, p. A4.

Solinger, Dorothy. *Contesting Citizenship in Urban China: Peasant Migrants, the State, and the Logic of the Market.* Berkeley: University of California Press, 1999.

Song Ping. "Zai quanguo zuzhi buzhang huiyi shang de jianghua" [Talk to a national meeting of organization department heads]. In *Shisanda yilai,* vol. 2, pp. 566–77.

Song Qiang, Zhang Zangzang, and Qiao Bian. *Zhongguo haishi neng shuobu* [China can still say no]. Hong Kong: Ming bao, 1996.

Song Qiang, Zhang Zangzang, and Qiao Bian. *Zhongguo keyi shuobu* [China can say no]. Beijing: Zhonghua gongshang lianhe chubanshe, 1996.

"Speech by Jiang Zemin at the Fourth Plenary Session of the Commission for Discipline Inspection." *Dangjian yanjiu* 4 as transmitted by Xinhua, April 1, 2000, in FBIS-CHI-2000-0401, April 1, 2000.

Steinfeld, Edward. *Forging Reform in China.* Cambridge University Press, 1998.

Stiglitz, Joseph E. *Whither Socialism.* Cambridge, MA: MIT Press, 1997.

Su Shaozhi (Ed.). *Marxism in China.* Nottingham, U.K.: Russell Press, 1983.

Su Shaozhi. *Shinian fengyu: Wengehou de dalu lilunjie* [Ten years of storms: The mainland's theoretical circles after the Cultural Revolution]. Taipei: Shibao chuban gongsi, 1996.

Su Xiaokang and Wang Luxiang. *He Shang* [River Elegy]. Beijing: Xiandai chubanshe, 1988.

"Summary of Tian Jiyun's Speech before Party School." *Pai hsing* 266, June 16, 1992, pp. 4–5, trans. FBIS-CHI, June 18, 1992, pp. 16–18.

Sun Hong. "Anecdotes about Deng Xiaoping's Political Career and Family Life." *Ching pao* 11, November 5, 1993, pp. 26–31, trans. FBIS-CHI, November 18, 1993, pp. 34–9.

Sun Liping. "Pingmin zhuyi yu Zhongguo gaige" [Populism and China's Reform]. *Zhanlüe yu guanli* 5 (October 1994): 1–10.

Sun Yushan. "Chen Xitong Points Out at a Municipal Supervision Work Conference That Supervision Departments Should Emancipate Their Minds in Carrying Out Work." *Beijing ribao,* March 8, 1991, pp. 1–2, trans. FBIS-CHI, March 29, 1991, p. 38.

Tan Shaowen. "Emancipate the Mind, Seek Truth from Facts, Be United as One, and Do Solid Work." *Tianjin ribao,* April 17, 1991, trans. FBIS-CHI, June 18, 1991, pp. 62–8.

Tanner, Murray Scot. *The Politics of Lawmaking in China: Institutions, Processes, and Democratic Prospects.* Oxford University Press, 1999.

"The CCP Issues Document No. 4, Fully Expounding Expansion of Opening Up." *Ta kung pao,* June 18, 1992, trans. FBIS-CHI, June 18, 1992, pp. 19–20.

Tseng Hui-yen. "*Looking at China With a Third Eye* Reportedly Written by Pan Yue." *Lien ho pao,* September 16, 1994, p. 10, trans. FBIS-CHI, September 16, 1994, p. 31.

Tseng Pin. "Party Struggle Exposed by Senior Statesmen Themselves; Meanwhile, the New Leading Group is Trying Hard to Build New Image." *Ching pao* 145, August 10, 1989, trans. FBIS-CHI, August 10, 1989.

Tsou, Tang. "Chinese Politics at the Top: Factionalism of Informal Politics? Balance-of-Power Politics or a Game to Win All?" *China Journal* 34 (July 1995): 95–156.

Tsou, Tang. *The Cultural Revolution and Post-Mao Reforms: A Historical Perspective.* University of Chicago Press, 1986.

Tsou, Tang. "Political Change and Reform: The Middle Course." In Tang Tsou, *The Cultural Revolution and Post-Mao Reforms,* pp. 219–58.

Tsou, Tang. "Prolegomenon to the Study of Informal Groups in CCP Politics." In Tang Tsou, *The Cultural Revolution and Post-Mao Reforms,* pp. 95–111.

Tsou, Tang. "The Tiananmen Tragedy: The State–Society Relationship, Choices, and Mechanisms in Historical Perspective." In Brantly Womack (Ed.), *Contemporary Chinese Politics in Historical Perspective,* pp. 265–327. Cambridge University Press, 1991.

Tyler, Patrick. *A Great Wall: Six Presidents and China.* New York: Public Affairs, 1999.

Unger, Roberto Mangabeira. *Democratic Experimentalism.* London: Verso, 1998.

Vogel, Ezra (Ed.). *Living with China: U.S./China Relations in the Twenty-First Century.* New York: Norton, 1997.

Wakeman, Frederic. "All the Rage in China." *New York Review of Books,* March 2, 1989, pp. 19–21.

Wallerstein, Immanuel. *The Modern World System: Capitalist Agriculture and the Origins of the European World-Economy in the Sixteenth Century.* New York: Academic Press, 1974.

Wan Li. "Juece minzhuhua he kexuehua shi zhengzhi tizhi gaige de yige zhongyao keti" [Making decision-making democratic and scientific is an important subject in political structural reform]. Xinhua, August 14, 1986, in FBIS-CHI, August 19, 1986, pp. K22–K34.

Wang Chi, Zhao Zhiwen, and Zheng Hongfan. "Trading Power for Money Is Not Tolerated by Law." Xinhua, June 7, 1999, in FBIS-CHI, June 14, 1999.

Wang Hui. "Dangdai Zhongguo de sixiang zhuangkuang yu xiandaixing wenti" [The circumstances of contemporary Chinese thought and the problem of modernity]. *Wenyi zhengming* 6 (November 1998): 7–26.

Wang Hui. "Guanyu xiandaixing wenti dawen" [An interview on the question of modernity]. *Tianya* 1 (January 1999): 18–34.

Wang Hui. "Wenhua pipan lilun yu dangdai Zhongguo minzu zhuyi wenti" [Cultural critical theories and the problems of contemporary Chinese nationalism]. *Zhanlüe yu guanli* 4 (1994): 17–20.

Wang Hui and Yu Guoliang (Eds.). *90 niandai de "houxue" lunzheng* ["Post-ism" in the Nineties]. Hong Kong: Chinese University Press, 1998.

Wang Huning. "Chuji jieduan yu zhengzhi tizhi gaige" [The initial stage and political structural reform]. In *Wang Huning ji,* pp. 28–9.

Wang Huning. "Jifen pingheng: Zhongyang yu difang de xietong guanxi" [Equilibrium between concentration and dispersal: Harmonizing relations between the center and localities]. *Fudan xuebao* 2 (1991): 27–36.

Wang Huning. "Juece gongneng de shehuihua ji qi tiaojian" [The socialization of the policy-making function and its conditions]. In *Wang Huning ji,* pp. 74–80.

Wang Huning. "Lun minzhu zhengzhi jianshe" [On building democratic politics]. In *Wang Huning ji,* pp. 30–8.

Wang Huning. "Shehui ziyuan zongliang yu shehui tiaokong: Zhongguo yiyi" [Aggregate social resources and social control]. *Fudan xuebao* 4 (1990): 2–11, 35.

Wang Huning. *Wang Huning ji* [Collected essays of Wang Huning]. Harbin: Heilongjiang jiaoyu chubanshe, 1989.

Wang Huning. "Wenhua guozhang yu wenhua zhuquan: Dui zhuquan guannian de tiaozhan" [Cultural expansionism and cultural sovereignty: A challenge to the concept of sovereignty]. *Fudan xuebao* 3 (1994); reprinted in Wang Jisi (Ed.), *Wenming yu guoji zhengzhi,* pp. 340–56.

Wang Huning. "Zhengzhi shenmei yu zhengzhi fazhan" [Political aesthetics and political development]. *Shehui kexue zhanxian* 1 (January 1991): 134–41.

Wang Huning. "Zhiwei fenlei yu ganbu guanli tizhi" [Types of posts and the cadre management system]. In *Wang Huning ji,* pp. 88–95.

Wang Huning. "Zhongguo bianhua zhong de zhongyang he difang zhengfu de guanxi: Zhengzhi de hanyi" [Governmental relations between the center and localities in the course of China's changes: The political implications]. *Fudan xuebao* 5 (1988): 1–8, 30.

Wang Huning. "Zhongguo zhengzhi tizhi gaige de beijing yu qianjing" [The background and prospects for the reform of China's political system]. In *Wang Huning ji,* pp. 3–14.

Wang Huning. "Zhongguo zhengzhi – Xingzheng tizhi gaige de jingji fenxi" [Chinese politics – An economic analysis of the reform of the administrative structure]. *Shehui kexue zhanxian* 2 (1988): 107–15.

Wang, Jing. *High Culture Fever: Politics, Aesthetics, and Ideology in Deng's China.* Berkeley: University of California Press, 1996.

Wang Jisi (Ed.). *Wenming yu guoji zhengzhi: Zhongguo xuezhe ping Hengtingdun de wenming chongtu lun* [Culture and international relations: Chinese scholars critique Huntington's cultural clash thesis]. Shanghai: Renmin chubanshe, 1995.

Wang Jiye. "Several Questions on Achieving Overall Balance and Restructuring." *Renmin ribao,* December 8, 1989, trans. FBIS-CHI, January 19, 1990, pp. 30–3.

Wang Renzhi. "Guanyu fandui zichan jieji ziyouhua" [On opposing bourgeois liberalization]. *Renmin ribao,* February 22, 1990.

Wang Renzhi. "Lilun gongzuo mianlin de xin qingkuang he dangqian de zhuyao renwu" [The new situation confronting theoretical work and the primary task at the moment]. *Xuexi, yanjiu, cankao* 11 (1990): 8–17.

Wang Ruoshui. *Hu Yaobang xiatai de beijing* [Behind Hu Yaobang's stepping down]. Hong Kong: Mingjing chubanshe, 1997.

Wang Ruoshui. *Wei rendao zhuyi bianhu* [In defense of humanism]. Beijing: Sanlian, 1986.

Wang Shan [Luo yi ning ge er]. *Disanzhi yanjing kan Zhongguo* [Looking at China through a third eye]. Taiyuan: Shanxi renmin chubanshe, 1994.

Wang Shaoguang. " 'Jiegui' haishi 'nalai': Zhengzhixue bentuhua de kaolu" ['Joining tracks' or 'borrowing': Thoughts about the nativization of political science]. Part 1, *Zhongguo yu shijie,* October 2000, ⟨www.chinabulletin.com/2000/zs0010b.txt⟩; Part 2, *Zhongguo yu shijie,* November 2000, ⟨www.chinabulletin.com/2000/zs0011b.htm⟩.

Wang Shaoguang. "The Social and Political Implications of China's WTO Membership." *Journal of Contemporary China* 9 (2000): 373–405.

Wang, Shaoguang and Hu Angang. *The Political Economy of Uneven Development: The Case of China.* Armonk, NY: M.E. Sharpe, 1999.

Wang Shuo. *Playing for Thrills,* trans. Howard Goldblatt. New York: Penguin, 1998.

Wang Shuo. *Please Don't Call Me Human,* trans. Howard Goldblatt. New York: Hyperion East, 2000.

"Wang Shuo zibai" [Wang Shuo's Self-Defense]. *Wenyi zhengming* 1 (1993): 65–6.

Wang Xiaodong [Shi Zhong], no title. Posting under "Guanyu Zhongguo minzu zhuyi de taolun (er)" [Discussion of China's nationalism (two)] on ⟨www.jczs.com.cn⟩, June 9, 1999.

Wang Xiaodong [Shi Zhong]. "Ping liangzhong butong de gaige guan" [Evaluating two different views of reform]. *Dangdai sichao* 1 (January 1992): 10–26.

Wang Xiaodong [Shi Zhong]. "Weilai de chongtu" [The coming clash]. *Zhanlüe yu guanli* 1 (November 1993): 46–50.

Wang Xiaodong [Shi Zhong]. "The West in the Eyes of a Chinese Nationalist." *Heartland: Eurasian Review of Geopolitics* 1 (2000): 17–30.

Wang Xiaodong [Shi Zhong]. "Zai pingmin yu jingying zhijian xunqiu pingheng" [Seeking a balance between populism and elitism]. *Zhanlüe yu guanli* 5 (October 1994): 11–14.

Wang Xiaodong [Shi Zhong]. "Zhongguo de minzu zhuyi he Zhongguo de weilai" [Chinese nationalism and the future of China]. *Mingbao yuekan* 9 (1996); trans. Stanley Rosen (Ed.), *Chinese Law and Government* 30 (November/December 1997): 8–27.

Wang Xiaodong and Qiu Tiancao. "Jiqing de yinying: Ping dianshi xiliepian 'He shang'" [The shadow of passion: Critique of the television series 'River Elegy']. *Zhongguo qingnianbao,* July 10, 1988, p. 4.

Wang Xiaoming. "Kuangyeshang de feixu" [Ruins on the wilderness]. In Wang Xiaoming (Ed.), *Renwen jingshen xunsilu* [Pondering the humanistic spirit]. Shanghai: Wenhui chubanshe, 1996.

Wang Ying. "Xin jiti zhuyi yu Zhongguo tese de shichang jingji" [New collectivism and a market economy with Chinese characteristics]. *Ershiyi shiji* 10 (October 1994): 11–14.

Wang Yizhou. "Minzu zhuyi gainian de xiandai sikao" [Contemporary reflections on the concept of nationalism]. *Zhanlüe yu guanli* 3 (June 1994): 7–12.

Wang, Yong. "China's Accession to WTO: An Institutional Perspective." Unpublished manuscript.

Wang Youfu. "Wang Zhen Inspects Xinjiang." *Renmin ribao,* August 26, 1991, p. 1, trans. FBIS-CHI, August 29, 1991, p. 21.

Wang Yungui. "Kan RiMeiFa zhengfu ruhe baohu benguo gongye" [Looking at how Japan, the United States, and France protected their domestic industries]. *Jingji ribao,* July 17, 1996, pp. 1, 3.

"We Must Not Only Persevere in Reform and Opening Up but Also Speed Them Up." *Renmin ribao* editorial, May 22, 1987, trans. FBIS-CHI, May 22, 1987, pp. K1–K3.

Wei Ming. "Yijiu jiu'er nian yilai zichan jieji ziyouhua de dongtai he tedian" [The movements and characteristics of bourgeois liberals since 1992]. *Zhongguo yu shijie,* March 1998, ⟨http://www.chinabulletin.com/98/zs9803d.htm⟩.

Wei Yung-cheng. "Reveal the Mystery of Huangfu Ping." *Ta kung pao,* October 7, 1992, trans. FBIS-CHI, October 16, 1992, p. 19.

"Weilai yi, ershinian woguo guojia anquan de neiwai xingshi ji zhuyao weixie de chubu tantao" [A preliminary investigation of China's domestic and international situation and primary threats in the next ten to twenty years]. In Shi Liaozi (Ed.), *Beijing dixia "wanyanshu,"* pp. 134–5.

Wen Jin (Ed.). *Zhongguo "Zuo" huo* [China's 'leftist' peril]. Beijing: Chaohua chubanshe, 1993.

Weng Jieming, Zhang Ximing, Zhang Qiang, and Qu Kemin (Eds.). *Yu zongshuji tanxin* [Heart-to-heart talks with the general secretary]. Beijing: Zhongguo shehui kexue chubanshe, 1996.

"Why Must We Unremittingly Oppose Bourgeois Liberalization?" *Renmin ribao,* April 24, 1991, p. 5, trans. FBIS-CHI, April 26, 1991, pp. 18–21.

World Bank. *The State in a Changing World.* New York: Oxford University Press, 1997.

Wu Bangguo. "Guanyu guoyou qiye gaige yu fazhan de jige wenti" [Several problems regarding the reform and development of SOEs]. *Zhongyang dangxiao baogaoxuan* 18 (1996): 3.

Wu, Guoguang. "Documentary Politics: Hypotheses, Process, and Case Studies." In Carol Lee Hamrin and Suisheng Zhao (Eds.), *Decision-Making in Deng's China: Perspectives from Insiders,* pp. 24–38. Armonk, NY: M.E. Sharpe, 1995.

Wu, Guoguang. *Zhulu shiwuda: Zhongguo quanli qiju* [Toward the Fifteenth Party Congress: China's Power Game]. Hong Kong: Taipingyang shiji yanjiusuo, 1997.

Wu Jiaxiang. "Xin quanwei zhuyi shuping" [Discussing the new authoritarianism]. *Shijie jingji daobao,* January 16, 1989; reprinted in Qi Mo (Ed.), *Xin quanwei zhuyi,* pp. 4–8.

Wu Jinglian. "Guanyu gaige zhanlüe xuanze de ruogan sikao" [Some thoughts about choices in reform strategy]. *Jingji yanjiu* 2 (February 1987): 3–14.

Wu Jinglian. *Jihua jingji haishi shichang jingji* [Planned economy or market economy]. Beijing: Zhongguo jingji chubanshe, 1993.

Wu Yan and Gu Zhaonong. "Jiji yinzi mo panghuang" [We should not hestitate to import capital]. *Renmin ribao,* July 16, 1996, pp. 1–2.

Xiang Jingquan. "Review and Prospects of China's Economic Development." *Guangming ribao,* trans. FBIS-CHI, March 19, 1993, pp. 48–50.

"Xiangqile 'zai mai yetian xin butong'" [Thinking of 'the lout who sells his grandfather's land without remorse']. *Baokan wenzhai,* April 27, 2000, p. 2.

Xiao Gongqin. "Jingti jiduan minzu zhuyi" [Be careful of extreme nationalism]. Posted under "Guanyu Zhongguo minzu zhuyi de taolun (yi)" [Discussion of China's nationalism (one)] on ⟨www.jczs.com.cn⟩, June 9, 1999.

Xiao Gongqin. "Qingmo xinzheng yu Zhongguo xiandaihua yanjiu" [The new policies of the late Qing and the study of Chinese modernization]. *Zhanlüe yu guanli* 1 (November 1993): 61–6.

Xiao Gongqin. *Weijizhong de biange: Qingmo xiandaihua jinchengzhong de jijin yu baoshou* [Change in the midst of crisis: Radicalism and conservatism in the course of modernization in the late Qing]. Shanghai: Sanlian, 1999.

Xiao Gongqin. "Wuxu bianfa de zai fanxing" [A new reflection on the reform of 1898]. *Zhanlüe yu guanli* 4 (1995): 11–20.

Xiao Gongqin. *Xiao Gongqin ji* [Collected essays of Xiao Gongqin]. Harbin: Heilongjiang jiaoyu chubanshe, 1995.

Xiao Gongqin. " 'Yan Fu beilun' yu jindai xinbaoshou zhuyi biange guan" [The 'Yanfu paradox' and the neoconservative view of change]. In *Xiao Gongqin ji,* pp. 18–41.

Xiao He. "Yuanhua an he dangjun gaoceng de guanxi" [The relationship between the Yuanhua case and the upper echelons of the party and army]. *Kaifang,* October 2000, pp. 15–18.

Xibu dakaifa zhanlüe juece ruogan wenti [Several issues concerning the strategic decision to open widely the west]. Beijing: Zhongyang wenxian chubanshe, 2000.

Xin Mao. "Gaige yu jingjiren" [Reform and economic man]. In Shi Liaozi (Ed.), *Beijing dixia "wanyanshu,"* pp. 201–30.

Xing Bensi. "Emphasis on Study, Politics, and Uprightness as Fine Party Traditions." *Qiushi* 7 (April 1997): 2–10, trans. FBIS-CHI-97-106, June 5, 1997.

Xing Bensi. "Jianchi Makesi zhuyi bu dongyao" [Uphold Marxism without wavering]. *Renmin ribao,* June 6, 1996, p. 9.

Xu, Ben. *Disenchanted Democracy.* Ann Arbor: University of Michigan Press, 2000.

Xu Ben. "Shenma shi Zhongguo de 'houxin shiqi'?" [What is China's "post-new period"?]. *Ershiyi shiji* 8 (1996): 74–83.

Xu Bing. "Wang Shan qi ren" [This person, Wang Shan]. In Liu Zhifeng, *Jieshi Zhongguo,* pp. 25–63.

Xu Jilin. *Ling yizhong qimeng* [Another type of enlightenment]. Guangzhou: Huacheng chubanshe, 1999.

Xu Jilin. "Xunqiu 'disantiao daolu' – guanyu 'ziyouzhuyi' yu 'xinzuopai' de duihua" [Searching for a 'third way'– a conversation on 'liberalism' and the 'new left']. In Xu Jilin, *Ling yizhong qimeng* [Another type of enlightenment], pp. 276–302.

Xu Ming (Ed.). *Guanjian shike: Dangdai Zhongguo jindai jiejue de ershiqi ge wenti* [The critical moment: Twenty-seven problems in contemporary China that need solving urgently]. Beijing: Jinri Zhongguo chubanshe, 1997.

Yan Jiaqi. *Toward a Democratic China: The Intellectual Biography of Yan Jiaqi,* trans. David S. K. Hong and Denis C. Mair. Honolulu: University of Hawaii Press, 1992.

Yan Yunxiang. "The Politics of Consumerism in Chinese Society." In Tyrene White (Ed.), *China Briefing 2000: The Continuing Transformation,* pp. 159–93. Armonk, NY: M.E. Sharpe, 2000.

Yang Dali. "Dui 'binweilun' de jidian fanbo" [Some points in refutation of the 'thesis of proximate crisis']. *Ershiyi shiji* 2 (1994): 15–18.

Yang Peixin. "Shenhua gaige de zhongxin shi shenma?" [What is the focus of deepening reform?]. *Zhanlüe yu guanli* 1 (1994): 76–80.

Yang Ping. "The Third Eye – Commenting on *Seeing China through a Third Eye.*" *Beijing qingnian bao,* June 25, 1994, p. 3, trans. FBIS-CHI, August 11, 1994, pp. 20–1.

Yang Qixian. "Guanyu guoyou qiye gaige de lixing sikao" [Thinking rationally about reform of state-owned enterprises]. *Jingji yanjiu cankao* 13 (February 7, 1997): 2–18.

Yang Shangkun. "Zai jinian Xinhai geming bashi zhounian dahuishang de jianghua" [Talk at the meeting to commemorate the eightieth anniversary of the Revolution of 1911]. In *Shisanda yilai,* vol. 3, pp. 1713–19.

Yang Zhongmei. *Jiang Zemin zhuan* [Biography of Jiang Zemin]. Taipei: Shibao wenhua, 1996.

Yao Fan. "How Comrade Zhao Ziyang Weakened the Party's Ideological and Political Work." *Guangming ribao,* August 25, 1989, p. 1, trans. FBIS-CHI, August 29, 1989, pp. 8–10.

Yen Shen-tsun. "Deng Xiaoping's Talk during His Inspection of Shoudu Iron and Steel Complex." *Kuang chiao ching* 238, July 16, 1992, pp. 6–7, trans. FBIS-CHI, July 17, 1992, pp. 7–8.

"Yi gaige cu wending zhong fazhan," *Jingji yanjiu* 7 (July 1990): 3–19.

Yi jia yan [pseud.]. " 'He Shang' xuanyangle shenma?" [What is 'River Elegy' propagating?]. *Renmin ribao,* July 19, 1989.

Yi Ren. "Zhuozhuo huiyi de qianqian houhou" [Before and after the Zhuozhuo meeting]. *Renmin ribao,* February 14, 1990.

Yin Baoyun. "Minzu zhuyi yu xiandai jingji fazhan" [Nationalism and contemporary economic development]. *Zhanlüe yu guanli* 3 (June 1994): 13–15.

Yin Yen. "Hu Jiwei Served with Warning after Releasing Articles Criticizing CCP Autocracy and Exposing Its Errors in June 4 Incident." *Sing tao jih pao,* January 23, 1998, trans. FBIS-CHI, January 27, 1998.

"Yingxiang woguo guojia anquan de ruogan yinsu" [Several factors influencing our country's national security]. In Shi Liaozi (Ed.), *Beijing dixia "wanyanshu,"* pp. 25–48.

"Yiwei yanjiusheng guanyu gaoxiao sixiang zhandi wenti de laixin" [A letter from a graduate student on the question of the ideological front at schools of higher learning]. *Guangming ribao,* March 29, 2000, p. 1.

"Yongyuan baochi he fayang jianku fendou jingshen" [Hold on to and develop the spirit of bitter struggle forever]. *Jiefangjun bao,* April 22, 1996, pp. 1, 6.

Yu Guanghua. "Xin quanwei zhuyi de shehui jichu ji huanxiang" [The social foundation and illusions of the new authoritarianism]. *Zhengming* 4 (1989): 42.

Yu Haocheng. "Zhongguo xuyao xin quanwei zhuyi ma?" [Does China Need the New Authoritarianism?]. In Rosen and Zou (Eds.), "The Chinese Debate on the New Authoritarianism (III)," pp. 44–55.

Yu Quanyu. "Qianyan: Women de guojia dayou xiwang" [Preface: There is great hope for China]. In Fang Ning et al. (Eds.), *Quanqiuhua yinyingxia de Zhongguo zhilu,* pp. 1–4.

Yu Quanyu. "Zan dangdai qingnian de 'sixiang jiefang' " [Praising the 'open-mindedness' of contemporary youth]. *Zhenli de zhuiqiu* 1 (January 2000): 1–3.

Yu Xinyan [pseud. Xu Welcheng]. "Preface to *Practice and Future of Contemporary Socialism.*" *Renmin ribao,* August 19, 1991, trans. FBIS-CHI, August 27, 1991, pp. 29–30.

Yu Yingshi. "Zailun Zhongguo xiandai sixiang zhongde jijin yu baoshou" [Again discussing radicalism and conservatism in the history of modern Chinese thought]. *Ershiyi shiji* 10 (1992): 143–9.

Yu Yingshi. "Zhongguo jindai sixiangshi zhongde jijin yu baoshou" [Radicalism and conservatism in the history of modern Chinese thought]. *Lishi yuekan* 6 (June 1990): 135–46.

Yuan Mu. "Firmly, Accurately, and Comprehensively Implement the Party's Basic Line – Preface to 'Guidance for Studying the Government Work Report to the Fifth Session of the Seventh NPC'." *Renmin ribao,* April 14, 1992, trans. FBIS-CHI, April 16, 1992, pp. 20–3.

Yuan Mu. "Zhongguo gongren jieji shi Zhongguo gongchandang bu ke dongyao de jieji jichu" [China's working class is the unshakable class basis of the Communist Party of China]. *Dangdai sichao* 1 (February 20, 1997): 2–19.

Yuan Yongsong and Wang Junwei (Eds.). *Zuoqing ershinian, 1957–1976* [Twenty years of leftism, 1957–1976]. Beijing: Nongcun duwu chubanshe, 1993.

Yue Daiyun. "Shijie wenhua duihua zhongde Zhongguo xiandai baoshou zhuyi – Jian lun *Xueheng* zazhi" [China's contemporary conservatism in the world cultural discourse – On the journal *Xueheng*]. In Beijing daxue shehui kexuechu (Ed.), *Beijing daxue jinian wusi yundong qishi zhounian lunwenji* [Essays from Beijing University's commemoration of the seventieth anniversary of the May Fourth Movement]. Beijing daxue chubanshe, 1990.

Yue Daiyun and Carolyn Wakeman. *To the Storm: The Odyssey of a Revolutionary Chinese Woman*. Berkeley: University of California Press, 1985.

Yueh Shan. "Central Advisory Commission Submits Letter to CCP Central Committee Opposing 'Rightist' Tendency." *Zhengming* 175, May 1, 1992, pp. 13–14, trans. FBIS-CHI, April 30, 1992, pp. 15–16.

"Zai duiwai kaifang zhong hongyang aiguo zhuyi jingshen" [Continue to hold high the patriotic spirit in the course of opening to the outside world]. *Jiefangjun bao,* April 8, 1996, pp. 1, 6.

"Zao gai zheyang taolunle" [There should have been this discussion long ago]. *Jingji ribao,* July 18, 1996, p. 1.

Zha, Jianying. *China Pop: How Soap Operas, Tabloids, and Bestsellers are Transforming a Culture*. New York: New Press, 1995.

Zhang Bingjiu. "Jingji tizhi gaige he zhengzhi tizhi gaige de jincheng yu xietiao" [The progress and coordination between economic and political system reform]. In Liu Jun and Li Lin (Eds.), *Xinquanwei zhuyi*, pp. 1–26, trans. Rosen and Zou (Eds.), "The Chinese Debate on the New Authoritarianism (I)," pp. 8–35.

Zhang Fa, Zhang Yiwu, and Wang Yichuan. "Cong 'xiandaixing' dao 'Zhonghuaxing'" [From 'modernity' to 'Chineseness']. *Wenyi zhengming* 2 (March 1994): 10–20.

Zhang Houyi and Ming Lizhi (Eds.). *Zhongguo siying qiye fazhan baogao* [Report on the development of private enterprises in China]. Beijing: Shehui kexue wenxian chubanshe, 2000.

Zhang Kuan. "OuMeiren yanzhong de 'feiwo zulei'" ['Other races' in the eyes of Europeans and Americans]. *Dushu* (September 1993): 3–9

Zhang Kuan. "Sayide de 'dongfang zhuyi' yu xifang de hanxue yanjiu" [Said's 'Orientalism' and Western sinology]. *Liaowang* 27 (July 3, 1995): 36–7.

Zhang Kuan. "Wenhua xinzhimin de keneng" [The possibility of cultural neocolonialism]. *Tianya* 2 (1996): 16–23.

Zhang Kuan. "Zaitan Sayide" [Another discussion of Said]. *Dushu* (October 1994): 8–14.

Zhang Longxi. "Duoyuan shehui zhongde wenhua piping" [Cultural criticism in a pluralistic society]. *Ershiyi shiji* 2 (1996): 18–25.

Zhang Ming and Li Shitao (Eds.). *Zhishi fenzi lichang* [The standpoint of intellectuals], 3 vols. Changchun: Shidai wenyi chubanshe, 1999.

Zhang Shuguang. "Guojia nengli yu zhidu biange he shehui zhuanxing" [State capacity, system change, and social transformation]. In Zhang Shuguang, *Zhang Shuguang jingjixue shupingji* [Collected economic book reviews of Zhang Shuguang]. Beijing: Zhongguo caizheng jingji chubanshe, 1996.

Zhang Shuguang. "Zhengfu de caizheng guanxi: Yizhong teshu de jiaoyi" [Fiscal relations of government: A special type of exchange]. In Zhang Shuguang, *Zhang Shuguang jingjixue shupingji* [Collected economic book reviews of Zhang Shuguang]. Beijing: Zhongguo caizheng jingji chubanshe, 1996.

Zhang Weiguo. "Chen Xitong an yu quanli douzheng" [The Chen Xitong case and the struggle for power]. *Beijing zhi chun* 30 (November 1995): 30–2.

Zhang Weiying. *Qiye de qiyejia – Qiyue lilun* [Entrepreneurs of enterprises – Contract theory]. Shanghai: Sanlian, 1995.

Zhang Weiying. "Suoyouzhi, zhili jiegou ji weituo – daili guanxi – jian ping Cui Zhiyuan he Zhou Qiren de yixie guandian" [Ownership, management structure, and principal–agent relations – Also critiquing some views of Cui Zhiyuan and Zhou Qiren]. *Jingji yanjiu* 9 (September 1996): 3–15, 53.

Zhang Wenmin et al. (Eds.). *Zhongguo jingji dalunzhan* [Great debates on the Chinese economy]. Beijing: Jingji guanli chubanshe, 1996 (vol. 1) and 1997 (vol. 2).

Zhang Xiangping. "Qimeng, mincui, daminzhu de lishi fansi" [Reflections on the history of enlightenment, populism, and great democracy]. *Zhanlüe yu guanli* 5 (October 1994): 15–19.

Zhang Ximang. "Xinwen fazhi yu shehui fazhan" [Journalism, rule by law, and social development]. *Fangfa* 3 (1998): 4–6.

Zhang Xueli. *Zhongguo heyi shuobu* [How China says no]. Beijing: Hualing chubanshe, 1996.

Zhang Xuwu, Li Ding, and Xie Minggan (Eds.). *Zhongguo siying jingji nianjian, 1996* [Yearbook of China's private economy, 1996]. Beijing: Zhonghua gongshang lianhe chubanshe, 1996.

Zhang Yiwu. "Chanshi 'Zhongguo' de jiaolu" [Explaining 'China's' anxieties]. *Ershiyi shiji* 28 (April 1995); reprinted in Wang Hui and Yu Guoliang (Eds.), *90 niandai de "houxue" lunzheng*, pp. 43–55.

Zhang Yiwu. "Miandui quanqiuhua de tiaozhan" [Facing the challenge of globalization]. *Ershiyi shiji* 38 (December 1996); reprinted in Wang Hui and Yu Guoliang (Eds.), *90 niandai de "houxue" lunzheng*, pp. 67–75.

Zhang Zhuoyuan. "Promoting Economic Rectification by Deepening Reform." *Renmin ribao*, November 27, 1989, trans. FBIS-CIII, December 7, 1989, pp. 28–31.

Zhao Guoliang and Cui Jianlin (Eds.). *Lixiang zhi guang – Nanjieren kaizhan gongyouzhi dataolun* [A ray of idealism – People of Nanjie open a discussion on public ownership], 3 vols. Beijing: Zhonggong zhongyang dangxiao chubanshe, 1998.

Zhao Shilin (Ed.). *Fang "zuo" beiwanglu* [Memorandum on opposing "leftism"]. Taiyuan: Shuhai chubanshe, 1992.

Zhao, Suisheng. "Deng Xiaoping's Southern Tour: Elite Politics in Post-Tiananmen China." *Asian Survey* 33 (August 1993): 739–56.

Zhao, Suisheng. *In Search of a Right Place? Chinese Nationalism in the Post–Cold War World*. Hong Kong Institute for Asia–Pacific Studies, Chinese University of Hong Kong, 1997.

Zhao Yiheng. " 'Houxue' yu Zhongguo xinbaoshou zhuyi" ['Post-ism' and China's neoconservatism]. *Ersihyi shiji* 2 (1995): 4–15.

301

Zhao Ziyang. "Further Emancipate the Mind and Further Liberate the Productive Forces." *Renmin ribao,* February 8, 1988, trans. FBIS-CHI, February 8, 1988, pp. 12–14.

Zheng Bijian. " 'Sange daibiao' zhongyao lunshu yu mianxiang ershiyi shiji de Zhong-guo gongchandang" [The important exposition of the 'three representatives' and the CCP facing the twenty-first century]. In *Shenru xuexi "sange daibiao" quanmian luoshi "sange daibiao"* [Study deeply the "three representatives"; comprehensively implement the "three representatives"], pp. 119–33. Beijing: Xuexi chuban-she, 2000.

Zheng, Yongnian. *Discovering Chinese Nationalism in China.* Cambridge University Press, 1999.

"Zhonggong Zhongyang guanyu jinyibu zhili zhengdun he shenhua gaige de jueding (zhaiyao)" [CCP Central Committee decision on furthering improvement and rectification and deepening reform (outline)]. In *Shisanda yilai,* vol. 2, pp. 680–708.

"Zhonggong Zhongyang, Guowuyuan guanyu jinqi zuo jijian qunzhong guanxin de shi de jueding" [Decision of the CCP Central Committee and State Council regarding doing a few things of concern to the masses in the present period]. In *Shisanda yilai,* vol. 2, pp. 555–7.

Zhonggong zhongyang wenxuan yanjiushi (Ed.). *Shehui zhuyi jingshen wenming jianshe wenxian xuanbian* [Selected documents on building socialist spiritual civilization]. Beijing: Zhonggong zhongyang wenxuan yanjiushi, 1996.

"Zhongguo gongchandang dishisanjie zhongyang weiyuanhui disice quanti huiyi gong-bao" [Communiqué of the fourth plenary session of the thirteenth CCP Central Committee]. In *Shisanda yilai,* vol. 2, pp. 543–6.

"Zhongguo gongchandang dishisanjie zhongyang weiyuanhui diqice quanti huiyi gong-bao" [Communiqué of the seventh plenary session of the thirteenth CCP Central Committee]. In *Shisanda yilai,* vol. 2, pp. 1420–6.

Zhongguo jingji nianjian 1995 [Chinese economic yearbook 1995]. Beijing: Zhongguo jingji nianjianshe, 1995.

Zhongguo jushi fenxi zhongxin (Ed.). *Beijing zaochun de jiaofeng* [Crossing swords in the early spring in Beijing]. Hong Kong: Mingjing chubanshe, 1998.

Zhongguo kexueyuan guoqing fenxi yanjiu xiaozu. *Shengcun yu fazhan* [Survival and development]. Beijing kexue chubanshe, 1996.

"Zhongguo shehui jiegou zhuanxing de zhongjinqi qushi yu yinhuan" [Trends and hidden difficulties in the transformation of China's social structure in the near and mid-term]. *Zhanlüe yu guanli* 5 (October 1998): 1–17.

"Zhongliu Loses Lawsuit against 'Jiaofeng'." *Ming pao,* April 23, 1999, p. B15, trans. FBIS-CHI-1999-0423, April 23, 1999.

Zhu Jianhong and Jiang Yaping. "Development and Standardization Are Necessary – Perspective of Real Estate Business." *Renmin ribao,* May 11, 1993, trans. FBIS-CHI, May 24, 1993, pp. 56–7.

Zhu Rongji. "Summarize Experiences in Clearing Debt Defaults and Preventing New Defaults to Ensure Sound Development of the National Economy." Xinhua, December 25, 1992, in FBIS-CHI, December 28, 1992, pp. 36–9.

Zhu Tao. "A Brief Introduction to the Special Zones Debate." *Neibu wengao,* trans. Stanley Rosen (Ed.), *Debates over Special Economic Zones, Income Polarization, and Other Related Issues* (*Chinese Economic Studies* 29(3): 36–46, May/June 1996).

Zi Yu. "Shei zai zhanling daxuesheng de sixiang zhandi" [Who is occupying the ideo-logical front of university students?]. *Zhongliu* 4 (April 2000): 42–4.

Zou Dang [Tsou Tang]. *Ershi shiji Zhongguo zhengzhi: Cong hongguan lishi yu weiguan xingdong jiaodu kan* [Twentieth century Chinese politics: Viewed from the perspec-tive of macro history and micro action]. Hong Kong: Oxford University Press, 1994.

Zysman, John. *Government, Markets, and Growth*. Ithaca, NY: Cornell University Press, 1983.

OTHER SOURCES

AFP. Agence France Presse
Beijing qingnian bao
Beijing radio
Beijing television service
Beijing zhi chun
China Central Television
China Daily
Ching chi tao pao
Ching pao
FBIS-CHI. Foreign Broadcast Information Service, *Daily Report: China*
Financial Times
Guangdong radio
Guangming ribao
Hong Kong Standard
Hsin pao
Jiefangjun bao
Jingji daobao
Jingji ribao
Jinrong shibao
Kaifang
Kuang chiao ching
Lien ho pao
Ming pao
Minzhu yu fazhi
Nanfang ribao
New York Times
Renmin ribao
Shijie ribao
Sing tao jih pao
South China Morning Post
Ta kung pao
Tangtai
Wall Street Journal
Washington Post
Wen wei po
Xinhua News Service

Xinjiang television
Xinwanbao
Zhengming
Zhongguo qingnian bao
Zhongguo tongxun she

Index

Academy of Chinese Culture: 12, 108
Anshan Iron and Steel Factory Constitution: 119
anti-Americanism: and Chinese nationalism, 133; and embassy bombing, 211–14; of He Xin, 94–5; and popular nationalism, 151, 154–6; WTO membership, 215–17
authoritarianism: *see* new authoritarianism

Babbitt, Irving: 110
Bai Hua: 67
Bao Zunxin: 12
Beijing Municipality: and corruption investigation, 166
Beijing spring: 193, 196–201
Beijing University: 2, 17, 200
Beijing Young Economists Association: 84
Berlin, Isaiah: 128
Bernstein, Richard: 2
Bo Yibo: 55; and decision to declare martial law, 28
bourgeois liberalism: 31–2, 33, 50, 182–3; and leftist critique of reform, 169; Zhao charged with promoting, 30
Brzezinski, Zbigniew: *Out of Control,* 125
Buchanan, James, 81

Cai Yuanpei: 198
Cao Siyuan: on role of state owned enterprises (SOEs): 178
Capital Iron and Steel (Shougang): 62
censorship: and crackdown on publishing, 227–8
center–local relationship: 21, 40–2, 83–6, 88–9, 163; and regional inequalities, 137–9; and state capacity, 134–6; *see also* taxation; extractive capacity
Central Advisory Commission: abolished, 66
Chen Daixi: and critique of Zhao, 37
Chen Xiaoping: on private enterprise, 172–3
Chen Xitong: 24, 64, 69; and corruption investigation, 166–7; and criticism of

Zhao, 29–30; and support for Deng's reforms, 46
Chen Yaoqing: and corruption scandal, 225
Chen Yeping: 54
Chen Yinke: 111, 198
Chen Yuan: 98, 100, 111; and Deng's reforms, 49–50; as exponent of neoconservatism, 84–6
Chen Yun: 139, 233; and Deng's reforms, 33, 34, 35, 36, 49–50, 61–2; and Jiang Zemin, 23; on threat of peaceful evolution, 55, 59; and Zhu Rongji, 48, 53
Chen Zili: and closure of *World Economic Herald,* 26
Chen Ziming: 25
Cheng Nien: *see* Zheng Nian
Cheng Weigao: and provincial support for Deng's reforms, 46
Chi Haotian: and corruption scandal, 227
China Can Say No: 154–6
China's Road under the Shadow of Globalization (Fang Ning, Wang Xiaodong, and Song Qiang): 218
Chinese Communist Party (CCP): 99; divisions within, 28–31
Chinese intellectuals: *see* intellectuals
Christopher, Warren: 144
civil society: 6
Clinton, Bill: 3, 17, 144; and China's WTO membership, 207, 209, 210, 223
Coase, Ronald: 81, 110
Collected Writings of Wang Huning: 87, 88
commercialization: 102–5
Confucian capitalism: 108, 144
Confucianism: in cultural debates of 1980s, 82; and nationalism, 100; and Yan Fu, 91
conservatives: and critique of Deng's economic reforms, 35–7, 49–50; *see also* leftists and leftism
Contemporary Trends (Dangdai sichao): and conservative critique of Deng's policies, 50; and 10,000-character manifesto, 188